Communicating in English

Talk, Text, Technology

This book is part of the series *Worlds of English* published by Routledge in association with The Open University. The three books in the series are:

English in the World: History, Diversity, Change
(edited by Philip Seargeant and Joan Swann)

ISBN 978-0-415-67421-8 (paperback)

ISBN 978-0-415-67420-1 (hardback)

ISBN 978-0-203-12456-7 (ebook)

Communicating in English: Talk, Text, Technology
(edited by Daniel Allington and Barbara Mayor)

ISBN 978-0-415-67423-2 (paperback)

ISBN 978-0-415-67422-5 (hardback)

ISBN 978-0-203-12454-3 (ebook)

The Politics of English: Conflict, Competition, Co-existence
(edited by Ann Hewings and Caroline Tagg)

ISBN 978-0-415-67424-9 (paperback)

ISBN 978-0-415-67425-6 (hardback)

This publication forms part of the Open University module U214 *Worlds of English*. Details of this and other Open University modules can be obtained from the Student Registration and Enquiry Service, The Open University, PO Box 197, Milton Keynes, MK7 6BJ, United Kingdom (Tel. +44 (0845 300 60 90, email general-enquiries@open.ac.uk).

www.open.ac.uk

Communicating in English

Talk, Text, Technology

Edited by Daniel Allington and Barbara Mayor

Published by

Routledge
2 Park Square
Milton Park
Abingdon OX14 4RN

in association with

The Open University
Walton Hall
Milton Keynes MK7 6AA

Simultaneously published in the USA and Canada by

Routledge
711 Third Avenue
New York, NY 10017

Routledge is an imprint of the Taylor & Francis Group, an informa business

First published 2012

Edited and designed by The Open University.

Typeset by The Open University.

Printed and bound in the United Kingdom by Latimer Trend & Company Ltd., Plymouth.

British Library Cataloguing in Publication Data: A catalogue record for this book is available from the British Library.

Library of Congress Cataloging-in-Publication Data

Communicating in English: Talk, Text, Technology / edited by Daniel Allington and Barbara Mayor.

p. cm. -- (Worlds of English)

ISBN 978-0-415-67422-5 (hardback) -- ISBN 978-0-415-67423-2 (pbk.) -- ISBN 978-0-203-12454-3 (ebook) 1. English language--Textbooks for foreign speakers. 2. English language--Spoken English. 3. Text messages (Telephone systems) 4. Communication. I. Allington, Daniel. II. Mayor, Barbara M., 1949-
PE1128.C69388 2012

428.2'4--dc23

2011037885

ISBN 978-0-415-67423-2 (paperback)

ISBN 978-0-415-67422-5 (hardback)

ISBN 978-0-203-12454-3 (ebook)

1.1

Contents

Series preface

The books in this series provide an introduction to the study of English, both for students of the English language and the general reader. They are core texts for the Open University module U214 *Worlds of English*. The series aims to provide students with:

- an understanding of the history and development of English, and a critical approach to its current global status and influence

- skills and knowledge to use in analysing English-language texts

- an appreciation of variation in the English language between different speakers and writers, and across different regional and social contexts

- examples of the diversity of English language practices in different parts of the world

- an understanding of how English is learned as a first language or as an additional language, and of its role as a language of formal education around the world

- an appreciation of how media, from print to the internet, have affected the English language and contributed to its position in the world today

- an understanding of how English is promoted around the world and the controversies surrounding the politics and economics of such decisions and its impact on other languages and the people who speak them

- informed reflections on the likely future role of English.

The readings which accompany each chapter have been chosen to exemplify key points made in the chapters, often by exploring related data, or experiences and practices involving the English language in different parts of the world. The readings also represent an additional 'voice' or viewpoint on key themes or issues raised in the chapter.

Each chapter includes:

- **activities** to stimulate further understanding or analysis of the material

- **boxes** containing illustrative or supplementary material

- **key terms** which are set in coloured type at the point where they are explained; the terms also appear in colour in the index so that they are easy to find in the chapters.

The other books in this series are:

Seargeant, P. and Swann, J. (eds) (2012) *English in the World: History, Diversity, Change*, Abingdon, Routledge/Milton Keynes, The Open University.

Hewings, A. and Tagg, C. (eds) (2012) *The Politics of English: Conflict, Competition, Coexistence*, Abingdon, Routledge/Milton Keynes, The Open University.

Ann Hewings
Series Editor

Biographical information

Daniel Allington

Daniel Allington is Lecturer in English Language Studies and Applied Linguistics at the Open University, although he has also worked as an illustrator and taught English in the UK and abroad. His research into the production and consumption of culture has appeared in major journals and edited collections, and he is part of an international team of scholars writing a history of the book in Britain.

Guy Cook

Guy Cook is Professor of Language and Education at the Open University. He has published extensively on various aspects of applied linguistics. From 2004–2009, he was co-editor of the journal *Applied Linguistics*. He is Chair of the British Association for Applied Linguistics (2009–2012) and is an Academician of the Academy for the Social Sciences. His books include *Translation in Language Teaching* (2010), Winner of the International House Ben Warren Prize.

Ann Hewings

Ann Hewings is Senior Lecturer in Language and Communication at the Open University. She has taught English in a variety of countries to children, young people and adults. Her research and teaching interests focus on academic literacy in English and interdisciplinary and global perspectives on English language. Her publications include *Grammar and Context* (2005, co-edited with Martin Hewings).

Almut Koester

Almut Koester is Senior Lecturer in English Language in the Department of English, University of Birmingham. Her research focuses on spoken workplace discourse and she is author of *The Language of Work* (2004), *Investigating Workplace Discourse* (2006) and *Workplace Discourse* (2010). She also writes Business English materials and is interested in the application of research to English language teaching.

Barbara Mayor

Barbara Mayor is Lecturer in the Centre for Language and Communication at the Open University, where she has contributed extensively to courses in applied linguistics. Her research interests include the pragmatics of bilingual interaction, English as a global language of education and linguistic landscapes. Recent publications include 'Perspectives on children learning English' in Maybin and Swann (2010, eds) *The Routledge Companion to English Language Studies*.

Joan Swann

Joan Swann is Director of the Centre for Language and Communication in the Faculty of Education and Language Studies at the Open University. Recent books include *Creativity in Language and Literature* (2011, co-edited with Ronald Carter and Rob Pope) and the *Companion to English Language Studies* (2010, co-edited with Janet Maybin).

Caroline Tagg

Caroline Tagg is Lecturer in Applied Linguistics in the Centre for English Language Studies at the University of Birmingham. Her research interests include the application of discourse analysis and corpus linguistics to digital interaction, particularly text messaging and social network sites. She is author of *The Discourse of Text Messaging* (forthcoming) and has published articles in journals such as *World Englishes* and *Writing Systems Research*.

General introduction

Daniel Allington and Barbara Mayor

This is a book about the relationship between communication, technology and the English language. It is often remarked that language and communication have been transformed in the digital age. But new communications technologies do not force people to communicate in particular ways: they simply provide their users with possibilities that they may or may not take up. There is thus continuity as well as change, and this book is able to draw on decades of scholarship while simultaneously keeping up with the cutting edge of research.

The focus throughout is on *people communicating*. This means that the contributors to this book discuss neither language nor communication in the abstract. When we use language to communicate, it is never language in general that we use, but always a *specific* language or language variety: one that may have an association with a particular community, with high or low social status, with work, with education, and so on. English has a unique place in the contemporary world – both as an official language of many countries and as the most widely used international language for business, trade, diplomacy and the mass media – and this must be remembered in any account of how it is used.

'Talk' and 'text'

In linguistics, the term 'text' is often used to mean 'any passage, spoken or written, of whatever length, that … form[s] a unified whole' (Halliday and Hasan, 1976, p. 1). However, this book is centrally concerned with the distinctions between speech, writing and other forms of language use. For this reason, communication will generally be referred to as **talk** if the words involved are composed of sounds produced by the human mouth, and as **text** if the words involved are composed of visual or other symbols. These are fairly commonsensical definitions, but by no means perfect. When people type messages in online chat, are they speaking or writing? And when we listen to a speech that was prepared in written form, is it talk or text that we are hearing? In some circumstances, it may be more helpful to use the word 'talk' to refer to communications produced in a situation of rapid interaction, and the word 'text' to refer to more extended and deliberately crafted communications that take a relatively stable and permanent form. Even this leaves grey areas, however. We might want to classify songs as texts, for example – but what if the lyrics vary from one performer or performance to the next? The words 'talk' and 'text' are useful because they remind us that people communicate in different ways, some of which require the mediation of technology. But it is important to bear in mind that such terms do not necessarily refer to discrete or easily separable things in the real world.

It is also important to remember that when we study talk (in the sense of speech), we generally do so through the medium of text (in the sense of writing). In this book, for instance, examples of spoken language are given in written (or rather, printed) form. This is not unusual: when linguists and other scholars research speech, they often capture it using an audio recorder, and then transcribe it (write it down) using letters, punctuation marks and other symbols. In fact, the technological ability to record speech and render it into textual form has been of fundamental importance to language study since the mid-twentieth century. However, a transcript (and even a recording) can never be any more than a *representation* of what somebody said: it is not *talk itself*, and, while some transcripts include more information than others, many details will always be left out. On the other hand, the process of **transcription** can help us to focus on what is useful for our purposes. If we want to know about the role of silence in speech, for example, then we can choose to transcribe every slight pause and hesitation. But if we are interested in other aspects of speech, such as pronunciation or vocabulary, then it may be more helpful to leave out such details. In this book, you will see that different authors have taken different approaches to transcription, depending on their particular focus, purpose or disciplinary background.

The focus and structure of the book

The first two chapters of the book, 'Talking in English' and 'Reading and writing in English', look at how people use talk and text to communicate in English. As these chapters show, communication is always shaped by habitual activities and social situations. These chapters use a wide range of real-world examples (from conversations over dinner to online journals) and introduce some of the most important theories in the field of discourse analysis. There is a special focus on the importance of 'paralinguistic' forms of communication such as tone of voice and typography, and the two chapters provide a grounding of skills and ideas that will be built on throughout the remainder of the book.

Chapter 3, 'Growing up with English', looks at how children, whether monolingual or bilingual, learn to participate in spoken and written communication involving English. It explores both cognitive and social factors in language acquisition, weighing up the respective roles of a child's individual meaning-making and of the ways of communicating that are prevalent in the child's community. Chapter 4, 'Working in English', moves forward in the life of the individual, focusing on the use of English in the adult world of work. It shows how English is used for social and professional purposes at work and how international business communication is changing assumptions about 'correct' English – but it also shows how difficulty in speaking the right kind of English can lead to disadvantage in the job market.

Chapters 5 and 6, 'Everyday creativity in English' and 'Persuasion in English', address fundamental questions about how language is used and what it is used for by investigating two familiar phenomena that can be found in many contexts. These phenomena are the playful, creative use of the English language that we see not only in so-called 'creative writing', but also in everyday conversation; and the use of spoken and written English to persuade an audience, whether it be to make a purchase, support a cause or simply concede a point. As these chapters show, rhetorical and poetic features are not restricted to particular kinds of text, but infuse all human communication. The recognition of this has been vitally important to much recent research on language and communication.

Chapters 7 and 8, 'Material English' and 'Digital English', discuss the impact of communications technologies on the English language, and on how it is used to communicate. This is a new topic for language research. These two chapters take us from the development of the alphabet, through the invention of printing, to the world of digital communications. As these chapters show, it is always important to think about the material and technological basis of language and communication – but that basis is itself shaped by social and economic factors.

All these chapters balance theory with empirical research and provide opportunities to analyse data and reflect on ideas. They share a commitment to exploring the English language as it is used to communicate in real-world situations.

1 Talking in English

Barbara Mayor and Daniel Allington

With grateful acknowledgement to Janet Maybin for the inclusion of material from an earlier Open University publication.

1.1 Introduction

Figure 1.1 Maintaining relationships through talk

How do you keep in touch with friends and family? How do you keep track of work, study and day-to-day life? How do you express yourself and your feelings and organise your life? If you think about the many ways in which you communicate your thoughts with others and yourself, you are likely to focus first on speech and writing. These are made up of sounds and marks which we recognise as words. You might also think about the ways in which we experience speech and writing – face to face, on the telephone, in books and on screens. However, communication is rarely confined to words. The meaning of written words will be influenced by how they are laid out and where they are read. Similarly, the meaning of a spoken utterance will depend not only on what is said, but on the way in which it is said: tone of voice, pauses and gestures are central to the meaning of talk. We learn these forms of **paralanguage** as children, alongside language itself.

There are many approaches to the study of talk and text. In this book, we view communication in terms of **language practices**: routines or activities in which people take part for particular purposes (e.g. finding something out, persuading somebody to do something or simply building relationships with other people). A language practices approach focuses on how language is part of our daily routines and how it functions to help us get things done, establish and maintain relationships, and express creativity and playfulness. However, we will also sometimes focus in detail on the surface form of what people have said or written, looking carefully at the way they use language. This complementary approach is often called **discourse analysis**.

In this introductory chapter, our focus is on the ways in which people use spoken English to communicate and interact. One of the most important concepts in dealing with spoken communication (and any other form of language in use) is **context**. Context refers to the physical location and social circumstances in which a particular example of language use occurs. Context can include the following (overlapping) elements, all of which will influence the use and interpretation of particular words and phrases:

- the physical surroundings
- the relationship between the speakers
- their past shared experience, and current goals
- the social events of which the interaction is a part
- if applicable, the institutional setting (e.g. if the interaction takes place in somebody's place of work, or if one or more of the participants is speaking in an official or professional capacity)
- broader cultural values and expectations.

Anthropologists have found that, in order to use and interpret language, we draw on a considerable amount of cultural as well as linguistic knowledge. Within any single community there will also be a range of ways of speaking: different uses of language associated with particular institutions, particular relationships and particular social events. In order to understand the function and meaning of any spoken exchange, we need to know the values held by the speakers and their expectations about language use in that particular cultural context.

Talk and conversation

By **talk**, we mean any kind of spoken interaction between people. Although the word **conversation** is often used with the same meaning as 'talk', in this chapter we follow Emanuel Schegloff (1999) in defining conversation as the specific kind of talk that people engage in when their spoken interaction is *not* organised by institutional rules. Schegloff (1999) exemplifies this distinction by contrasting the classroom (where there are rules about who speaks when and in what way) with the playground or schoolyard (where there are no such rules, enabling conversation to occur). Other situations where people talk without necessarily engaging in conversation would include job interviews, legal hearings and service encounters (i.e. where one person sells a product or service to another).

1.2   The structure and functions of talk

What kind of knowledge do you need in order to be able to take part in everyday English-language talk? How do you know when it is appropriate to speak and when not, how best to express yourself, and what response you are likely to elicit from your interlocutor? And how do people actually use talk to get things done and pursue relationships? These are the kinds of questions we will be pursuing in greater depth in this and the next section.

Informal talk is of course largely unplanned because it arises spontaneously out of fluid and changing everyday activities and relationships, and has to be produced and comprehended in real time. It is a normal feature of spoken language to contain inexplicit references, as well as unfinished and overlapping utterances which look nothing like what most English speakers are taught to regard as 'grammatical' sentences. However, in recent years, linguists such as Douglas Biber and colleagues (1999) and Ronald Carter and Michael McCarthy (2006), who have been able to base their understanding on large computerised data banks of transcribed talk, have come to recognise that spoken English has its own distinctive grammar. Moreover, people who have studied the structure of conversation have demonstrated that – despite first impressions – everyday talk is far from being chaotic or disorganised.

**Allow about
5 minutes**

Activity 1.1

Consider the following brief extract from an ongoing conversation. What
can you tell about the relationship between the two people concerned?
What do you notice about the content of the exchange? What do you
notice about the style of interaction?

Extract 1: Small talk

P: Have a nice day tomorrow.

C: Oh thanks, and thanks again for the things. This is lovely …
       cyclamen isn't it? Cyclamen …

P: Yeh, cyclamen, I think it is.

C: …'s gorgeous. Have a lovely time.

(adapted from Cheepen and Monaghan, 1990, p. 41)

Comment

A key point about everyday talk is that it is **dialogic**. This means that
each person's contributions are orientated towards other speakers: a
point that Mikhail Bakhtin (1986 [1952]) made with regard to all language
use. Especially in conversation, people constantly (although often
implicitly) refer to what previous speakers have said, anticipate what they
might say next and assume a large amount of shared experience
(Bakhtin, 1986 [1952], pp. 68–9). Obviously, Extract 1 is only a brief
extract from a longer exchange, but we have no difficulty in interpreting
the 'first' line as a reference to a shared context and previous
conversations between the speakers. It seems clear that this is an
informal exchange between two people who already know each other
well. Despite some simultaneous speech in the middle, the conversation
appears to proceed smoothly, with each speaker managing to accomplish
two turns in quick succession.

The purpose of this kind of talk, which the anthropologist Bronisław
Malinowski (1923) called 'phatic communion', is specifically to bind
people together and to establish an interactional framework for the
encounter. The linguist Roman Jakobson (1960) argued that any speech
event fulfils both a **referential function** (dealing with information) and a
phatic function (dealing with social relationships); following Michael
Halliday (1973), these are often now called the **ideational** and
interpersonal functions of language. Although interpersonal aspects

infuse all talk, it is not unusual for there to be specific phases of primarily interpersonal 'small talk', particularly at the beginning and (as here) at the ending of an interaction.

Doing things with words

In fact, talk can fulfil a wide range of functions. The philosopher J. L. Austin (1962) realised that in *saying* something (e.g. 'hello'), a speaker is usually also *doing* something (in this case, perhaps greeting somebody). Austin referred to actions that are carried out through speaking as **speech acts**. Some speech acts can be performed by anyone at almost any time (e.g. making a promise), and these have generally been the focus of the greatest discussion by linguists, since their power often seems to come from the words used to carry them out (e.g. 'I promise'). The sociologist Pierre Bourdieu (1992 [1982]), however, argues that more attention should be paid to the social conditions that make particular speech acts possible. The most powerful speech acts require particular institutional contexts and are not authorised for every speaker to perform. For example, '[o]nly a hopeless soldier … could imagine that it was possible to give his captain an order' (Bourdieu, 1992 [1982], p. 75): even if the soldier says something that sounds like an order, it won't count as a real order because, in the military, one has to be of a higher rank than another person to be able to give that person an order (see Figure 1.2).

Speech act theory has also been criticised for relying on invented or remembered examples instead of working with recordings of real talk (see, for example, Potter, 2001). In an attempt to reach an understanding of how people *actually* use spoken language to communicate, sociologists Harvey Sacks, Emanuel Schegloff and Gail Jefferson developed the discipline of **conversation analysis**, which examines naturally occurring talk in an extremely detailed and methodical way (Sacks et al., 1974; Sacks, 1998 [1995]). This is one of the most important forms of discourse analysis and, through it, researchers have come to appreciate the intricate patterns evident in the management of conversation and other forms of everyday talk.

Figure 1.2 'Only a hopeless soldier … could imagine that it was possible to give his captain an order' (Bourdieu, 1992 [1982], p. 75).

Opening and closing a conversation

Harvey Sacks began his work on conversation by noticing the ways in which spoken interaction could go *wrong* when people rang in to the helpline at a psychiatric hospital. This set him thinking about the implicit cultural rules that underlie the conduct of talk.

Activity 1.2

Now turn to Reading A: *Rules of conversational sequence*, which is an extract from a lecture delivered by Harvey Sacks at the University of California, Los Angeles in the mid-1960s.

As you read, take particular note of the following:

1   the way in which one speaker's turn creates an expectation of what the following utterance will be, and may to some extent constrain the next speaker's turn

2   the way in which pairs of utterances constitute different kinds of social exchange

3   the distinction between the linguistic form of an utterance and its pragmatic function (the action performed in uttering it).

Then make a note of:

4   any other typical pairs of utterances that you can think of that perform other social functions

5   the different kinds of opening utterance that you regularly use yourself in telephone calls.

Comment

1   Sacks talks about 'procedural rules' (elsewhere 'rules of etiquette') which people tend to follow when one person addresses another. He argues that in any spoken exchange the first speaker has the social right to choose the form of address, and that there are then predictable 'returns' that the second speaker may routinely choose from to fill the next speaker 'slot'. However, although this to some extent constrains the second speaker's choices, all speakers have the choice of whether or not to respond predictably, and more deviant choices (Sacks calls all options conversational 'devices') remain open to either speaker.

2   Sacks argues that spoken exchanges are composed of 'single units' or 'composites', which tend to function together in pairs: for example, a greeting followed by a reciprocal greeting or a question followed by an answer. They are composed of particular kinds of speech act that tend to follow one another. Sacks later came to call these units **adjacency pairs** (Schegloff and Sacks, 1973). If you say the first part of an adjacency pair to somebody else, that person will usually realise that they (to use Sacks's phrase) 'properly ought' to respond with the second part. Conversation analysts refer to this 'proper' way of responding as the **preferred response**, in other words the response that the first speaker would be assumed to expect. As Sacks illustrates, a speaker does not always get the preferred response – for example, a question may be followed by a change of topic or a greeting by silence. This is referred to as a **dispreferred response** – a response that the first speaker would not be assumed to expect. As Sacks recognised, speakers have a number of strategies open to them when they want to avoid giving the preferred response – for example, he suggests that a telephone caller can say 'I can't hear you' instead of openly refusing to provide his or her name.

3   Sacks gives the example of 'May I help you?', which has the form of a question but, as conventionally used, is intended to serve as an opening or offer, inviting the other to express a query or request.

4   Your list may have included some of the following typical pairs of utterances: an offer or invitation, followed by either acceptance or refusal; an apology or a compliment, followed by either acceptance or rejection; a directive, followed by either compliance or refusal; a reprimand, followed by either apology or retaliation; and so on.

5   Your list may have included a range of more or less formal greetings, depending on the context and whether you know (or think you know!) who you are talking to.

It is not only the openings of spoken interactions that are structured so regularly. There are also important rituals for closing a conversation and withdrawing from the roles it involves, as illustrated by the full version of the exchange that you met at the start of this chapter. In line with the tradition launched by conversation analysis, this has been re-punctuated to represent more accurately some of the features of its delivery and is beginning to look less like ordinary written language. We can also now reveal to you that P and C are English women in their thirties who became friends because they both had children at the same school, and that P has been spending the afternoon at C's house.

Extract 2: Saying goodbye properly

P: I must go (.) taking up your time (.) have a nice day tomorrow

C: oh thanks and thanks again for the things (.) this is lovely (.) cyclamen isn't it (.) cyclamen

P: yeh (.) cyclamen (.) I think it is

C: 's gorgeous (.) have a lovely time

P: all this evening to look forward to (.) oh [*a squeak is heard*]

C: enjoy it

P: I will

C: have a lovely time and thanks again

P: thanks (.) bye

C: bye

P: bye

(adapted from Cheepen and Monaghan, 1990, p. 41)

Transcription conventions

(.) indicates a brief pause
[*square brackets*] enclose description of background noises

The role of transcription conventions

After a transcript such as Extract 2, a key is often provided
explaining the symbols used to represent features of spoken
language. Transcription requires more or less detailed symbols
depending on the purposes for which it will be used. For example,
many of the transcriptions in this chapter were produced for the
purposes of conversation analysis, so symbols are needed to
represent overlaps, pauses, laughter and other such features.
Research in the tradition of conversation analysis often goes into
even more detail, however; for example, the original version of
Extract 2 included symbols to represent the speaker's breathing,
vocal pitch and speed of speaking, and some conversation analysts
also transcribe gesture, eye movement and body posture. Other
forms of discourse analysis frequently employ less detailed
transcripts: if we want to focus on *what* is said, we may need less
information about exactly *how* it is said.

In terms of structure, conversation endings are often highly repetitive:
this is partly because they refer back to topics raised earlier (*all this
evening to look forward to*), and partly because (as with greetings) farewells
form adjacency pairs: here, P's first 'bye' is followed by C's 'bye', which
is in turn followed by P's second 'bye'. This repetition is part of the
emphasis on solidarity at the closing point of an encounter. Before
parting, speakers often express positive evaluations of their time
together (*thanks again*), and the person initiating the closing often cites
an external reason for needing to go or effaces her- or himself in some
way (e.g. *taking up your time*).

Turn taking

As conversation analysts have shown, everyday conversations have an
organised (and often orderly) structure, despite the fact that they are
neither scripted nor rehearsed. This can be seen in the phenomenon of
turn taking between speakers. In the 1970s, a great deal of research on
this phenomenon was conducted among speakers of standard British
and American varieties of English. On this basis, it was observed that

one person typically spoke at a time and that **overlap** (simultaneous speech) was generally kept to a minimum. Since then, research has been conducted among more diverse communities, and it has been shown that patterns of turn taking are in practice more variable. But, regardless of context, speakers need to cooperate with one another if communication is not to break down, and they can do this by a number of means, including the use of adjacency pairs.

As well as following particular forms of turn taking, speakers have been argued to unconsciously use their grammatical knowledge of English, coupled with their knowledge of paralinguistic cues, such as intonation and eye contact, in order to respond to their interlocutors at the *end* of a unit of speech rather than in the middle. At the end of each unit comes what Sacks (1998 [1995]) calls a **transition relevance place** (frequently abbreviated to TRP). When this is reached, it may sometimes happen that the speaker will pause very briefly for a response, but it is equally likely that other speakers (having anticipated the opportunity) will come in with their next turn, perhaps leading to a slight overlap. Overlap that occurs before a transition relevance place may be considered an interruption, although how participants react to an interruption will depend on their cultural expectations as well as the immediate context.

Allow about 5 minutes

Activity 1.3

The extract below represents a family's conversation over dinner. Russell and Maggie are children (aged twelve and seven respectively) and Jen is their mother. Look at the transcript carefully and try to identify any adjacency pairs (with preferred and dispreferred responses) and overlaps (including whether or not they seem to involve interruption). You will probably have to read the transcript several times to make sense of what is happening.

Extract 3: Keeping order at the dinner table

1	Jen:	Have some chee- put some cheese on your potato now and it will melt (10.0)
2		((Maggie starts to get up)) Sit down I'll get you a drink
3	Russell:	And me please
4	Maggie:	*Milk*
5	Jen:	Milk or water Russ?
6	Russell:	Water please (1.0) *SIT DOWN*
7	Maggie:	*I KNOW I SLIPPED*
8	Jen:	*Ok* there's no need to [shout] at her

9	Russell:	[If you] slipped you're just standing there goin'=
		((does action of Maggie's claimed slipping))
10	Maggie:	=[*No*]=
11	Russell:	=[Ooh] [I slipped!] ((mimicking))
12	Maggie:	=[*I went back*]*wards like that*
13	(1.5)	
14	Russell:	*SIT DO::WN*
15	Maggie:	*I KNOW* [*don't talk*] *with your mouth open*
16	Jen:	[She is love]y ((sotto voce))
17	Russell:	Hmm How am I meant to talk then?
18	Jen:	*Russell*

(adapted from Hester and Hester, 2010, p. 35)

Transcription conventions

(10.0) a number in parentheses indicates the length of a pause in seconds
: indicates that the preceding sound was lengthened
= at the end of one turn and the beginning of the next indicates that there was no pause between them
italics indicate particularly strong emphasis
CAPITALS indicate shouting
((parentheses)) enclose descriptive comments from the transcriber (sotto voce = 'in a soft voice')
[square brackets] enclose overlapping speech

Comment

In the extract, there is just one adjacency pair in which the preferred response is received: this is Jen's offer of a drink in line 5 and Russell's acceptance in line 6. Other adjacency pairs involve dispreferred responses. For example, in line 6, Russell goes on to give Maggie a directive (*SIT DOWN*), but Maggie responds by rejecting the directive as unnecessary (*I KNOW*), implying that she would already be sitting down had she not accidentally slipped. In line 14, Russell issues the same directive, getting almost the same rejection in line 15; then, Maggie issues a directive of her own (*don't talk with your mouth open*), which Russell rejects (line 17). In the discussion of speech acts earlier in this section, we observed that not everyone has the authority to perform every speech act; here, neither of the children accepts the other's authority to tell him or her what to do. This authority might be assumed to belong to Jen as the children's mother – and as Sally and Stephen Hester (2010) note in their analysis of this data, Russell's directives to

Maggie repeat a directive that Jen had earlier issued to Maggie (line 2). By not responding to her mother, Maggie left an adjacency pair incomplete, and Russell appears to take advantage of this in order to present his directives as being 'reiterated on behalf of his mother' (Hester and Hester, 2010, p. 38). When he does this for the second time, Jen defends Maggie by implying that the directive is unnecessary, stating that Maggie is by now already sitting down (line 16), though she softens the reprimand to Russell by addressing him as 'lovey'. (See also line 18, where Jen is more direct in her reprimand.)

There are three cases of overlap. Russell appears to interrupt Jen in line 9: there is no transition relevance place between *to* and *shout*, since these words form part of the same grammatical unit. Then in line 10, Maggie appears to interrupt Russell: in this context, *goin'* is a transitive verb (meaning 'saying'), so it is not a complete grammatical unit and must be followed by something else; however, Maggie breaks in with *No*. Overlap also occurs in lines 11 and 12, but you might not consider it to be interruption: *standing there goin' Ooh* could be heard as a complete grammatical unit, followed by a transition relevance place at which both Russell and Maggie start speaking simultaneously. *I KNOW* is a complete grammatical unit, so when Jen starts speaking in line 16, she is probably not interrupting Maggie.

As readers of the transcript alone, we cannot know how the participants felt about any of the interruptions or dispreferred responses, nor can we know what is normal for this family, except insofar as we can deduce these things from the way the conversation develops and from paralinguistic features (such as shouting). Conversation analysts always try to work in this way, basing their claims only on the recordings and transcripts that they analyse, but discourse analysts working in other traditions may also refer to additional information about the participants and context.

1.3 Politeness and interpersonal meaning

Face needs and relationship constraints

Social interactions through talk, like those in the examples above, involve the constant management of one's own and other people's **face**, a term used by the American sociologist Erving Goffman (1967) for people's public self-image. Loss of face for any speaker is disruptive and may need to be 'repaired'; for instance, by the rephrasing of a comment or by an explicit apology. Effort to maintain one's own or others' face is known as **face work** and may involve strategic talk to boost or maintain status: an aspect of the interpersonal function of language use. Thus, we may speak of speech acts as **face threatening** (possibly causing someone to lose face) or **face saving** (enabling a speaker to escape from potential loss of face).

Politeness also involves using strategies such as appropriate **terms of address** and degrees of directness and formality. These vary according to people's **relative status**, the degree of **social distance** between them and the extent of their **solidarity** with one another. For example, *Eat up your lunch, dear!* might be an appropriate command to a child, or even to an intimate friend, but not to one's line manager at work, and possibly not to one's grandmother, depending on the formality of status relationships within the family. If you live in a cool climate and find yourself in a hot and stuffy meeting room at work, and a close colleague of yours is sitting next to the window, you might say *Open that window, will you?* However, if it is a very senior colleague who is by the window you might use more politeness markers in your utterance, as in *Excuse me, I wonder if you'd mind just opening that window slightly for me please?* Or you might be even more indirect with the statement *Does anyone else find it hot in here?* and hope that the colleague infers your indirect request accordingly. Generally speaking, people in a lower status position pay more attention to the face needs of those in a higher status position than the other way round.

Being linguistically polite also involves sensitivity to the social and cultural context (especially the formality of the occasion) and to sociolinguistic rules about behaviour: how to accept or refuse an invitation, the appropriate language practices around giving and receiving hospitality, greetings formulae, terms of address, taboo terms, and so on. These conventions vary in different English-speaking communities, as do the values governing the way formality, social distance and status are expressed.

Bearing all this in mind, let's look at one particular practice in English, to see what kinds of factors influence the use and interpretation of language to convey interpersonal meaning.

Terms of address

In some languages the relationship between speakers is encoded grammatically; for example, the distinction between formal and informal 'you' in many European languages, or in Japanese the use of distinctive verb endings to acknowledge the relative positions of speaker and addressee in the social hierarchy. In English, however (where the distinction between familiar *thou/thee* and polite *you* has died out in standard varieties), relationships between speakers are not so immediately obvious. One has to look across a whole interaction to gather clues from the way language is used to see how particular relationships are being marked, negotiated or contested. However, one way in which relationships are quite explicitly marked in English is in the terms people use to address each other.

Allow about
10 minutes

Activity 1.4

Make a note of all the names or terms that people use to address you (in English or other languages). What are the reasons for people calling you one name rather than another? And would it be appropriate for you to address them in an equivalent manner?

Comment

We asked some of our colleagues and students to think about this activity, and their lists included variations on first and last names, together with *Miss, Ms, Mrs, Mr, Dr* or *Professor*, nicknames, *mum, dad, aunty, uncle*, etc. and their non-English equivalents (within the family), *sir/madam/ma'am* (in certain public settings, including service encounters), *mate/love* and the local variant *me duck* (in less formal ones), *miss/sir* (in schools), and various terms of endearment and abuse. One of our students from Singapore noted that she bears both an English name (*Debbie*) and a Chinese one (*Wing Yu*), both of which have been used, and differently pronounced, by different people at different times in her life.

We reflect further on the meaning of all these choices below.

Some of the names in our list are kinship terms (with some variation between more and less formal versions), while *sir/miss* used by children in schools signals a particular work role (like *doctor* or *your honour*) as well as maintaining social distance. Honorific terms, like *sir/madam*, mark not just formal respect, but also certain genteel politeness conventions – hence the difference between the ways in which we may be addressed in smart department stores and in the local market. Some family terms, like *mother* and *father*, which were used until relatively recently as terms of address in the UK, are now largely used only for reference to third parties.

Finally, you may have observed that the same term can mean rather different things in different relationships or contexts; for instance, the various uses of *sir* identified above, or the way in which a woman (less often a man) may be addressed as *love/dear/honey/sweetheart* by her partner, a female relation or friend, an older male colleague or a local tradesman, all with very different meaning and impact. You may also have noticed that many of these terms are not used reciprocally, and that the person in the lower status position may have less freedom of choice. In the UK, many people comment on the increasing tendency of commercial organisations to adopt rather informal terms of address for their clients, presumably to try to establish, or mimic, a close, trusting relationship. And even the same name can convey different meaning when abbreviated: in Extract 3, for example, Jen used the familiar form of Russell's name ('Russ', line 5) when asking him a question, but used his full name ('Russell', line 18) when telling him off.

If further proof of the potential communicative force of terms of address is needed, consider this classic example from the 1960s involving an African-American doctor:

'What's your name, boy?' the policeman asked ...
'Dr Poussaint. I'm a physician ...'
'What's your first name, boy? ...'
'Alvin.'

The policeman manages to insult Dr Poussaint three times in this short exchange; once by his initial use of the term 'boy' which denies adult status on the grounds of race, secondly because he ignores the doctor's stated preference for how he should be addressed, and thirdly by repeating the denigrating term 'boy' even when he knows the doctor's name. Dr Poussaint's own experience of the encounter was 'profound humiliation' – 'For the moment, my manhood had been ripped from me.'

(Ervin-Tripp, 1969, pp. 93, 98)

So are there sociolinguistic rules that tell us who has the right to use which terms to whom? As explained above, terms of address are a part of politeness conventions, and will depend on difference in status between the speakers, how well they know each other, the formality of the situation, and the cultural and linguistic context. In 1960s America, for example, the issue of segregation and civil rights was to the fore of the public conscience, so the policeman's use of *boy* carried deep and troubling social connotations.

As the example of Dr Poussaint and the policeman shows, terms of address are powerful ways of expressing and asserting relationships. In multilingual communities, speakers have access to a range of conventions deriving from different cultures and languages and may use their choice of terms of address to invoke a particular set of values. For example, speakers of many of the new Englishes (e.g. Indian English, Hawaiian English, Singaporean English, Nigerian English) address a wider range of people as *aunty* and *uncle* than do most British or American English speakers, reflecting the greater social importance of kinship for these speakers. They may also choose kinship terms from their other languages: for instance, an Indian English speaker may address a listener who is not a blood relative as *didi* or *di* (elder sister), to indicate respect and affection. In such ways speakers can signal that they want to invoke local conventions, rather than those associated with British or American culture (Pandharipande, 1992).

1.4   Communicative strategies and conversational style

Apart from the universal function of everyday talk in cementing human relationships and getting things done, and some basic structural constraints on turn taking, it will already have become apparent that the particular rules and strategies for how these interactional goals are achieved are very variable, even within English. A growing body of work exists on the ways in which conversational style varies systematically from context to context.

In its broadest definition, **conversational style** refers to a combination of features relating to the meaning and management of conversation, including prosody (rhythm and intonation), overlapping, repetition, use of laughter, tolerance of noise and silence, and ways of using anecdotes, asking questions, linking topics and expressing particular emotions (Tannen, 1984), as well as paralinguistic features such as gesture, stance and gaze. At the individual level we all have our own particular conversational style – the way we use stories, for instance, or how much personal information we tend to reveal, or how we express politeness.

However, aspects of our conversational style can also be traced to social variables, such as place of origin, social class, ethnicity, age group and gender.

How do conversational styles vary?

There can be a remarkable diversity of styles even among speakers of standard varieties of English, as Deborah Tannen (1984) found in a now classic work of discourse analysis. Tannen analysed the conversation of five friends and herself during a Thanksgiving dinner party in the USA. These friends came from different geographical backgrounds: two were Californian men, three (two men and Tannen) were New Yorkers, and there was one English woman. Tannen was intrigued by the striking difference between the New Yorkers and the rest when she asked them afterwards how much they had enjoyed the conversation during the meal. Whereas the New Yorkers remembered it as lively and satisfying, the others had found it 'all over the place and frenetic' and had felt bulldozed and marginalised.

In contrasting the New Yorkers' conversational style with those of the others, Tannen highlights the following differences:

- expectations about what it is appropriate to talk about; for example, whether 'personal' topics are ruled out
- how turn taking is managed; for instance, whether pauses and silence are tolerated and whether interruptions are meant to encourage or stop the other speaker
- the degree of directness in questions and whether these are perceived as supportive or off-putting
- use of intonation and voice quality (to signal enthusiasm, the punch line of a story, and so on)
- willingness to enter ironic routines or story rounds, and expectations about what constitutes a joke or story worth telling.

Some of the differences in communication strategies that Tannen identifies between her friends are also highlighted in studies of different cultural groups and of gender and talk. In the next two subsections, questioning strategies, ways of seeking and expressing personal information, and the role of pauses and silence crop up again as important aspects of communication style that can have quite far-reaching effects if they are not used in the same way by people trying to talk to each other.

Cultural differences: a case study of Aboriginal English

Diana Eades, an Australian linguist, studies Aboriginal English speakers' ways of speaking and the effects these have on their experience of communicating with white Australians. She suggests that Aboriginal ways of using English are closely related to Aboriginal lifestyle and culture, and to their beliefs about how people should relate to one another.

Activity 1.5

Now turn to Reading B: *Communicative strategies in Aboriginal English* by Diana Eades. As you read this classic study based on research from the 1980s, note the features of Aboriginal communicative style that Eades identifies. What explanations does she advance for this? What kinds of misunderstanding may arise between speakers of Aboriginal English and white Australians as a result of these differences in communicative style? To what extent do you think the communicative style that Eades identifies is restricted to Aboriginal speakers?

Comment

Eades suggests that the lack of personal privacy in the Aboriginal lifestyle may have led to an indirect verbal style. Aboriginal people, she argues, are reluctant to express personal opinions, supply information or account for actions directly. Indirectness is often achieved through the 'multifunctional' nature of utterances; for example, whether a question is also interpreted as a request for a favour can be negotiated between the speakers concerned. Aboriginal responses to the directness of white interactions often include 'gratuitous concurrence', an apparent agreement with the previous utterance, when all that may be intended is that the conversation should move on. According to Eades' evidence, this can cause significant misunderstanding whenever direct questions are used in legal, medical and educational settings.

You may have felt that indirectness is not unique to Aboriginal speakers, but is a common feature of the speech of many groups who lack social power. The phenomenon of 'gratuitous concurrence', on the other hand, may be rather less widespread. It was in the context of Aboriginal English that it was first observed and labelled (by Liberman, 1981).

Gender differences

Another way of identifying significant aspects of style is to compare the conversational behaviours of men and women. Research in this area tended initially to be carried out among middle-class, white women from the UK or USA, but, as we shall see, ideas developed in those relatively limited contexts are beginning to be applied more broadly to other contexts.

Figure 1.3 Women's talk?

Activity 1.6

Spend a few moments noting down your personal experience of any differences between men's and women's talk – the way they interact, their choice of words and phrases, the topics they like to discuss. Why might differences exist (or seem to exist)? Our comments follow.

Allow about 10 minutes

It is often argued that in conversation, women are less competitive and more cooperative than men, and work harder to make the interaction run smoothly – for instance, by encouraging others to talk and using more face-saving politeness strategies. The linguist Robin Lakoff (1975) influentially argued that this is because women are brought up to occupy a less powerful position in society, and to display deference towards men, which they do through being more hesitant and indirect. Lakoff suggested that women use more tag questions (e.g. *isn't it? don't you think?*) and more indirect polite forms (e.g. *could you possibly?*), intensifiers (e.g. *I'm so glad*), euphemisms and what she saw as generally weaker vocabulary (e.g. words such as *nice* and *Oh dear*). Lakoff's observations were largely intuitive and anecdotal, and they received elements of both challenge and support in later studies, some (but not all) of which found men to dominate mixed gender conversation, interrupting more and giving less feedback and support (see Coates, 1996, 2003; Cameron, 2007).

Other linguists have argued that men and women speak differently, not because of an asymmetrical power relationship between them, but because they are socialised into different gender subcultures as children through play. In her study of African-American children playing in the street, Marjorie Harness Goodwin (Goodwin, 1998) found that, while boys played in hierarchical groups, with those higher up issuing clear directives such as *Gimme the pliers*, the girls organised themselves into more cooperative groups and made more indirect suggestions, such as *Let's do it this way*. Boys' arguments involved challenges to the group hierarchy and were sorted out straight away through direct competition and verbal confrontation, while girls who organised their friendships through inclusion and exclusion tended to have protracted discussions about other girls in their absence. Here then might be the seeds of a non-confrontational, collaborative speech style for women, with an interest in topics concerning people's motives and feelings, and a more directly competitive style for men, with a focus on the physical world.

These two approaches towards men's and women's talk have been referred to respectively as the 'dominance' and the 'difference' approach: the former suggests that men dominate women in spoken interaction, the latter that men and women simply communicate differently. Other researchers, however, have pointed out that neither of these approaches seriously addresses the ways in which men and women use language differently in different contexts, or the considerable range of speaking styles within each gender group. There has recently been a shift in the study of gender and language, away from simply matching up particular language features to men or to women, and towards examining how people 'do' or 'perform' their gender through language. The performance of gender involves *what* is said as well as *how* it is said. For instance, Deborah Cameron's (1998) discourse analysis of a conversation between a group of male college students showed that their talk had both cooperative and competitive aspects, including solidarity-signalling features that some researchers had associated with 'women's talk'. Cameron argues that, in this private conversation among male friends, gender is not expressed through speaking style so much as through the content of talk: the speakers' references to sexual exploits with women and their derogatory comments about other males whom they describe as 'gay'. Cameron suggests that, through what they say, these young men define themselves *against* these other groups (women and gay men), in a performance of the gender identity of 'red-blooded heterosexual males'.

Recently, Cameron has taken this critique further still. In *The Myth of Mars and Venus* (2007) she argues that popular conceptions of linguistic variation across the gender divide are not supported by the evidence: men and women are not as alien to each other as relationship counsellor John Gray's (1992) *Men are from Mars, Women are from Venus* would have us believe. Cameron argues that, as long as gender is a key element of our social identity, we will continue to magnify the significance of discrepancies between male and female behaviour, including language use. In fact, there are far more similarities in the way the sexes use language than there are differences. Moreover, Cameron gives examples of cultures from around the world (including Madagascar and Papua New Guinea) where men are recognised for their cooperative talk and women for their confrontational talk. Instead of gender, Cameron suggests that we should focus on social roles to explain the predisposition to cooperative or competitive talk. When in the 'public realm', both sexes are adept at using assertive, direct language. Conversely, women and men alike display a more sympathetic, convivial style of language in the private sphere of family and close relationships. So for Cameron, the distinction between 'female' and 'male' talk has acquired too great a significance at the expense of other, more significant social markers. She concludes that ideas of typical, gendered communication themselves promulgate traditional ideas of gender roles, obstructing the path to a more equitable society.

To summarise, while both the dominance and difference arguments provide useful explanations for certain language behaviour patterns between men and women, more recent studies show how style, function and meaning vary across different contexts, and suggest that there may be more complex reasons underlying the patterns of women's and men's language use. Thus, particular language features and communicative strategies may be used more often by *some* men or women in *some* contexts.

Style, identity and performativity

Many researchers, such as Penelope Eckert and Sally McConnell-Ginet (2003), now argue that a focus on individual language features is less revealing than a focus on *combinations* of features. It is particular patterns of language features, along with the content of the talk, that communicate social messages and serve to **index** (literally, 'point to') a particular social identity on the part of the speaker. Eckert and McConnell-Ginet suggest that linguistic behaviour is also tied in with other aspects of personal style. They argue that style and performance are part both of the *formation* and of the *expression* of identity: each of us has a 'toolbox' of communicative resources, both linguistic and paralinguistic, and uses that toolbox – whether unconsciously or strategically – to produce a 'communicative style, which combines with other components of style such as dress, ways of walking, hairdo, and so on to constitute the presentation of a persona, a self' (Eckert and McConnell-Ginet, 2003, pp. 305–6; see Figure 1.4).

The question of what constitutes a language is explored in greater depth in another book in this series: Seargeant and Swann (eds) (2012) *English in the World*, Chapter 1.

In a multilingual context, speakers are able to draw on linguistic resources from more than one language, performing complex identities. Multilingual speakers in their everyday talk often use **codeswitching** between languages, whether symbolically to signal shared ethnicity or group allegiance with the person they are addressing, or pragmatically to achieve particular effects. In some communities, such as the various Hispanic communities in the USA, a mixed code may be used routinely; this practice has been termed **plurilanguaging** (García, 2007) and calls the very idea of separate languages into question. The corresponding process within a purely English-medium conversation would be termed **style shifting**, whereby speakers adopt different accents or dialects or use a more or less formal register, in order to serve particular purposes or to achieve particular effects.

From the way you dress, to the way you say 'hello', you will be influencing an interviewer's opinion of you....

Figure 1.4 'Communicative style ... combines with other components of style ... to constitute the presentation of a persona, a self' (Eckert and McConnell-Ginet, 2003, pp. 305–6).

Activity 1.7

Allow about
5 minutes

Read the following example of informal talk in English, Spanish and Chinese recorded in a Vietnamese butcher's shop in San Francisco. What languages does each speaker appear to know, and what do you think motivates them to change languages as they do?

Extract 4: Haggling over the price of meat

1	Butcher A:	you need two leg ... 20 pound each so I order two.	
2	Anne ((TO BELA)):	*pregúntele si es más barato*	[ask if it's cheaper]
3	Bela:	*¿si?*	[yes?]
4	Butcher A:	oh *¿habla español?*	[you speak Spanish?]
5	Bela:	*es más barato*	[it's cheaper]

6		uh huh	
7	Butcher A:	oh ((SPEAKS TO BUTCHER B IN WHAT SEEMS TO BE CHINESE))	
8		he said OK	
9	Butcher B:	*uno cincuenta y nueve la libra*	[$1.59 a pound]
10	Anne:	*uno cincuenta y nueve si compramos más?* ... (3)	[$1.59 if we buy more?]
11		if we buy more?	
12		ok. (??)	
13	Butcher B:	*¿quiere?*	[you want it?]
14	Anne:	ah ...	

(adapted from Kramsch and Whiteside, 2008, pp. 653–4, lines 60–75)

Transcription conventions

[ ] indicates translation
(( )) indicates comment
( ) indicates pause in seconds
(??) indicates unintelligible

Comment

It is apparent even from this short extract that all the participants are *able* to speak at least some Spanish, and yet they choose not to use this common language consistently throughout the interaction. Why is this? Although the mixture of languages may at first seem random to an outsider, on closer scrutiny it appears that a language is sometimes deployed to address a particular person (as in the 'asides' between Anne and Bela at lines 2–3 or between the two butchers at lines 7–8), sometimes to exclude other participants (as when the two butchers formally haggle in Chinese over the price at lines 7–8) and sometimes to reinforce a particular point (as when Anne re-emphasises the terms of her purchase in both Spanish and English at lines 10–11). Other interpretations are of course possible, and the participants themselves may have insights into what was going on that even the most expert observer would not be able to recognise.

The purpose of such codeswitching, therefore, is not only to communicate most effectively with the addressee, but also simultaneously to signal a symbolic allegiance to different parts of one's identity. In general, people are remarkably adept at interpreting the implicit references and implications that abound in conversation, so that conversations become essentially collaborative communicative affairs between speakers and listeners.

1.5 Stories, accounts and identity

Figure 1.5 Sharing a story

When people talk together, they often share experiences in the form of spoken narratives, and such conversational storytelling has attracted a great deal of research interest. Based on interviews conducted with African-American men, the sociolinguists William Labov and Joshua Waletzky argued that informal spoken narratives are composed of up to six kinds of 'narrative clause', five of which occur in a predictable order (Labov and Waletzky, 1967; Labov, 1972):

Abstract: a brief preview of what the narrative is about.

Orientation: an explanation of where and when the story took place and who was involved.

Complicating action: an unusual or unexpected action. Events are told in the order in which they happened.

Resolution: the way in which the complicating action came to an end. Again, events are told in chronological order.

Coda: the end of the telling, which brings the focus back to the present and out of 'story-time'.

Evaluation: the point of the story. While the other narrative clauses typically occur in the order above, evaluation can appear at any point within the story.

Allow about
10 minutes

Activity 1.8

The following narrative was taken from a focus group discussion. In contrast to the earlier extracts, this one has been transcribed using the normal conventions of written English. Because the surrounding discussion has been removed, the narrative lacks an abstract. See if you can identify the remaining elements from Labov's model of narrative structure. (For convenience of analysis, the individual sentences have been numbered.)

Extract 5: 'There are certain patterns that happen'

Context: A focus group of four middle-aged African-American men are discussing the topic of police relations with minority ethnic communities in the city of Portland, Oregon. The speaker ('George') takes a very critical line regarding the police and what he alleges to be the racist tendencies of the police administration. One of the other men in the group has been arguing in support of the police.

1. Tony Stevens was ex-Marine, Vietnam era. 2. He had a guy came in. 3. Robbed a gas station. 4. Tony grabbed the guy and held him down. 5. The police came in. 6. In spite of what everybody in the surrounding area was telling them, the police jumped on Tony, and choked him to death. 7. Why? 8. The perpetrator was white and Tony was black. 9. And this was a detective that did it. 10. This was when Potter was chief of police. 11. There are certain patterns that happen.

(adapted from Ritchie, 2010, p. 129)

Comment

Your analysis may look something like this:

Orientation: 1.

Complicating action: 2–3 (plus, arguably, 4–5).

Resolution: 4–5 (if not seen as part of the complicating action) and the second part of 6 (*the police jumped on Tony, and choked him to death*).

Coda: 11.

Evaluation: first part of 6 (*In spite of what everybody in the surrounding area was telling them*) and 7–10.

Even though the story is so short, it is quite complicated: as L. David Ritchie (2010, p. 129) observes, the complicating action is followed by an 'attempted resolution' (Stevens's attempt to deal with the robber), a 'reversal' (the arrival of the police) and a 'final resolution' (the killing of Stevens). It is hard to decide whether the 'attempted resolution' should be analysed as part of the resolution proper or as part of the complicating action in Labov and Waletzky's basic framework. But it is clearly the evaluation that reveals why George tells the story: he is presenting what happened as evidence supporting his low opinion of the local police force.

It has been argued that the structure described by Labov and Waletzky (1967) is produced partly by the conditions of the research interview, where 'the prototypical interviewer tends to avoid interruptions or challenges in the course of a story's telling' while 'the prototypical interviewee … tells the story to attentive ears, fills in the gaps, and creates the missing frames of mutual reference' (Georgakopoulou, 2006, p. 237). In other situations (e.g. in ordinary conversation), this does not necessarily apply: tellers of stories may assume that their listeners already know something about the events they are relating, and listeners may challenge the storyteller's interpretation of events. The result may be a form of storytelling in which '[m]ost of the talk is occupied with evaluating the events in moral and ethical terms, while information about what actually happened is relatively sparse' (Bamberg, 2004, p. 340).

1.6 Collaborative storytelling

Stories are often told collaboratively. In the next example, eleven-year-old Karlie provides an evaluation at the beginning of a story that she tells together with her friend Nicole. The interviewer, Janet Maybin, had asked Nicole who else lived at her house and Karlie had mentioned that Nicole's sister Terri had recently had a baby.

Extract 6: Terri did the best thing

1	Janet:	So does your sister live quite near you?
2	Nicole:	She lives with us
3	Karlie:	Cause she's only quite young
4	Nicole:	She's young, she's sixteen
5	Janet:	Ah right
6	Karlie:	She did the best thing about it though, didn't she, Nicole?
7	Nicole:	She didn't tell a soul, no one, that she was pregnant
8	Karlie:	Until she was due, when she got into hospital, then she told them
9	Nicole:	On Saturday night she had pains in her stomach, and come the
10		following Sunday my mum was at work and my sister come to the pub
11		and my aunt Ella was in it and my sister went in there and said 'I've got
12		pains in my stomach!', so my aunt Ella went and got my mum, and took
13		her to hospital, and my mum asked her if she was due on and she said 'No,
14		I've just come off' and when they got her to hospital they said 'Take her
15		to Maternity!' My mum was crying
16	Janet:	Your mum didn't realise she was pregnant?
17	Nicole:	No. And my mum slept with her when she was ill!
		…
18	Karlie:	/My dad said she did, Terri did the best thing about it. Her sister's Terri
19	Nicole:	Or if she did tell, as she's so young, she weren't allowed to have him

(adapted from Maybin, 2006, pp. 117–18)

Transcription conventions

… indicates omitted talk
/ indicates where another speaker interrupts or cuts in

After Karlie's evaluation (line 6), Nicole and Karlie give the abstract of the story (lines 7–8). In line 17, Nicole provides an evaluation in the form of additional information which emphasises the extraordinary nature of the story: *my mum slept with her when she was ill* (i.e. *and still didn't notice that she was pregnant*).

Interestingly, although Karlie's initial evaluation is presented as her own, later in the interview we learn that it was her father's (line 18). Karlie seems to have presented her father's judgement of Terri's actions as if it were her own. This occurrence might remind you of Extract 3, where Russell repeated his mother's words in order to boss his younger sister around. Mikhail Bakhtin (1981 [1975]) suggests that such taking on of other people's voices is a common feature of language use. He argues that whenever we take on a voice, we also take on an evaluative stance towards that voice – here, Karlie clearly aligns herself with her father's opinion.

1.7 Conclusion

Talk is a central part of most of our lives. Through it we carry out activities, negotiate relationships, try to construct understandings about the world around us and develop our own sense of identity. In this chapter we have looked at the structure of informal talk, particularly at the level of conversational management, where there are predictable structures around turn taking and adjacency pairs. Particular spoken language practices also have predictable structures – for instance, storytelling or conversational openings and closings. But we saw above that structure is closely tied up with both the ideational and the interpersonal function of language. As well as conveying and negotiating ideas, talk is used to pursue social relationships: through it, intimacy and status are negotiated, and people position themselves, and are positioned, in various ways.

We have seen how people and groups may vary in their conversational style, but that these differences are also cross cut by contextual factors. Not only do people speak differently according to the context, but the language forms they use may have different significance and meaning depending on where and when they are used. Practices to do with questioning, the disclosure of personal information and the use of silence vary across cultures, gender and even individuals, depending on the context of the talk and the relationships involved.

In any community, there exist patterned ways of using language to talk about experience which encode particular evaluative positions, and we inevitably invoke these through the voices we take on and reproduce. The English language provides a variety of resources for pursuing individual purposes, but it also shapes our purposes, even as we use it.

Chapter 2 moves on to consider how the purposes of English speakers are pursued in written language and how the resources of written language have shaped, and continue to shape, English-speaking societies.

READING A: Rules of conversational sequence

Harvey Sacks

Source: Sacks, H. (1998 [1995]) *Lectures on Conversation*, Vol. 1 (ed. G. Jefferson), Malden, MA, Blackwell, pp. 3–11. (Compiled from audio recordings of lectures given by Harvey Sacks in 1964 and 1965.)

I'll start off by giving some quotations.

[Conversation] (1)	A:	Hello
	B:	Hello
[Conversation] (2)	A:	This is Mr Smith may I help you
	B:	Yes, this is Mr Brown
[Conversation] (3)	A:	This is Mr Smith may I help you
	B:	I can't hear you.
	A:	This is Mr <u>Smith</u>.
	B:	Smith.

These are some first exchanges in telephone conversations collected at an emergency psychiatric hospital. They are occurring between persons who haven't talked to each other before. One of them, A, is a staff member of this psychiatric hospital. B can be either somebody calling about themselves, that is to say in trouble in one way or another, or somebody calling about somebody else.

I have a large collection of these conversations, and I got started looking at these first exchanges as follows. A series of persons who called this place would not give their names. The hospital's concern was, can anything be done about it? One question I wanted to address was, where in the course of the conversation could you tell that somebody would not give their name? So I began to look at the materials. It was in fact on the basis of that question that I began to try to deal in detail with conversations.

I found something that struck me as fairly interesting quite early. And that was that if the staff member used 'This is Mr Smith may I help you' as their opening line, then overwhelmingly, any answer other than 'Yes, this is Mr Brown' (for example, 'I can't hear you,' 'I don't know,' 'How do you spell your name?') meant that you would have serious trouble getting the caller's name, if you got the name at all.

I'm going to show some of the ways that I've been developing of analyzing stuff like this. [...] I'll be focussing on a variety of things, starting off with what I'll call 'rules of conversational sequence.'

Looking at the first exchange compared to the second, we can be struck by two things. First of all, there seems to be a fit between what the first person who speaks uses as their greeting, and what the person who is given that greeting returns. So that if A says 'Hello,' then B tends to say 'Hello.' If A says 'This is Mr Smith may I help you,' B tends to say 'Yes, this is Mr Brown.' We can say there's a procedural rule there, that a person who speaks first in a telephone conversation can choose their form of address, and in choosing their form of address they can thereby choose the form of address the other uses.

By 'form' I mean in part that the exchanges occur as 'units.' That is, 'Hello' 'Hello' is a unit, and 'This is Mr Smith may I help you' 'Yes, this is Mr Brown' is a unit. They come in pairs. Saying 'This is Mr Smith may I help you' thereby provides a 'slot' to the other wherein they properly would answer 'Yes, this is Mr Brown.' The procedural rule would describe the occurrences in the first two exchanges. [...]

Secondly, if it is so that there is a rule that the person who goes first can choose their form of address and thereby choose the other's, then for the unit, 'This is Mr Smith may I help you' 'Yes, this is Mr Brown,' if a person uses 'This is Mr Smith ...' they have a way of asking for the other's name – without, however, asking the question, 'What is your name?' And there is a difference between saying 'This is Mr Smith may I help you' – thereby providing a slot to the other wherein they properly would answer "Yes, this is Mr Brown" – and asking the question 'What is your name?' at some point in the conversation. They are very different phenomena.

For one, in almost all of the cases where the person doesn't give their name originally, then at some point in the conversation they're asked for their name. One way of asking is just the question 'Would you give me your name?' To that, there are alternative returns, including 'No' and 'Why?' If a caller says 'Why?' the staff member may say something like, 'I want to have something to call you' or 'It's just for our records.' If a caller says 'No', then the staff member says 'Why?' and may get something like 'I'm not ready to do that' or 'I'm ashamed.' [...]

Now, given the fact that such a greeting as 'This is Mr Smith ...' provides for the other giving his own name as an answer, one can see what the advantage of 'Hello' is for someone who doesn't want to give their name. And I found in the first instance that while sometimes the staff members use 'Hello' as their opening line, if it ever occurred that the persons calling the agency spoke first, they always said 'Hello.'

Persons calling could come to speak first because at this agency, caller and staff member are connected by an operator. The operator says 'Go ahead please' and now the two parties are on an open line, and one can start talking or the other can start talking. This stands in contrast to, for example, calling someone's home. There, the rights are clearly assigned; the person who answers the phone speaks first. If they speak first, they have the right to choose their form. If they have the right to choose their form, they have the right thereby to choose the other's. Here, where the rights are not clearly assigned, the caller could move to speak first and thereby choose the form. And when callers to this agency speak first, the form they choose is the unit 'Hello' 'Hello.' Since such a unit involves no exchange of names, they can speak without giving their name and be going about things in a perfectly appropriate way.

Now, there are variant returns to 'This is Mr Smith may I help you?' one of which is in our set of three exchanges: 'I can't hear you.' I want to talk of that as an 'occasionally usable' device. That is to say, there doesn't have to be a particular sort of thing preceding it; it can come at any place in a conversation. [...]

Our third exchange from the psychiatric hospital has the device used at the beginning of the conversation.

A: This is Mr Smith may I help you

B: I can't hear you.

A: This is Mr <u>Smith</u>.

B: Smith.

What kind of a device is it? What you can see is this. When you say 'I can't hear you,' you provide that the other person can repeat what they said. Now what does that repetition do for you? Imagine you're in a game. One of the questions relevant to the game would be, is there a way in that game of skipping a move? It seems that something like 'I can't hear you' can do such a job. If you introduce it you provide for the other to do some version of a repeat following which you yourself can repeat. And then it's the other's turn to talk again. What we find is that the slot where the return would go – your name in return to 'This is Mr Smith ...' – never occurs.

It is not simply that the caller ignores what they properly ought to do, but something rather more exquisite. That is, they have ways of providing that the place where the return name fits is never opened. So that their name is not absent. Their name would be absent if they just went ahead and talked. But that very rarely occurs. The rules of etiquette – if you want to call them that, though we take etiquette to be something very light and uninteresting and to be breached as you please – seem to be quite strong. Persons will use ways to not ignore what they properly ought to do by providing that the place for them to do it is never opened.

I hope it can also be seen that a device like 'I can't hear you' – the repeat device, providing for a repetition of the thing that was first said, which is then repeated by the person who said 'I can't hear you' – is not necessarily designed for skipping a move. It is not specific to providing a way of keeping in the conversation and behaving properly while not giving one's name. It can be used for other purposes and do other tasks, and it can be used with other items. That's why I talk about it as an 'occasional device.' But where that is what one is trying to do, it's a rather neat device.

Let me turn now to a consideration which deals with a variant return to 'May I help you?' That is, not 'Yes …' but 'I don't know.' I'll show a rather elaborate exchange in which the staff member opens with a version of 'This is Mr Smith may I help you' but the combination gets split. The name is dealt with, and when the 'can I help you' is offered, it occurs in such a way that it can be answered independent of the name.[1]

Op: Go ahead please

A: This is Mr Smith (B: Hello) of the Emergency Psychiatric Center can I help you.

B: Hello?

A: Hello

B: I can't hear you.

A: I see. Can you hear me now?

B: Barely. Where are you, in the womb?

A: Where are you calling from?

---

[1] The fragment of data is reproduced pretty much as Sacks transcribed it, preserving his attempts to deal with simultaneous talk […].

B: Hollywood.

A: Hollywood.

B: I can hear you a little better.

A: Okay. Uh I was saying my name is Smith and I'm with the Emergency Psychiatric Center.

B: Your name is what?

A: Smith.

B: Smith?

A: Yes.

A: Can I help you?

B: I don't know   hhheh I hope you can.

A: Uh hah   Tell me about your problems.

B: I uh   Now that you're here I'm embar[r]assed to talk about it. I don't want you telling me I'm emotionally immature 'cause I know I am

I was very puzzled by 'I don't know' in return to 'May I help you.' I couldn't figure out what they were doing with it. And the reason I was puzzled was that having listened to so many of these things and having been through the scene so many times, I heard 'May I help you' as something like an idiom. I'm going to call these idiom-like things 'composites.' That means you hear the whole thing as a form, a single unit. And as a single unit, it has a proper return. As a composite, 'May I help you' is a piece of etiquette; a way of introducing oneself as someone who is in the business of helping somebody, the answer to which is 'Yes' and then some statement of what it is one wants. We can consider this item in terms of what I'll call the 'base environment' of its use.

By 'base environment' I mean, if you go into a department store, somebody is liable to come up to you and say 'May I help you.' And in business-type phone calls this item is routinely used. And if you come into a place and you don't know what it's like, and somebody comes up to you and uses such an item, that's one way of informing you what kind of a place it is. [...]

Now the thing about at least some composites is that they can be heard not only as composites, but as ordinary sentences, which we could call 'constructives,' which are understood by taking the pieces and adding them up in some way. As a composite, 'May I help you' is a piece of etiquette, a signal for stating your request – what you want to be helped with. Alternatively, as a constructive, 'May I help you' is a question. If one hears it as a question, [...] 'I don't know' is a perfectly proper answer.

Further, 'I don't know' may be locating a problem which 'May I help you' is designed, in the first place, to avoid. In its base environment, for example a department store, it's pretty much the case that for a customer, the question of whether some person 'can help' is a matter of the department store having made them the person who does that. [...] But we're dealing with a psychiatric hospital. In a department store, being selected to do a job and having credentials to do it are essentially the same thing. In a psychiatric hospital and lots of other places, however, they are very different things. That is, whether somebody can help you if you have a mental disorder, is not solved or is not even presumptively solved by the fact that they've been selected by somebody to do that job. [...]

Now let me just make a few general points. Clearly enough, things like 'This is Mr Smith,' 'May I help you?' and 'I can't hear you' are social objects. And if you begin to look at what they do, you can see that they, and things like them, provide the makings of activities. You assemble activities by using these things. [...] What we want then to find out is, can we first of all construct the objects that get used to make up ranges of activities, and then see how it is those objects do get used. [...]

One final note. When people start to analyze social phenomena, if it looks like things occur with the sort of immediacy we find in some of these exchanges, [...] then you figure that they couldn't have thought that fast. I want to suggest that you have to forget that completely. Don't worry about how fast they're thinking. First of all, don't worry about whether they're 'thinking.' Just try to come to terms with how it is that the thing comes off.

READING B: Communicative strategies in Aboriginal English

Diana Eades

Source: adapted from Eades, D. (1991) 'Communicative strategies in Aboriginal English' in Romaine, S. (ed.) *Language in Australia*, Cambridge, Cambridge University Press, pp. 84–93.

Sociocultural context of Aboriginal English

Varieties of Aboriginal English are spoken as the first language of Aboriginal people living in most areas of Australia, primarily in urban and rural parts of 'settled' Australia (as opposed to remote Australia). The majority of speakers of Aboriginal English are of mixed descent, and many are undeniably biculturally competent, increasingly participating in mainstream Australian institutions, such as education and employment.

Irrespective of the language spoken, Aboriginal people throughout Australia today belong to overlapping kin-based networks sharing social life, responsibilities and rights, and a common history, culture, experience of racism and ethnic consciousness. Social relations are characterised by on-going family commitments within groups, and the highest priority is placed on the maintenance and development of these commitments (rather than, for example, on financial security, employment, or individual fulfilment). Moreover, Aboriginal social life is very public. In towns and cities the openness of traditional Aboriginal camp life has been replaced by the openness of frequently overcrowded housing and vehicles. Much of the business of day-to-day living occurs in open outside areas, for example, in parks and other public places, on the main streets of towns, and on verandahs of houses. Because people have on-going commitments to a wide network of kin (far beyond the nuclear family) virtually every aspect of their lives is shared in some way with a number of relatives.

While Aboriginal societies place a high priority on constantly maintaining and developing social relations, there is also provision for considerable personal privacy. This personal privacy is ensured not in terms of physical privacy as it is, for example, in mainstream Australian society, where walls, an indoor lifestyle and a strong prohibition on directly observing many of the actions of others, are all essential factors in the maintenance of personal privacy. It is through their indirect style of verbal interaction that Aboriginal people experience much personal privacy [...].

Figure 1   The public nature of social life in an Aboriginal community

Indirectness in Aboriginal English

Seeking information

While questions are frequently used in Aboriginal English in certain contexts and functions, there are constraints on their use which protect individual privacy [...] Direct questions are [...] used to elicit orientation information, for example in a typical greeting such as 'Where you been?' Frequently, however, the orientation question takes the form of a statement uttered with rising intonation, e.g. 'You been to town?' Rather than asking directly, the speaker presents known or supposed information for confirmation or denial.

This strategy of seeking information by presenting information is also seen clearly in the ways in which English is used by Aboriginal speakers to seek substantial information, such as important personal details, a full account of an event, or the explanation of some event or situation. In these situations questions are not used, but the person seeking information contributes some of their own knowledge on the topic, followed often by silence. This strategy serves as an invitation (or hint) for another participant to impart information on this topic. There is no obligation on the knowledgeable person to respond, and, further, it is rare for silences to be negatively valued in Aboriginal conversations. Important aspects of substantial information seeking are the two-way exchange of information, the positive, non-awkward use of silence, and the often considerable time delays (frequently of several days) between the initiation of substantial information seeking and the imparting of such information.

Making and refusing requests

Aboriginal people rarely make direct requests. A question frequently serves to make an indirect request, as well as to seek orientation information. For example, a typical Aboriginal way of asking for a ride is to ask a car owner a question, such as 'You going to town?' or 'What time are you leaving?' Such questions can be interpreted as information seeking of a kind common in Aboriginal conversations, but they can also be interpreted as a request for a ride, depending on the relationship between speakers. Even if speakers understand questions such as these as requests for a ride, the ambiguity enables a person to refuse a request in a similar indirect fashion, for example, 'Might be later', 'Not sure'. In this way Aboriginal people can negotiate requests and refusals without directly exposing their motives (see Eades, 1988).

Seeking and giving reasons

Research with Aboriginal speakers of English in south-east Queensland reveals that the questioning of a person's motives or reasons for action is always carried out indirectly through the use of multifunctional linguistic forms (Eades, 1983).

Thus, for example, an orientation question such as 'You went to town yesterday?' would be used to seek information concerning a person's movements, but this answer might also provide evidence of the reasons behind some of their actions. The use of multifunctional forms makes the requests for reasons indirect and ambiguous, and it gives people considerable privacy; they are never confronted with an inescapable request for a reason (e.g. 'Why didn't you visit us yesterday?').

Just as the seeking of reasons relies on the use of multifunctional forms, so too does the expression of reason. There is frequently no unambiguous linguistic marker of reasons (cf. Standard Australian English *because, in order to, so*). Speakers rely on the non-linguistic context for their interpretation of a statement as a reason. Specifically, it is shared experiences and knowledge which provide the evidence that a multifunctional statement is intended as a reason. [...]

Expressing opinions

A number of studies of Aboriginal communicative strategies provide evidence that it is important for Aboriginal people to present opinions cautiously and with a degree of circumspection. Von Sturmer first discussed the use of disclaimers as a strategy of 'not presenting oneself too forcefully and not linking oneself too closely with one's own ideas'. Examples of such disclaimers are 'might be I right or wrong' (Von Sturmer, 1981, p. 29), and 'this is just what I think' (Eades, 1988) […] Many Aboriginal people in south-east Queensland do not express a firm or biased opinion, even if they hold one. A common strategy involves general discussions on a topic, while speakers gauge each other's views gradually, before a definite presentation. When speakers realise a difference between their views and those of others, they tend to understate their own views. This style of gradually and indirectly expressing an opinion is a significant factor in cross-cultural miscommunication, and will be discussed below.

Also relevant here is the widespread Aboriginal notion of 'shame', which is a combination of shyness and embarrassment occurring in 'situations where a person has been singled out for any purpose, scolding or praise or simply attention, where he/she loses the security and anonymity provided by the group' (Kaldor and Malcolm, 1979, p. 429).

Aboriginal communicative strategies in cross-cultural communication

Aboriginal people have developed a number of ways of accommodating the directions of non-Aboriginal interactions but some of these ways of accommodating can actually lead to further misunderstanding. For instance, one way in which they respond to the much more direct communication style of [W]hite speakers is through the use of **'gratuitous concurrence'** (Liberman, 1981, 1982, 1985), where Aboriginal speakers say 'yes' not necessarily to signal agreement with a statement or proposition, but to facilitate the on-going interaction, or to hasten its conclusion. Occasionally, Aboriginal people switch to a vociferous, confrontational style which they perceive as appropriate to interactions with Whites. In some situations the Aboriginal participants are, in fact, more direct and confrontational than the White participants.

Aboriginal speakers' use of gratuitous concurrence has serious implications for all cross-cultural situations in Australia where direct questioning is used, in particular in police interviews, law courts, employment interviews, medical consultations, classrooms at all levels, and government consultations. Differences in degrees of directness lead to misunderstandings in many settings. In meetings, for example, Aboriginal people are often offended and feel dominated by the White participants, who express forceful opinions, often in direct opposition to those expressed by a previous speaker. On the other hand, White people often mistakenly assume Aboriginal agreement with a particular viewpoint after listening to the initial statements of an Aboriginal speaker, and not allowing time for the expression of a different opinion. If asked directly whether they agree with a particular issue Aboriginal speakers may frequently respond with the 'yes' of gratuitous concurrence. The indirect and roundabout Aboriginal style requires a non-linear meeting organisation and a much longer time span than is typical of White meetings, before participants can express important contradictory viewpoints. Thus, in meetings of Aboriginal organisations, for example, the lengthy discussion of issues often causes non-Aboriginal participants to become frustrated with the seeming lack of organisation and inability to make decisions.

My current research with Queensland Aboriginal students at University and College indicates that the bicultural competence of many, but not all, of these students includes the ability to participate successfully in the mainstream strategies of information seeking, which are so central to the western education system. For some Aboriginal students, however, the direct interrogative style used in tutorials is quite unsuccessful in involving them in discussion, and in assessing the extent of their knowledge of a topic. These students are often uncomfortable and annoyed about views expressed by non-Aboriginal students, and the forceful manner of their expression, but are unable to respond in the same manner. Without the Aboriginal students' feedback, non-Aboriginal students continue in the direct expression of opinions upsetting to Aboriginal students, who in their turn become more resentful of the non-Aboriginal students.

Such situations of miscommunication, potentially disastrous in a cross-cultural setting, are being constructively approached by discussions between Aboriginal students, fellow students and staff (some of whom are Aboriginal and some of whom are non-Aboriginal, with some bicultural competence). The resulting processes of in-group discussion and analysis, and particularly the support and responsibility assumed by the successfully bicultural Aboriginal students, is an important factor in the on-going positive resolution of such challenges.

References for this reading

Eades, D. M. (1983) 'English as an Aboriginal language in South-east Queensland', PhD thesis, University of Queensland.

Eades, D. M. (1988) 'They don't speak an Aboriginal language, or do they?' in Keen, I. (ed.) *Being Black: Aboriginal Cultural Continuity in Settled Australia*, Canberra, Aboriginal Studies Press.

Kaldor, S. and Malcolm, I. G. (1979) 'The language of the school and the language of the Western Australian Aboriginal school child – implications for education' in Berndt, R. M. and Berndt, C. H. (eds) *Aborigines of the West: Their Past and Their Present*, Nedlands, University of Western Australia Press, pp. 407–37.

Liberman, K. (1981) 'Understanding Aborigines in Australian courts of law', *Human Organization*, vol. 40, no. 3, pp. 247–54.

Liberman, K. (1982) 'Intercultural communication in Central Australia', *Working Papers in Sociolinguistics*, vol. 104, Austin, TX, South West Educational Development Laboratory.

Liberman, K. (1985) *Understanding Interaction in Central Australia: An Ethnomethodological Study of Australian Aboriginal People*, Boston, MA, Routledge & Kegan Paul.

Von Sturmer, J. (1981) 'Talking with Aborigines', *Australian Institute of Aboriginal Studies Newsletter*, 15.

2 Reading and writing in English

Daniel Allington and Ann Hewings

2.1 Introduction

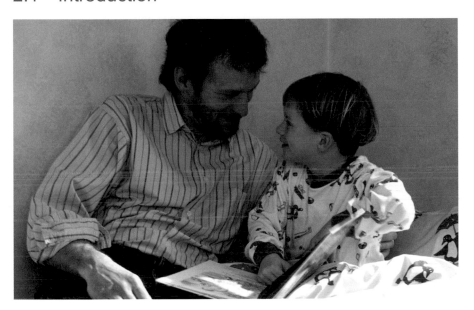

Figure 2.1 Enjoying a book together

Now that you have looked at how people communicate by talking, it is time to look at how they communicate by writing and reading. Throughout this chapter, we discuss these activities in social and historical terms, showing how writers and readers rely on context to make texts meaningful. We repeatedly draw attention to the **literacy practices** that people engage in: the ways in which they interact with texts (and with one another, through the use of texts). The concept of the literacy practice was proposed by the anthropologist Brian Street (1984), who used it to emphasise the connection between an individual's use of written language and his or her social identity. In many societies, for example, adults with young children are encouraged to see it as part of their role as parents or carers to provide the sort of shared reading experience that we see in Figure 2.1 – but this literacy practice is far from universal.

This chapter will also introduce several influential approaches to the analysis of texts. We begin by thinking about written language in terms of **signs**: forms (e.g. words) that are conventionally associated with particular concepts (e.g. the meanings of words). This approach is known broadly as **semiotics** and is founded on the work of the linguist Ferdinand de Saussure (1960 [1916]). Saussure argued that signs are only meaningful because they belong to accepted **sign systems**. As we shall see, however, understanding texts requires us to consider the purposes for which people *use* them, and this requires us to think about the **genre**, or conventional type, of any text we analyse. Moreover, just as the meaning of talk is communicated through gesture and tone of voice as well as through language, the meaning of text is usually communicated in a range of different ways. For this reason, writing is considered here in **multimodal** terms, with attention to its visual as well as to its linguistic aspects.

2.2 Reading signs and images

Let's start with the most basic elements of a text in modern English: the letters of the English alphabet. According to Saussure (1960 [1916], pp. 119–20), an alphabet can be understood as a sign system in which letters play the role of signs: each letter has particular visual characteristics and is (on the whole, somewhat loosely) associated with particular sounds. Moreover, letters can be combined to convey more complex meanings. In English, for example, the letters A, I, L, N and P can be arranged to produce the words 'lapin' and 'plain'. Other languages use different sign systems, and the signs in those systems always work differently – even if they are superficially similar. For example, the Polish letter N is not the same sign as the English letter N, because it belongs to a set of thirty-two letters rather than to a set of twenty-six: you can combine the Polish letter N with the letter Ł in a word like 'bawełna', but you can't do that with the English letter N because there is no letter Ł in the sign system that we call the English alphabet. One of Saussure's key insights was that signs are only meaningful insofar as they exist in opposition to other signs: he suggested that it doesn't matter exactly what a letter looks like in your handwriting, provided that it won't get confused with other letters in the same alphabet. This means that outside a sign system, signs lose their meaning. Without an alphabet to be part of, the N shape would not be a letter – it would just be a zig-zag, and we wouldn't be able to use it to write words with.

Saussure regarded the vocabulary of a language as a sign system functioning in the same basic way. Although many linguists now reject this view (e.g. Harris, 1981), it can still be a useful point from which to start thinking about communication, particularly if we reflect on the differences between vocabulary and a fixed code like an alphabet. To add letters to an established alphabet is relatively difficult: the English alphabet settled on its current, twenty-six letter form several centuries ago, for example, and it is unlikely to expand or contract in the foreseeable future. But living languages accept new words all the time, both in the form of **coinages** (i.e. newly invented words) and in the form of **borrowings** (i.e. words originating in other languages). Semiotic theory would suggest that, in order to enter a new language, an existing word must change in some way, becoming a new sign in a new sign system – and this is what we see when we look at actual cases of borrowing. In French, for example, 'lapin' is the ordinary word for a particular species of animal, but English already had a word for that ('rabbit'), so 'lapin' was borrowed as a specialist word for one of its products (rabbit fur): there would be no sense in a system's having two signs with the same meaning. Thus, Saussure argued that '[w]ithin the same language, all words used to express related ideas limit each other reciprocally' and if a word were lost, 'all its content would go to its competitors' (Saussure, 1960 [1916], p. 116). This is a simplification, but it clearly contains an element of truth.

Although semiotics was originally conceived as a theory of language rather than a means of analysing texts, it has suggested some valuable methods for textual analysis. If it is the oppositions between signs that are truly meaningful, for example, then it is no good trying to think about the meaning of a word in isolation – we have to compare that word to words with related meanings. And this in turn suggests that, when we analyse a text, it may be very helpful to think about how its overall meaning or effect would be changed if different words had been used.

Sometimes, the change can be very subtle. Switching 'rabbit' for 'lapin' would produce a very obvious change to a sentence, since the words signify different concepts (in this case, a type of animal and a type of animal product). Switching 'rabbit' for 'bunny', on the other hand, would produce a less obvious change, since both words apparently signify the same concept (i.e. they are **synonyms**). The change here is not at the level of **denotation** (the concept associated with the word), but at the level of **connotation** (what the word suggests or implies). Like the word 'rabbit', the word 'bunny' denotes a particular species of animal – but unlike that word, it also carries affectionate (and possibly childish) connotations. Connotation was established as a key area of semiotic theory by Roland Barthes (1967 [1964]), arguably the foremost proponent of semiotics as an approach to textual analysis.

Allow about
10 minutes

Activity 2.1

The following lyrics are taken from a song by the rock singer Lou Reed. Would it be different if the third and fifth words were not 'ladies' but 'women'? If so, what does that tell you about the original lyrics?

> Goodnight, sweet ladies
> Ah ladies, goodnight

(Reed, 1971)

Comment

In terms of denotation, 'ladies' can signify several concepts: it is **polyvalent**. It can denote female holders of aristocratic rank. In addition, it can denote the same concept as the word 'women', while holding very different connotations. As a term of address (see Chapter 1), 'ladies' may have respectful connotations (as in the phrase 'ladies and gentlemen'), although many women also find it to have patronising connotations. Patronising connotations are shared by the adjective 'sweet', which is more of a compliment when applied to children or to pets than when applied to adults. So we might want to interpret Reed's lyrics as patronising – but of course we could also interpret them as ironic. A purely semiotic approach can't help us decide between these two interpretations: whether a statement is ironic depends on how it was meant, not on what the words mean.

Other interpretations may have occurred to you if you recognised that the phrase 'sweet ladies' had already been used by two very famous writers before Reed put it into his song. The words 'good night, sweet ladies, good night, good night' appeared in T. S. Eliot's poem *The Waste Land* (2004 [1922], l. 172), where they were ironically addressed to some very un-ladylike and not at all sweet characters. And Eliot's phrase was lifted directly from Shakespeare: in *Hamlet* (1604), it is one of the last things Ophelia says before she drowns herself. Using similar words in a song may suggest similarly morbid events. As the literary critics William Wimsatt and Monroe Beardsley (1946, p. 478) observe, '[t]he meaning of words is the history of words': a word or other sign has whatever meaning it does because of the history of the ways in which people have used it.

We might also note that, because it is so close to lines used by two of the English language's most celebrated poets, Reed's line seems much more 'intellectual' than it would have done otherwise. As we saw in the previous chapter, people often take on one another's voices when they speak (see Bakhtin, 1981 [1975]). When the voice taken on is that of a 'great' writer, this is called literary allusion, and the effect may be to identify the speaker as a 'cultivated' person (see Bourdieu and Passeron, 1990 [1970], p. 134). By alluding to the works of Eliot and Shakespeare, Reed arguably indexed (pointed to) a 'highbrow' social identity for himself.

These points show how we must go beyond the idea of a sign system to understand writing: thinking deeply about the meaning of a text leads us to consider what the language user who produced it was *doing* and what other language users had previously *done*.

Semiotic analysis has been applied not only to texts, but also to a huge range of other cultural products, including photographs and food (Barthes, 1972 [1957]). The extent of its usefulness when applied in this way is contentious, however, as it is not obvious that every form of communication should be analysed in the same way as language. Some scholars propose that visual images can be parsed like sentences, for example, with picture elements such as lines and colours being treated analogously to parts of speech (Dondis, 1973; Kress and van Leeuwen, 1996). However, others deny that 'classifying and dissecting images will uncover their meanings' and argue that the idea of 'visual language' is no more than 'a loose analogy at best' (Raney, 1999, p. 43).

A more fundamental problem is that to understand communication, we have to think about how signs are being used by human beings in specific situations – and not just about those signs' systematic relationships to other signs. For this reason, Pierre Bourdieu complains that the influence of Saussure has left us 'looking within words for the power of words' (Bourdieu, 1992 [1975], p. 107) when that power is to be found elsewhere, in the social and institutional contexts within which language is used.

Despite these problems, Saussure's focus on *meaningful difference* is undeniably useful and you should practise applying it to all sorts of texts. As a start, you might like to try changing other words in the lyrics above (e.g. 'night' to 'day': semiotic analysis often focuses on opposites or **antonyms** as well as synonyms). And such an approach can be taken even when you are not carrying out an explicitly semiotic analysis. For example, if we return to the most basic elements of written English – letters – we can see that they communicate meaning not only thanks to their inclusion in the English alphabet, but also thanks to their visual appearance: think, for example, of the way that this book uses differences in the colour, size and style of lettering to indicate the conceptual difference between a heading, a subheading, a comment and an ordinary paragraph.

2.3   Meaning and typeface

> ### 'Typeface' and 'font'
>
> Strictly speaking, a font is a complete set of letters, numerals and punctuation marks in a single size (e.g. 10- or 12-point) and a single style (e.g. bold or italic), while a typeface is a design for a complete set of fonts (e.g. Times New Roman or Calibri). In recent years, however, the two words have come to be treated as synonyms.

One of the most important non-linguistic communicators of meaning is typography. Just as writers may agonise over a choice between words, graphic designers will agonise over a choice between typefaces. It would make little sense to see a typeface as a sign in the way that the English letter N can be seen as a sign. But a typeface can be used to associate a text with previous uses made of the same or similar typefaces, and in advertising and in politics this is used to index particular identities for people and products. For example, some deeply considered typographic choices were made by presidential candidates' campaign teams in the run-up to the 2008 US elections. Barack Obama's team set his publicity materials in a typeface called Gotham (see Figure 2.2). As Simon Garfield (2010) shows, this twenty-first century typeface had been designed for the men's style magazine *GQ* and adopted by the educational TV channel, *Discovery*: associations in keeping with Obama's modern, stylish and intellectual image. The campaign team for Obama's rival, John McCain, by contrast chose a mid-twentieth century typeface called Optima (see Figure 2.3), 'perhaps [in] an attempt to remind voters of his war record (Optima is the type on the Vietnam Veterans Memorial in Washington DC)' (Garfield, 2010, p. 214).

Figure 2.2 President (then, Senator) Barack Obama and the Gotham typeface

Figure 2.3 Senator John McCain and the Optima typeface

Until relatively recently, only printers and designers had to worry about this sort of thing on a day-to-day basis, but thanks to the popularity of WYSIWYG ('what you see is what you get') word processing software, typographic choice has become a part of language use for almost everyone who uses digital technology to produce texts. While it was difficult to change the appearance of letters typed on old-style mechanical typewriters, popular computer operating systems are distributed with a range of digital fonts, giving millions of people access both to modern typefaces such as Helvetica, Gill Sans and Calibri, and to centuries-old typefaces such as those of the Garamond family. Such opportunities can be viewed as a distraction, which is why many scientists reject word processors in favour of LaTeX: a document markup language that encourages the user to forget about what the text is going to look like and concentrate instead on its conceptual structure. But if the choice of typeface is so distracting, that is because it is so meaningful.

A text needs a typeface if it is to be printed on paper or printed to a computer screen, and a typeface always says something about the text it makes visible. Jerome McGann has theorised texts in terms of a metaphor drawn from genetics: a text is a 'double helix' of 'linguistic codes' and 'bibliographic codes' twined around one another (McGann, 1991, p. 77). Linguistic codes would include punctuation marks and the letters of the alphabet, while bibliographic codes would encompass the visual and material characteristics of a printed text. These characteristics often give clues as to the ways in which a text was produced and used. In the nineteenth century, for example, there was a direct relationship between a book's page size and the wealth of its intended readers, with large format 'octavo' editions being produced for much more exclusive audiences than small format 'sextodecimo' editions of the same works (which typically appeared only after years of delay).

Perhaps the relationship between the linguistic and the bibliographic is becoming easier to understand in the age of the internet. Digital devices can process information only in numerical form, so the letters and punctuation marks we see on web pages have to be stored in the form of numbers, using conventions such as ASCII (which was designed around the English alphabet) and Unicode (ASCII's multilingual successor). When a human being reads a web page, these computer-friendly numbers have to be turned back into user-friendly letters and punctuation marks. If no extra information about the original text's appearance was stored, then the appearance of the text displayed will be determined largely by the hardware and software used to display it. This is what happens if you open the 'Plain Text' version of a book digitised by Project Gutenberg (www.gutenberg.org). Figure 2.4 shows how the beginning of Project Gutenberg's version of a very famous novel appeared on the screen of one of the computers used to write this chapter.

Allow about 5 minutes

Activity 2.2

What do you notice about the look of Figure 2.4? How do you respond to it?

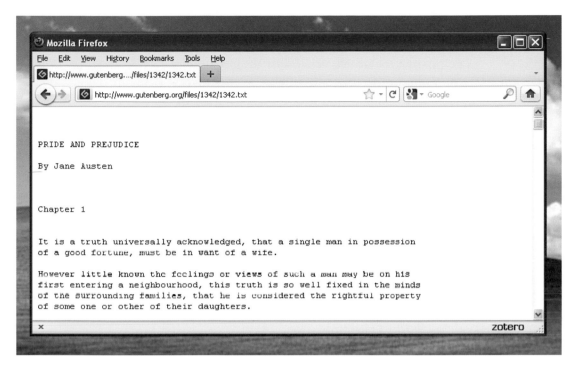

Figure 2.4 Extract from the Project Gutenberg plain text edition of Jane Austen's *Pride and Prejudice*

Comment

Because I (Daniel) viewed the text on a computer provided by my employer, it appeared in the Courier New typeface, which is the default plain text font for the Windows XP operating system; had I viewed it on my own laptop, which runs on Xubuntu Linux, the text would have appeared in a different font (as it happens, DejaVu Sans Mono) and its jagged edges would have been smoothed. Courier New has a somewhat utilitarian appearance that few people find easy on the eye, and you might not want to read a whole novel in it for fun! Below, we will look at why that might be.

It should be noted that the look of the text was not *entirely* determined by the technology used to make it visible. The line breaks (and thus the lengths of the lines) were encoded into the text file, as were the upper-case letters that mark out the initial letters of sentences and make clear that the words 'Pride and Prejudice' constitute the title of the text.

Just as there are always different ways to say the same words, there are always different ways a text can be made to look. You might like to try comparing the above version of the beginning of *Pride and Prejudice* with the same words in a new edition of the novel – or in an old edition, such as you might find in a research library or on the website of a digitisation project that (unlike Project Gutenberg) provides scans of the original pages. One such digitisation project, the Rossetti Archive, aims to facilitate this kind of comparison by including high-quality images of *every version* of every text by Dante Gabriel Rossetti from 1848 to 1920 (www.rossettiarchive.org): if you have access to the internet, you might like to have a look, and see just how different these sometimes were. Bibliographic codes were perhaps more important to Rossetti than to the average nineteenth-century poet, since (also being a painter) he took an especially great interest in how his poems looked. But typography is becoming a conscious part of communicative practice for more and more of us, as the digital era's multitude of amateur graphic designers continues to expand.

Take Courier New, which has already been mentioned. If this has a somewhat mechanical look, that is because it was modelled on Courier, a typeface designed for mid-twentieth century office typewriters. These machines required every letter, space and punctuation mark to take up the same amount of horizontal space, which is why texts in Courier New have a grid-like appearance: in the extract from *Pride and Prejudice* in Figure 2.4, the 't' of 'truth' is directly above the 'd' of 'good' and the 'l' of 'little', and directly below the '1' of 'Chapter 1' and the 'A' of 'Austen'. Because of Courier's association with office typewriters, Courier New has somewhat bureaucratic connotations. Furthermore, it is rarely used for long published texts such as novels because it is not considered to be sufficiently legible: most readers of English are better accustomed to styles of lettering in which a capital 'M' will take up rather more line space than a comma than they are to 'monospaced' typefaces like Courier New (and DejaVu Sans Mono). On the other hand, the regularity of such typefaces makes them suitable for certain literacy practices. Many computer programmers choose monospaced typefaces so that they can precisely line up related bits of code and easily identify individual symbols. And in Hollywood, Courier is the standard font for screenplays (scripts), because it makes it easy to estimate the amount of time represented by a given volume of text: provided that it is printed to the right size with the right margins and the right amount of line spacing, a page of Courier will generally amount to about a minute of screen time.

'Black-letter' – or, as they are popularly known, 'gothic' – typefaces provide an even clearer example of the relationship between visual appearance and literacy practices. If there is a black-letter typeface installed on a computer that you use, it is likely that you use it only for decorative purposes or leave it well alone, but at one time, such typefaces were the standard. In fact, the very first typefaces to be used in Europe were the black-letters created by Johannes Gutenberg. Gutenberg's most famous work was a Latin Bible, but black-letter typefaces were also used for early printed books in English, including the very first to be printed in England – William Caxton's 1477 edition of the fourteenth-century poem known as *The Canterbury Tales* (Chaucer, 1477). You can see the opening lines of that historic edition in Figure 2.5 overleaf.

Activity 2.3

Allow about
10 minutes

Think about how you respond to the look of the page in Figure 2.5. What meaning does its visual style hold for you? How easy do you find it to read the text? And why do you think that is?

Comment

The poem begins 'Whan that Apprill with his shouris sote // And the droughte of marche hath p[er]cid [the] rote'. The second line contains two scribal abbreviations (one from Latin – a crossed p for 'per'; and one from English – a y with a superscript e for 'the'), its first word could be considered a mistake, and there is probably a missing preposition near the end. Corrected to reflect what the author is now believed to have written, these lines might be translated as 'When April with his sweet showers // Has pierced the drought of March to the root'.

Together with the deliciously ironic first sentences of *Pride and Prejudice*, Geoffrey Chaucer's opening couplet is among the most celebrated beginnings in English literature: it is echoed, for example, in the first two lines of *The Waste Land* ('April is the cruellest month, breeding // Lilacs out of the dead land, mixing': Eliot, 2004 [1922], l. 1–2). But in this form, it is likely to seem alien, even indecipherable, to most readers – a relic of an earlier stage of history. This is partly because the lines were composed in Middle English. But it is also partly because of the use of black-letter and because of another typographic practice that has since passed out of general use: the text begins with (and is indented around) a large, ornamental capital letter W (apparently drawn over a lower-case w on the second line). The ornamental letter is fully three lines tall and looks very different not only from a modern capital W, but also from the

Middle English is discussed in another book in this series: Seargeant and Swann (eds) (2012) *English in the World*, Chapter 2.

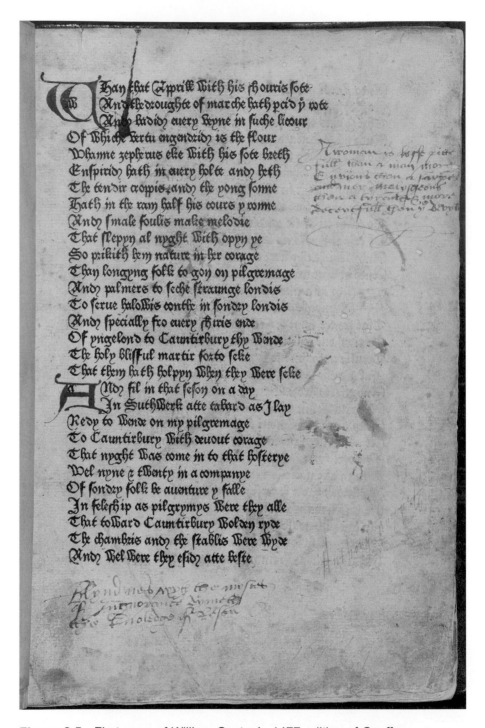

Figure 2.5 First page of William Caxton's 1477 edition of Geoffrey Chaucer's *Canterbury Tales*

lower-case w that appears later in the same line. It is quite possible that you did not recognise it as a W; seeing it in isolation, many twenty-first century readers of English would not even realise that it was a letter.

This is largely a matter of what you are used to, however, and to Caxton's literate contemporaries, the extract would have seemed much more familiar and legible than the paragraph you are reading now. Black-letter typefaces were modelled on styles of handwriting common in fifteenth-century Europe, and the use of ornamental initial capitals was a tradition directly deriving from handwritten texts of the day: in photographs, museums or rare book collections you may have seen medieval manuscripts with beautifully painted capital letters at the beginnings of chapters and paragraphs. Black-letter and ornamental capitals continued to be used in English for a long time, including for the first edition of the King James Bible (1611), but they have been considered obsolete for centuries. So if the visual style of Figure 2.5 has 'medieval' connotations for you, that's for good reason!

So far, you have started to consider how communication integrates language with other ways of expressing meaning, such as images and font choice. Digital technology facilitates more complicated forms of multimodality by enabling moving images, sound files and hyperlinks to be embedded in a text. In the next section, we will consider how texts are perceived to belong to identifiable types whose nature is evolving in the digital world.

2.4   Genre

You may have come across the word 'genre' in relation to literature. It is the French word for 'type' or 'kind' and it is often used to refer to specific literary forms, especially the classical genres of tragedy, comedy, epic, lyric and satire. In language study, however, the term is used differently. Bakhtin, for example, used the term 'speech genres' to describe the 'relatively stable types' of spoken utterance or written text that have developed within 'each sphere in which language is used' (Bakhtin, 1986, [1979], p. 60). And Carolyn Miller (1984) builds on speech act theory (see Chapter 1 of this book) to argue that each genre is a social action that one carries out through writing. For example, writing a text of the *book review* genre would mean carrying out the social action of *reviewing a book* (see Grafton, 2010). Following Bakhtin's and Miller's arguments, sociolinguists now define genres 'according to their function, formal characteristics and/or rhetorical purposes' (Swann et al., 2004, p. 124). On this definition, tragedies are a genre – but so are bills, insults, sermons and menus.

Activity 2.4

In the online world, genres and literacy practices are realised through digital technology. Now turn to Reading A: *Genre under construction: the diary on the internet* by Laurie McNeill. There are striking differences between the blog and the older but related genre of the print or manuscript diary. However, there are also many similarities, suggesting that some aspects of genre may remain stable even when technologies change. What similarities and differences can you think of?

Comment

One of the most important differences between blogging and diary writing is that a public blog can be accessed by virtually unlimited numbers of people unknown to the author, which would only be the case for a diary if it were published. As McNeill emphasises, blogs can also incorporate technical features specific to the internet, such as links and page view counters. Another point you may have considered is that although both diary entries and blog postings are arranged chronologically, the chronology usually runs in different directions: the latest entry to a diary will be the one closest to the back, while the latest posting to a blog will be the one closest to the front. This is because blogs are designed to be read as they are being written, so it makes sense to help the reader find the most recent postings first. Although many people want their diaries to be read, it is quite uncommon for them to hand their diaries around after each entry is completed, so there is no need to use reverse chronological order. And when blogs are republished as books, such as *Wasting Police Time* (Copperfield, 2006), the postings tend to be reordered chronologically, like the entries in a diary. Already at this level, then, we can see the complex interactions of genre, technology and literacy practices. We should not imagine technology as the driving force, however, since it is clear that people did not *have to* use blogging technology as a way of publishing information about their 'private' lives.

Carolyn Miller and Dawn Shepherd (2004) point out that the blog genre developed at a time when celebrities and politicians were disclosing more and more personal information to the media and when ordinary people were beginning to expose their private lives on 'reality television' shows. Miller and Shepherd suggest that the social action of blogging is performed in response to a growing demand for the public 'cultivation' of the individual self: a demand that is not technological but cultural. And McNeill suggests that some of the possibilities of blogging technology (such as the ability to revise postings) appear to be used reluctantly because readers still come to blogs with expectations that derive from print or manuscript diaries. In this way, McNeill suggests that the history of the blog genre (including its historical origins in the culture of pre-digital diary writing) is 'activated' in every blog posting.

Further similarities and differences can be seen if we compare extracts from a blog and a diary that cover similar topics (Figures 2.6 and 2.7 overleaf). The diary entry was written in 1846 by Susan Shelby Magoffin; the blog posting was published in 2010 by a pseudonymous internet user, o-jenny, and is shown as it appeared on the screen of one of the computers used to create this chapter. Below is an extract from a printed version of Magoffin's diary, published over a century after her death. The text corresponds to what is written on the left-hand page seen in Figure 2.6, although note that where Magoffin used underlining for emphasis, the printed version switches to italic font (a common change when handwritten texts are prepared for publication) – a change that required a certain degree of interpretation on the part of the editor, since Magoffin's underlines were so short.

Saturday 29th. I have visited this morning the ruins of an ancient pueblo, or village, now desolate and a home for the wild beast and bird of the forest.

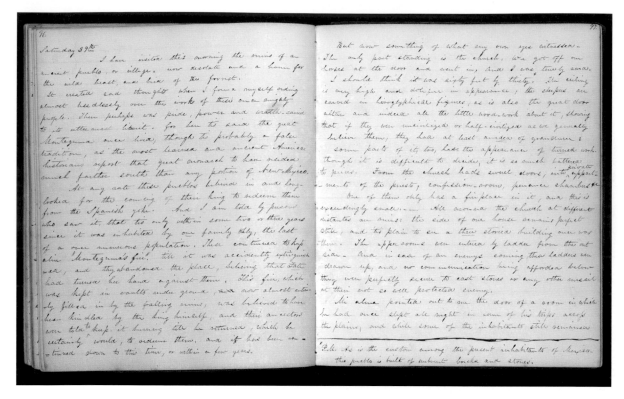

Figure 2.6 Extract from Susan Shelby Magoffin's diary, 1846

It created sad thoughts when I found myself riding almost heedlessly over the work of these once mighty people. There perhaps was pride, power, and wealth carried to its utter most limit, for here tis said the great Montezuma once lived, though tis probably a false tradition, as the most learned and ancient American historians report that great monarch to have resided much farther south than any portion of New Mexico.

At any rate these pueblos believed in and long-looked for the coming of their kind to redeem them from the *Spanish yoke*. And I am told by persons who saw it, that tis only within some two or three years since it was inhabited by one family only, the last of a once numerous population. These continued to keep alive 'Montezuma's fire,' till it was accidently extinguished, and they abandoned the place, believing that *Fate* had turned her hand against them. This fire, which was kept in vaults under ground, now almost entirely filled in by the falling ruins, was believed to have been kindled by the king himself, and their ancestors were told to keep it burning till he returned, which he certainly would, to redeem them, and it has been continued down to this time, or within a few years.

(Magoffin, 1962 [1846], pp. 99–100; see Figure 2.6)

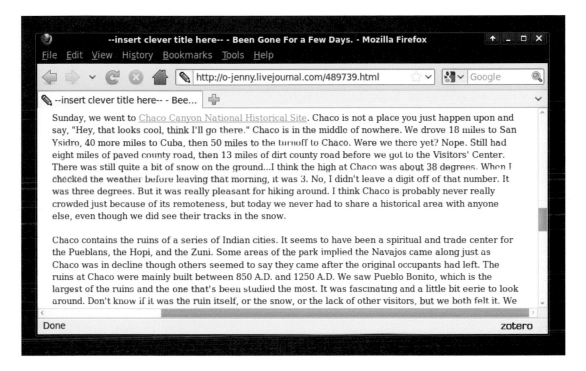

Figure 2.7 Extract from o-jenny's blog, 2010

Magoffin's text shows us how different her situation was from o-jenny's. There was no 'Visitors' Center' at the ruins she passed through, because there was no tourist industry in the New Mexico of the time. In fact, when Magoffin wrote the above, the annexation of New Mexico by the United States was still in progress – with news of an important (and bloodless) American victory having reached her just a few days earlier. Thus, while the blog posting appears to include historical details simply as a matter of curiosity, the diary entry's discussion of the last Aztec emperor and the 'Spanish yoke' has an implicit political relevance: Magoffin suggests that the Pueblos were now to be set free from Spanish rule, although not by what she calls 'their kind' but by American soldiers.

Much of what the two travellers write is strikingly similar, though, which shows the extent to which the blog genre has inherited the functions of the diary genre. Each writer refers to her means of transport, although indirectly: one writes that she drives (a car), the other that she rides (a horse). Each writes about the emotions stirred by what she encounters, and on the face of it these are not very different: one notices an 'eerie' feeling, the other has 'sad thoughts'. And though each discusses the history of New Mexico, it is without claiming any personal authority on the matter or providing evidence beyond a summary of what others claim. We can, then, see a great deal of continuity between these texts.

Magoffin's diary has long been known to have been influenced by a book published shortly before her journey began, Josiah Gregg's *Commerce of the Prairies* (1844) – and, as it happens, the informational content of this particular extract can be seen to derive largely from Gregg's account of the same ruined pueblo, Pecos. Even some of the language Magoffin uses was clearly influenced by Gregg: for example, her 'Spanish yoke' echoes his 'yoke of the Spaniards' (Gregg, 1844, p. 271). But Gregg's businesslike account is very different in tone from Magoffin's emotional one. It was written to accomplish a very different purpose: which is to say, it belonged to a different genre. Gregg's book was written as an authoritative account of the history, geography, social structure and economics of the region, for use by traders like Gregg himself. Gregg thus dismisses the local Montezuma traditions as 'deluded' (p. 271), for example, rather than musing on their emotional resonance. The diary entry is much closer to the blog posting in this respect, because both were written to convey an impression of what it *felt like* to be a particular person in a particular place at a particular time. This function is part of the print and manuscript heritage of blogging.

Whatever the similarities, the practices associated with blogging also appear to encourage some very different uses of language than diary writing, and it is likely that if somebody posted Magoffin's text on a blog, it would appear stilted and pretentious in comparison to o-jenny's. It is not that there is anything inherently pretentious about the way Magoffin wrote – just that expectations of a twenty-first century blog are different from expectations of a nineteenth-century diary. Typically for a blog posting, the example in Figure 2.7 gives the impression of being written quickly and without too much polish. We see this, for instance, in the omission of the subject pronoun 'we' from the statement 'Still had eight miles of paved county road'. The blog directly mimics colloquial speech in its representation of things people would not say ('Hey, that looks cool') and things they may have said ('Nope'). It also involves a feature that linguist Greg Myers has found to be typical of blog style: the 'enact[ment of] conversational interaction' through 'conversational self-interruption' (Myers, 2010, pp. 84–5). This can be seen in the sentence 'No, I didn't leave a digit off of that number' (note the colloquial 'off of', in place of the standard English 'off'), which responds to an imaginary question from the reader (i.e. 'Did you leave a digit off of that number?').

By contrast, the diary entry is much less conversational in tone – although some of Magoffin's word choices would have seemed much less old-fashioned at the time she made them. This is certainly the case with her use of 'tis', rather than 'it's' – both these contractions of 'it is' have been in use since at least the seventeenth century, but Magoffin's preferred form has fallen out of popularity since her time of writing. The 'bookish' quality of the diary entry is not simply an effect of time, however. In the highly figurative (and somewhat melodramatic) '*Fate* had turned her hand against them', Magoffin's writing takes on a distinctly poetic tone, as it does in her picturesque description of the pueblo as 'desolate and a home for the wild beast and bird of the forest'. All these points flag Magoffin's diary entry as a text that is to be treated as worthy of attention *for the care that has gone into writing it*. Instead of adopting characteristics of spontaneous speech, it adopts characteristics of printed literature. It was not written for publication, but it had an intended audience – Magoffin's family – and in it, the writer tells a spooky story to be enjoyed in years to come.

Activity 2.5

Allow about
10 minutes

Look at a text you have written recently: a blog posting, a diary entry, a letter, an email, an essay, a poem, a shopping list or anything at all. What was its purpose? What technologies did you use to create it? Who did you write it for? What did you expect that person or those people to do with it? And in what ways is it typical of its genre?

Comment

It is worth emphasising that every communicative text has a genre and will be typical of that genre in some way. Some people might feel this to be a bad thing: 'it's rather generic' is a negative comment. But that is not necessarily fair. Just like tools (and toys), texts are designed to be used for particular purposes, and use necessarily affects form. A menu that was completely unlike any other menu might be very difficult for restaurant customers to make use of, for example, and even experimental poetry is a genre.

2.5 Literacy practices

We have moved from thinking about texts as arrangements of signs, through consideration of the meanings carried by choices of font, to thinking about texts as actions fulfilling typical social needs. As we have seen again and again, we need to look beyond text to understand communication. Take the letter of recommendation. Such a letter's effectiveness as an action will often depend less on *how it is written* than on *who it is from*: the signatory must be someone whose opinion will carry weight with the recipient. There are, moreover, many social actions that can be carried out only by people in authority – and as we saw with the example of the soldier and the captain (Chapter 1), 'authority comes to language from outside' (Bourdieu, 1992 [1975], p. 109). Writing and reading cannot be understood in isolation from the world in which they are carried out.

Think about this page. Are you reading it on paper or on an electronic device? Are you alone? If there is a computer nearby, are you also using it to write notes or to search websites? What is your purpose in reading? Are you studying the English language or reading for general interest? If you are studying, do you annotate the page you are reading and, if so, how – by highlighting, underlining or making notes in the margin? When you make notes on a page or on a screen, do you just use words or do you use colour, symbols or images as well? Perhaps you draw 'mind maps' or link things with arrows, for example. Think too of the ways in which your literacy practices may be institutionally determined; for example, if you are studying for a qualification, your note taking may help you to be successful when your knowledge is examined or assessed.

Activity 2.6

Allow about
15 minutes

In Figure 2.8, you can see an example of a multimodal text – notes made by a first year undergraduate chemistry student. He uses symbols originating in chemistry and in a sign system developed for expressing propositions in mathematics and formal logic. Even if you are unfamiliar with these systems, can you understand anything about the student's literacy practices by reading this extract? Use the questions in the paragraph above to guide your thinking about literacy practices.

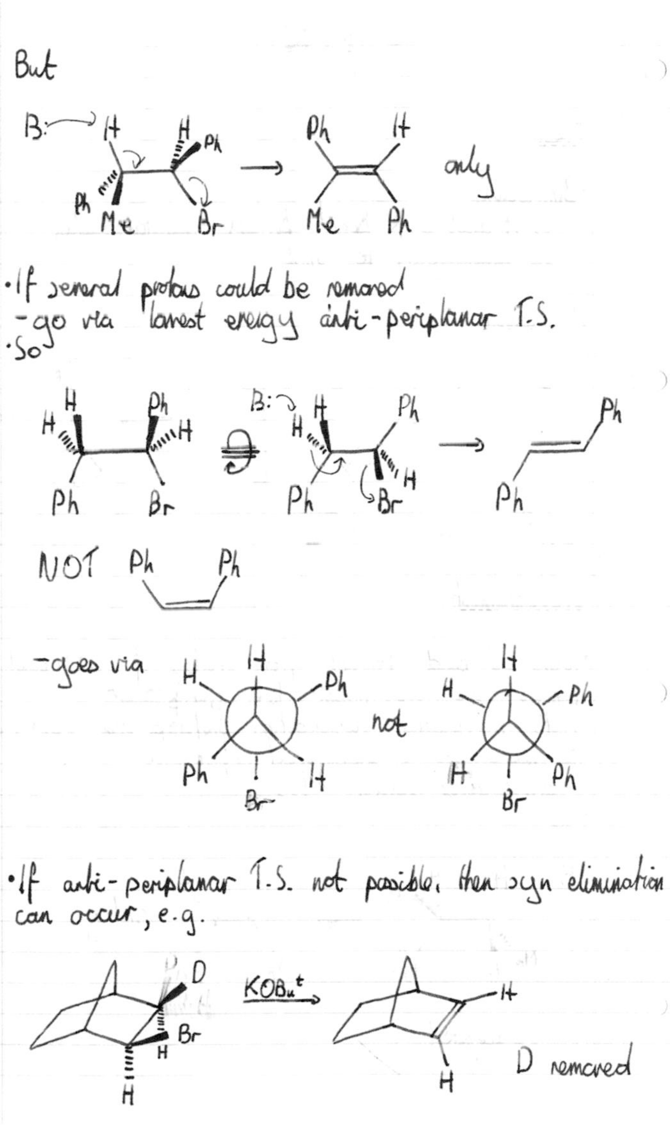

Figure 2.8 Undergraduate chemistry notes (David Hewings)

Comment

The notes look very different from anything I (Ann) would write. The first thing I noticed is how few words there are and yet it clearly conveys information to the author (David). He uses predominantly diagrammatic representations of molecules, as well as letters and other symbols, and uses a pen and a pencil to produce two different colours. The diagrams of molecules represent information and are linked together with words (especially conjunctions such as 'if'), much as sentences are. When I emailed David about this he responded:

> I think the formation of 'sentences' out of symbolic representations joined by so, not etc. borrows from logic and maths. Often we even use logical and other mathematical symbols ($\Rightarrow$, $\rightarrow$, $\therefore$, $\sim$, $\equiv$, $\neq$, iff) albeit in a non-rigorous or idiosyncratic way to form an argument (A happens since B, but C implies D). You can see I used $\equiv$ but modified it by putting an arrow round it (that's just something I made up!) to say 'these two representations are equivalent if you rotate the molecule'. So that's not standard notation, but people would work out what it meant.
>
> (personal email communication)

David suggests that although chemists adapt symbols from sign systems that are agreed for use in mathematics and logic, they are able to play with those symbols to create new meanings that do not strictly arise from the original sign systems. It is likely that much of what he has written would be comprehensible to chemists who did not know English as they would share sufficient knowledge of the other semiotic systems he uses. What you can't tell about his literacy practices from looking at Figure 2.8 is that his notes were written up when he was alone, sitting at a desk with a computer in his room at university and are based on photocopied sheets from his lecturers' notes made in class, printed textbooks and journal articles accessed online. They were for his personal use, not for sharing with others, and the literacy practice of creating them is an integral part of his learning process.

A chemistry student's literacy practices are likely to be different from those you engage in as you read this book and learn about the English language. If you have the opportunity, ask others how, where and when they study. What are their literacy practices with regard to reading, note taking, assignment writing? Are their practices multimodal? Do they use colour, underlining, diagrams?

Activity 2.7

Over the period of a day

Your literacy practices are not only associated with studying, they are also closely tied to your work and social life. For one day, keep a literacy diary of the things that you read and write by noting them down every hour or so. Consider:

- **The context**: do you read and write alone, in company or collaboratively?
- **The medium**: do digital devices, such as mobile phones or computers, play a role?
- **The form**: when you write do you use full sentences, notes, symbols or other forms of notation?

Are your own practices linked to ideas of social identity and expectations about behaviour and role? Do you see yourself in the role of student, parent, worker? Does this identity change with different literacy practices?

Comment

- Read election posters outside my house.
- Read food packets to distinguish breakfast cereal I wanted.
- Flicked through clothes catalogue.
- Noted need to buy more coffee on kitchen white board.
- Wrote and received text message from friend.
- Read emails and wrote responses.
- Noted appointments in my diary (paper).
- Finished reading and wrote comments on part of a book chapter by a colleague.

The brief list above refers to the first couple of hours of my (Ann's) morning. My reading was all done alone and the writing in my diary was for my benefit. All the other writing was aimed at communicating with people. The note about coffee was a reminder to my husband for when he next went shopping. The text messages were affective, a way of maintaining contact with a friend and wishing her well in her new home. It used some common text messaging conventions such as 'u' for 'you'. This level of informality is often associated with text messaging between friends. The emails, on the other hand, all related to my work role and involved communication between myself and other individuals and groups of people. As such, they were slightly more formal, although for short interactions I often didn't bother to correct typing errors. The final activity – commenting on a book chapter I am writing with a colleague – was part of a collaborative exercise. Such writing is more carefully crafted and will go through many changes before being finalised as it represents our professional selves. As you can see, because of my job my day revolves around literacy practices of different types, and some days, if I am working at home, I need to use talk for work very little. This is probably quite an extreme example and your own practices may well be a very different mix.

Figure 2.9 shows a man in a parked taxi reading the world's best-selling English-language newspaper: *The Times of India*. Thinking about this picture enables us to reflect on the diversity of literacy practices in which English-language texts are taken up. In the scene pictured, a text is being made to perform functions that have implications for the social identity of the reader. We cannot know precisely what these are. But we can make some guesses, based on what we may know about the context.

Figure 2.9 Reading *The Times of India*

Many people find reading to be a useful way of managing the boredom and discomfort of waiting; it turns a part of the day that might otherwise be considered wasted into an opportunity for learning and entertainment. The physical size of a broadsheet newspaper (such as the one in the picture) also forms an effective barrier between oneself and the world, excluding unwanted attention and providing an often welcome sense of privacy: a function less easily performed by a handheld digital device! And focusing attention on a text makes it socially acceptable to refrain from interacting with other people (note the second newspaper reader behind the first).

The language of the text being read is also highly significant. While an outsider might assume that someone who chooses to read an English-language newspaper in India is identifying him- or herself with a foreign culture, this does not reflect the complexities of language use in India. English is a national language of India and although Hindi is spoken by far more people, it is not a first language for the majority of Indians; especially outside the 'Hindi belt' of northern India, therefore, many Indians prefer to use English rather than Hindi. English is a language associated with the middle and upper classes in India, so in some contexts, reading texts in English can help to index the reader as a person with aspirations. It is a very important language for the Indian higher education system, so reading texts of almost any kind in English can suggest an educated identity for the reader. And it is also one of the key languages for large-scale commerce and administration within India, so keeping up with the news in this language may be a way of expressing or maintaining an affiliation with business culture.

Diaries, blogs and lecture notes can all be considered examples of ordinary everyday writing and of what David Barton and Mary Hamilton (1998) call 'vernacular literacy practices'. Such practices play important personal roles in helping to *organise life* through the keeping of financial records or lists of birthdays; keeping in contact with friends and relatives through *personal communication*; and *documenting life* through diaries and albums. Examination of these practices can provide insights into the lives of ordinary people in ways that writing viewed as 'literature' might not. An example of ordinary writing is that associated with sending postcards, which has been the subject of research by Julia Gillen and Nigel Hall. These scholars collected over 2000 postcards sent in the first decade of the twentieth century and examined their significance in everyday communication practices.

Activity 2.8

Now turn to Reading B: *The Edwardian postcard* by Julia Gillen and Nigel Hall. Consider the writing of postcards as a literacy practice. What roles in society were played by people who wrote postcards? Why might their writing be considered 'vernacular'? How does the *writing* of a postcard connect to the postcard's visual characteristics? Are there significant differences from more modern communications media, such as email?

Comment

In early twentieth-century Britain, postcards were widely used across different strata of society, but because they were largely unregulated and not subject to rules of style they were able to fulfil a variety of useful functions in the lives of huge numbers of people, from keeping in touch to arranging a meeting. The use of pictures on postcards allowed senders to supplement their writing with reference to the image. Sometimes the images were personal photographs, a practice similar to picture messaging via mobile phones today. One significant difference relates to how ephemeral the medium may be. Postcards were not necessarily expected to be long lasting, but as material objects they have survived. It remains to be seen how long emails and text messages may be preserved in the digital archives of the future.

2.6   Multimodal literacy and cultural difference

Literacy practices may vary considerably between groups of people and between different cultures, and so may the multimodal characteristics of the texts taken up in those literacy practices. This is because visual representations have genres – from the self-portrait to the road sign to the assembly diagram – and, like the genres of speech and text, those genres are social actions that have undergone a history of development in order to serve recurrent needs in a conventional way. A simple illustration of this is the genre of the cartoon strip, which combines image and text.

Activity 2.9

Look at the cartoon strip in Figure 2.10. As you do so, try to monitor what you are doing as you 'read' it. What do you look at first? What assumptions do you make about the setting or the people?

COMICS IN THE CLASSROOM   **BY MRKAISER**

WWW.BITSTRIPS.COM

Figure 2.10   Comics in the classroom by MrKaiser

Comment

As you looked at the cartoon, the chances are that you started on the left-hand side and moved sequentially to the right. Did you recognise the figure in the first picture as a teacher because he was in a classroom setting, behind a desk and wearing more conservative clothes? What about the other three characters who were positioned next to desks, wore less formal clothes and were shorter? You may have assumed they were school students. In the first picture, the eyebrow raised in a frown, the hunched shoulders and the downturned mouth index the teacher's unhappiness. In the final picture, smiles and raised hands index the students' pleasure. Words indicate the causes of the unhappiness and the happy response to the teacher's suggestion.

Some of the above meanings may be recognisable to almost anyone. Smiles seem to express happiness in all human cultures, for example. On the other hand, there are many cultural contexts in which the teacher's clothes would index not a conservative but a *Western* identity. Moreover, although the meaning of the words in the cartoon will be clear to most people who can read English, the status of those words as thought or speech is communicated not by the words themselves but by the solid white shapes within which they are printed. These containers for words (or rather, the oppositions between these containers!) would seem a good example of a visual sign system. In contemporary comics, rectangles signify that any words within them are to be understood as narration, oval 'speech bubbles' with sharp tails (Figure 2.12) signify that any words within them are to be understood as spoken aloud by the characters to whom the tails point, and cloud-like 'think bubbles' trailing lines of little circles (Figure 2.13) signify that any words within them are to be understood as the unspoken thoughts of the characters towards whom the circles trail. As is often the case, however, there is more flexibility than the idea of a system might imply. Bubbles can be rectangular. Newspaper cartoons often leave out speech bubble outlines, keeping only the tails. And in Figure 2.10, the edge of the rightmost speech bubble is jagged rather than smooth, presumably to suggest that the words are shouted rather than spoken.

These meanings are entirely conventional. Eighteenth-century English-language caricatures often show spoken words scrolling out of people's mouths in a speech bubble-like manner, for example, but do not feature think bubbles and do not place narrative text in rectangular boxes (see Figure 2.11, which satirises judicial approval of domestic violence). A study of Vietnamese students learning English found them unable to derive the expected meaning from cartoons, but subsequently discovered that it was the speech and thought bubbles that were causing the confusion (M. Hewings, 1991). The symbol in Figure 2.12 was not recognised as indicating speech and the symbol in Figure 2.13 was not recognised as indicating thought.

The direction of reading is also conventional. The students' exclamation 'Yeaaaaah!!' (Figure 2.10) follows the teacher's announcement about comics because it is printed to the right of it: like pages of English text, Western comics are intended to be scanned from left to right and top to bottom. By contrast, Japanese comics, or manga, are read in the opposite direction. When they are published for mass audiences in the West, they are not only translated into other languages, but also visually 'flipped' – although some enthusiasts demand translations that retain the original right-to-left, bottom-to-top picture order. Moreover, although a left-to-right, top-to-bottom approach may now seem natural to most readers of English-language cartoons, it was not expected by eighteenth-century caricaturists: in Figure 2.11, for example, the words of the man beating the woman are in cruel answer to her cries for help, but they are above and to the left of them on the page. In text, very little is genuinely universal.

Figure 2.11   'JUDGE THUMB. or – Patent Sticks for Family Correction: Warranted Lawful!', James Gillray, 1782

Figure 2.12   Speech bubble

Figure 2.13   Think bubble

It should be clear by now that making sense of a text involves recognising the complex interactions of both visual elements and verbal elements, and relating these to contextual knowledge. What we understand, then, depends not only upon the image itself, but also on the context and on the other images or words on the page. And it is only in the course of the reader's interactions with the multimodal text as a whole that 'meaning' takes shape.

2.7   Conclusion

In this chapter, we have begun to explore the complexities of written, printed and digital communication, looking in detail at texts, their genres and the technologies that have made them possible. The complex interrelationships that come into play prevent a study of communication from limiting itself to artificially circumscribed categories, such as 'speaking', 'writing' and even 'language': thus, while communication through language is the primary focus in this book, we never pretend that a discussion of language alone is sufficient. Indeed, the notion of 'language alone' is meaningful only on a theoretical level, because real-world uses of language are invariably structured by one or more genres, realised through particular media and accompanied by forms of paralanguage (one cannot speak without taking a tone of voice, for example, and a text without letterforms would not be readable by humans). Above all, any such uses are embedded in social, historical, cultural and institutional contexts without which they could carry neither meaning nor power. To understand communication in English, we must therefore study a great deal else besides the English language.

READING A: Genre under construction: the diary on the internet

Laurie McNeill

Source: McNeill, L. (2005) 'Genre under construction: the diary on the internet', *Language@Internet*, vol. 2, article 2, Digital Peer Publishing, http://www.dipp.nrw.de/

Diaries began to appear on the Internet in 1995, typically developing out of the personal home pages of individuals already involved with Internet technologies (Astruc, Leitch-Thompson, & Wade, n.p.). In 1997 people started creating pages that became known as weblogs (or 'blogs') – these were daily lists of annotated links to other sites, without extended commentary or personal narratives. They acted as filters for the burgeoning content of the Web and directed readers to material the blogger found particularly worthwhile. In 1999 free software became available that allowed users who did not know HTML to make and post a blog or diary. As a result, blogging became an accessible activity for significantly more people, and the numbers of both diaries and blogs mushroomed (Blood 'Weblogs' 8). […] With the huge influx of new writers into the blogging and online diary communities, both forms evolved to suit these users' needs. Collapsing these related forms into one, the latest generation of writers marry personal narratives (like a diary) with critical commentary about the Web and its content (like a blog), drawing on the Internet culture to speak to and for other 'Netizens.'

As these formerly distinct text-types merged and the resulting hybrid form became hugely popular, writers talked openly in their texts about what they saw themselves doing and why, seeking to understand the genre by examining their own practices. Since the online diary – whether called a diary or a blog, a contentious issue of terminology that I will return to in a moment – has a relatively short history and challenges stereotypes of the offline version, many readers and writers see the genre as an emerging form. Consequently, its practitioners make particular efforts to tell readers how to read and other writers how to write. This commentary can be characterized as what Giltrow and others have called meta-genre, which is discourse about genres by its users. By advising and even prescribing how writing should be produced, what it should look or sound like, meta-genre acts to typify a genre. Because meta-genre comes from within the community formed by the genre, it indicates how the community, to paraphrase Burke, 'acts together' through genre, using genre to accomplish purposes that serve and establish the group.

The appearance of such meta-genre is, perhaps, unexpected in a genre so frequently characterized as artless, without rules, fragmentary, and personal rather than professional. Despite the booming self-help market for journalling 'how-to' guides, the print diary is typically considered a genre that requires no analysis or instruction. Because of the popular notion that the personal manuscript diary never circulates, new diarists apparently know how they are supposed to write through some kind of cultural osmosis. And since ostensibly no one else should be reading these diaries, it hardly matters whether or not a diarist successfully reproduces the genre.

Online diarists, on the other hand, who write diaries explicitly for external readers, will be evaluated on their generic performance. The consistent appearance of meta-genre in online diaries indicates bloggers' awareness of this potential evaluation, as well as their sense that they are doing something new, even transgressive, and therefore requiring commentary. Web-diarists comment on all aspects of their texts, holding forth on topics including style, ethics, connections to other genres, and audience. These discussions, in which writers explain, justify, teach, or philosophize, illuminate cultural values, reading practices, and discourse features. In addition, such commentary allows diarists to address their desired readers specifically, distinguishing their community members from the hundreds of thousands of 'lurkers' who read blogs without becoming part of the diary's communities. Understanding genre and making a genre claim are therefore not simply academic concerns for practitioners. Internet diarists need to be clear about what kind of text they see themselves producing in order to attract the kinds of readers they seek. Building a faithful audience is one of the key social actions that diaries perform in this context, and the establishment of community is arguably the exigence to which bloggers use diaries to respond. Failure to understand or adequately perform the genre, to live up to the expectations it creates, may well mean a failure to attract and keep readers – and a lack of readership causes the demise of many blogs. While writing to an actual reader in a print diary may be seen as breaking generic 'rules,' doing so online is not just expected but demanded. Internet diarists ignore their readers and their desires at their own (textual) peril. Advising readers how to read their texts allows diarists to anticipate readers' misunderstandings about the nature of their texts, and avoid offending potential new audiences.

Looking at what bloggers say about the texts they are producing, and how they see their work in both a digital and literary context, demonstrates the careful negotiations these writers make in producing texts that will build the communities they seek. But their commentaries also underscore the tension and confusion that surrounds claims for 'newness' in these personal sites. Recognizing that 'a lot of people are quite insistent' that journals and blogs are different forms, for example, blogger Jane Pinckard discusses her decision to create separate pages for her journal and her blog. She explains, 'for me the weblog and the journal have very different functions. The weblog is sort of my "instant fix" for when I feel like I just have to write about something, even if I don't necessarily have a lot of time.' In contrast to this off-the-cuff writing, the journal calls upon a more literary tradition: she says, 'It takes me longer to write, I think about it more, and it tends to be much more rambling, introspective what have you' (http://www. umamitsunami.com). More forcefully, blogger Neale Talbot argues that blogs and diaries are distinct genres and should remain that way. He acknowledges that blogs 'share similar elements to the journal world,' but concludes, 'that don't mean one will eat the other. Distinct places. Distinct genres. You say it's the same old shit in the same old package. Well I say it's a lot less shit in a much smaller package' (157). Echoing Pinckard, he explains, 'They're different styles for different audiences about different things' (157–158). The aggressiveness of his rant, a tone picked up by many bloggers – 'Why your moveable type blog must die' – demonstrates high anxiety about generic contamination, an anxiety perhaps fuelled by the diary's offline reputation as a feminine genre of no consequence.

'Old school' bloggers like Talbot may want to see themselves as participating in a new enterprise, one without the cultural baggage of an existing (print) genre, and consequently disavow any connection to related or similar genres. While the term 'online diaries' clearly connects these texts to the print world, to the traditions of the diary and the generic rules and expectations that come with them, the expression 'blogs' invites a reading of these writings as a new form. However, as Pinckard's definitions illustrate, generic (and, correspondingly, community) lines may not be any easier to keep clean online than off. Though bloggers clearly want to align themselves with a new genre and culture, reflective of their participation in the so-called 'New Media,' their practices tie them to the traditions of the diary, too. Pinckard describes journal-writing as an activity requiring time, thought, and meditation, a characterization that reflects traditional uses of the diary as a spiritual exercise, personal therapy tool, and literary production. Despite the public nature of the online journal, it still focuses on the personal and introspective. Her characterization of the blog as off-the-cuff, capturing her thoughts in the instant of writing, though, is a style also popularly associated with the diary genre as an artless, spontaneous text.

In reality even the scantiest of blog narratives incorporates trademark diary features, with regular, dated entries that focus on the diarist's experiences or at least his or her interests. Few practitioners separate their writings as Pinckard does, making instead texts that do a little bit of everything, and eliding the artificial distinction between the blog and the diary (just as the line between 'diary' and 'journal' is untenable when we look at actual writing practices). Despite their difference in name and occasionally in format, then, weblogs draw upon the diary form and tradition, and perhaps we can read the blog as simply another kind or function of the diary genre, one particularly well-suited to contemporary diarists. Online participation in this genre allows writers to carry on public diary conversations that will no longer be monologic, where the response will not be just imagined but actual. These conversations may be in-depth discussions, as in Pinckard's journal, or simply chats, as in her blog, with varying degrees of personal disclosure and intimacy – the 'different styles for different audiences' that Talbot highlights. But even in this new context, bloggers do not write in a vacuum; they participate in a generic activity with a long history, and this history will be activated each time the genre is used. They know that their diaries will be recognized by and understandable to their audiences in part because of this generic precedent, even as the genre evolves in this different situation. The fact that both bloggers felt the need to acknowledge this generic confusion and outline their approach underscores the importance of genre to their own projects and to the communities they address. Participation in a genre attracts particular kinds of readers, and Pinckard and Talbot's meta-genre suggests that 'blogs' and 'journals' can hail very different groups, particularly if the writer denies that any cross-over exists between the old and new forms.

Writers who identify their texts as 'Internet diaries,' as opposed to 'blogs,' in particular must keep a delicate balance between old and new practices and expectations. Readers again are central to this exercise, since they provide explicit feedback in comments pages and guestbooks that demonstrates their expectations and whether or not these are being met. Steve Schalchlin, who was one of the first Internet diarists when he began posting in 1996, incorporated his readers' responses into his meta-genre, clearly indicating to his audience their instrumental role in the entries he writes. […] By September 1997, he records the impulse to change an old entry in which he had been extremely angry, but concludes, 'My diary page from yesterday will stay as it is (because readers have now laid down the law about me changing a single word of anything I write)' (12 Sept. 1997). To Schalchlin's audience, his going back and changing entries that cast him in an unfavorable light would be 'cheating,' inauthentic, inaccurate. They seek a text that cannot be altered after the fact, a 'finished' version that would most resemble the fixed nature of the entries in a published diary. They look for their experiences of the traditional journal to be replicated in this new context, despite the changes Internet technology has made to that experience of genre.

The fact that readers have 'laid down the law,' and that Schalchlin is respecting that (legalistic) decision, provides evidence of an implicit mutual agreement about the new rules of the diary, one formulated to suit this particular community's understandings of the genre. As Schalchlin's experiences suggest, these genre rules are produced in collaboration between writers and readers, a distinct departure in practice from manuscript diaries. Playing by these 'rules' therefore both upholds community norms and assists in attracting readers, whose presence, as we have noted, is key to the Internet diary's social actions. Bloggers operate under an unwritten code of conduct that governs the appropriate uses of an Internet diary, a code based again on the generic traditions of the print diary but adapted to the genre's new online capacity. Readers still expect texts that are personal, even intimate, even while they hope to become part of a community through the shared experience of reading these 'private' texts.

These opposing ideals can produce friction within a particular community when diarists infringe upon any of these sequestered expectations. I was not surprised to see this confusion and negotiation around generic practices when Schalchlin began — at that point Internet diaries had been on the scene for less than a year and very few of them existed. But his experiences in 1996 and 1997 with angry and rule-making readers are not in fact unusual for bloggers, nor have the issues his case highlights — issues including disclosure, truth claims, intimacy — been satisfactorily resolved. In May 2004, Justin Hall, another Web pioneer who has kept an online diary in various forms since 1994, ignited a firestorm of response when a reader posted a comment questioning whether Hall had been being truthful with his readers about his decision to go to grad school. Within hours of the original response, 64 replies appeared, and similar numbers of readers responded to each of Hall's subsequent posts. Hall was either pilloried or defended – some readers made point-by-point refutations of Hall's version of his experiences, while others came up with explanations or defended his right not to tell all. (Hall himself never directly addressed the debate.) These unhappy readers clearly expected Hall's diary to be an exact mirror of his offline life – expectations that arise out of the stereotype of the contemporary diary. [...]

Since online diaries incorporate the familiar alongside the strange, they are unsettling generic territory. Producing texts that consciously bridge both print and Internet cultures, online diarists work to give new audiences a context within which to understand their texts and help them develop expectations for the genre and its producers. Concerned with creating texts that serve functions for both themselves and their readers, online diarists write with an awareness of, and a desire for, a reading public unprecedented for the traditional concept of the diary and diarist. Carrying over to the Internet such expected features as dated, distinct entries, a confiding if not confessional tone, and a concern with the everyday details of one's own life, Web-diarists reassure readers of the print diary that their narrative expectations will be met online. But these diarists also expand the form to fit new uses and users, adding [page view] counters, e-mail addresses, links, and discussion boards, addressing the range of possibilities the technology of the Internet opens up for the diary genre. The combination of new technologies and an old form generates what has become a productive tension within the loose community formed by participation in the online diary. Both readers and writers work together to establish a definition of the genre and its consequences that suits their particular needs. As such, they make the Internet diary a useful response to the situations of contemporary society and culture.

References for this reading

Giltrow, Janet (2001). Meta-Genre. In Coe, Richard & Lorelei Lingard & Tatiana Teslenko (eds.) The Rhetoric and Ideology of Genre: Strategies for Stability and Change. Cresskill, NJ: Hampton. 187–205.

Hall, Justin. Justin's Links. 22 June 2004. < http://www.links.net/ >.

Joyce, James A. Why your Movable Type blog must die. Kuro5hin. 3 Feb. 2004. < http://www.kuro5hin.org/story/2004/2/2/171117/8823 >.

Pinckard, Jane. Umami Tsunami. 30 June 2004. < http://www.umamitsunami. com/ >.

Rodzvilla, John (ed.) (2002). We've Got Blog: How Weblogs are Changing Our Culture. Cambridge, MA: Perseus.

Schalchlin, Steve. Living in the Bonus Round. 30 June 2004. < http://www.bonusround.com >.

Talbot, Neale (2002). Put the Keyboard Down and Back Away from the Weblog. In Rodzvilla, John (ed.) We've Got Blog: How Weblogs are Changing Our Culture, Cambridge, MA: Perseus. 47–56.

READING B: The Edwardian postcard

Julia Gillen and Nigel Hall

Source: Gillen, J. and Hall, N. (2010) 'Edwardian postcards: illuminating ordinary writing' in Barton, D. and Papen, U. (eds) *The Anthropology of Writing: Understanding Textually Mediated Words*, London, Continuum, pp. 169–79.

> *People today wonder how our fathers and mothers got on without those useful adjuncts of civilization – postcards.*
>
> Anon, 1901

[…] During the reign of Edward VII (1901–1910) the total number of postcards posted in Britain was 5,920,933,334, almost six billion, getting on for 200 cards per person. Although the postcard had been first developed in Austria in 1869 it was very quickly adopted across the world. […] By 1902 Britain had experienced almost 30 years of compulsory education, and while literacy levels may not have necessarily been high, the postcard did not make huge demands on writers. Everyone could use postcards: they were cheap and attractive objects and nobody was looking over a writer's shoulder checking for errors. Most people, save for the very poor and the totally illiterate, found that postcards had great value in their increasingly fast and complex social lives. […]

It is because the postcard was so widely used during the Edwardian period that it has great potential for anyone interested in the history of writing. Ordinary writing from England's past represents an elusive quarry. The writing that has survived in archives, libraries and personal collections is often that of elite writers, their clerks and scribes, or belongs to distinctive educated individuals, often diarists. The absence of other people's ordinary writing is not only because limited educational opportunities restricted access to writing skills, but also because any such texts were not seen as worth preserving. [...]

The explosion in use of the postcard in Edwardian times, reaching nearly one billion annually, bears a striking parallel to today's growth in electronic communications. A downward shift in costs and improvements in technologies led to a dramatic increase in writings that reached their addressees quickly wherever they were. Multiple daily deliveries in some centres meant that multimodal communications could be exchanged more rapidly than ever before. The postal service was so efficient that up to six deliveries a day were being made in major cities. For the first time in British history there was a literacy-related object that did not demand too much writing or reading, could be posted extremely cheaply, in which a significant part of the overall message could be conveyed by a printed picture and in its relative informality was ideally suited to vernacular writing. The consequence was the use of the postcards by most sectors of society for a great range of purposes.

In their easy multimodality, postcards may be seen to transcend the comparable communicative tools of a century later. In the first decade of the twenty-first century, it is very possible to send multimedia text messages, but this is still a relatively unusual mode in comparison with all the messages that feature words, with a highly constrained range of additional graphical features such as emoticons. Multimodal emails are common for those sent by commercial organizations to their target markets, but the majority of 1:1 emails we send in our personal and professional lives are essentially verbal. By contrast, Edwardian postcards by default give the sender the opportunity to combine a choice of image with their text, at very little cost: it has been estimated that in real terms sending a postcard cost about one fortieth the amount in this period in comparison with the 1970s (Monahan, 1980; Staff, 1979). The postcard even offered the chance of avoiding writing at all. As one writer in *The Picture Postcard* wrote, 'As a picture is far easier to read than print, so superior is the pictorial card to the written word' (1901: 145). Indeed, many of the cards being sold during the Edwardian period have a pictorial side that included a printed text (e.g. 'Why haven't you written?' or 'I'm sorry I haven't written').

The Edwardian postcard did bring with it two issues that have also affected digital communications. The first is privacy. Unlike the letter, a postcard is a very open and public form of communication, and any message written on a card will be exposed to scrutiny beyond that of its intended recipient. [...]

The second issue relates to concerns about standards. First, for some the postcard transgressed social standards. When the postcard first appeared, it was rejected by some as being below their dignity. The journalist James Douglas wrote in 1907, 'There are still some ancient purists who regard postcards as vulgar, fit only for tradesmen' (cited in Staff, 1979: 81). For others, just as it is for some with today's texting and email, the new medium was going to ruin the English language. Douglas (ibid.) also claimed that 'The picture postcard carries rudeness to the fullest extremity. There is no room for anything polite' while another critic said 'The postcard is utterly destructive of style' (Sims, 1900). However, one author suggested that 'The postcard with its entire freedom from ceremony of formality, is such an obvious boon to thousands, if not millions, of correspondents in these days' (*The Times*, 1.11.1899, p. 13).

[... P]ostcards represent the kind of writing that has been characterized in a number of ways by different academics, such as 'ordinary writing' (Sinor, 2002) and 'vernacular' and 'everyday writing' (Barton & Hamilton, 1998).

So what kind of writing is it on Edwardian postcards? Is it 'ordinary writing' as defined by Sinor (2002)? She claims that ordinary writing is 'writing that is typically unseen or ignored, and is primarily defined by its status as discardable' (p. 5). She borrows from Langbauer's formulation that it is an example of the 'very things we cannot read because they are so commonplace as to be boring, to refuse our regard or interpretation (p. 126). [...]

[...] It is clear that while the handwritten messages have not necessarily been physically discarded, they have nevertheless been largely refused our regard and interpretation. Ordinary writing has been too easily represented as mundane or insignificant, but as Thurlow, Jaworski and Ylänne (in press) point out it is the 'apparent' banality which makes postcards so communicatively important. Being positioned as banal obscures the complex range of functions embedded within such texts.

Barton and Hamilton (1998) offer another perspective that relates to the ordinariness of writing on postcards. They discuss vernacular literacies and describe them as 'essentially ones which are not regulated by the formal rules and procedures of dominant social institutions and which have their origins in everyday life'. Postcards do not escape some of the rules of dominant social institutions for in many respects usage was regulated by the British Post Office; when they began they had to be of certain sizes, cost a specified amount and certain parts of [a] postcard could only be used in certain ways […] Postcard writers developed many creative solutions to how they could write on postcards and the composition of messages was restricted only by Britain's libel and obscenity laws. Most importantly, no-one sought to restrict the quality of composition, spelling, grammar and punctuation. No-one set acceptable standards for postcard writing and no-one assessed what people wrote. […] Thus, postcard texts essentially evolved out of the practice of writing them and these practices were situated in people's ordinary, everyday lives. Postcards might contain no writing, a couple of words or up to, in some cases, well over a hundred words, they could have drawings, codes, or symbols, and the writing could be oriented in many different directions. The evidence of the millions of Edwardian cards that have survived is that their authors took every opportunity to explore their freedoms. […]

Three quarters of our sample are views or buildings; there is a scattering of other topics including comic subjects, photographs of ordinary people and representations of fine art. We have categorized two thirds as essentially 'photographic' and almost all the rest as 'professionally illustrated' although the boundary between the two is impossible to draw finitely. Very many cards feature adapted images: for example, personal photographs turned into postcards or, very commonly, professional photographic images that have been coloured, tinted or 'improved' in some way. So we see that a great deal of the image editing that goes on today as part of both professional and personal practices has clear ancestry in the practices of the Edwardians. Occasionally we suspect that the image selected was of secondary importance; the message was vital and the writer sent the first card that came to hand. However, far more frequently, there is some relationship between the image and the reason for sending it; some cards make explicit reference to supplying the card as a gift to supplement the addressee's collection. Others draw some feature of the illustration to the addressee's attention, for example: 'Do you not think this is a saucy card' or 'My house is further along on the right.' […]

Figure [1]   An Edwardian postcard, picture side

Figure [2]   An Edwardian postcard, message side

[… W]e will present some analysis of one randomly selected card […]

The card (as in Figure [1]) has on one side a poor quality colour reproduction of a church, St Peter's in Bramley, Leeds. [… A]n extremely local publisher of postcards, Fairbank's of Bramley and Pudsey issued the card which was sent by a 'Rob C' to a Mr Harry Jones of 47 Ermine Road, Hoole in Chester. The illustration is not mentioned at all by the writer.

On the address side Rob C stuck the stamp on upside down, whether by accident or intent. The postmark is of Bramley, Yorkshire, at 9 p.m. on 29 August 1907, a Thursday (see Figure [2]). We have begun calculating the distances between sender and addressee on a random sample of our cards and the distance of this one, 86 miles is actually very typical of our results of this exercise so far. The layout of the card illustrates the regulatory framework within which some elements of postcards continued to be controlled after 1902 in specifying very clearly where the message and address were to be written. The card was 'inland use only' as some other countries had different regulations about how cards were to be laid out. The writer has stuck very precisely to the framing of the card, although he does write right down the bottom edge of the card. The cursive handwriting, written in ink, is fairly neat and very legible (save for one word). The message contains 69 words.

> Mr H. Jones
> 47 Ermine Rd
> Hoole
> Chester
> Dear Harry
> Pleased to hear
> that you have had such a
> pleasant holiday. We were
> quite expecting to see you
> on your way through, and
> were very much disappointed
> you did not turn up. I had
> a grand holiday & will let
> you know all about it soon.
> My people are all well & join
> me in kindest regards. Will
> write soon. Yours to a cinder
> (Rob) C.

The card begins with a salutation which both marks it as an epistolary genre, clearly drawing from letter writing conventions, and informalizes the rendition of the addressee's name elsewhere on the card intended for the Post Office's use. Such salutations shift the tone from (relatively) public to (relatively) private, personalizing the communication. Typical of postcard authors is the elliptical omission of self-reference in the opening sentence, going straight into 'Pleased to hear;' this structure is mirrored in the pre-pre closing at the other end of the message: 'will write soon' (symmetries of structure in openings and closings have been noted as characteristic of telephone conversations, [Hopper, 1992]). As with contemporary written communications constrained by extremely limited use of space, there is some use of abbreviation and short forms: here use of the ampersand rather than spelling out 'and'.

The body of the message, as typically with our sample, consists of fairly short sentences, lacking amplification and moving rapidly from one topic to another; underlying may be a sense that the receiver will make use of their background knowledge in interpretation.

The card contains an interesting phrase at the end: 'Yours to a cinder', a friendly catch-phrase of the Edwardian period. Although not appearing in the 1898 Dictionary of Phrase and Fable it was used in the following decade by Lord Fisher in many letters to Winston Churchill and by Banjo Patterson, the Australian bush poet. In 1907 the phrase appeared in a postcard at the centre of a notorious *cause celebre*, it was written by a young commercial artist Robert Wood on a card to Phyliss Dimmock who was murdered soon afterwards; he was tried for the crime but eventually acquitted (Hogarth, 1954).

References for this reading

Anon, *The Picture Postcard*, July 1901, 101.

Barton, D. & M. Hamilton (1998), *Local Literacies: Reading and Writing in One Community*. London: Routledge.

Hogarth, B. (1954), 'Robert Wood, 1907'. In J. Hodge (ed.), *Famous Trials 4*. London: Penguin Books, 176–221.

Hopper, R. (1992), *Telephone Conversation*. Bloomington, IN: Indiana University Press.

Monahan, V. (1980), *Collecting Postcards in Colour 1914–1930*. Poole: Blandford Press.

Sims, G. (1900), Untitled article in *The Picture Postcard*, January, 22.

Sinor, J. (2002), *The Extraordinary Work of Ordinary Writing: Annie Ray's Diary*. Iowa City: University of Iowa Press.

Staff, F. (1979), *The Picture Postcard and its origins 2nd edn*. London: Lutterworth Press.

Thurlow, C., A. Jaworski & V. Ylänne (in press), '"New" mobilities, transient identities: holiday postcards'. In C. Thurlow & A. Jaworski (eds.), *Tourism Discourse*. Basingstoke: Palgrave Macmillan.

3   Growing up with English

Barbara Mayor

With grateful acknowledgement to Dennis Bancroft and Pam Czerniewska for the inclusion of material from earlier Open University publications.

3.1   Introduction

Chapters 1 and 2 have considered a range of practices in spoken and written English involving English-speaking adults. In this chapter I consider how English-speaking children learn to take part in such practices – how they learn to make *sense* of the English language as a system, and how they learn to make *meaning* in English. I also consider what extra processes are involved in learning to crack the code of written language, and whether the writing and spelling systems of English pose any special challenges to learners of any age.

According to David Crystal, 'approximately one in three of the world's [seven billion] population are now capable of communicating to a useful level in English' (Crystal, 2012, p. 155) and daily exposure to English has become a fact of life for many millions of children on all six inhabited continents. David Graddol envisages 'a new generation of English-knowing children' around the world, for whom English represents a 'basic skill' (Graddol, 2006, pp. 101, 72). The focus of this chapter is on how children in the preschool years, whether monolingual or bilingual, come to understand what it means to be an English user.

Throughout this book, the term 'bilingual' is used to encompass multilingual people and contexts.

3.2   Learning to talk in English

Activity 3.1

What knowledge and skills do you think the task of learning English involves for children? Think about everything from producing the right sounds to learning how best to get one's way.

**Allow about
5 minutes**

Comment

Crystal (1995, p. 426) outlines the knowledge that children need to acquire in order to speak English: the twenty or so vowels and twenty-four or so consonants of a particular spoken dialect, and over 300 ways of combining these; an active vocabulary of around 50,000 words and a passive ability to understand about half as many again; at least a thousand aspects of grammatical construction; several hundred ways of using the **prosodic features** of pitch, volume, speed and rhythm to convey meaning; a large number of rules governing the ways in which sentences can be combined into spoken discourse; a large number of conventions governing the ways in which varieties of English differ; and an even larger number of strategies governing the ways in which all the above rules can be bent or broken in order to achieve special effects. The various aspects of this task develop at different rates at different stages of life, with some continuing into adulthood.

How infants communicate

Theoretical linguist Noam Chomsky (1980, 1986) was the first to argue for a so-called 'nativist' position that language is an innate human ability which is biologically determined and follows a predictable developmental path. Chomsky acknowledged, however, that some minimal language input is required to trigger the language learning process, and that this needs to occur in the very early years of life; in other words, that there is a 'critical period' for language acquisition. Evidence from the small number of children tragically isolated from social contact in their early years provides support for this claim, since such linguistically deprived children neither spontaneously develop language in isolation nor go on to develop normal language competence beyond a certain stage of maturation.

Obviously, no baby is pre-programmed to speak English or any other language, but it has been observed both before and after birth (through the monitoring of such things as movement, gaze and natural cries) that babies are primed even within the womb to attend to the particular 'melody' of the language that surrounds them (see, for example, Mampe et al., 2009). Infants come to recognise the boundaries of English words by the frequent stress on the first syllable, and their early experimentation with babbling soon differentiates the particular sounds which are meaningful in their linguistic community from those which are not.

Allow as much time as you like

Activity 3.2

Choose some typical sounds produced by an infant, such as *mmm* or *ooh* or *dada*, and try saying them to convey the following:

- pleasure
- disgust
- resignation
- a request.

If you are able to recruit family or friends to help in this exercise, do so, but it works equally well as a solo effort. Listen carefully to the way in which your utterances change according to your communicative purpose.

Comment

You will probably have noticed how it is possible to have a one-word vocabulary and yet be capable of expressing a range of different meanings – or performing a range of different speech acts (see Chapter 1) – by varying the intonation and the body language. When infants exercise their vocal cords and facial muscles in the first months of life, regardless of the language or languages they are acquiring, they are taking control of a system which will be useful to them in later communicative exchanges with others.

Anthropologists Elinor Ochs and Bambi Schieffelin (1979) were among the first to argue that children begin by learning the meaning of speech acts and only gradually learn the language that corresponds to these in the community around them. Ochs identifies a range of 'pragmatic alternatives that are available to young children even before single words emerge … touching, pointing, and eye gaze … reaching, holding up, waving … pushing away, head shaking, and the like' (Ochs, 1979, p. 13). Gordon Wells has likened this to a 'conversation without words' between infants and their caregivers; he argues that 'infants come to be able to have and express communicative intentions by being treated as if they could already have them' (Wells, 1985, p. 24). So it could be said that learning to speak is initially a matter of learning the rules of social behaviour and meaning making and only later a matter of learning the grammatical rules by which these are realised in English or any other language.

A baby's first experience of language across many cultures is likely to be in dialogue with a caregiver (i.e. an adult of either sex who takes regular care of a child). When communicating with babies, adults in many English-speaking cultures tend to use a simplified style of speech with exaggerated intonation, referred to as child-directed speech (CDS) or, more colloquially, 'baby talk'. This was vividly described by Jean Berko Gleason, who carried out her studies in the USA:

> Briefly we can say [caregivers] raised the fundamental frequency of
> their voices, used simple short sentences with concrete nouns,

diminutives, and terms of endearment, expanded the children's utterances and in general performed the linguistic operations that constitute baby-talk style. ... One mother, for instance, spoke in a normal voice to her husband, a high voice to her 4-year-old, a slightly raised voice to her 8-year-old and when she talked to her baby she fairly squeaked.

(Gleason, 1973, pp. 160–1)

Allow about
5 minutes

Activity 3.3

What do you think might be the function of CDS? How useful is it? Do you think it would be possible to learn a first language without it?

Comment

CDS, although not universal, appears to serve at least three possible useful functions in learning English. On the one hand, as Usha Goswami (2010, p. 112) has observed, it may help children attune their ear to the characteristic strong–weak **stress pattern** of English words (like '*func*tion', '*chil*dren' and '*pat*tern' in this paragraph) by retaining this same pattern in diminutives like 'Mummy', 'Daddy' and 'baby' and extending it to other words like 'doggie' and 'milkie'.

Second, by use of exaggerated stress at the sentence level, CDS may serve to direct the child's attention to the key elements (usually the **content words**) in an utterance.

Third, by means of exaggerated intonation patterns involving rising or falling pitch, CDS may also help to facilitate turn taking in conversation by emphasising question-and-answer exchanges and other adjacency pairs (see Chapter 1).

However, cross-cultural studies (such as Pye, 1986) have demonstrated that CDS is by no means essential to language acquisition since children are able to acquire language in cultures where CDS is not practised. The difference in adult input, however, may well have an effect on the kind of language a child goes on to produce.

Allow about
15 minutes

Activity 3.4

Consider the following examples of children's early utterances. How would you best explain what is going on in each case? What do you think has prompted the child to say what they do? Are they likely to be imitating something they have heard someone else say? If not, what else do you think may be going on?

1   Delia aged 0;2 in 2011: 'orrr … heeee … laaahh' (personal communication).

2   Child's first word in 1877: 'mum' (associated with food) (Charles Darwin, 1877, quoted in Gillen, 2003, p. 59).

3   English child Max aged 1;2: 'Dada!' (pointing to book) (Gillen, 2003, p. 73).

4   Ellen aged 1;9: 'time for a cup of coffee' (quoted in Wray, 2002, p. 107).

5   Mexican boy Edgardo aged 3, temporarily resident in the UK: 'The tractor green, the *camión* yellow' (The Open University, 1997, p. 46).

6   Canadian boy Lawrence aged 3;6: 'I don't want to go to your ami' [= 'I don't want to go to Miami'] (Pinker, 1994, p. 267).

7   English girl Susie aged 4;7: 'And we saw a jellyfish, and we had to bury it. And we – we did holding crabs and we – we holded him in by the spade' (Crystal, 1986, p. 9).

In research on child language, ages are usually given in the form 1;2 or 1:2, indicating 1 year and 2 months.

Figure 3.1   Edgardo and his mother

Comment

The first thing to say is that we can rarely be *certain* what is going on in a child's mind and in some cases we can only guess what words may have been intended, let alone the communicative intent. In all but the first three examples, the words that are reproduced in standard English spelling here may well have sounded very different when uttered by the child. I offer a few brief comments on each.

1 You may have attributed Delia's babbling either to the human baby's *instinct* to make sounds or as her early attempts to *imitate* those around her, and there may indeed be elements of both processes in operation. In addition, Delia's father told me he had just been 'vocalising' with her, in which case he was doubtless reinforcing some of the sounds she produced and ignoring sounds which were less familiar to his English-speaking ear.

2 and 3. Both Max and Darwin's young subject are recorded here as producing the words that are often reported as being children's first recognisable English 'words', although the processes by which they settled on these particular sequences of syllables may have been similar to those at play for Delia. However, the contextual information for each of these examples casts doubt as to whether they were simply referring to their parents. Darwin's baby may indeed have been greeting Mum, but Darwin speculated that the baby was more probably smacking his or her lips in anticipation of food. In Max's case we are even less sure out of context what this single word was meant to convey – possibly a whole phrase such as 'Daddy, please read me the picture book!' or 'That picture looks like you, Daddy!'

4 Ellen's utterance was interpreted by her caregiver as meaning 'please may I have a biscuit', presumably because this expression was associated in Ellen's mind with the daily routine of stopping for a snack.

5 Edgardo's switch to Spanish for the word *camión* may partly be to plug a gap in his English vocabulary, but also indicates that he is aware that his audience (in this case his big brother) is capable of understanding either language.

6 and 7. There can be little doubt that neither Lawrence nor Susie has heard these particular stretches of language before, so there seems to be no imitation at play here. However, they both show signs of great linguistic analysis and creativity in the original language that they produce.

I will return later to some of these examples.

Interest in how children learn to talk has a long history across a range of academic disciplines, including linguistics, psychology, sociology, biology, neurology, anthropology and philosophy. Prior to the 1960s, the dominant understanding was that children learn to speak largely by *imitation* of the language modelled around them. Subsequent work in the tradition of Chomsky emphasised the role of *instinct*: human infants are programmed to process such language input, in order to generate *hypotheses* about its underlying structure and develop *rules of use*. More recent research findings have taken a step back in the direction of imitation, recognising that, although much of any language is probably stored as a set of rules, there is also a large element of *habit formation*. In other words, children learn much of their early language in 'chunks' as part of *interactional routines* with those around them.

In the next two subsections I look at the influential cognitive and social traditions in the study of how children acquire their first language.

Cognitive perspectives on learning to talk

Research in the cognitive tradition seeks to understand the mental processes within children's minds, focusing on the relationship between the outward *form* of their utterances (especially their grammar and vocabulary) and what these may reveal about their developing understanding of language and the world. A cognitive perspective generally seeks to investigate what is common to all normally developing children, rather than what makes each child different. It has provided a body of evidence that the linguistic development of monolingual English-speaking children follows a predictable path, and that the key stages in the acquisition of English are constant, even though each child's rate of progress and actual linguistic output will differ.

Grammatical development

With particular regard to how children learn grammar, Chomsky (1986) argues that there are 'universal principles' (such as, arguably, the concepts of noun and verb) that are common to the grammars of all human languages, but that 'parameters of variation' (such as word order or details of morphology) need to be set differently according to the language to which children are exposed. Put more simply, all children are born with an awareness that language is composed of certain building blocks (e.g. noun phrases and verb phrases), but they do not know how to combine these elements into sentences until they are exposed to some input in a particular language. So, in English, they would learn first that the basic order of a sentence is Subject–Verb–Object, and only later that you need to add a few special endings, like *-s* for the 'third person' or the plural. Once they have the benefit of input to trigger the learning process, children very rarely opt for word orders that are not permitted in the language spoken around them. According to Stephen Pinker (1994, p. 268), they get it right 95 per cent of the time.

One of the most widely reported phenomena is that English-speaking children roughly between the ages of eighteen months and two years start to produce two-word 'mini sentences' expressing simple semantic relations such as actions or belonging. This kind of emergent grammar has been termed **telegraphic language**.

Allow about 10 minutes

Activity 3.5

In the following examples, what do you notice is missing from the children's 'telegraphic' versions, as compared to the conventional adult versions?

Child's utterance	Assumed meaning in context
Dolly hat	(That's) Dolly's hat
Bottle juice	(I want) a bottle of juice
Shoe wet	My shoe is wet
Chocolate gone	The chocolate has gone
Hayley talk	Hayley is talking
Want Teddy	I want Teddy
Bang bottom	I banged my bottom

(adapted from Radford, 1990, pp. 68, 62, 76, 161, 148, 70, 70)

Comment

You may have noticed that such early 'sentences' usually consist of content words only. It seems that **function words**, like articles (*a* or *the*), pronouns (*my*), prepositions (*of*) and auxiliary verbs (*is* or *has*), as well as morphological inflections (like *-ing* or *-ed* or possessive *-'s*), are normally acquired relatively late. This has been attributed in part to the stress patterns of English, since 'in stressed languages generally, it is the unstressed items that are omitted in early utterances' (Wells, 1985, p. 27).

Once grammatical inflections start to appear, it has been observed that normally developing English-speaking children actually appear to move 'backwards' in their learning and start making more mistakes. This is because they gradually replace simple imitation (as in *she held two mice*) by the application of a set of rules (as in *she hold-ed two mouse-s*), before finally settling on the unique mix of rules and special cases that constitutes their local variety of English. Susie from Activity 3.4 illustrates this unstable phase very well, as she experiments with *did holding* and *holded*. Children's early mistakes in generalising rules are thus a sign of creative minds at play, rather than the mere imitation of adult speech. Pinker remarks that '[a] child who echoed back a parent's sentences verbatim would be called [a poor communicator] not a powerful learner' (Pinker, 1994, p. 416). You will remember Lawrence in Activity 3.4 saying *I don't want to go to your ami* (meaning *I don't want to go to Miami*) (Pinker, 1994, p. 267). This is clearly not an utterance that Lawrence had ever heard spoken, but rather evidence of independent analysis and creative rule generation.

Drawing on Chomsky's ideas (e.g. 1986), a distinction is often drawn between the child's active **linguistic performance** and their underlying knowledge of the language system or **linguistic competence**. A child may thus be sensitive to a distinction between their own developing language and that of a mature speaker, even though they are unable to reproduce precisely what they hear. For example, Frederick (aged 3;6) objects when his (psycholinguist!) father mimics his own immature use of language:

Father: Where's mommy?

Frederick: Mommy goed to the store.

Father: Mommy goed to the store?

Frederick: NO! (annoyed) Daddy, *I* say it that way, not you.

Father: Mommy *wented* to the store?

Frederick: No!

Father: Mommy went to the store.

Frederick: That's right, mommy wennn … mommy goed to the store.

(adapted from Bever, 1975, quoted in Lachter and Bever, 1988, p. 219)

The argument here is that children have an abstract model of the English language in their minds (their competence) which may differ from their ability to produce the language (their performance). This disparity between linguistic competence and performance is particularly salient in young children, but is a phenomenon which exists throughout life, as manifested in the slips of the tongue and incomplete grammar which characterise even the unscripted speech of adults.

Vocabulary development

Another strand of research in the cognitive tradition treats language learning as closely related to a child's experiences and understandings of the world. Much work in this tradition has concentrated on children's lexical development, with the emphasis on both the size of vocabulary and the types of words produced. Thus, there are established inventories of young learners' comprehension and production of English words (e.g. Bancroft, 2007, p. 20) and attempts to categorise the functions of these early words (e.g. Aitchison, 1994, p. 170ff). It has been widely observed that young children tend to 'over-extend' (or less commonly 'under-extend') the meanings of words, as they try to maximise their limited vocabulary and develop a sense of conceptual boundaries in English. Drawing on a range of diary studies of children's early word use, psycholinguists Peter de Villiers and Jill de Villiers classify some typical **over-extensions** according to the apparent grounds for similarity. For example:

- movement ('bird' used for any moving creature)
- shape ('moon' for round objects such as cakes, postmarks, the letter O)
- size ('fly' for crumbs, specks of dirt, toes)
- sound ('koko' = cockerel, for music of all kinds)
- texture ('bow-wow' for toy animals, slippers, fur coat).

(adapted from de Villiers and de Villiers, 1979, p. 36)

To this inventory Jean Stilwell Peccei (1994, p. 8) adds similarity in:
- function (quoting a child who extends the notion of 'hat' to other objects that come into contact with the head, like 'scarf, ribbon, hairbrush').

Bilingual children

So far, I have been talking as if all children learn English monolingually, but of course many infants are learning English around the world quite naturally alongside one or more other languages. Yet others acquire it as a *second* language in childhood in contexts outside the home. Research with the latter group lends support to the idea that there may be a natural order of acquisition of grammatical structures within English, regardless of the child's first language. Indeed, many of the errors made by such children resemble the developmental stages of monolingual English speakers. For example, Roar Ravem (1974) studied the acquisition of English *wh-* questions (beginning with *who, what, which, where* or *why*) by his Norwegian-speaking son and daughter. He found that, like monolingual English-speaking children, they used reduced structures like *Where Daddy go?* and faulty analogies like *Where Daddy is going?* before they produced the mature form *Where is Daddy going?* According to Ravem, this did not reflect interference from their native Norwegian, which would probably have led to a form like *Where go Daddy?*

But how do bilingual children come to know what is 'English' and what is not? Research with infants growing up bilingual suggests that they tend first to distinguish the different sound systems of their languages, followed by the vocabularies and then the grammars. However, the question of whether they have effectively one linguistic system or two has long been an area of research (with good overviews in Romaine, 1995; Deuchar and Quay, 1998; Genesee, 2000). The answer may well be related to the kind of language practices to which an individual child has been exposed; in other words, whether the languages are kept separate or regularly used side by side. This leads us to the second major tradition of research into learning to talk.

Social perspectives on learning to talk

Whereas cognitive perspectives on language learning focus on processes internal to the child's mind in making sense of language as a *system*, social perspectives focus on the role of language in social context, with the emphasis on communicative *function* (see Chapter 1). According to this view, language learning is seen as part of the child's socialisation into a community with distinctive language practices, and language itself is seen as a resource for its users. As Michael Halliday observed, from an early age a child 'uses his [*sic*] voice to order people about, to get them to do things for him; he uses it to demand certain objects or services; he uses it to make contact with people, to feel close to them' (Halliday, 1975, p. 11). Social perspectives therefore emphasise the 'pragmatics' of language use, focusing on how children learn to take part in conversations with others, and how they use language to perform particular speech acts and to express social identity (see Chapter 1).

Meaning making

Pioneer researcher into child language Roger Brown (1973) was one of the first to attempt to classify the range of meanings he observed young children trying to express. As illustrated in Activity 3.4, children's early utterances are open to diverse interpretation, but Brown identified what he believed to be the eight most basic semantic relations expressed by children at the two-word stage, including Agent–Action (as in *mail come* or *daddy hit*), Action–Object (*want more* or *hit ball*) and Agent–Object (*mommy sandwich* or *daddy ball*) (Brown, 1973, pp. 114, 173).

Building on Brown's seminal work, de Villiers and de Villiers (1979) established that normally developing two-year-olds favour a limited range of meanings in their first sentences:

> English-speaking children ... talk about actions, what happened to what and who does what: *Me fall. ... Car go vroom!* They are concerned, not to say obsessed, with the relationship of possession: *My teddy. Mommy hat.* ... Equally prevalent is the relationship of location: *Cup in box. Car garage.* ... Among other early meanings that find frequent expression at this stage are recurrence ... labelling ... and nonexistence ... Children learning many different languages, among them Samoan, German, French, Hebrew, Luo (in Kenya), and Russian, seem to encode the same limited set of meanings in their first sentences.
>
> (adapted from de Villiers and de Villiers, 1979, pp. 48–50)

De Villiers and de Villiers conclude that young children's meaning making, regardless of the language they are learning, is restricted by 'the two-year-old's understanding of the world' (de Villiers and de Villiers, 1979, p. 50).

Formulaic language

Despite the human capacity for analysing language, much of what children are heard to say seems to be acquired simply by copying those around them. Wray has observed that 'although we have tremendous capacity for grammatical processing, this is not our only, nor even our preferred, way of coping with language … much of our entirely regular input and output is not processed analytically, even though it could be', but rather in socially contextualised chunks of **formulaic language** (Wray, 2002, p. 10). In other words, children are able to deduce the meaning of whole phrases from the communicative context, without necessarily analysing them into their component parts. You may remember Ellen's *time for a cup of coffee* in Activity 3.4. Similarly, even quite young children learning English as a second language have been recorded as producing phrases like *Get out of here!, Good-bye, see you tomorrow* (Huang and Hatch, 1978, p. 122), *Don't do that!* and *That's not yours* (Hakuta, 1986, p. 126).

Activity 3.6

In what ways do you think formulaic language differs from telegraphic language?

Allow about
5 minutes

Comment

The two processes seem to be operating simultaneously but from different bases. Formulaic language is reproduced holistically by imitation, with the emphasis on its social function, whereas telegraphic language is generated independently of any adult model and appears to reflect a deeper level of grammatical analysis.

Although all children probably learn language through a combination of analysis (with a focus on the form) and holistic processing (with a focus on the function), some researchers have argued that individual children may have a tendency towards one or the other. Katherine Nelson (1981) was among the first to speculate that family patterns of interaction might influence the extent to which young children acquiring English learn how to name objects (what she called the 'referential function') or engage in social interactions (the 'expressive function'). More recently, Alison Wray (2002, pp. 116–17), reviewing a range of evidence, has observed that a high level of parental education, as well as a child's position in the family as first born, appear to correlate with referential language. Conversely, children whose dominant experience of language has been in social interaction with older siblings are more likely to be 'expressive' in their own use of language.

Children as cooperative conversationalists

Allow about 10 minutes

Activity 3.7

Here is a longer extract from the dialogue between Susie, whom you met in Activity 3.4, talking to her babysitter, at the age of 4;7. What skills has Susie acquired in order to take part in a conversation? What skills does she still appear to be developing?

1	Susie:	Oh, look, a crab. We seen – we were been to the seaside.
2	Babysitter:	Have you?
3	Susie:	We saw cr – fishes and crabs. And we saw a jellyfish, and we had to bury it. And we – we did holding crabs, and we – we holded him in by the spade.
4	Babysitter:	Did you?
5	Susie:	Yes, to kill them, so they won't bite our feet.
6	Babysitter:	Oh.
7	Susie:	If you stand on them, they hurt you, won't they.
8	Babysitter:	They would do. They'd pinch you.
9	Susie:	You'd have to – and we put them under the sand, where the sea was. And they were going to the sea.
10	Babysitter:	Mhm.
11	Susie:	And we saw some shells. And we picked them up, and we heard the sea in them. And we saw a crab on a lid. And we saw lots of crabs on the sea side. And I picked the – fishes up – no, the shells, and the feathers from the birds. – And I saw a pig.
12	Babysitter:	Gosh, that was fun.
13	Susie:	Yes, and I know a story about pigs.
14	Babysitter:	Are you going to tell it to me?

(adapted from Crystal, 1986, pp. 9–10)

Transcription convention

– indicates a pause

Comment

Susie is clearly a competent conversationalist, able to take turns and produce appropriate adjacency pairs in response to specific prompts and questions from her babysitter (see turns 4–5, 7–9, 12–13). On the other hand, she is relentless in maintaining her seaside topic at turn 11, and shoehorns in her pig story with scant regard for her listener! In other words, she is still producing something of a monologue.

Even before children utter their first recognisable word, there are many ways in which the patterns of discourse between children and caregivers differ according to the culture or cultures in which they are being brought up. It is often the social routines of language that children learn first. Anthea Fraser Gupta quotes the following example of a typically Singaporean 'checking sequence' between a father and his daughter (aged 2;11). Note the use of the 'pragmatic particles' *meh* and *a* in the questions (indicating, respectively, relatively strong contradiction and a straightforward query) — an influence of Chinese languages on Singaporean English. 'Aunty' here is a general term of address in Singaporean English (see Chapter 1), used here to refer to an adult female friend of the family.

GIRL   Aunty wear red red one, the Aunty wear red shoes.
FATHER   Who wear red shoes?
GIRL   Aunty.
FATHER   Aunty wore red shoes *meh*?
GIRL   Red red.
FATHER   Red shoes *a*?
GIRL   Yes.

(Fraser Gupta, 1994, p. 81)

In their different ways, Susie and the Singaporean girl are being exposed to what it means to carry on a conversation. Children are, in the memorable phrase coined by Evelyn Hatch (1978, p. 384), 'co-operative conversationalists' and, according to a social perspective, language learning evolves out of learning how to carry on conversations, rather than the other way round.

Whereas more cognitive approaches to language learning focus on children's *linguistic* competence, the focus of social approaches is on their **communicative competence**, a term generally attributed to linguist Del Hymes: '[A] normal child acquires knowledge of sentences, not only as grammatical, but also as appropriate. He or she acquires competence as to when to speak, when not, and as to what to talk about with whom, when, where, in what manner' (Hymes, 1972, p. 277). Because only a small proportion of the sentences permitted by the grammar of English are routinely used, children have to learn what is socially appropriate in the course of social interaction.

Allow about 5 minutes

Activity 3.8

Consider the following exchange between a little girl and her father at meal time. What is interactionally odd about it?

Child: Want other one spoon, Daddy.

Father: You mean, you want *the other spoon*.

Child: Yes, I want other one spoon, please, Daddy.

Father: Can you say 'the other spoon'?

Child: Other … one … spoon.

Father: Say … 'other'.

Child: Other.

Father: 'Spoon.'

Child: Spoon.

Father: 'Other … spoon.'

Child: Other … spoon. Now give me other one spoon?

(Braine, 1971, p. 160)

Comment

Unlike some language teachers, who might see this as their role, caregivers do not normally give explicit feedback on the *form* of a child's utterance, but generally react to the *function* of what the child says. As Pinker puts it, 'parents are remarkably unconcerned about their children's grammar; they care about truthfulness and good behavior' (Pinker, 1994, p. 280). Indeed, in interactional terms, the kind of adult feedback seen in this example seems irregular, and appears to have little effect. As soon as the 'language lesson' is over and the 'conversation' resumes, the little girl immediately reverts to her preferred expression, which has presumably functioned well enough for her so far.

Shoshana Blum-Kulka and Catherine Snow (2002, pp. 4–9) observe that, when children interact with larger social groups, not only are turn-taking boundaries more challenging to negotiate, but children are also exposed to greater variation in role and need to design their utterances more carefully to achieve the desired effect: it's a matter of 'knowing what to say and knowing the rules of interaction that allow one to say it' (Snow and Blum-Kulka, 2002, p. 328).

Speaking as a child

There are particular kinds of social acts that children regularly get to perform *as children*, and this has led to increasing interest in children's language as an object of study in its own right (see Goodwin, 1990, 2006; Hoyle and Adger, 1996; Sealey, 2000). Sensitivity to relative status in relationships is particularly apparent if we look at children's developing recognition and use of the different ways of performing the speech acts of making requests and issuing commands in English. It would appear that children take some time to develop sensitivity to the full adult repertoire for 'getting people to do things'. Although they understand the force of adult commands, because of their relative lack of social power children are rarely in a position to issue instructions or make direct requests themselves, unless it is to even younger children, and it is easy to get things wrong:

7-year-old boy: *[to 11-year-old girl]* Bring your li'l self here.

Bystander: Who you think you are?

7-year-old boy: I think I'm somebody big.

(adapted from Mitchell-Kernan and Kernan, 1977, p. 204)

In order to choose the appropriate expression for the occasion, a child not only needs to be aware of the range of linguistic forms available to perform the speech acts of requesting or demanding, but also needs to have a sense of how likely the addressee is to comply with the request. In many (but by no means all) English-speaking communities, the word 'please' serves a powerful interpersonal function, and even very young children – perhaps because of explicit teaching – seem to be sensitive to its effect, especially when addressing adults. Children also resort to indirect means of getting what they want, such as asking questions or making hints. Roger Shuy (1978, p. 272) relates how five-year-old Joanna got herself invited to dinner by making three 'statements': about the absence of the family car, the fact that her mother worried if she missed meals, and finally 'You know, I eat almost anything'!

Figure 3.2   Speaking as a child

It is important to remember that adult–child role relationships are not reciprocal. When one adult researcher tried jokingly to use language more typical of a child, it caused some bemusement in the young listener:

> one of the authors said ... in an accusatory tone similar to the one the children often used when hinting ... *Oh, you washed Karen's car.* The child responded with a puzzled look and it was a few seconds before he realized that the researcher was jokingly requesting that he wash her car.

(Mitchell-Kernan and Kernan, 1977, p. 200)

Summary of issues in the acquisition of spoken English

As you have seen, the more cognitive perspectives on the language learning process give greater prominence to analytic processes and rule formation, along with the child's general understanding of the world, while the more social perspectives give greater prominence to imitation and habit formation, along with developing skills of social interaction. These parallel accounts, which reflect a relative emphasis on linguistic structures or on communicative practices, work in a complementary way, enabling us to view the language learning process through different lenses.

3.3   Learning to read and write in English

Emergent literacy

I now turn to consider some of the ways in which children learn to read and write in English. From the beginning of life, children growing up in communities where literacy plays an important part react to the written environment around them, making sense of its functions and forms. Taking part in literacy practices (see Chapter 2) does not depend on being able to read and write in the adult sense. Particular genres of text, such as product labels, restaurant signs, street banners, and so on, may be recognised long before individual letters are known. Where children are encouraged to experiment with writing even before their marks are intelligible to others, they will often produce 'pretend' shop signs, shopping lists, telephone messages, newspapers, and so on. In an environment of written texts, children will use many strategies to work out what adults are doing with magazines, pens, computers and all the other things associated with literacy, and will attempt to join the adult literate world in different ways. These first discoveries of reading and writing have been described by some (e.g. Teale and Sulzby, 1988) as **emergent literacy**.

Activity 3.9

Allow about
10 minutes

Consider the following four examples. What understandings do you think these children may be forming about the nature and function of written language?

Examples 1 and 2

Figure 3.3   Christopher's 'shop sign' (aged 2;10)

Figure 3.4   Joe's page of 'writing' and 'drawing' (aged 3;3)

Example 3

> Alison, aged 4 years, attending a nursery school in [England], discovered that it was not her turn to join her favourite 'Soft Play' activity. Several minutes later she … presented her [teacher] with a piece of paper saying: 'I can go to Soft Play because I'm on the list. Look!'

(National Writing Project, 1989, p. 13)

Figure 3.5 Alison's 'list' (aged 4)

Example 4

In an Australian nursery, four-year-old Heidi drew a large detailed picture of a dog. Down the side she wrote some letters (many from her own name). Asked by her teacher what her writing said, she replied, 'I don't know'. 'Well, you wrote it', her teacher replied; 'I know', said Heidi, 'but I can't read yet'.

(adapted from Cambourne and Turbill, 1987, p. 12)

Comment

The children in these examples are finding out what it means to be a reader and writer in the communities in which they live. It is clear that they associate writing with particular social practices, and that they are beginning to understand how literacy affects people's lives and what it has the power to do for them.

All the children have developed some reader-like and writer-like behaviours. At this stage, it is probably fair to say that they are mainly imitating without analysis – although Joe is already exploring the boundary between 'writing' and 'drawing' (you may have speculated as to which was which), and Heidi evidently associates some individual letters with her own name. It is interesting that she is so categorical in distinguishing between the productive skill of writing, which is under her control, and the receptive skill of reading, which stretches her beyond her limits.

Cognitive perspectives on learning to read and write

A child's-eye view

A walk in any local shopping area where English features in the environment will demonstrate the diversity of visual symbols which confront children. For example, depending on where they are growing up in the world, there may be any combination of the following:

- street signs, posters, shop names, notices and leaflets which use the Roman alphabet (as in English)
- a similar array of signage using other scripts (e.g. Chinese characters)
- some rather arbitrary abbreviations (e.g. Co., Pte., Ltd.)
- **logographs**, also known as 'logograms' (where a symbol stands for a whole word), as in the Arabic-based numeral system, various weights and measures and company logos, for example, 1K for £1000, H for hospital, M for McDonald's, or the heart shape sometimes used to mean 'love'
- **pictographs**, also known as 'pictograms' (where an image denotes an entire phrase or concept), such as many road traffic signs and pictorial symbols for male and female toilets.

However, the child's world of written texts is not limited by the adult divisions into 'writing' and 'not-writing', and part of the task facing them is what to identify as 'English'. Mathematical and musical notation, map signs, computer graphics, bar codes, punctuation marks, road signs, and so on are also part of the literacy learning process and need to be worked out for their individual meaning as well as their place as part of a system. Just as Joe's concepts of 'writing' and 'drawing' in Activity 3.9 were virtually indistinguishable, many young English-speaking children often use the words 'number' and 'letter' fairly interchangeably. In due course they will learn that, whereas the *numeral* 6 stands for the whole word 'six', the visually very similar lower case b is a *letter* that has no individual meaning and must be combined with other letters to spell a word (see Chapter 2).

After observing the writing of three- to six-year-olds in the USA, Jerome Harste et al. (1981) commented:

> It is as if ... every convention that has been adopted by written language users worldwide was being reinvented and tested by this group of very young language users. Some tried writing right to left, others bottom to top, and a not surprising majority, given the culture they were in, wrote left-to-right, top-to-bottom. ... Some used space and distance freely about the page, others drew dots between conceptual units, some drew circles around sets of markings, others wrote in columns to preserve order, while still others spaced their concepts using what we would see as the conventional form for this society ... Children's markings, while having many English language features, ranged from pictorial graphs to symbol-like strings.
>
> (Harste et al., 1981, p. 137, cited in Bissex, 1984, p. 101)

Just as with spoken language, children face the task of sorting through the available information about writing in order to work out the principles underlying their home or community writing system.

Is English literacy harder to acquire than literacy in other languages?

One critical task in the early stages of learning to read is to work out which unit of speech is coded by any particular language. Two principles are usually identified as the basis of the different writing systems: that symbols should represent *meaning*, as in logographs or pictographs, or that symbols should represent *sound*, as in alphabets or syllabaries. (There is a much fuller discussion of this in Chapter 7.) In addition, children need to work out how the temporal order of speech relates to the spatial order of writing. For example, English words are conventionally written from left to right, whereas in Hebrew and Arabic, which are both alphabetic, words are written from right to left. The classical way of writing Chinese, which is predominantly logographic, was from top to bottom, and in Japanese, which may be written with syllabic or logographic symbols, writing may be either vertical or horizontal.

The advantage of learning to read in an alphabetic or a syllabic system is that, once the initial breakthrough in understanding happens, any new word can (more or less) be worked out, while the learning of new logographs has to continue for many years. However, alphabetic systems may represent another kind of learning challenge in terms of their spelling system or **orthography**. In some languages – for example, Finnish, Spanish or Welsh – there is a very close relationship between the phonemes and the letters. This means that a fluent reader familiar with alphabetic systems would soon be able to read aloud in Finnish, although unless they knew some Finnish they would not understand what they read. English writing is more complex, as there are fewer symbols in the twenty-six-letter alphabet of English than there are sounds in the spoken language, and the standard orthography does not correspond precisely to any particular accent.

Children learning to read and write English have to become aware of many inconsistencies. For example, some symbols are used to represent more than one sound, such as the letter 'a' in the words 'cat', 'play' and 'are'. Within English, there are also many letter combinations which may have to be memorised as though they were logographs (e.g. *knight, through*) and others as though they were morpheme or syllable based (e.g. the ending *-tion*). The young child learning to read and write English seems to face a more challenging task than, say, the child learning to write Spanish or Welsh, with their more regular spelling conventions.

There have been a number of major international studies that cast light on how children's experience of becoming literate varies from one language to another (e.g. Downing, 1973; Downing and Leong, 1982; Seymour et al., 2003; Mullis et al., 2007; OECD, 2010). A recent study by J. Richard Hanley reported on the different challenges facing children learning to read respectively in Welsh and English.

Activity 3.10

Now turn to Reading A: *English is a difficult writing system for children to learn* by J. Richard Hanley. As you read, make a note of what Hanley regards as the advantages and disadvantages of English orthography, and what strategies he thinks might help young learners to overcome the disadvantages.

Note that Hanley refers at one point to 'CV structure', by which he means a syllable consisting of Consonant + Vowel, as in *he* or *to*. He also refers at several points to the notions of **onset** and **rime**, which denote the letter combinations used respectively at the beginnings and endings of English words, as in *bl-ock*, *st-ock*, *r-ock*, *l-ock* etc., where *bl-* etc. is the onset and *-ock* the rime.

Comment

You probably noted the following major disadvantage of English orthography:

- It is 'opaque' in the sense that there is relatively little consistency in the **grapheme–phoneme relationships**, partly as a result of 'frozen' spellings reflecting an earlier pronunciation and partly because of the large number of words imported from other languages, which makes it difficult to predict the pronunciation of a word from its written form.

On the other hand, potential advantages include the facts that:

- homophones with different etymologies (like *knight* and *night*) may be distinguishable by spelling
- morphemes may retain the same surface form in different contexts; for example, plural *-s* in words like *rocks* and *rods* (compare the past tense morpheme *-ed*, which varies in pronunciation in words like *wanted, laughed* and *called*).

Hanley, drawing on the work of Goswami, suggests that learners' attention might be drawn to:

- the greater orthographic consistency of English spelling at the level of the syllable or morpheme
- the way in which words break down into onset and rime.

Making sense of the written word

Literacy in any language, however, is not just about 'decoding' a script or learning a conventional orthography. Children may struggle at a deeper level to make *sense* of the words they hear and to attempt to convey this sense in the words they write.

Allow about 5 minutes

Activity 3.11

Gunther Kress (2003, pp. 160–2) provides the illustrations of two six-year-old children's attempts to spell the word 'frogspawn' shown in Figures 3.6 and 3.7. What hypotheses do you think the two children are making, and what knowledge might they be drawing on?

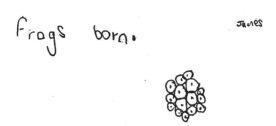

Frogs born.

'When Frogs are born, there called frogs born and there in littel rond bits of jelly so they cont do nofing.

Figure 3.6   Six-year-old James: 'Frogs born'

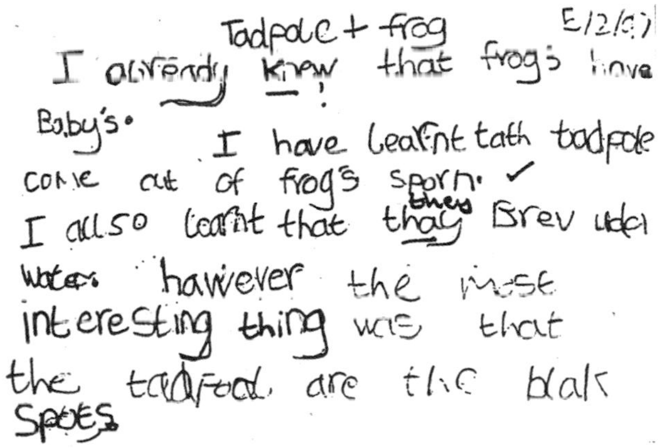

Tadpole + frog   8/2/97

I already knew that frogs have Baby's.   I have learnt tath tadpole come aut of frog's sporn. ✓ I allso learnt that thay brev uder water hawever the most interesting thing was that the tadpool are the blak spots.

Figure 3.7   Six-year-old 'Amy' (a pseudonym): 'Frog's sporn'

Comment

Kress argues that James is drawing mainly on his experience of the world: frogs are *born* from frogspawn. Amy, on the other hand, is drawing on her knowledge of the English spelling system: if a frog has 'sporn', it must be '*frog's* sporn'.

Social perspectives on learning to read and write

Engaging in literacy practices

The paths taken to literacy do not only vary at an individual level. In different communities, written and spoken language are intertwined in different ways, and there is variation in both the types of practices that are encouraged and the value placed on literacy.

A classic ethnographic study by Shirley Brice Heath (Heath, 1982, 1983) was influential in revealing differences in preschool literacy practices among three communities in the American Piedmont Carolinas that she called Trackton, Roadville and Maintown. Her focus was on 'any occasion in which a piece of writing is integral to the nature of the participants' interactions and their interpretive processes' (Heath, 1982, p. 93). Thus, it included events from filling in a form to singing with a hymn book. All of the communities were English-speaking and all the observed literacy was in English.

Allow about 20 minutes

Activity 3.12

Consider the following three scenarios, based on Heath's (1982) observations. How did the communities differ in terms of what the children were learning about literacy? How easy would it be to transfer such learning to the school context?

Scenario 1

Children in Maintown, a middle-class community, lived in an environment filled with print and with information derived from print. From six months on, these children heard and responded to books and referred to book-related incidents in their interactions. As they got older, Maintown children learnt certain rules about book reading, such as the types of questions that can be asked and the fact that interruptions are allowed. They also learnt ways of talking about texts and began to use the types of language structures more often heard in books than in speech.

Scenario 2

In Roadville, a white working-class community, books also played a central role in children's lives, and their rooms were full of alphabet friezes, mobiles and the like. However, books were widely regarded as 'teaching opportunities', times when children 'got it right', rather than as opportunities for stories to be explored. The world of books was distinct from 'real life', and book reading was less interactive between adult and child than in Maintown, especially when a child reached school age.

Scenario 3

Children from Trackton, an African-American working-class community, did not experience the baby paraphernalia of mobiles, friezes and pop-up books. The rich language opportunities came not from books, but from adult talk and oral narratives. Reading in Trackton was not a private affair, it was highly social, a time for discussion and negotiation of meaning. A letter, a set of instructions or a story might be interpreted, reshaped and reworked through a lot of talk.

Comment

In Heath's words, the three communities introduced children to different 'ways of taking' meaning from literacy events. Each of the communities intertwined talk and writing in very different ways that challenge any simple oral–literate division. For example, Maintown and Trackton valued imagination and fictionalisation, while Roadville did not. Direct teaching about language was valued in Maintown and Roadville but not in Trackton. Negotiation over the meaning of a book or letter happened in Trackton and to some extent Maintown, but was not valued in Roadville. Children were seen as needing their own specially designed reading materials in Maintown and Roadville but not in Trackton. When these children, with their different experiences of interacting with print, enter school they will find that only some of their literacy practices are valued. For some children, then, school literacy may seem very different from the literacy found in their own homes, whereas for others it may be very familiar.

Becoming biliterate

It will already have become apparent that *all* children experience a range of forms and functions of writing. However, children acquiring literacy in bilingual or multilingual communities are additionally faced with working out the particular forms and functions of a variety of different scripts or orthographies. Mukul Saxena (1993) described the complex choices available for spoken and written communication among the British Panjabi community in Southall, London, where the three main cultural groups – Muslims, Hindus and Sikhs – respectively use predominantly Urdu (usually written in Arabic script), Hindi (normally written in Devanagari script) and Panjabi (normally written in Gurmukhi script) – although each language can be and sometimes is written in the script usually associated with another. Factors such as religion, age, schooling and social roles all affect the language(s) used in both speech and writing, with many people speaking and writing more than one. Literacy events in the home and community will involve a complex interaction of different spoken languages and literacies. In planning a letter, for example, people might discuss the contents in one language and write the letter in another, even switching between languages and scripts within a letter.

It is clear that young children who have the opportunity to do so are able to develop two or more literacy systems alongside each other with relative ease. The text in Figure 3.8, produced by Raki (who was attending an east London primary school where the pupils were nearly all bilingual), includes English, Urdu (visible above the A–F in the lower left-hand corner) and Bengali (visible above the A–E in the lower right-hand corner). Interestingly, all scripts were written left-to-right. Raki had not yet adopted Urdu right-to-left orientation.

Figure 3.8 Raki's text (National Writing Project, 1990, p. 40)

Charmian Kenner's study of biliterate children in a nursery class in London explores the complexity of the everyday learning process for biliterate children. She studied three pairs of children learning to read and write in English in parallel with becoming literate in their own community language, respectively Chinese, Arabic and Spanish.

Activity 3.13

Now turn to Reading B: *Young children learning different writing systems* by Charmian Kenner. As you read, make a note of any special skills or attributes that the biliterate children seem to be acquiring.

Comment

You may have noted some of the following at various points in the reading:

- Biliterate children develop a wider range of 'visual and actional capabilities'.

- They learn to 'recognise what counts as important in each script' and to 'identify what really matters when distinguishing one letter or character from another'; in so doing, they build up 'a vocabulary for concepts of shape, angle and size'.
- They learn to 'adapt to different contexts' and in particular, to recognise that their classmates 'might not have the same expertise'.
- They develop an interest in 'exploring connections' between their writing systems.
- They can use their different scripts to express a distinctive personal identity.

Summary of issues in the acquisition of English literacy

Many young children have a continuous involvement with literacy from their earliest years. Literacy is part of their social world, and many children will experiment with its forms and functions long before they are formally introduced to it. When children learn to read, they also have to sort out how literacy is used in their own particular culture. They can take different paths to this understanding, but they will do so by trying to make sense of the written texts they encounter and the literacy practices they observe and become involved in.

3.4 Conclusion

This chapter has shown how the processes of learning to speak and to read in English require children, on the one hand, to make sense of how spoken and written language operate as systems and, on the other, to become sensitive to the role of language and literacy practices in their communities. Only on the basis of these insights can they begin to use the English language to make meaning for themselves. Language and literacy thus act as key instruments for socialisation into the adult world.

READING A: English is a difficult writing system for children to learn

J. Richard Hanley

Source: Hanley, J. R. (2010) 'English is a difficult writing system for children to learn: evidence from children learning to read in Wales' in Hall, K., Goswami, U., Harrison, C., Ellis, S. and Soler, J. (eds) *Interdisciplinary Perspectives on Leaning to Read: Culture, Cognition and Pedagogy*, London and New York, Routledge, pp. 117–29.

Introduction

In 2003, Seymour, Aro and Erskine reported the results of a comprehensive investigation of written word recognition skills at the end of first grade in 14 different European countries. Results showed that children who were learning to read English performed far worse than the children of any other nationality at reading both real words and non-words with a similar structure to real words. Whereas children from most of the 14 countries read over 90 per cent of real words accurately, the children learning to read English were correct on only 34 per cent. The next lowest score was 71 per cent of words read correctly by children from Denmark.

Following Wimmer and Hummer (1990), this is just one of many studies published in the last 20 years to show that the word recognition skills of children learning to read English take longer to develop than those of children from countries such as Austria, Croatia, Greece, Germany, the Netherlands, Italy, Turkey, Serbia and Spain. Although the reading speed of children from these countries increases as they get older, the accuracy of their decoding skills is at a very high level by the end of their first year of formal instruction.

Why do children from the UK consistently perform so much worse in these cross-cultural comparisons? Seymour *et al.* (2003) highlighted two important differences between the English language and European languages where children's word recognition skills develop particularly quickly. The first is the opaque nature of the English writing system (or 'orthography'). The second is the complex nature of the syllabic structure of spoken English. The reasons why both the spoken and written form of English might be associated with relatively slow development of reading skills are discussed below.

The English writing system

In common with all European and American languages, English employs an alphabetic writing system in which letters (or *graphemes*) represent the spoken sounds of words (*phonemes*). A phoneme is the smallest unit of sound that can affect the meaning of a word, and a grapheme is the representation of a phoneme in written form. The problem with English is that there is less consistency in grapheme–phoneme relationships than in almost any other alphabetic writing system. Graphemes for vowels in particular can represent a large number of different phonemes in different words. Hence English is said to have a *deep* or *opaque* orthography in contrast with languages that are written in *shallow* or *transparent* orthographies where each grapheme represents the same phoneme in every word in which it appears.

There are two obvious reasons why English is not transparent. First, although the pronunciation of many words has changed over the centuries, their spelling remains frozen in its earlier form. For example the now silent *k* at the start of the word *knight* was sounded out at the time when its written form was established. Second, when foreign words are imported into English, we generally keep the written form of the word in the language from which it originated. For example, the spelling of the word *café* was retained when it entered English from French instead of being changed to *caffay*. In languages with transparent orthographies such as Spanish or Welsh, spelling reform ensures that the written form of a word is congruent with its current spoken form. Consequently, frozen spellings and spellings of imported words are altered to ensure that they are consistent with the letter–sound rules of the transparent orthography.

There are some advantages for English in not having a completely regular orthography. For example, skilled readers of English can distinguish the meanings of homophones such as *colonel* and *kernel* directly from their written form. In a transparent orthography, they would be spelled the same way. The disadvantage of an opaque orthography is the existence of many irregular words whose pronunciation cannot be predicted from their spelling. Moreover, many frequent and early-acquired English words are irregular.

The existence of irregular words means that a child learning to read English faces two potential problems that are not encountered by most of his or her counterparts in Continental Europe. When children read a word in a transparent orthography that is part of their speech vocabulary, they can reliably generate its spoken form and hence access its meaning even if they have never encountered the word in print before. Such a strategy will not be successful for many words in English because letter–sound rules will not produce the correct pronunciation. The second problem is that the existence of exceptions means that the letter–sound correspondences that apply in regular English words are likely to be more difficult for children to learn. Decoding skills may therefore take longer to develop in opaque writing systems.

The syllabic structure of English

In many languages, including Italian and Spanish, words typically contain simple syllabic structures in which a vowel is preceded by a single consonant. English is more complex because clusters containing two or more consonants can occur either at the start or end of syllables. According to Ziegler and Goswami (2005), the preponderance of consonant clusters in English affects the acquisition of literacy by making it more difficult for children to learn grapheme–phoneme consistencies.

Before they start to read, many children become aware that spoken languages have smaller units than words and can count the number of syllables that spoken words contain (Liberman, Shankweiler, Fischer & Carter 1974). Later, awareness of the sub-syllabic units of onset and rime develops in pre-literate children, particularly in the UK where nursery rhymes are part of the culture (e.g. Bradley & Bryant 1983). However, alphabetic writing systems do not contain visual symbols for onsets, rimes or syllables. Instead they represent phonemes. As Usha Goswami [2010] makes clear, phonemes are not natural units of speech and cannot be produced or perceived in isolation. Furthermore, sounds that are physically different in words or syllables (e.g. the /p/ sound in *spoon* and *pit*) must be mapped onto the same phoneme. As a consequence, awareness of phonemes does not develop automatically […] [and it] appears that speakers do not know about the existence of phonemes until they learn an alphabet.

Children whose languages have a simple syllabic structure may find the transition from representations based on onset and rime to representations based on phonemes easier to master. This is because onsets and rimes will frequently be single phonemes in languages where there are relatively few consonant clusters. Consequently, splitting an Italian or Spanish word into its onset and rime will often automatically produce two phonemes. It may therefore be relatively easy for Italian or Spanish children to learn the relationship between the letter sounds that they are taught in school and the words that these letters represent when the words are written down. However, only 5 per cent of English [syllables] have a CV structure (De Cara & Goswami 2002), which means that English onsets and rimes will both typically contain more than one phoneme. English children may therefore need much more explicit training before awareness of phonemes develops.

[…]

Research study of learning to read in Wales

Between 1996 and 2004, my colleagues and I conducted a research programme that investigated some of the reasons why early reading skills develop relatively slowly in children learning English. In this investigation, the ease of learning to read English was compared with learning to read Welsh (Hanley 2010; Hanley, Masterson, Spencer & Evans 2004; Spencer & Hanley 2003, 2004). The research was conducted in Denbighshire in North Wales, where 27 per cent of the population described themselves as Welsh speakers in the 1991 Office of Population Censuses and Surveys. Some towns in this county contain both English- and Welsh-speaking Primary schools, and parents can choose which school their child will attend. […]

If they attend Welsh speaking schools, children are taught to read in Welsh, a transparent alphabetic orthography in which letter–sound relationships are relatively consistent and irregular words are virtually non-existent […]

Despite the differences in the transparency of the orthographies, the Welsh- and English-speaking children in our studies lived in the same area of North Wales, commenced reading instruction at the same age, and were taught by similar methods of instruction. Welsh syllables also contain consonant clusters that can occur either at the beginning or end of words. It is therefore possible to compare the acquisition of a shallow and deep orthography in children of a similar age whose languages contain words with complex syllabic structures, all of whom receive phonic instruction. Wales therefore offers a unique opportunity to investigate the influence of orthographic consistency on reading development. […]

When the children were ten years old, we compared their reading accuracy on a set of 60 words that varied according to their regularity and their frequency (i.e. how often they occur in written English). For example, the words *horse* (*ceffyl*), *tooth* (*dant*) and *grill* (*gril*) are regular words of high, medium and low frequency, and *bowl* (*bowlen*), *glove* (*maneg*) and *sword* (*cleddyf*) are irregular words of high, medium and low frequency. The English children read the regular words and the high frequency irregular words as accurately as did the Welsh children. […] This suggests that the decoding skills of the English children have by now caught up with those of their Welsh counterparts. Significantly superior performance by the Welsh children was only observed on the medium and low frequency irregular words. The lower frequency irregular words will have been encountered less often in print and many of them do not yet appear to be part of the English children's sight vocabulary. If English children try to use decoding skills to read these words, they will pronounce them incorrectly. The absence of irregular words in Welsh means that Welsh children will be able to read aloud correctly the Welsh equivalents of these words even though they are equally unlikely to have encountered them in print very often.

It therefore appears to be the case that the opaque nature of the English orthography slows down the acquisition of decoding skills, but even when these skills have caught up at ten years old, children learning to read English have not received sufficient print exposure to many irregular words to allow them to be read accurately. Because of the absence of irregular words, a much larger reading vocabulary is available to readers of Welsh immediately they have developed competence in decoding. […]

Pedagogy

Improving children's reading attainment in the future by reform of the English orthography is clearly a utopian pipe-dream. […]

[In its simplest form, phonics involves teaching children to associate individual letters with particular sounds.]

A more realistic strategy than reforming the orthography might be to acknowledge that English probably requires more extensive training in phonics than transparent orthographies. […]

[However] it is […] possible that English requires a different type of phonic reading instruction. According to *grain-size* theory (Ziegler & Goswami 2005), teaching should not be exclusively focused on grapheme–phoneme correspondences. Children should also be made aware of correspondences between larger phonological and orthographic units. Most obviously, the correct pronunciation of many irregular words can only be taught by word-specific training. Nevertheless teaching a child to read an irregular word such as *friend* will allow him or her to read all words that contain 'friend' as their root morpheme (e.g. *friend, friendship, friendly, friendlier, unfriendly, befriend, friendliness,* etc.).

In some irregular words, however, there are higher order consistencies that provide information about how the irregular portion of the word should be pronounced. In particular, there are important orthographic consistencies at the level of onsets and rimes even in words that are irregular in terms of their grapheme–phoneme mappings (Treiman, Mullennix, Bijeljac-Babic & Richmond-Welty 1995). For example, the pronunciation of the *ea* vowel in *health* differs from the regular pronunciation of *ea* (as in *heat*). However, *ea* is pronounced as it is in *health* in all words in which –*ealth* is the rime segment *wealth, stealth*, etc.). Consequently, if they are taught the correspondences between rime segments and their pronunciation, Ziegler and Goswami argue that children should be able to successfully decode words that contain consistently spelled rime segments even if they are irregular. A teaching schedule that concentrates exclusively on grapheme–phoneme relationships ignores this important source of information about the English writing system. [...]

Morphemes (defined as the smallest units of meaning in a language) contain another important source of information about how English words are written because English orthography often preserves morpheme identity at the expense of phonology. For example, *the* is always spelled the same way even though its pronunciation differs according to whether it precedes a vowel or consonant. In a highly impressive series of studies, Nunes and Bryant (2006) provide a powerful demonstration that interventions based on the teaching of morphemes to children significantly improve their spelling ability. For example, they point out, teaching children that the plural inflection at the end of a word is consistently represented by the letter *s* should prevent them from spelling *rocks* as *rox* even if they have learnt to spell *fox* correctly. [...]

In conclusion, it is evident that English is a particularly difficult writing system to learn. The transparent alphabetic orthographies that are commonly used in other European countries including Wales allow children to develop phonological awareness and decoding skills much more easily. [...] It appears that children learning English require more extensive phonics instruction than is required for children learning transparent orthographies. [...] However, the unpredictable nature of the English writing system can be reduced if children's attention is [...] drawn to the relationships between larger units than graphemes and phonemes (Nunes & Bryant 2006; Ziegler & Goswami 2005). Knowledge of the relationships between the orthography and phonology of onsets, rimes, and morphemes is likely to make it easier for children to achieve mastery over the notoriously complex English writing system.

Acknowledgements

The work reported in this paper was funded by the ESRC in the form of a project grant (No. R000238437) and an earlier research studentship to Llinos Spencer. I am grateful to Llinos Spencer, Jackie Masterson, and Dylan Evans for the contribution that they made to the research discussed in this chapter. I would also like to thank the teachers and staff of a number of primary schools in Denbighshire, North Wales for permission to test the children in their classes.

References for this reading

Bradley, I., & Bryant, P.E. (1983) 'Categorising sounds and learning to read: A causal connection', *Nature*, *310*: 419–421.

De Cara, B., & Goswami, U. (2002) 'Statistical analysis of similarity relations among spoken words: Evidence for the special status of rimes in English', *Behavioral Research Methods and Instrumentation*, *34*: 416–423.

Goswami, U. (2010) 'Phonology, reading and reading difficulties', in K. Hall, U. Goswami, C. Harrison, S. Ellis & J. Soler (eds), *Interdisciplinary perspectives on learning to read: culture, cognition and pedagogy*. London and New York, Routledge.

Hanley, J.R., Masterson, J., Spencer, L., & Evans, D. (2004) 'How long do the advantages of learning to read a transparent orthography last? An investigation of the reading skills and incidence of dyslexia in Welsh children at 10 years of age', *Quarterly Journal of Experimental Psychology*, *57*: 1393–1410.

Hanley, J.R. (2010) 'Differences in reading ability between children attending Welsh- and English-speaking primary schools in Wales', in N. Brunswick, S. McDougall & P. de Mornay Davies (eds), *The role of orthographies in reading and spelling*. Hove, Psychology Press.

Liberman, I.Y., Shankweiler, D., Fischer, F.W., & Carter, B. (1974) 'Explicit syllable and phoneme segmentation in the young child', *Journal of Experimental Child Psychology, 18*: 201–212.

Nunes, T., & Bryant, P. (2006) *Improving literacy by teaching morphemes*. London, Routledge.

Office of Population Censuses and Surveys (1991) *1991 census report for Wales (Part 1)*. London, HMSO.

Seymour, P.H.K., Aro, M., & Erskine, J.M. (2003) 'Foundation literacy acquisition in European orthographies', *British Journal of Psychology, 94*: 143–174.

Spencer, L., & Hanley, J.R. (2003) 'The effects of orthographic consistency on reading development and phonological awareness: Evidence from children learning to read in Wales', *British Journal of Psychology, 94*: 1–28.

Spencer, L., & Hanley, J.R. (2004) 'Learning a transparent orthography at 5 years old: Reading development of children during the first year of formal reading instruction in Wales', *Journal of Research in Reading, 27*: 1–14.

Treiman, R., Mullennix, J., Bijeljac-Babic, R., & Richmond-Welty, E.D. (1995) 'The special role of rimes in the description, use, and acquisition of English orthography', *Journal of Experimental Psychology: General, 124*: 107–136.

Wimmer, H., & Hummer, P. (1990) 'How German-speaking first graders read and spell: Doubts on the importance of the logographic stage', *Applied Psycholinguistics, 11*: 349–368.

Ziegler, J.C., & Goswami, U. (2005) 'Reading acquisition, developmental dyslexia and skilled reading across languages: A psycholinguistic grain size theory', *Psychological Bulletin, 131*: 3–29.

READING B: Young children learning different writing systems

Charmian Kenner

Source: adapted from Kenner, C. (2004) *Becoming Biliterate: Young Children Learning Different Writing Systems*, Stoke-on-Trent, Trentham Books, pp. 73–89 and 103–8. This reading draws on research conducted in the context of the ESRC-funded project, 'Signs of Difference', for which the research team consisted of Gunther Kress, Hayat Al-Khatib, Gwen Kwok, Roy Kam and Kuan-Chun Tsai.

Figure 1   Selina's drawing of her mother and sister

Figure 1 shows Selina's drawings of her mother and sister, with the words 'I love my mum' and 'I love my sister' written below in English. Above the picture of her mother Selina [a six-year-old Chinese-English bilingual] has written 'love' in Chinese, whilst above her sister's head she has placed Chinese characters representing the concept of 'Girl Power'.

Here Selina has chosen to combine her writing systems, linking images of two of the people closest to her with ideas holding special significance. Love for her mother is expressed in both Chinese and English. 'Girl Power' is a slogan coined in English by one of Selina's favourite all-female Western pop groups, but Selina uses a translation available in Chinese and links the idea to her ten-year-old sister Susannah.

Selina's representation shows us the world of a six-year-old whose life is lived simultaneously in Chinese and English – a world in which symbols and concepts from two languages co-exist. For Selina, these bilingual links are an important part of her emotional and intellectual development. Yet the institutions of [British] society, including primary schools, tend to separate out the languages in children's lives. Often children are required to use only English at school and other languages are restricted to home and community. The justification usually given is that children will experience confusion if allowed to think and write in more than one language, or that their learning of English will be held back. Our research, however, found a very different story.

The bilingual children in our project were well aware of the differences between their languages and literacies [...] But they were also interested in exploring connections between these systems. When writing, they had two sets of resources present in their minds and could draw on either or both of them to make a text. This is the potential creativity and learning power of living in simultaneous worlds. [...]

Writing different scripts

[...] Children becoming biliterate find out that different scripts operate by different rules. Even scripts which look similar have their special attributes. As Brian [a six-year-old Spanish-English bilingual] remarked when comparing English to Spanish, 'They haven't got a N with *this* on top' (referring to the letter 'ñ' as in 'España').

Biliterate children widen their horizons with respect to the making and placing of marks on the page. They have to recognise what counts as important in each script and be able to produce their own version, whether this involves writing [in an unfamiliar orientation] or using Chinese stroke patterns as compared to English 'joined-up writing'. The children in our research project were developing an impressive range of visual and actional capabilities, due to their experience of different scripts. [...]

Kress [1997] explains that all modes of representation offer different potentials and limitations. Each writing system uses the visual and actional modes in particular ways. When children produce written symbols they have to pay attention to a number of different facets – the type of stroke to be used, directionality, shape, size, spatial orientation, placement on the page – and these will be culturally specified in the teaching experienced by the child.

From these features, children create their own repertoire of representational resources [...] [E]ach child forms particular interpretations of what is important in the act of writing. [...] From this they ma[k]e decisions about how symbols are created and positioned in each writing system. [...]

The design of symbols

The precision of Chinese characters

[...] In [a British] primary school, children are not expected to show [fine] pen control at the age of five. However, this capability is necessary in order to write in Chinese. Children also need to be able to recognise small differences in stroke patterns, to check that they have written each character correctly. Selina [and her] classmates at Chinese school were developing their visual and actional capacities through close attention and continual practice, so that they could produce these complex patterns.

They were helped by their teachers, who would write similar-looking stroke patterns on the board and ask children to spot the difference. Children would volunteer that 'it's too straight' (when the stroke should be curved) or 'it's too far away' (when two strokes should be placed closer together). The teacher would remind them to be precise when writing each stroke, saying for example 'Make sure it's only like a little one – a short line'. As teacher and pupils discussed the stroke pattern together, children built up a vocabulary for concepts of shape, angle and size in both English and Cantonese.

The children themselves were concerned to produce characters which were beautifully written as well as correct. They brought an array of pencils and rubbers to class, sharpening their pencils frequently to produce clearer strokes, and rubbing out over and over again. [...]

Key differences in stroke patterns

Ming's family did not put so much emphasis on teaching stroke production, and Ming [another six-year-old Chinese-English bilingual] was less concerned with complete accuracy when teaching his classmates at primary school. However, he showed that he was aware of criteria such as the correct length, angle and balance of strokes when he made comments such as 'Make it even more bigger' or criticised his own writing by saying 'That's too lumpy'. He decided to do a circle round one offending character 'cos that's what my Chinese teacher does when I get it wrong'.

Ming also knew that small variations in stroke pattern could differentiate between two potentially similar characters. When teaching his classmate Roberto to write the character meaning 'six' (Figure 2), Ming suddenly became dissatisfied with his pupil's efforts. He complained that at some points Roberto's writing of the upper vertical stroke was 'too long', and that the lower part of the character was wrong 'because it's next to each other' (the two strokes under the horizontal line were supposed to be further apart). It turned out that these details were indeed significant in differentiating this character from the one meaning 'big' [...]

Figure 2   The Chinese characters for (*left*) 'six' and (*right*) 'big'

Joined letter forms in Arabic

Arabic, like English and Spanish, is an alphabetic system, so symbols do not have to be written quite as accurately as in Chinese. Instead of having thousands of characters that are subtly different from one another, alphabetic scripts have a defined set of letters which can be more easily distinguished. Readers usually encounter letters in the context of a word, giving further clues as to what the letter might be.

However, in Arabic a number of concerns still arise for learners about certain details of each letter, because the letters take different forms when they are at the beginning, in the middle or at the end of a word.

Children have to know how to produce each shape and how to join it to others. They also need to guard against letters looking too similar to each other when joined.

At Arabic school, teachers helped children to develop their abilities for visual discrimination by writing words on the board and asking which letters they were composed of. They also requested children themselves to write words on the board so that the whole class could decide if the letters had been correctly formed and joined. If children needed help to remember these characteristics and to write the script appropriately, teachers provided support through a join-the-dots model of a word on the board or in exercise books. This was an aid both to perception and action. [...]

'You forgot to do that little wiggly line'

Tala [a six-year-old Arabic-English bilingual] decided to teach the word 'mama' (mum) to her friends Tina and Bhumi. Just like her teachers in Arabic school, she provided a join-the-dots version to help her pupils to write the word. She then decided to write over the dots herself, giving them a model to follow (Figure 3). One of the original dots can still be seen in the loop of the first syllable.

Figure 3 Tala's writing of the Arabic word 'mama' (mum). The symbol on the left shows a pronounced 'wiggle'.

Writing the word 'mama' in Arabic involves joining the letter 'mim' (for the sound 'm') to the letter 'alif' (for the sound 'a'), twice over. First you have to write the initial form of 'mim', and join it to the middle form of 'alif', making 'ma'. Since 'alif' is one of the 'stubborn' letters which cannot join to the [next letter, which would be on the] left, you then have to leave a gap before starting the next syllable. The second syllable is identical to the first.

When Tina began writing the word, using the model provided, Tala shrieked and grabbed the sheet of paper from her, saying 'Tina, you ain't doing the stick so good – do the circle here and then you do the line'. Tracing the letters with her finger, she emphasised the necessary action for connecting the 'circle' of 'mim' to the 'stick' of 'alif'.

Tina began again, but Tala was still dissatisfied. She said 'you got to do the line, there', tracing the shape with her finger once more, and rubbing out Tina's new version. The 'line' at issue seemed to be the wiggle which follows the loop of 'mim' as it joins to the vertical stroke of 'alif' – this is clearly visible in the left-hand part of Figure 3. This time Tala gave Tina more precise instructions: 'you're doing a circle, right, but you always forget to do the line', while demonstrating writing a circle followed by a pronounced wiggle. Tina understood, and responded by including a wiggle in her next version. Later Tala explained to her other pupil Bhumi, who was trying to write the same word, 'you done it wrong because you forgot to do that little wiggly line'. [...]

Just as Selina and Ming focused on specific details of Chinese characters which they considered to alter the meaning, so Tala picked out the 'wiggle' as the key attribute when [distinguishing] two particular letters. This is a complex task for children; out of all the instruction they receive on the act of writing, they have to identify what really matters when distinguishing one letter or character from another. Teachers at Chinese and Arabic school helped children to understand significant details of this kind by emphasising them in discussion. [...]

Making your mark

Children also like to develop their own style, particularly when writing their name. Producing a signature is the most personal and self-defining act of writing, and children recognise it as such. This can explain why children's signatures are often unconventional. Brian, for example, wrote his name in a combination of upper- and lower-case letters. It could be assumed that this was because he was still working out the difference between the two types of lettering. However, it also seems that this particular representation of his name became important to Brian, because he continued to use it throughout the year of the research project.

Part of his signature involved the upper-case form of the letter 'N' (see Figure 4). Brian was especially attached to this form of 'N' when writing other words too, probably because he linked it with his name. [...]

Figure 4 Brian's drawing of a bear with wings, with the caption
'un oso que vuele' (a bear which flies)

Children often feel strongly about their particular design of a written
symbol and are prepared to argue for it. At stake is the issue of social
acceptability – does their version fall within the boundaries of
conventional meaning? – and also the desire to produce an individual
flourish. [...]

Embodied knowledges

From their experience of different scripts, the children in the research
project were developing different kinds of knowledge in several areas:
ways of designing symbols and using the graphic space of the page, and
the physical process of writing. The term 'embodied knowledges' can be
used to describe this learning, because it simultaneously involves visual,
actional and cognitive aspects.

Embodied knowledges are part of understanding how a writing system
works. As well as knowing what symbols stand for, children recognise
that the visual characteristics of symbols and the actions needed to
produce them also hold significance. [...] The children realised that
their primary school classmates might not have the same expertise in
these areas, and sought to give advice. [...]

These biliterate children seemed to adapt to different contexts, drawing
on their multisemiotic resources in ways they found appropriate.
Mainstream educators sometimes think that children will find it hard to

switch between ways of writing in different scripts. For example, it is said that children who have learned the precision of writing Chinese will find it difficult to adapt to the relative freedom of the emergent writing they are encouraged to do in [British] schools. However, children like Selina who have grown up with Chinese and English develop capacities from both writing systems, and can use either to their advantage.

Reference for this reading

Kress, G. (1997) *Before Writing: Rethinking the Paths to Literacy*, London, Routledge.

4 Working in English

Almut Koester

4.1 Introduction

This chapter looks at how English is used at work. Before you begin reading, think about the following questions:

- Do you speak in the same way when you speak to your friends as when you speak to your boss, a doctor or someone at the bank?
- If not, what are some of the differences?
- What are the reasons for the differences? Is it because of your relationship with the person? Is it because of what you are trying to get done?

By the end of this chapter, you will know how these questions have been approached and to some extent answered by applied linguistics. I start by looking at how English used in everyday situations can be distinguished from English used in the workplace (which could be a physical location or a virtual space), and at the special characteristics of language and interaction patterns in the workplace. We shall see how people working together interact using structured and goal-oriented genres that have evolved over time. This leads into a consideration of multimodal literacy in professional practice, using the example of architecture, and to a discussion of English as an international language. Finally, I explore the topic of business relationships, by considering the role of humour and power in managing workplace interactions and the connection between language and power in job interviews. The chapter deals mainly with the use of English by 'white collar' office workers, managers and professionals, since that has been the focus of recent research. Routine manual work is by definition less centrally concerned with the use of language and other symbolic systems. But it involves the exchange of instructions and information in linguistic form, and those who carry it out use language to interact socially, insofar as working conditions permit this. And as we shall see, access to such work may be restricted to those who can produce the right kind of language under interview conditions.

Figure 4.1   Talk and text in a business meeting

4.2   How does workplace talk differ from ordinary conversation?

This chapter explores the special characteristics of the language used at work. Chapter 1 contrasted everyday conversation with the sorts of talk that take place in institutional settings such as places of work. Following Emmanuel Schegloff, it was noted that turn taking often has to follow institutional rules, and following Pierre Bourdieu, it was emphasised that certain speech acts can only be carried out by a holder of institutional authority. These two points are related. For example, Greg Myers observes that in a meeting, '[t]urns are typically assigned ... by the chair ... and the ... chair but not others may interrupt' (Myers, 2004, p. 53): this means that the chair has the unique authority to carry out certain speech acts, including the speech acts of permitting other people to speak and of cutting them off when they have spoken for too long. However, it is important to recognise that much workplace talk is not structured in this way, being conversational and informal. Discourse analysis can help us to understand the subtle differences between more and less formal kinds of workplace interaction.

Activity 4.1

Allow about 15 minutes

Look at the following two brief extracts: the first involves informal talk and the second is from a workplace meeting. As you do so, keep these questions in mind:

- How are the two extracts structured?
- What are the differences between them?
- What makes the second extract typical of a workplace interaction?

Think too about the vocabulary used and the roles the speakers play.

Extract 1: Chatting about food

Helga, Andy and Don are talking about a jar of French chestnut paste that Don brought back from Paris for Andy.

1	Helga:	What you got?
2	Andy:	[I got this /??/
3	Andy:	Yeah. Chestnut?
4	Helga:	*Oh! I* thought you were were a *real* gour*met*!
5	Andy:	[I'd never-
6	\<Don:\>	Heheheh
7	Andy:	Well, I guess, I'm *not-* heheheh
8	Andy:	I never heard of it before.
9	Helga:	You know you put it in a dish-
10	Don:	Well I've never seen it here.
11	Andy:	Well I went- I went *home*, I went *home*,
12	Helga:	Yeah.
13	Andy:	And … looked on my shelf and there was a- a- *jar* of it.
14	[1]	
15	Don:	You're *joking!*
16	Andy:	[Someone obviously gave it to us for Christmas
17	Don:	[That's hilarious!

(author's own data)

Extract 2: Management meeting

Chris is chairing a management meeting in a small North American company. The participants discuss how to redistribute the database of a sales representative who is leaving (David Johnson), and arrangements for a new one starting (Jim Murray).

1	Chris:	Okay ... the uh topics I wanted to handle when we get together right
2		now were ... uhm distribution of David Johnson's database after he's
3		gone, and that's something we have to decide kind of now. And uh
4		and that relates to the fact that Jim Murray is uh ... likely gonna start
5		working with us within the week. Uh he'd like to- by the way, he'd
6		like to start working with us right away if he can, without coming up
7		first, and so we gotta talk about that a little bit too.
8	Amy:	Well we have to have signed agreement before ... we give him anything
9	Chris:	[Yeah
10	Chris:	Yeah, but I mean that can be done by fax. [3] Uhm ...
11	Amy:	What's the downside of having him start before ... really isn't one, is
12		there?
13	Chris:	Well the only downside is that we ha- then we have to have a written
14		agreement before we actually *ever* meet him face to face.
15	[2]	
16	Tom:	We've met him face to face.
17	Chris:	Well, in a totally different context, though. (Tom: Mm)
18		Uhm so anyway that's- *one* thing is what to do about David
19		Johnson's database, the second thing is ... uh consolidated sales force
20		idea that ... John would like to propose ...

(author's own data)

Transcription conventions used for author's own data in this chapter

[indicates overlapping speech
< > indicates that the identity of the speaker is uncertain
... indicates noticeable pause of less than 1 second
[2] indicates a pause of more than one second; number in square
brackets indicates duration
( ) around utterances interjected by a speaker within another speaker's
turn
italics indicate emphatic stress
: indicates a sound that was drawn out for longer than usual
- indicates an interrupted word or utterance
/?/ indicates inaudible utterances: one ? for each syllable
{comment} curly brackets indicate a comment
The dialogue has been punctuated to aid understanding

Comment

Some of the differences you observed probably included the following:

- Extract 1 seems much 'messier', with speakers interrupting each
  other and overlapping with one another, whereas Extract 2 appears
  more orderly, with one person speaking at a time.

- The vocabulary and intonation used in Extract 1 show the speakers' emotions and personal opinions (e.g. 'You're *joking*!', 'That's hilarious!'), whereas the language used in Extract 2 appears more neutral.

- In Extract 2, the speakers are clearly talking about things related to their work (sales) and they use special business vocabulary (*database*, *signed agreement*, *sales force*) to indicate this. But their interaction is also typical of workplace interaction in that the participants are speaking with a clear purpose and are trying to arrive at a decision, rather than 'just chatting'.

According to Paul Drew and John Heritage (1992), 'institutional talk', as they call workplace and professional talk, differs from ordinary conversation in three ways:

1   It is **goal oriented**: participants usually focus on some core goal, task or identity ... associated with the institution or workplace.

2   There are **constraints** on what participants will treat as 'allowable contributions', i.e. on what participants may say.

3   There are **inferential frameworks and procedures** that are particular to the specific institutional or workplace context.

(Drew and Heritage, 1992, p. 22)

Using Drew and Heritage's categories gives another way of answering the questions in Activity 4.1. Each of these characteristics of workplace interactions can be found in Extract 2. There are clear goals – that is, things the participants aim to achieve in the meeting – and this extract shows Chris going over what the goals are by setting the agenda for the meeting. A result of this goal orientation is that the meeting is quite structured, with one topic (or agenda item) being dealt with at a time and speakers taking orderly turns. In Extract 1, it is more difficult to identify a clear goal, except perhaps to exchange opinions and share an anecdote.

Second, there are few constraints on what the speakers in Extract 1 can say and when they can speak. This is not the case in the meeting, where Chris, as the chair, has the right to guide the discussion and where it is expected that the participants will restrict their contributions to items on the agenda. Notice, however, that Amy nevertheless interrupts Chris (line 11) as he goes over the agenda in order to raise a point. This shows that in this kind of workplace interaction, the restrictions as to who can speak when are not absolute. This might be different in more formal institutional contexts, such as a parliament or courtroom.

The inferential frameworks the participants in the meeting draw on include their assumptions about how such management meetings in their organisation are normally conducted, as well as background knowledge about the business and its procedures, such as the database they refer to, and the contract that the new sales representative will need to sign. Related to this is the fact that special professional or technical lexis is often used, such as the terms used here relating to business or technology.

Finally, a further feature of workplace interactions linked to all three characteristics listed above is the fact that interactions are often **asymmetrical**; that is, some speakers often have more power and/or special knowledge than others. Chris chairs the meeting and therefore has a more powerful role than the other speakers. However, Tom is actually the chief executive officer (or CEO) – the head of the company – so is a more powerful person in the organisation. Another kind of asymmetry can result from differential knowledge; for example, in interactions between professionals and lay people (e.g. a doctor and a patient), where the professional has knowledge of a specialist subject and of institutional procedures. This means that participants in workplace interactions have **institutional identities** (or professional roles) which interact with their personal and discursive identities (the role they are playing at any particular time in the interaction). Although we have been looking at the special characteristics of workplace language in spoken interactions, all these distinguishing features, except turn-taking structures, are also relevant for written workplace communication.

Another way of referring to the goal orientation of workplace interactions is to say that they are **transactional**, which means that participants focus on doing a particular workplace task. Extract 2 clearly involves transactional talk, whereas Extract 1 does not, and can therefore be described as **relational**; that is, the purpose is more of a social one. (Compare this to the discussion of the ideational and interpersonal functions of language in Chapter 1.) This kind of casual talk allows the participants to bond socially, and thus contributes to building a good relationship. Extract 1 is very typical of informal talk between friends, but interestingly, it is actually an example of small talk between colleagues at work: the three speakers all work in the administrative office of a university. This shows that not all workplace talk is transactional and that relationship building at work is important. I shall return to this point later in the chapter.

Frontstage and backstage

Although the two extracts above are quite different in their orientation (transactional or relational), what they have in common is that they both involve interactions between co-workers in the same organisation. However, many professionals or people working for organisations also deal with lay members of the public in the course of their work. We can therefore distinguish between two kinds of interaction in which English can be used as a working language:

- *Interactions among co-workers*, where people are working together in the same workplace, occupation or profession.

- *Interactions between experts in an organisation or profession and members of the public*; that is, between 'insiders' in particular areas of work and 'outsiders'. This includes lay–professional encounters; for example, interactions between health professionals and patients, or service encounters, where service providers interact with customers.

These two general types of workplace interaction correspond to two sites in which, according to the sociologist Erving Goffman, social life can be studied: front regions (or **frontstage**) and back regions (or **backstage**). Front regions are areas 'where a particular performance is or may be in progress', whereas back regions are 'where action occurs that is related to the performance but inconsistent with the appearance fostered by the performance' (Goffman, 1959, p. 135). The dramaturgical metaphor used by Goffman implies the presence of an audience in frontstage activity, as in interactions between lay people and professionals, and a setting in which 'best behaviour' is expected. The backstage setting, on the other hand, is more relaxed and 'allows minor acts which might easily be taken as symbolic of intimacy and disrespect for others present' (Goffman, 1959, p. 129). This kind of relaxed behaviour at work is most evident in Extract 1, where co-workers are laughing, talking over each other and teasing (e.g. '*I thought you were were a real gourmet!*'). But even in the transactional meeting situation in Extract 2, the interaction is quite informal, and participants interrupt each other and disagree in a fairly direct manner (e.g. *Yeah, but I mean that can be done by fax*).

Figure 4.2 Backstage interaction in the workplace

Allow about
15 minutes

Activity 4.2

Compare Don's language in Extract 1 with a frontstage encounter in Extract 3 below, in which he interacts with a student, rather than with his colleagues.

How do the two speakers play different roles in Extract 3? For example, what linguistic evidence is there in the extract of Don being an 'insider' and Wendy an 'outsider' – how is asymmetry in terms of knowledge shown, for instance?

Extract 3: The spring programme

The student, Wendy, wants to look at the spring course programme.

1	Wendy:	Hi. I suppose … [1] Ah! You only have one copy, and it's a prelim?
2	Don:	We haven't printed those yet.
3	Wendy:	Okay.
4	Don:	W- they … We should have 'em … within about a week.
5	Wendy:	Within a week? Okay. Is it okay if I look at it now?
6	Don:	That's what it's there for
7	Wendy:	[i-
8	Wendy:	Okay! Super.
9	[3 sec: student leafs through programme]
10	Wendy:	Am I allowed to take it over and copy it? [1] At a … the library? Or
11		would that be …
12	Don:	If you really want to?

| 13 | Wendy: | Is that okay? Thanks. I'll be back in three minutes. |
| 14 | Don: | Okay. |

(author's own data)

Comment

The roles of the two speakers are quite distinct: Wendy, the 'outsider', is the one who asks questions, and Don provides the answers. There is clearly asymmetry of knowledge, with Don having insider knowledge that Wendy does not have, such as the fact that the final version of the schedule hasn't been printed yet, and that it will be ready in about a week. There is also asymmetry in the power difference between the two speakers, with Wendy having to ask Don for permission to borrow the one copy of the programme so that she can photocopy it, and this is reflected in the language she uses (lines 10–11).

Extracts 1, 2 and 3 illustrate the fact that working in English can involve a range of different types of encounter and uses of language. The same person often has to switch between frontstage and backstage interactions at work; and while workplace interactions are mainly goal oriented and transactional, relational language, which is quite similar to small talk outside the workplace, also occurs. This means that the distinction between workplace language and everyday language is not a hard and fast or absolute one.

4.3   Workplace genres

Discourse communities

Another concept that is often used to talk about groups of people who use particular ways of communicating in order to pursue a common goal is that of **discourse community**. In a discourse community the members do not necessarily work closely together or form relationships involving mutual engagement. However, their spoken and written interactions may still be characterised by a particular **register**: a set of conventions for language use, possibly including specialist vocabulary. A discourse community may be geographically dispersed, yet its members use language to pursue common goals in ways that distinguish them from other groups. This concept was originally developed by the linguist John Swales (1990), who was interested in the ways in which professional groups such as scientists have developed and used specific genres of speech and text (e.g. academic articles, conference papers and laboratory reports) as an integral part of their professional practice.

Genres

According to Swales, genres are: 'class[es] of communicative events … which share some set of communicative purposes … [The] rationale shapes the schematic structure of the discourse and influences and constrains choice of content and style' (Swales, 1990, p. 58). This is similar to the definition of genre in Chapter 2 and highlights two aspects of genres:

- Different texts or utterances can be said to belong to the same genre because they share the same communicative purpose.
- Genres follow particular patterns or 'schematic structures', which may involve participants playing specific roles, and using particular vocabulary or a particular style of speaking or writing.

For example, in frontstage service encounters, such as the one in Extract 3 above, the communicative purpose for the customer or service recipient is to obtain goods or services. The interaction usually begins with a greeting and request for service and ends with a service provision and a closing, and it is characterised by the use of politeness features (e.g. 'Thanks' in line 13). In the backstage workplace interaction in Extract 2, the communicative purpose is to reach a decision. The meeting begins with an overview of the agenda (in lines 1–7), followed by a discussion of each of the items on the agenda, with Chris playing the role of chair.

Allow about 15 minutes

Activity 4.3

Extract 4 is from a workplace conversation I recorded between two people who work in the back office of a US food cooperative (see Koester, 2004, 2006): a book-keeper, Ann, who is talking to Meg, a new assistant she is training. The interaction involves instruction giving, which is a genre that occurs frequently in many different types of work. As you read the transcript, answer the following questions:

- How does the instruction-giving dialogue start?
- Do you notice any particular patterns in the structure of the conversation?
- What role does each speaker play in the conversation?
- Is there any specialised vocabulary or any language that is typical of instruction giving?

Extract 4: Sorting delivery documents

1   Meg: Before I get going to onto another computer, here I wanna ask you ...
2   (Ann: Okay.) about things I wasn't sure about sorting.
3   [1.5] Bills of *la*ding?
4   Ann: That is ... comes with every delivery an' it can be thrown away.
5   Meg: Okay.
6   {Meg shows Ann something}
7   Ann: Uhm ... *that* is for the Save the Earth stuff, and ... I will- it will
8   *even*tually probably get thrown away, but ... if you haven't come
9   across a packing list for Save the Earth products
10 Meg: Okay.
11 Ann: hang onto it.
12 Meg: Okay.
13 Ann: 'Cause I'm just I'll show you what to do with it.
14 Meg: Okay.
{a number of turns have been omitted}
15 Ann: Then the next thing you do is ... There *should* also be a packing slip
16   for this one here. So ... I would do this ... staple that bill of lading
17   onto that *in*voice, 'cause we know *those* two go together.
18 [9]
19 Meg: So they're all in this /?/
20 [8]
21 Ann: Okay, and ... just- assuming that our packing slip's gonna come from
22   upstairs, you can go ahead an' put it back in here. An' then at- like at
23   the end o' the month ... we'll look through here an' say wait a
24   second, what happened to that packing slip an' figure it out then.
25 Meg: [Okay. ... Alright.
26   An' the:n: ... other things I had /????/ This ... uh- is this just a- d- do
27   I just treat this-
28 Ann: Hmmm ... let's treat that as an invoice for one case at twenty-seven
29   bucks, an' that's it.
30 Meg: [Okay.

(author's own data)

Comment

The interaction begins with Meg, the subordinate, indicating that she has
some queries (lines 1–2: *I wanna ask you about things I wasn't sure
about sorting*). Advance summaries like this of what an enquiry or
meeting will be about are common in workplace or professional
conversations, and are often a clue to the genre being performed. A
clear pattern emerges in the talk: Meg asks questions or simply shows

Ann the document relating to her query (lines 3, 6, 19) and Ann responds with instructions and explanations (lines 4, 7–9, 11, 13, 21–24, 28–29); Meg then acknowledges she has understood, usually by simply saying *okay* (lines 5, 10, 12, 14, 19, 25, 30). The speakers each have clearly defined roles in this conversation: Ann as the instruction giver and manager, Meg as the one receiving instruction and training. The structure of the conversation reflects these respective roles: whereas Meg's turns often consist of a single word, Ann's turns are substantially longer than Meg's. There is also some specialised vocabulary to do with delivery and sales: *bills of lading, packing list, packing slip.* Typical language for instruction giving includes verbs such as *show, do, put,* and imperatives like *hang onto it* (line 11). However, it is interesting that Ann often gives instructions in a more indirect way:

- *I would do this ...* (line 16)

- *you can go ahead an' put it back in here* (line 22)

- *we'll look through here ...* (line 23)

- *let's treat that as an invoice* (line 28)

This conversational, interactive way in which Ann gives instructions, even phrasing the instruction as a joint activity (*we'll, let's*), shows that, although she is pursuing a transactional goal (training and instruction giving), she is also trying to build a good relationship with her new trainee. This example illustrates the fact that genres have predictable structures and characteristics but can also vary; for example, in the range of language used for instruction giving.

Genres in a changing world of work: the example of the business email

In the early twenty-first century, email has emerged as one of the most important means of communicating information in English for commercial purposes. The business email has now to a great extent replaced the traditional business letter, as well as some kinds of telephone communication. Like the blog (examined in Chapter 2), the business email has features of both written and spoken language, and has been influenced by a variety of other genres, providing a good example of how genres are not fixed and immutable, but change over time (e.g. as a result of changing technology).

There are different theories about how the conventions of business emails developed. According to JoAnne Yates and Wanda Orlikowski (1992), the business email developed from the genre of written memos, which are company-internal messages circulated between employees, and were once distributed in typed or handwritten form. However, as Yates and Orlikowski (1992, p. 317) remark, email is also used for other kinds of messages; for example, very informal exchanges between individual colleagues, such as a two-line invitation or a one-word response to a question. Therefore Yates and Orlikowski see email as a 'medium', rather than a genre.

Julio Gimenez (2000), on the other hand, claims that many features of email communication were carried over from telephone communication. Table 4.1 shows some of the typical characteristics of written compared to spoken English mentioned by Gimenez.

Table 4.1 Typical characteristics of written and spoken English

Written English	Spoken English
Elaborate syntactic structures	Simple syntactic structures: short sentences or simple clauses linked with 'and'
Explicit constructions	Reliance on context: reference to shared background knowledge
Complete information units	Elliptical forms: words 'left out'
Formal language	Informal language

(adapted from Gimenez, 2000, p. 240)

Now consider the examples below comparing extracts from business letters and emails. They show that while business letters use language that is typical of written language, business emails tend to use language that is more typical of spoken English.

Syntactic structures:

[Letter:] We would appreciate your letting us know which models of used *(brands)* copiers you can make available, as also the quantities and unit prices thereof.

[Email:] Pls e-mail us your ... *(brand)* inventory and price lists.

(Gimenez, 2000, p. 247)

Explicit constructions vs. reliance on context:

[Letter:]   Should you have any queries at all about the review or what to include in your report, please do not hesitate to contact me …

[Email:]   Christine or myself will be available if you have any questions.

(Koester, 2004, pp. 31, 33)

Complete vs. elliptical forms:

[Letter:]   I would appreciate if you let me know at your earliest convenience.

[Email:]   if interested, notify us accordingly,

(Gimenez, 2000, p. 242)

Formal vs. informal (e.g. use of contractions):

[Letter:]   … please do not hesitate to contact me …

[Email:]   Please don't hesitate to contact me if you have any questions.

(Koester, 2004, pp. 49, 32)

Allow about 10 minutes

Activity 4.4

Look at the email below. It is from the editor-in-chief of a magazine to one of his journalists and concerns the blogs hosted by the magazine. (Magazine and newspaper blogs arguably belong to a different genre from the more personal, diary-like blogs or online journals discussed in Chapter 2.) As you read it, think about these questions:

- What features of spoken English identified by Gimenez and shown in Table 4.1 can you find?
- Are there any other features you notice that are typical of email?
- How well do you think the writers know each other?

Extract 5: Email

Subject: More on blogging …

Hi Jenny

Had a chat with Geoff Dixon on the phone today. He was asking whether we have any figures about the PIs for the blogs and what (if anything) we can do to get more comments.

Also, he'd appreciate a quick bloggers meeting sometime when you're in London so the four of us can get together to discuss things. Not urgent, but a good idea sometime I think.

: –)

Scott McKensie

Editor-in-chief

(author's own data, with grateful acknowledgement to Ian McMaster)

Comment

You will probably have noticed that this email has many features of spoken English, such as:

- simple syntactic structures: *Had a chat with Geoff Dixon on the phone today*
- reliance on context: reference to people (*Geoff Dixon, the four of us*) and things (*figures about the PIs*) both the sender and the recipient know
- elliptical forms: *[I] Had a chat with …, [It's] Not urgent*
- informal language: contractions: *he'd, you're*; abbreviations: *PIs*; vocabulary: *chat, get together*.

Another feature that is typical of many kinds of email (but which cannot be used in speaking) is the use of an 'emoticon'. The writer does not actually sign the email with his name, but uses the symbol : –) instead. He can do this, because his name and position appear at the bottom of the message in his 'signature file', which is a regular feature of emails at work. It is of course also a very informal way of ending this message, and this, as well as the many features of informal spoken English in the email, indicates that Scott probably knows Jenny very well and works with her on a regular basis. Although emails in general are less formal than business letters and use many features of spoken English, there are of course differences in formality between emails too, depending on the purpose of the message and how well the writers know each other. Some emails can be quite similar to business letters and use more features that are typical of written English.

As mentioned earlier, the example of the business email shows that genres change and evolve to adapt to changing demands in communication and technology in the workplace. Leena Louhiala-Salminen (1999) suggests that one reason for the increased use of email may be the need, with the increasing globalisation of business, to communicate across time zones, which means that people may choose email for types of communication that might have been done via the telephone in the past. A more recent study by Astrid Jensen (2009) shows that email is even being used for international business negotiations, which until a short time before were being conducted face-to-face.

Activity 4.5

Spoken and written communication are vitally important to most forms of non-manual work in the modern world – not only for people who work in obviously 'verbal' fields such as magazine publishing, but also for people who work in 'visual' fields such as architecture and design. Now turn to Reading A: *The discourse of architecture* by Thomas A. Markus and Deborah Cameron. In these extracts from their book on language and architecture, Markus and Cameron first discuss the importance of register and of particular textual genres within architectural working practices, and then subject documents from an architectural competition to **critical discourse analysis** (Fairclough, 1995). This means that they examine the visual and linguistic construction of the texts (see Chapter 2) in order to critique the ways in which those texts represent reality.

As you read, answer the following questions:

- According to Markus and Cameron, why do architects use a professional register?
- What relationship do Markus and Cameron see between the design briefs issued by the UK government and the multimodal exhibition boards on which the winning architects presented their proposed design?

Comment

Although Markus and Cameron admit that it may also exclude non-architects from discussions of architecture, they argue that the specific register used by architects helps them to think in a way that other architects will understand. Markus and Cameron's critical discourse analysis shows that the design briefs for the Scottish Parliament contained a range of subtexts, such as security, national identity and history, and that these themes were repeated in the exhibition boards submitted by the competition finalists. Interestingly, they find that the winning entry did not reproduce these subtexts as obviously as some of the unsuccessful entries (e.g. the one that modelled part of the proposed building on Scotland's flag), but rather responded to them in a 'more subtle and more powerful' way, by repeatedly emphasising the Scottish *land* in text, images and building materials. Markus and Cameron suggest that this emphasis was effective not only because of an association between Scottish national identity and the Scottish land, but because of the use of nature as 'a metaphor for ageless tradition, permanence, strength, and growth'. These associations and metaphors were constructed through multimodal means on the exhibition boards, through the use of colours, pictures and written statements.

4.4 English as an international language and intercultural communication

English as an international language

Another factor that distinguishes English used for work from English used in social encounters or family settings is that the speakers or writers are often not **native speakers** of English. This term is loosely used to describe a person who grew up using a language to communicate (as opposed to a person who learnt it as an adult or studied it at school as a so-called 'foreign language'). For many years, people who are native speakers of different languages have used English as a **lingua franca** (or 'contact language') for purposes of trade. More recently, English has become the international language, not only for trade, but for all kinds of business and other forms of international communication. In fact, there are now many more people using English in this way than people who use it as a native language.

The term 'native speaker' is discussed in more detail in another book in this series; Seargeant and Swann (eds) (2012), *English in the World*, Chapter 1.

There has been a growing interest in recent years in what the characteristics of English as a lingua franca (or ELF) are, and whether there are significant differences between the way lingua franca speakers and native speakers use English; see, for example, the work of Barbara Seidlhofer (2004) and her team of researchers. Activity 4.6 explores some of the possible differences between standard English and the English used as a lingua franca by non-native speakers.

Allow about 10 minutes

Activity 4.6

Think of some features that typically characterise the English usage of speakers whose native language is not English. Write down at least one example in each of the following categories:

- pronunciation
- grammar.

Do you think features like this generally cause problems for communication?

Comment

Seidlhofer (2004) and others have identified a number of features of pronunciation, vocabulary and grammar, as well as discourse features, that seem to be common to lingua franca interactions and deviate from native speaker English. Jennifer Jenkins (2000) suggests that there is a 'lingua franca core' of pronunciation features essential for mutual comprehension among ELF speakers, such as the contrast between long and short vowels. For example:

- /ɪ/ (l_i_ve) and /iː/ (l_ea_ve)

Some other sound distinctions that native speakers make do not seem to be considered essential by ELF speakers, such as the various sounds that correspond to the letters TH. For example:

- /θ/ (_th_ink) and /ð/ (_th_e)

Grammatical features that occur frequently in lingua franca interactions and deviate from standard English include (Seidlhofer, 2004):

- dropping the third person -s (e.g. _she say_)
- invariant question tags (e.g. general use of _isn't it?_ instead of forms such as _doesn't she?_ and _aren't you?_)
- 'non-standard' use of articles (e.g. omitting or inserting _a_ or _the_)
- 'non-standard' use of prepositional patterns (e.g. _study about_ ...)

These would often be considered 'errors' in grammar, but Seidlhofer and other researchers in ELF argue that, as they do not cause any problems for comprehension among lingua franca speakers (and may even aid understanding in some cases), they should be considered typical features of ELF, rather than 'mistakes'. This point relates to a wider argument made by researchers in ELF that as English is now used as an international language, native speakers of English no longer 'own' English, and it is therefore not up to them to determine what is or is not acceptable – at least in international English usage.

As far as discourse features are concerned, Alan Firth (1996), who was one of the first researchers to analyse ELF business interactions, identified something referred to as the '"let it pass" strategy'. He found that in telephone conversations between a Danish cheese seller and his international clients, the speakers would regularly 'let pass' things that were said that could potentially cause misunderstanding. That is, speakers were quite tolerant of and would not focus on language 'errors', and there was rarely a breakdown in communication.

Another feature of lingua franca discourse identified in many interactions is the use of **accommodation** strategies. 'Accommodation' involves adapting to the speech and behaviour of the person you are speaking to (Giles et al., 1991). Typical accommodation strategies in ELF interactions include repetition, paraphrasing, simplification and codeswitching (switching to a native language of the other speaker). We will look at examples of some of these strategies being used by ELF speakers or writers in international business situations.

The examples in Activity 4.7 are from some correspondence collected by Ulla Connor (1999) consisting of faxes sent by a Finnish broker in the fish importing/exporting business to an Estonian supplier.

Activity 4.7

Allow about 10 minutes

Look at the fax from the Finnish broker to the Estonian supplier, shown in Figure 4.3. In what way does the Finnish broker accommodate to the Estonian supplier? That is, how does he adapt his English so that it can be understood by the Estonian supplier?

Barrels of head-off herring is OK.

Documents: Health/Sanitary/Quality certificates
  Certificate of origin

Your invoice to [*Company name*] should not
follow the truck. It will send to Helsinki.

Enclosed two documents will follow the truck.

Number of copies:
  Please give the truck driver two sets of original documents and
  keep one set in your file.

[*Company name*] is asking as soon as possible a
set of documents to Helsinki by fax.

OBS! [*Company name*]'s contract is based on
100kg per barrel. Is that correct?

Best regards

Figure 4.3 Fax sent by Finnish broker to an Estonian fish supplier
(Connor, 1999, p. 123, Figure 3)

Comment

The Finnish broker accommodates to the Estonian supplier in a number
of ways. The language used in the fax consists of short, simple
sentences, and ellipsis of 'unnecessary' words. For example:

- *[Company name] is asking as soon as possible [for] a*
  set of documents

The vocabulary also is very simple; for example, the term 'head-off
herring', which may be a simplification of a more technical description.
The fax even contains a grammatical 'error': the use of the active voice
instead of the passive:

- *It will send to Helsinki.* (Standard English: *It will be sent to Helsinki.*)

Faxes sent by the same broker to other business partners show that he is perfectly capable of using standard grammar and more sophisticated English, and that he therefore simplifies his language deliberately in the communication with the Estonian supplier. For example, a fax sent to a Japanese buyer shown in Figure 4.4 uses the passive voice according to the rules of standard English, as well as more polite forms and sophisticated expressions.

```
[Seller company name ] has not
yet received any payments of
green roe. Could you please
check what is causing the
delays or when it has been
paid in Tokyo.
```

Figure 4.4 Fax sent by Finnish broker to a Japanese buyer (Connor, 1999, p. 126, Figure 5(1))

According to Connor, the broker's language is influenced not only by the level of English of his business partner, but also by factors such as the business partner's cultural background, the broker's own role in the interaction (as buyer or seller) and his relationship with the business partner. For example, his language is more polite in the fax to the Japanese buyer because he is showing deference to him as the customer and also because he believes (as he said in an interview) that 'the Japanese are polite people' (Connor, 1999, p. 125). Connor also discusses examples (not shown here) of codeswitching by the broker in his correspondence with Estonian and Norwegian suppliers where he used Estonian or Norwegian words. For instance, he uses the term *mandel fisk* (literally 'almond fish') to refer to a type of fish they are both familiar with. The reasons for codeswitching, according to Connor, were: 'in most cases for clarity, sometimes for fun or to create solidarity' (Connor, 1999, p. 122).

Intercultural business communication

Connor's discussion of the written communication between the Finnish broker and his international business partners mentions the role that culture can play in international business interactions. Her study, as well as other studies of the use of English in lingua franca interactions, shows that non-standard language usage causes very few problems. Interestingly, studies of **intercultural communication** have shown that misunderstandings can be caused by cultural differences, rather than linguistic difficulties. Helen Spencer-Oatey (2000) has carried out research on intercultural communication between people from significantly different cultural backgrounds: British and Chinese. One instance of a cultural misunderstanding she describes arose during the visit of a group of Chinese business people to a British company. The visit ended badly with both the Chinese visitors and the British hosts feeling annoyed with each other. As Spencer-Oatey describes, things started out very badly in the first welcome meeting on the premises of the British company. Spencer-Oatey shows that for both the Chinese and the British, the need for group face (rather than individual face; see Chapter 1) to be respected was important in this situation. Many of the problems were due to the British company misjudging the status of the visitors, rather than to cultural differences as such. However, cultural differences also played a role, in particular the level of formality expected and what the respective rights and obligations of hosts and guests were assumed to be. In the UK, there is a preference for informality and minimising hierarchical differences, whereas China is a culture with a 'large power distance' (Hofstede, 2005), which means that status differences are recognised and respected. As a result, the British hosts were not aware that such things as seating arrangements or lack of formal protocol (e.g. the Chinese visitors not having a chance to give a welcome speech) could be interpreted as a lack of respect for their status.

Spencer-Oatey's study shows that intercultural misunderstandings can arise, even when both sides act with the best of intentions. However, many (maybe even the majority of) international business interactions occur without any problems or misunderstandings. Gina Poncini (2002) studied an Italian company's meetings with its international distributors from twelve to fifteen different countries at which English was used as a lingua franca. Despite the fact that participants were from such a range of different cultures, Poncini describes these meetings as being highly successful. The company referred to as *Alta* below (not its real name) makes products for skiing and other outdoor sports. Poncini was interested in how the use of certain linguistic items, such as personal pronouns (e.g. *we*), technical terms and evaluative language, were used to create a sense of group identity and build a positive relationship between the company and its distributors. The example below illustrates the way in which one of the company representatives uses evaluative language (highlighted) in order to build a positive image of the company.

Extract 6: Multicultural business meeting

uh Edo yesterday explained to you that (+) our **success** (.) the **success** of *Alta* (+) has grown together (+) parallel (.) to the **success** of our athletes (++)

the the best example in this case is Rossi (++) ((well known Italian skier))

where Rossi (+) began to **win** (+) uh he **won** (.) thanks (.) to (.) *Alta* (.) to products of *Alta* (.) also- not only (.) of course ((smiles, almost laughs))

(adapted from Poncini, 2002, p. 361)

Transcription conventions

(.) short pause under 0.3 seconds
(I) pause of about 0.4–0.7 seconds
(++) pause of about 0.8–1.7 seconds
(( )) contextual information
bold font indicates explicit positive evaluation

Poncini suggests that 'the company speaker uses evaluation strategically to create a shared image of the company, its products, … activities and strategy so that the image comes to represent what is highly valued by the group' (Poncini, 2002, p. 361). Poncini's study shows that national culture may not necessarily be an impediment to communication in intercultural business interactions. It also shows that, even in a situation where English is used as a lingua franca, language is used not only for transactional or utilitarian purposes, but also for relationship building. In the multicultural meeting, positive evaluation is used to build a sense of group identity among participants with diverse national and cultural backgrounds. This illustrates the point made at the beginning of this chapter, that relational as well as transactional goals are achieved through workplace language use.

The examples of spoken and written international business interactions given in this section show that the language used in such situations can differ in a number of ways from that of people interacting as native speakers of English. It may be simplified, with an emphasis on clear communication and a tolerance of non-standard linguistic features, and speakers will accommodate to each other's language to ensure smooth communication. Furthermore, cultural factors may influence the interaction in a number of ways. Nevertheless, the examples also show that there is a great deal of variation in the level and function of the English used in such situations (even by the same writer or speaker) and that it fulfils both transactional and relational purposes.

4.5 Relationships at work

In this chapter, we have already seen examples of ways in which language is used for relationship building in workplace and business interactions; for instance, through small talk between co-workers, as in Extract 1, or through the use of evaluative language, as in the multicultural business meeting (Extract 6). This section begins by looking at a highly influential theory of how people interact at work, and then looks at an important device used for relationship building in the workplace: the use of humour.

Communities of practice

So far we have been trying to identify what makes workplace language distinctive. But of course, workplaces also differ from one another, and people working together share background knowledge, a set of procedures and a particular workplace culture. This is why, as an outsider, it is sometimes difficult to make sense of transcripts of workplace conversations. For example, we don't know what Chris means when he refers to the 'consolidated sales force idea' in Extract 2, but clearly the other participants do. Groups or teams of people who regularly interact for a particular purpose, for example at work, have been referred to as **communities of practice** (Wenger, 1998). The term 'practice' indicates that people in such groups are trying to get things done and that they have developed routine procedures for this. According to Etienne Wenger (1998, pp. 72–3), 'communities of practice' are characterised by three criteria:

1 mutual engagement

2 joint enterprise

3 a shared repertoire.

'Mutual engagement' means more than simply working together; it also indicates that people working together develop a relationship. 'Joint enterprise' refers to working together for a common purpose to achieve particular goals, and 'shared repertoire' refers to the means by which the members of a community of practice communicate with one another. This category is of particular interest to us, as it includes the language and jargon that are specific to a workplace. However, shared repertoire consists of more than just language; according to Wenger (1998, p. 83), it includes 'routines, words, tools, ways of doing things, stories, gestures, symbols, genres, actions, or concepts'.

Activity 4.8

Allow about
5 minutes

Think about a group of people with whom you interact regularly; for example, your co-workers, family or fellow students. Is it a community of practice? To decide whether or not it is, think about whether it conforms to the three criteria:

1 **Mutual engagement**: do you have a relationship with the other people in the group, based on the things you do together?

2 **Joint enterprise**: does the group have a common purpose or set of purposes?

3 **A shared repertoire**: do you have special ways of communicating or doing things, or any specific words or abbreviations you use regularly?

We will look at some specific examples of the ways in which different workplace communities of practice interact later in this chapter.

Humour and workplace culture

Janet Holmes, who led a project (the Language in the Workplace Project) to collect spoken interactions at work in a range of different workplaces in New Zealand, has looked at the role of humour in the workplace and how its use can be linked to workplace culture. In her study, she draws on the notion of community of practice (CoP), which was introduced above.

Activity 4.9

Now turn to Reading B: *Humour and workplace culture* by Janet Holmes and Maria Stubbe.

Before you read, consider the following points:

• Think of places you have worked. Do you think humour was part of the workplace culture?

• If so, what role do you think it played?

As you read, answer the following question:

- How is the use of humour different in each of the two communities of practice discussed?

Comment

Holmes and Stubbe's discussion of two case studies shows that humour can be a distinctive feature of workplace culture and can form an integral part of a community of practice. In the reading they describe how the type of humour used, and its functions, can be quite different in different communities of practice. Humour can be supportive and collaborative, or it can be contestive and competitive, involving 'jocular abuse'. Both types of humour are used predominately to maintain good relationships, but Holmes and Stubbe show that humour can also be used to deal with conflict and to exercise power in a mutually acceptable way.

The role of power in workplace relationships will be the topic of the final section in this chapter. This section will also illustrate how things can go wrong when the participants in the interaction do *not* manage to establish a relationship.

Figure 4.5 Routine manual work may provide fewer opportunities for verbal interaction.

4.6   Language and power

This chapter began by outlining some of the distinctive characteristics of workplace language, one of which is the asymmetry and power difference in many workplace interactions. Such asymmetry is particularly apparent in 'frontstage' encounters between professionals and lay people; for example, doctors and patients. One obvious but nevertheless critical aspect of many communications between 'professionals' and 'lay' people is the extent to which the professional is willing and able to talk about relevant topics in a way that is clear to the uninitiated outsider. While there may be cases of professionals trying to maintain control and exert power over a lay person by 'blinding with science', failure to make allowances for the lack of familiarity of non-professionals with professional discourse is not necessarily deliberate. Professionals often simply find it very hard to speak of their work in any language other than that of their discourse community.

In Section 4.4, I referred to Spencer-Oatey's research on intercultural business encounters. As in intercultural encounters, the lack of common knowledge and understanding between a professional and a client may not be confined to technical matters, but may be related to differences in the cultural and linguistic experiences of the people involved. Celia Roberts and Sarah Campbell (2006) have directly addressed this issue by recording and analysing interviews for low-paid jobs in the UK. Roberts and Campbell aimed to discover whether ethnic minority candidates were disadvantaged in **gate-keeping encounters** of this kind. Interestingly, they found that 'ethnicity itself was not the major indicator of success', since '[c]andidates who were born abroad were much less likely to be successful than British candidates, whether they were white British or EM British [i.e. members of minority ethnic communities within Britain]' (Roberts and Campbell, 2006, p. 29). Roberts and Campbell argue that the problem for candidates born outside the UK was not their general competence in speaking English, but their lack of what Pierre Bourdieu calls **linguistic capital**: the ability to produce utterances that will be considered appropriate in a range of specific social and institutional situations; for example, using just the right level of formality to make a good impression when interacting with people in authority (Bourdieu, 1986 [1983]; Bourdieu and Passeron, 1990 [1970]).

Activity 4.10

Allow about 10 minutes

Look at the extract overleaf from a job interview with an Ethiopian-born candidate. The candidate was not successful. Why do you think this is?

- What should he have said in answer to the question?
- What 'ground rules' is the candidate not aware of?

Extract 7: Job interview

I = Interviewer

C = Candidate

1.	I:	Okay what would you then say the advantages are (.) by
2.		working as a team
3.	C:	er:m the advantage wherev- wherever you go are the e-
4.		if you apply other jobs you won't find it difficult (.)
5.		you already integrate
6.		(nine seconds of talk deleted)
7.	C:	then wh- wherever you go in say (.) in (xxxxxx) job
8.		(.) or in a community job (.) and you won't get hard you
9.		won't be a- feel ashamed or if y- you (won't feel) a shy
10.		person (.) you get more powerful a:nd (1)
11.	I:	yeah (.) what more would you say
12.	C:	e:r (1) you would be open minded you don't have [to
13.	I:	okay yeah]
14.	C:	be worried (4)

(Roberts and Campbell, 2006, p. 49)

Transcription conventions

(text) text within parentheses indicates a comment by the transcriber
(.) a full stop within parentheses indicates an untimed brief pause
(1) a number within parentheses indicates the length in seconds of a longer pause
(xxx) uncertain transcription
[ ] overlapping utterances

Comment

The candidate responds to the interviewer's question about the advantages of working in a team using 'personal discourse': he talks about the personal benefits to himself. However, according to Roberts and Campbell, this question requires a response using 'institutional discourse': the candidate is expected to show that he understands how teamwork benefits the organisation; for example, by improving efficiency. There are thus unwritten rules about the kinds of responses that are considered to be appropriate to certain types of questions in job interviews, and successful candidates are able to 'align' themselves to the expectations of the interviewers. In order to make a good impression, candidates need to achieve the right balance between institutional discourse, which deals with the candidates' qualifications, and personal discourse, which is more informal and allows the interviewers to judge the candidate's 'personality' (Roberts and Campbell, 2006, p. 56). This analysis shows that job interviews place a very high demand on candidates in terms of the linguistic skills required. They not only need to demonstrate their qualifications and relevant experience for the job, but they also need to align themselves to expectations, use the right level of formality and establish a good relationship with the interviewer. Roberts and Campbell found this to be the case even in interviews for routine manual jobs involving low levels of verbal interaction.

Roberts and Campbell stress that there is not usually any deliberate discrimination against non-British candidates on the part of the interviewers. However, '[m]isunderstandings' often arose when these candidates 'were expected to infer the hidden purpose of questions and to present their experience according to British interview norms and styles' (Roberts and Campbell, 2006, p. 6), with the result that they were disproportionately unlikely to be given work. This highlights the structural difficulties that outsiders or novices can face in trying to enter a professional or workplace community and access the economic opportunities that it would provide.

4.7 Conclusion

One of the main points made in this chapter is that when people are working through the medium of English, the language and discourse they use take on a range of distinctive forms as a result of the different workplace and professional settings in which they occur and the different purposes for which they are used. We can see the specialised nature of English at work in a variety of spoken and written genres, which fulfil particular communicative purposes and have characteristic linguistic and interactive structures. We can also see that language used at work performs not only the transactional function of getting things done, but also the relational function of developing and maintaining working relationships. When people work in English both within and between organisations, language fulfils not only the more obvious needs of effective information exchange, but also the social and emotive functions of relationship building. Moreover, it enacts power relationships between participants, possibly embedding inequality and lack of access.

READING A: The discourse of architecture

Thomas A. Markus and Deborah Cameron

Source: Markus, T. A. and Cameron, D. (2002) *The Words Between the Spaces: Buildings and Language*, London and New York, Routledge, pp. 1–3, 12–13, 15–16, 149–50 and 167–70.

[Language in architectural working practice]

Language is a neglected subject in discussions of architecture, which is conventionally regarded as a visual rather than verbal activity. 'Architects', observes theorist and practitioner Ellen Dunham-Jones, 'tend to refer to themselves as visual people' (1997: 16). This professional self-image is faithfully reflected in popular representations of architects, which typically show them poring over plans, making drawings and models, or manipulating images on computer screens. But in reality, architects' work is both visual *and* verbal: language plays some part in almost everything they do.

This point is underlined by Dana Cuff's detailed study of architectural practice (Cuff 1992), for which she observed and interviewed numerous professionals and students. In training, she notes, students are encouraged to spend long hours in the studio, where they do not only draw, but also talk with instructors and each other; at regular intervals they face 'crits' delivered by architect-teachers in the medium of spoken language. In practice, the talking continues. Cuff cites findings showing that the average architect has only about half an hour a day when his or her work is uninterrupted by some kind of interaction (the architects she spoke to herself thought this an overestimate). Even the most 'creative', schematic design phase of a project rarely matches the idealized picture in which a solitary designer spends long silent hours at the drawing board. Making a building is a collaborative process which involves continual dialogue – with clients, with colleagues, with other professionals like engineers and landscapers, with building contractors. Cuff aptly describes what goes on in these interactions as 'constructing a word-and-sketch building' (1992: 97). She also makes clear how much *written* language is produced in any architectural project. Meetings are recorded in memos and minutes; letters may have to be written to various authorities and community representatives; agreements and contracts must be drawn up. Other texts to which architects may refer include building and planning regulations, briefs or building programmes, design guides and handbooks. Many of these texts are linguistically dense and complex, with a high proportion of verbal to visual material.

The observation that language pervades architectural practice is in one sense very obvious and banal. Everyone knows that architects must talk to clients, hold meetings with contractors, write memos, read planning regulations, and so on. But although architects may spend a lot of time actually engaged in these activities, few would spend much time reflecting on them. Whereas architects are expected to reflect on issues of design in a way that might be called 'abstract', 'theoretical', or 'analytic', they are not expected or encouraged to reflect in the same way on issues of language and its relationship to design. Language may be all around them, but it remains very much a background phenomenon, a part of what the ethnomethodologist Harold Garfinkel called the 'seen but unnoticed' of everyday life. […]

The significance we claim for language in relation to the built environment is a function of its significance in human affairs more generally. Natural languages are the richest symbolic systems to which human beings have access, and the main purposes for which we use language are fundamental to the kind of creatures we are. One of those purposes is, of course, communication with other people. Humans are not telepathic, and it is mainly by way of language that we are able to get more than a rudimentary sense of what is going on in another person's mind. But we also use language as an aid to our thinking, whether or not we communicate our thoughts to others.

Both these functions of language are relevant to the activities of designing and making buildings. True, language is not the only symbolic system involved: architects need to make mathematical calculations, and to represent form and space in drawings and models of various kinds. But they also need to use language to conceptualize what they are doing and convey it to others (given that making a building is typically a collaborative process). We say, 'a picture is worth a thousand words', but people rarely communicate, or think, in pictures alone; if called upon to elaborate the meaning of a picture or a mathematical formula – or, as we shall see, a building – they will use language.

Architects, like many other professionals, make use of linguistic resources developed over time for the purpose of reflecting, in speech and writing, on the phenomena which are their distinctive concerns. Architecture has its own linguistic *register* (the term used by linguists to denote a set of conventions for language-use tailored to some particular situation or institution – other examples include 'legalese' and 'journalese'). One obvious feature of the register of architecture is the extensive technical vocabulary architects must learn in the course of their training. Learning what words to use is every bit as necessary as learning how to draw plans, calculate loads, or use computer software for modelling; for the technical vocabulary of architecture is not merely a convenient shorthand, it is a system for thinking with. It provides the classificatory schemes which enable architects to 'see' as they do – and, importantly, as other architects do. Professional registers are often criticized as mystifying jargon whose main purpose is to exclude outsiders; but while that may indeed be one of their functions, they also allow a professional community's accumulated knowledge to be codified and transmitted in precise detail. In architecture as in medicine or law, 'learning the language' is inseparable from mastering the craft as a whole. […]

[Critical discourse analysis and the language of architecture]

Some linguists who practise discourse analysis are interested primarily or exclusively in *describing* the workings of language in use. Others, however, adopt a self-consciously critical perspective. As well as asking the descriptivist's question 'how does this text work?', critical discourse analysts pose the question, 'what or whose interests does it serve for this text to work in this way?'

[…] In modern societies, one very significant kind of power is the power to represent reality in a particular way, and to have your representation accepted not merely as one choice among others […] but as 'the truth': the 'natural', 'obvious', or 'neutral' version of reality. Critical discourse analysis looks for patterns of linguistic choice which contribute to a particular construction of the reality being represented. It also tries to relate these patterns to the power relations which are operative in the relevant context, and to the interests which are at stake. […]

Buildings themselves are not representations. They are material objects which enclose and organize space. However […] buildings often do this (or more exactly, their designers do it) on the basis of texts which *are* representations. […] [T]he textual representations which architects and designers work with […] are products of linguistic choices which construct reality in particular ways. And the constructions of reality which are made apparent in discourse will very often also be apparent in the way a building organizes space. A building's users may never see any of the documents which preceded its construction, but because those documents condition the architect's decisions, their contents profoundly affect how the building will be experienced and used. [...]

[An architectural brief]

In the 1998 international competition for Scotland's new Parliament building in Edinburgh, one of the five finalists (who, in the event, was the chosen winning architect) submitted on the required six display boards texts which had a rich and complex mixture of language and image. [...] In the winner's submission we find these cryptic phrases: 'The people sit in the land. The Parliament is a fragment of a large gathering situation ... [it] is a form in people's mind, it is a mental place ... [it] should belong to a broader thought.' [Figure 1.] Because these phrases were written in a mixture of capitals and lower case, in various colours, scattered over the surface of the boards, interwoven with coloured sketches (of such places as a 'gathering field') they became an integral part of the text, in which they framed [...] the images. No one, including members of the jury, could have looked at or assessed the images without the words unavoidably occupying some, if not most, of their attention. It is therefore interesting and important to try to answer the questions: to what extent does the interaction of language and image affect the perception and evaluation – the reading – of such a text? To what extent did this language influence the jury in its assessment of this design, and hence ultimately shape the material reality of Scotland's capital? [...]

[After an] open worldwide invitation [...] was made to architects to design the new Scottish Parliament building on a site near the end of the Royal Mile [in Edinburgh] [...] the Scottish Office [of the UK government] drew up and published a 'Building User Brief' of some sixty-six pages (brief 1) in 1998. This was made available on the Internet to anyone interested. A second, more elaborate brief in two volumes totalling one hundred and thirty-one pages (brief 2) was published later that year and was used by the five shortlisted design teams. [...]

We are interested in the way the competitors responded to the briefs both in their designs and in the language of their submissions. [...]

[Two] of the central themes [of the briefs were] open government, and [...] security.

There were also four subtexts in the briefs.

The first is that of national identity. There is a specific mention of the 'Scottish people's authority (and) their aspirations as a nation'; 'a landmark building reflecting the aspirations of Scotland as a nation'; 'the first landmark, political building of the 21st Century … of which the Scottish people can be proud'.

The second is history. The chosen location is within both a UNESCO World Heritage Site and the Edinburgh Old Town Conservation Area. The scheme was to incorporate the seventeenth century Queensberry House, and one of the site boundaries, Canongate, is the 'historic regal processional route between the Castle and the Abbey and Palace of Holyroodhouse'.

The third subtext is modernity. The project must be 'modern'. The design 'must take account of the latest advances in technology … *IT* will play a prominent part in the management of information' – using electronic voting, television and broadcasting technologies, not to mention electronic surveillance.

Finally, the fourth subtext is a deeply traditional definition of architecture as art – large public sculpture. In brief 1 the success of the project was defined in terms of 'design *and* use' (our emphasis). This implies that design (by implication form) is something separate from function and use, as is indeed confirmed in brief 2 which […] requires the building to be 'a piece of art in its own right … [which] should reflect the cultural dimensions of the country'.

With this range of requirements, some contradictory, some cryptic, some reinforcing the myth of architecture-as-art, and all in the form of sweeping generalizations, it is not surprising that the submissions of the finalists, both as designs and even more so in their language, should have the same characteristics. Sometimes, the words reproduce the wish-thinking of the brief almost verbatim.

[The winning submission]

[W]e focus our discussion on the […] exhibition boards of the winners.

[…] [These] have a rich and informal mixture of language and image, colour, varied typography, with geometrically controlled and freehand drawings. This well matches the complexity and fragmentation of the design itself.

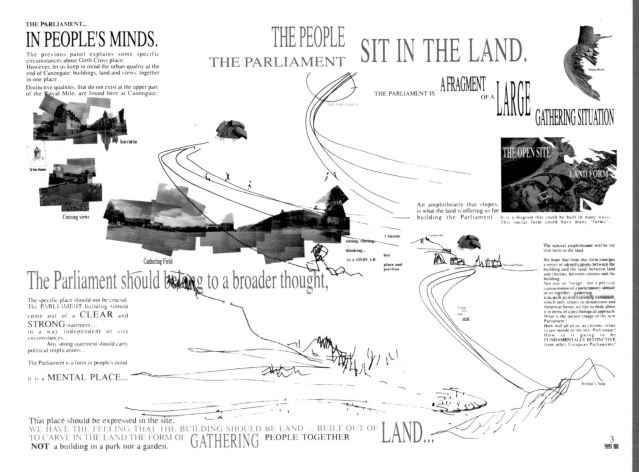

THE PARLIAMENT...
IN PEOPLE'S MINDS.

The previous panel explains some specific circumstances about Girth Cross place.
However, let us keep in mind the urban quality at the end of Canongate: buildings, land and views together in one place
Distinctive qualities, that do not exist at the upper part of the Royal Mile, are found here at Canongate.

Crossing views

THE PEOPLE
THE PARLIAMENT SIT IN THE LAND.

THE PARLIAMENT IS A FRAGMENT OF A LARGE GATHERING SITUATION

THE OPEN SITE
LAND FORM

An amphitheatre that slopes, is what the land is offering us for building the Parliament... It is a diagram that could be built in many ways... This social form could have many "forms"...

sitting, resting...
thinking...
in a SIMILAR

Citizens
but
place and
position

Gathering Field

The Parliament should belong to a broader thought,

The specific place should not be crucial.
The PARLIAMENT building should come out of a CLEAR and STRONG statement....
in a way independent of site circumstances...
Any strong statement should carry political implications...

The Parliament is a form in people's mind.

it is a MENTAL PLACE...

The natural amphitheater will be the first form in the land.

We hope that from this form emerges a series of identifications between the building and the land, between land and citizens, between citizens and the building.
'Not just an "image" but a physical representation of a participatory attitude to sit together - gathering - not as in an overwhelming monument, which only relates to dimensions and rhetorical forms, we like to think about it in terms of a psychological approach.
What is the mental image of the new Parliament?
How will all of us, as citizens, relate in our minds to the new Parliament?
How is it going to be FUNDAMENTALLY DISTINCTIVE from other European Parliaments?

That place should be expressed in the site.
WE HAVE THE FEELING THAT THE BUILDING SHOULD BE LAND ... BUILT OUT OF
TO CARVE IN THE LAND THE FORM OF GATHERING PEOPLE TOGETHER LAND...
NOT a building in a park nor a garden.

Arthur's Seat

Figure [1] Drawing by Enric Miralles, Benedetta Tagliabue with Robert Matthew, Johnson Marshall, for the Scottish Parliament competition entry

[...] [T]he architects based their entire scheme on the *land* of Scotland. It is worth repeating and expanding their articulation (on the boards) of this. 'The Parliament sits in the land … Scotland is a land … it is not a series of cities… The Parliament should be able to reflect the land which it represents.' 'The Parliament sits in the land because it belongs to the Scottish Land.' Indeed, 'the building should be land … built out of land … to carve in the land the form of gathering people together … almost out of the rock'. Thus its form derives from 'a series of identifications between the building and the land, between citizens and the building'. It is this focus which will make the building 'fundamentally distinctive from other European Parliaments'. Here nature has become a metaphor for ageless tradition, permanence, strength, and growth. In keeping with this metaphor, the dominant colours of both images and text are green and brown, and text is composed in blocks, lines, and typefaces which relate organically to the images. Moreover, buildings are seen, in themselves, as anthropomorphic living objects; along the Royal Mile 'one sees other buildings [...] sticking their noses out to look at each other'. On [one panel] a montage of landscape images and blocks of text are tied together by sweeping, freehand line sketches.

A number of other images are invoked. Some, such as the university campus and the monastery, are intended to create a place of 'rest … and meditation … an enclosed garden', and these descriptions are next to plans of enclosed courtyards. Another image, that of upside down boats 'offered by the land … [which] flout the landscape … [and are] a delicate presence in a place', occur not only in this language, but in images and in the design of the roofs. [...]

In keeping with these ambitions and metaphors the materials will be 'turf, stone, wood and glass'. Some of the other competitors interpreted the brief's aspirations to transparent government literally, by the use of glass [...] But to the winners this is too obvious; they propose a more introspective, solid, enclosed debating chamber, which should allow 'a clear atmosphere of concentration' on 'speeches and discussion', which 'makes glass and excessive transparency an inconvenient quality' – a statement that appears alongside an aerial view of a (wooden?) model of the proposed building, in which solid brown roof forms dominate.

Some designers used conventional metaphors. For instance [...] the upper part of [one design] is crossed by two pedestrian bridges 'in the form of a Saltire' (the diagonal St Andrew's cross on Scotland's flag).

The winners' text, with its language of land, boats and natural materials such as turf, rocks and water ('pumped from the foundations'), [...] when combined with the rustic images into complex and memorable visual compositions was more subtle and more powerful.

References for this reading

Cuff, Dana (1992) *Architecture: the Story of Practice*, Cambridge, MA: The MIT Press.

Dunham-Jones, Ellen (1997) 'Stars, Swatches and Sweets: Thoughts on Post-Fordist Production and the Star System in Architecture', *Thresholds* 15, Fall, 16–21.

READING B: Humour and workplace culture

Janet Holmes and Maria Stubbe

Source: Holmes, J. and Stubbe, M. (2003) *Power and Politeness in the Workplace*, Harlow, Longman. pp. 122–30, 134.

In this [study] we examine the ways in which humour contributes to the construction of a distinctive workplace culture in different communities of practice (CofPs).

Workplace culture comprises the knowledge and experience that enables people to function effectively at work [...] Humour is clearly one aspect of workplace culture. Knowing how to participate appropriately in workplace interaction is an important passport to social integration and managing humour is one aspect of this participation. Perhaps, most obviously, not 'getting' a joke brands you as an outsider.

[...] [M]embers of a CofP regularly engage with each other in the service of a joint enterprise. They share a repertoire of resources which enables them to communicate in a kind of verbal shorthand which is often difficult for outsiders to penetrate. Humour is one aspect of this. Ways of realising 'harmonious or conflictual workplace relationships' (Wenger 1998: 125), for instance, clearly include humour [...] 'Shared ways of engaging in doing things together' and 'certain styles recognized as displaying membership' (Wenger 1998: 125–6) point to the relevance of different styles of humour in constructing workgroup membership. The number and kinds of 'insider jokes' provide further obvious criteria for differentiating workplaces from one another. In what follows we focus on three work groups from different organisations as brief case studies, identifying relevant parameters for distinguishing the contribution humour makes to the contrasting workplace cultures, and in particular to the ways in which power and politeness are played out at work.

Case Study 1

The first case study is an office-based work unit in a relatively small, white-collar 'knowledge industry' organisation, with predominantly female staff. [...] Using Wenger's (1998) three criterial features for a CofP (mutual engagement, joint enterprise and shared repertoire), this group can be described as a relatively tightly knit, cohesive community of practice, with a high involvement communication style. They engaged with one another many times a day in a variety of ways: in formal meetings, informal problem-solving sessions and in social chat in their workspaces and at breaks. They shared a clear sense of joint enterprise which went beyond doing the tasks at hand to encompass the pursuit of certain ideals relating specifically to their organisation's objectives. And they often jointly constructed a highly interactive and typically supportive communicative style which was particularly evident in their humour.

Sequences of collaborative humour and amusing anecdotes were commonly interleaved with the business at hand during formal meetings and other discussions in this community of practice, indicating a workplace culture where relationships were valued and nurtured. In [another] meeting [...] the group worked very hard to reach consensus on a controversial issue. Leila, the manager and chair, was aware that Zoe, a senior member of the team, was unhappy about the solution being considered. In Example [1], Leila presents Zoe and herself [to Kerry] as in accord on a related matter, and then skilfully uses humour to compliment Zoe on her ability to 'mother' new staff, which raises a laugh from the group as a whole.

Example [1]

Context: Meeting of a work group in a white-collar professional organisation to plan changes to systems.

1	LEI:	Zoe Zoe and I'd been talking I mean one we're gonna need Zoe
2		um anyway to do handing over with the other librarians
3		when they come /on\ board and I think that
4	KER:	/yeah\
5	LEI:	they're probably going to feel a need for a little bit of mothering
6		and I think Zoe will be good at that
7		and the /other thing she's been\
8	KER:	/[laughs]\
9	LEI:	really good with Kerry I've watched her [laughs]
10		I've seen her doing it
11	EM:	mother librarian
12	LEI:	she'll be sort of the great aunt librarian /[laughs]\
		/[general laughter]\

[Transcription conventions are given at the end of this reading.]

Leila's humorous compliment indicates appreciation of Zoe's mentoring skills, eliciting agreement from Kerry (line 4) and a collaborative contribution from Emma *mother librarian* (line 11). The use of humour to lighten the tone and head off the threat of overt conflict is consistent with the team's preference for a consensual style of decision making.

Moreover, the characterisation of authority relationships in 'familial' terms is another typical strategy for defusing potential conflict and playing down power differences. [...]

Towards the end of the discussion in this meeting, as a solution begins to emerge, there is a good deal more collaborative, jointly constructed humour reflecting relief that a solution is in sight (Example [2]).

Example [2]

Context: Meeting of a work group in a white-collar professional organisation to plan changes to systems.

		[laughter throughout this section]
1	LEI:	Emma you are part of the solution in that I think that ( )
2	EM:	I only want to be part of the problem
3	XX:	really
4	LEI:	[laughs] [in fun growly tone] don't you dare be part of the problem
5		I'll keep on giving you vitamin c bananas [laughs] chocolate fish
6		[laughs] I gave I gave um I you know everyone had chocolate fish
7		last week but Emma had more chocolate fish than anybody
8		the only thing was she had holes in her teeth /[laughs]\
9	EM:	/I couldn't eat them\
10	LEI:	she couldn't eat them [laughs]
		[general laughter]

The way Leila shares information about the holes in Emma's teeth and jokingly threatens to feed her with various goodies simultaneously reinforces the supportive team culture and constructs Leila in a nurturing role. Once again 'family' roles provide a vehicle for the humour, which is collaboratively achieved. Emma plays the role of recalcitrant child (line 2) to Leila's benevolent, authority figure (lines 4–8). The extent to which they are 'in tune' is indicated by Emma's provision of the resolution to Leila's narrative *I couldn't eat them* (line 9), which is echoed and reinforced immediately by Leila *she couldn't eat them* (line 10). [...]

In terms of workplace culture, then, there is considerable emphasis on consensus-based decision making in this community of practice. Power and status differences are downplayed, and group membership is highly valued. The team's use of humour reflects these priorities. There is a good deal of laughter in the group's meetings, much of the humour is jointly constructed and collaboratively developed, and most of it is positive in its pragmatic effect. Where conflict arises, humour sometimes serves as a vehicle for the expression of dissatisfaction, or to mask a covert challenge to what is perceived as an overly 'managerial' style. Overall, however, the humour which characterises this workplace culture is an accurate reflection of the friendly, supportive work relationships of the group.

Case Study 2

The second case study is a blue-collar, multicultural, male-dominated but female-led, factory-based team within the manufacturing industry. On the three criterial features, this work group constitutes a very tightly knit and highly cohesive community of practice. Their level of mutual engagement on a day-to-day basis is not uniformly high, as the packers and manufacturers work on different floors of the factory, and there are long intervals where individual team members may not need to communicate with one another. However, the team has daily briefing sessions, individuals have regular contact with one another in the course of their 12-hour shifts, they see one another at 'smoko' (tea/coffee breaks), and there is regular social contact between many team members outside work hours. They are a very cohesive group with a real sense of joint enterprise and high motivation, both in terms of completing immediate tasks during each shift and meeting longer term goals, such as continuing to outperform other production teams. Teamwork is highly and explicitly valued, something which is further reinforced by the Polynesian cultural background of a majority of the team, which tends to privilege the group over individuals.

One of the more noticeable ways in which these characteristics are reflected in the discourse of this group is in the high proportion of humour which pervades their talk. [... T]here was a higher proportion of humour in the team meetings of this group than in any other work group we recorded. Moreover, the style of humour favoured by the group was sparky, contestive and competitive; i.e. rather different from the supportive, collaborative humour more characteristic of meetings between members of the team in Case Study 1. The factory team had a well-deserved reputation for uninhibited swearing and constantly joking around and 'having each other on'. Their particular blend of verbal humour, jocular abuse and practical jokes contributed to a unique team culture and generally helped to create positive relationships within the team. These kinds of playful yet highly competitive and 'in your face' strategies for building solidarity are well documented as common characteristics of all-male groups (e.g. Kuiper 1991; Coates 1997; Kiesling 2001).

Example [3] provides a typical illustration of how members embed the team culture and low-key humour into routine task-oriented interactions.

Example [3]

Context: Ginette the team leader talks to Russell in the manufacturing section via the intercom.

1	GIN:	copy Kiwi copy Kiwi
2	RUS:	what's up
3	GIN:	stand by and I'll give you the figures bro
4	RUS:	yep go
5	GIN:	for the line 1 acma rainbow flight we need 24 tonnes 24
6	RUS:	yo bro

Ginette, the manager, is participating in a longstanding team ritual when using the intercom, by the mock-serious use of ham radio conventions like *copy Kiwi* (line 1) and *stand by* (line 3) to initiate the interaction with Russell. Her use of his nickname *Kiwi* (line 1) and the familiar and friendly term of address *bro* (line 3) when addressing Russell, and his use in return of *bro* (line 6) are also characteristic of the way this team interacts.[1] Example [4] of humorous self-deprecation by Sam illustrates the way such low-key humour is endemic, naturally woven into team members' mundane workplace interactions.

Example [4]

Context: Sam and Helen are working side by side on the factory line.

1	SAM:	I dunno where my I dunno where my knife went (4) disappeared
2	MEL:	there it's there
3	SAM:	oh shit see that's what happens when you're running around
4		like a blue arsed fly [laughs] … you forget where you put things

Example [4] above is a more obvious example of the sort of no-holds-barred contestive humour that is commonplace between members of this team. This kind of teasing, focusing on personal characteristics, was common currency among team members, and an obvious way in which they constructed and reinforced team solidarity. Ginette, the team manager participated fully, often deliberately initiating humorous escapades to counteract boredom and maintain morale amongst the team. A classic example occurred on April Fools' Day when she tricked several team members into ringing the zoo to ask for 'Mr Lion', much to the mirth of their colleagues.

Ginette's routine use of humour to emphasise team cohesion and solidarity has much in common with Leila's use of humour to release tension and emphasise collegiality at strategic points in the meeting outlined in Case Study 1. What is very different, however, is first the type and style of humour which characterises the interactions within each team. The office-based team's humour is typically anecdotal, gentle and unthreatening, and often attracts support from others who collaborate to develop and extend it. The factory team's humour is largely abusive, robust and contestive, with team members frequently vying competitively for the floor to top each other's humorous sallies. In both cases, however, the effect is to reduce power differences between team members and their managers, and to emphasise social connection ahead of individual status (cf Tannen 1990).

A second difference is the way the factory team leader uses humour in conveying her more explicit face attack acts. The white-collar manager, Leila, is rarely overtly critical, especially in large meetings, preferring indirect strategies for indicating areas for improvement. Ginette, by contrast, is frequently extremely direct and critical, using explicit imperatives, often reinforced by strong expletives when addressing the group as a whole [...]. However, she is also skilled in using humour to ensure the team pay attention to her message. In Example [5] [...] she begins with a no punches pulled style, characterised by explicit directives, and appealing to individuals not to let the rest of the team down, but she ends with humorous bathos.

Example [5]

Context: Regular 6am team briefing meeting. Ginette is telling the packers that there have been serious delays caused by their mistakes with documenting the packing codes.

1	GIN:	check the case ... make sure you check them properly
2		cos like I said it's just one person's stupid mistake
3		makes the whole lot of us look like eggs +++
4		check them properly ...
5	GIN:	please fill them out properly fuck youse
		[general laughter]

Ginette uses very direct forcefully expressed imperative forms (lines 1, 4), but she includes an amusing simile (lines 2–3), based perhaps on the idea of getting egg on one's face, and she ends her long harangue (the example is edited) with the bathetic *please fill them out properly fuck youse.* The comic mix of imperative form and forceful expletive, alongside the formally polite *please*, and the friendly colloquial pronoun *youse*, an in-group solidarity signal, elicits appreciative laughter from the team.

This mix of critical abuse and humour is what distinguishes Case Study 2 from Case Stud[y] 1 [...] It is a distinctive interactional style which depends on close and trusting relationships between all group members. [...]

In terms of workplace culture, then, this community of practice can be described as a highly cohesive and solidarity oriented workplace, with team membership highly valued. Team members express their close relationships with a wide range of teasing, practical jokes and jocular abuse. By contrast to Case Study 1, decision making in this team is often unilateral and, in such cases, decisions are conveyed downwards clearly and explicitly. Directives and criticisms are commonplace. In this context, humour functions importantly to maintain good workplace relations. The team leader participates fully in the team horse-play, but she also uses humour as an attention-grabbing device and a means of rendering her most 'in your face' criticisms palatable. [...]

Conclusion

[...]

Humour can [...] be considered a distinctive feature of workplace culture, with considerable variation in the amount and type of humour which characterises workplace interaction in different communities of practice. Looking more closely at the humour of [two] specific work teams revealed interesting differences in the detailed interactional practices of each team. In the team in Case Study 1, where power and status were downplayed and smoothly attained consensus was an important goal, humour was predominantly supportive and positive in pragmatic effect and typically collaborative in style; jointly developed, supportive humour sequences were common. The team manager used humour to facilitate progress in areas where difficulties were apparent, and subversive or contestive humour was relatively rare.

A much more robust style of humour characterised the interaction of the team which was the focus of Case Study 2. Jocular abuse was the common currency and team members, including the team leader, were adept at 'roasting' each other in a variety of ways, including practical jokes. While jointly constructed sequences occurred, they typically involved trading jocular abuse. Often the boundaries between power and solidarity were fluid and humour was an interesting indication of this, with all team members, including the team leader, considered fair game. However, when necessary the team leader asserted her authority, skilfully using humour to convey unvarnished criticism and directives in attention-grabbing and acceptable ways.

Note

1 Although *bro* is an abbreviation of *brother*, and therefore more commonly used as a solidarity marker between males, it is nevertheless not unusual for it to be used in addressing women who are members of the in-group, particularly in Polynesian contexts.

References for this reading

Coates, J. 1997. One-at-a-time: the organization of men's talk. In S. Johnson and U.H. Meinhof (eds), *Language and Masculinity*. Oxford: Blackwell. 107–29.

Kiesling, S. 2001. 'Now I gotta watch what I say': shifting constructions of gender and dominance in discourse, *Journal of Linguistic Anthropology* 11, 2: 250–73.

Kuiper, K. 1991. Sporting formulae in New Zealand English: two models of male solidarity. In J. Cheshire (ed.), *English Around the World*. Cambridge: Cambridge University Press. 200–9

Tannen, D. 1990. *You Just Don't Understand: Men and Women in Conversation*. New York: Morrow.

Wenger, E. 1998. *Communities of Practice: Learning, Meaning and Identity*. Cambridge, Cambridge University Press.

Transcription conventions used in this reading

[laughs] Paralinguistic features in square brackets
+ Pause of up to one second
(3) Pause of specified number of seconds
… /…...\ … Simultaneous speech
(hello) Transcriber's best guess at an unclear utterance
 …. Section of transcript omitted

5 Everyday creativity in English

Joan Swann

5.1 Introduction

In a BBC radio broadcast on *A History of the World in 100 Objects*, Neil MacGregor, Director of the British Museum, discussed the properties of an ancient stone handaxe that was made about 1.2 million years ago. Although a practical object, it is a bit too large to use comfortably, and it is also pleasing to the eye. Was it designed intentionally to be a thing of beauty, the beginnings of art – perhaps a status symbol for someone powerful?

In speculating about the combination of practicality and art, Neil MacGregor was referring to people's actions on the material world, but in this chapter I examine similar ideas that apply to our use of the resources of English and other languages. The argument here is that the fabric of English (its linguistic structure and discursive patterns), while often associated with practical purposes such as conveying information (the 'ideational function' – see Chapter 1), is frequently drawn on creatively, even artfully, by speakers and writers. This happens principally in literature, and archetypally in poetry, as well as in rhetoric, which you will meet in Chapter 6. But much more routine uses of language – casual talk with friends, workplace meetings, various forms of electronic communication – are also characterised by creative episodes where people attend, even if momentarily, to the aesthetic properties of language. The phenomenon is so common that some linguists, such as Deborah Tannen, Ronald Carter and Guy Cook, whose work I discuss below, have suggested that it is a primary function of human communication.

Many intellectual traditions have seen an increasing interest in the creativity of everyday life. In education, for instance, Anna Craft discusses 'little c creativity', which is about 'acting effectively with flexibility, intelligence and novelty in the everyday rather than the extraordinary' (Craft, 2005, p. 19). While this is different from 'high' creativity (significant achievements, discoveries or inventions within a particular field – things that change the world), the distinction is not absolute. 'Everyday' and 'extraordinary' creativities are likely to lie at different points on a continuum rather than being entirely different phenomena. There is a parallel in the study of language, where linguists such as Tannen, Carter and Cook have suggested that there are links between even routine forms of linguistic creativity and 'high culture' forms such as literary language.

I return to these arguments in the sections that follow, where I examine some of the forms that everyday linguistic creativity may take; how it is embedded in communication in English; and also some of the communicative functions it serves – how it may be drawn on to manage relations with others, for instance, and to say something about the identities of speakers and listeners, and readers and writers.

5.2   Conversational poetics

poetry = the *best* words in the best order.

(Coleridge, 20 July 1827)

In much everyday language use there doesn't seem to be time to think about 'the best words'. Informal conversation, for instance, is an improvised activity, as people respond to one another off-the-cuff, often with little or no gap between speaking turns. There certainly isn't an opportunity for speakers carefully to polish up their utterances. Nevertheless, when people talk it isn't just what they say that's important, but also how they say things. You will remember from Chapter 1 that, in conversation, speakers make certain choices – adopting appropriate terms of address, for instance; switching between languages or language varieties; conveying evaluation in a narrative, or taking on a particular voice to animate a character. Language is routinely used strategically, to particular communicative effect, even if people are not fully aware of doing so. In this section I look at an argument that goes one step further, suggesting that everyday talk may, in various ways, be considered 'poetic'.

This idea relates to what linguist Roman Jakobson termed the poetic function of language: an occasion in which there is a 'focus on the message for its own sake' (Jakobson, 1960, p. 356). Jakobson is referring here to the highlighting of the linguistic form of a message (e.g. wordplay or a striking metaphor – an occasion when language draws attention to itself). While this is a dominant function of poetry, taking precedence over other functions such as conveying information, Jakobson argued that it was also evident in non-literary language.

Similar ideas have been developed more recently by researchers with an interest in everyday spoken interaction. For instance, sociolinguist Deborah Tannen has argued:

> [O]rdinary conversation is made up of linguistic strategies that have been thought quintessentially literary. These strategies, which are shaped and elaborated in literary discourse, are pervasive, spontaneous, and functional in ordinary conversation.

> (Tannen, 2007 [1989], p. 1)

As an illustration of this phenomenon, I shall look at the spontaneous, conversational use of two types of poetic language: imagery and descriptive detail; and play with the structures and patterns of English. Later in the chapter I return to Tannen's argument that such ways of using language are functional – that they serve particular purposes – in conversation.

Imagery and detail

Activity 5.1

Allow about 15 minutes

In the box overleaf Tannen presents an analysis of imagery in a tiny fragment from a conversation between two friends:

> 'I wish you were here to see the sweet peas coming up.'

Tannen notes that she felt moved by this reference to the appearance of summer flowers, and in seeking to understand her emotion was reminded of a line from T.S. Eliot:

> 'I am moved by fancies that are curled around these images and cling.'

- How do you respond to the conversational utterance?
- How convincing do you find Tannen's analysis in the box?

'I wish you were here to see the sweet peas coming up.'

A line of a poem? It could become one. But as it was, it was just a fragment of conversation, words uttered by a friend on one coast to a friend on the other. But these words have something in common with a poem: They spark a flash of feeling. They make us not just think about, but feel, the distance of the American continent separating two people, the longing to be in the presence of someone loved, to report not important events, but small ones, small perceptions.

'I wish you were here to see the sweet peas coming up.'

Why is this more moving than the simple, 'I wish you were here'? Partly because 'Wish you were here' is a fixed expression, a cliché. But mostly, I think, it is because of the sweet peas – small and ordinary and particular. The sweet peas coming up provide a detail of everyday life that brings everyday life to life. The sweet peas create an image – a picture of something, whereas 'Wish you were here' suggests only the abstract idea of absence. And the sound of 'sweet peas' is moving: the repeated high front vowel, /i/, suggests something small and tender, and this impression is intensified because it echoes the same sound in 'here' and 'see.' Similarly, the repeated, symmetrically bounding sibilants /s/ and /z/ in /switpiz/, almost adjacent to the /s/ of 'see,' are soothing and alluring. And semantic associations are at work as well: One is moved by the 'sweet' of 'sweet peas,' the word 'sweet' having gathered meaning associated with people, their character and their relationships. It would not have been quite as moving to say, 'I wish you were here to see the geraniums coming up,' or 'the tomatoes,' or 'the asparagus.'

(Tannen, 2007 [1989], pp. 133–4)

Comment

Although it relates to everyday discourse, Tannen's analysis is like a stylistic analysis of a poem, and indeed for Tannen the words used here have something in common with a poem. Her response is a personal one, but like literary criticism assumes common appreciation on the part of other readers: '[The words] make *us* not just think about, but feel ... [etc.]' (emphasis added). Tannen points to the detail of the sweet peas that creates an image for the listener, as well as certain linguistic features, such as alliteration and assonance, which add to the imagery. For Tannen, this combination of features makes the utterance moving. Interestingly she conveys this herself in language that, to me, feels quite literary: the 'detail of everyday life that brings everyday life to life'.

Like Tannen, I find the utterance quite moving, perhaps because it evokes recollections of the sight and smell of sweet peas in my parents' back garden in summer. Personal and cultural associations are important here – not everyone will respond in the same way. Students from China and the Philippines who tried out this activity did not share all of Tannen's intuitions. For instance, they could understand the emotion behind the sentence, but were unfamiliar with the imagery of sweet peas. One reader commented that a reference to vegetables could be just as powerful: 'Asparagus is my favourite dish. It is tender, juicy and crunchy. I would love to have the chance to see it coming out.' Arguably, the sentence needs to be considered and appreciated in relation to its context of utterance, between friends who do share common understandings and perceptions, but this does also mean that one cannot assume a similar level of appreciation from different listeners or readers.

Imagery often plays an important role in conversation, particularly in animating a narrative. Ronald Carter cites an example from an eye-witness account of the sight of a train carriage after its roof had been ripped off in an accident:

> the top peeled back as if it was a sardine can

> (data from Cornbleet, cited in Carter, 2004, p. 125)

The simile here adds to the visual imagery, and in comparing a train carriage with a sardine can it emphasises the scale of the accident.

Jennifer Coates has conducted studies of informal talk between both men and women. In the following extract from a story she collected, imagery contributes to the perceived point of the narrative.

Context: A woman, Bernie, recounts an incident in a London tube train, when a man took a seat before a pregnant woman could get to it:

1   … most of the seats were taken
2   but there was one spare seat opposite me

3   and you know how the seats are like in between two doors, *mhm*
4   one person got in this door,
5   one person got in this door,
6   one of them was like a typical commuter business-man type *mhm* man in his pin-stripe suit,
7   very *upright* holding himself very well,
8   very kind of you know fit and active,
9   the other one was a pregnant woman. *mhm*
10   Nike practically pushed pregnant woman out of the way so that he could sit down
11   *Really? [subdued laughter]*
12   *So who got the seat then?*
13   Well he did
14   but then about twenty people stood up to let this pregnant woman sit down *[sympathetic noises]*
15   including myself of course
16   *Yeah, good one, quite bad that that [unclear speech]*
17   *It is awful, the man was so horrible*

(adapted from Coates, 2003, pp. 130–1)

Transcription conventions

words in *italics* are contributions from other speakers
[square brackets] enclose descriptions of speech and other sounds

Here Bernie provides detail on the layout of seats in the tube, so that it's clear the two protagonists in her narrative would approach these from different directions. The detailed depiction of the businessman – he holds himself well, is fit and active – contributes to the point of the narrative – the man clearly has no need to claim the seat. The reference to the man as *Nike* is an example of metonymy, a figure of speech in which something is referred to by one of its attributes, or something associated with it – in this case a brand of trainers and sports clothing that emphasises the man's fitness. (The brand name Nike is itself a metaphorical allusion to the Winged Goddess of Victory, but we cannot know whether the speaker would have had this additional level of association in mind.) The imagery here probably wouldn't be considered beautiful or moving, in the same way as the sweet peas, but the narrative clearly holds the attention of its audience and there is evidence of appreciation, as listeners respond with laughter, questions and commentary.

Play with linguistic structures and patterns

Ronald Carter, like Tannen, has been concerned with the prevalence of literary-like features in everyday discourse. Carter focused partly on what he termed 'pattern-reforming' behaviour, known more traditionally as poetic **deviation** – where speakers or writers creatively bend linguistic rules and manipulate linguistic forms and structures. Utterances, here, don't follow expected patterns or norms, so that language stands out and draws attention to itself. While deviation is particularly associated with poetic language, it occurs frequently in advertisements and also, more spontaneously and often playfully, in everyday speech.

Activity 5.2

The extracts in the box below involve some form of play with the linguistic resources of English.

Allow about 15 minutes

How do you think these extracts work – in what precise ways are the speakers and writers playing with language?

English at play

1 *abcdefghijklmnop rstuvwxyz*
   (Advertisement for an airline company that boasts its business-class travellers have 'no queues') (cited in Carter, 2004, p. 1)

2 *Cutting Edge* (Hairdressers, Cape Town); *Special Branch* (Tree surgeon, Milton Keynes); *So.uk* (Middle Eastern restaurant, London)

3 *'We're plumbing shallows here we didn't know existed.'*
   (Compère critiquing a team on a British TV quiz show) (cited in Carter, 2004, p. 45)

4 *'I guess now you are over the moon, Mars, Jupiter and the whole galaxy'*
   (Sky TV sports reporter) (cited in Carter, 2004, p. 128)

5 *'If you don't strive, they won't thrive.'*
   (Singapore radio horticultural discussion) (cited in Carter, 2004, p. 167)

6 A and B are discussing the possibility of a mutual colleague repaying a debt:

(continued overleaf)

> A: He won't forget this time.
>
> B: Brian, can you see those pigs over my left shoulder moving slowly across the sky?
>
> [A and B both burst into laughter]
> (Conversational data) (cited in Carter, 2004, p. 23)

Comment

Extract 1 is a form of wordplay, a pun based on the fact that the letter *q* and the word *queue* have identical pronunciations in English – in linguistic terms they are 'homophones'.

The wordplay in Extract 2 is common in certain kinds of shop or business names. In the first two examples the play humorously exploits the potential for dual (metaphorical and literal) meaning in the set phrases *cutting edge* and *special branch*. *So.uk* plays on similarity in the written forms (in Roman script) of the Arabic word *souk* (i.e. street market) and the English *so UK*, with its spoof email address.

Extracts 3 and 4 derive their effect from the distortion of fixed metaphorical expressions, *plumbing (the) depths* and *over the moon*, whereas Extract 5 uses rhyme, and parallel rhythms and grammatical structures (*you don't strive/they won't thrive*).

In the conversation in Extract 6, B makes a more oblique reference to another fixed metaphorical expression, *pigs might fly*, implying the unlikelihood of the occurrence but here playfully taken as literal.

In all cases there is a point to the wordplay. In Extracts 1 and 2 this draws attention to an advertisement or a shop or business name. In Extract 1, the alphabet with its missing letter is also a kind of puzzle – it may require quite a bit of interpretive work on the part of the reader to understand its meaning, and this perhaps adds to its effectiveness. The particular associations of the phrases in Extract 2 are important – for instance *So.uk* brings together the Middle Eastern cuisine of the restaurant with its British location. The play with fixed expressions, and the use of rhyme and parallelism, in Extracts 3–6 add emphasis – for example, heightening critique or pointing up advice.

Carter himself studied such phenomena systematically in a five-million word corpus of spoken English, known as CANCODE – Cambridge and Nottingham Corpus of Discourse in English. Creativity was not Carter's original interest in working on the corpus – his main concern was to construct a grammar of spoken English. But he noticed that creativity, of various sorts, 'leaps out at researchers from almost every transcript of the data' (Carter, 1999, p. 196), so much so that he began to see this as a key feature of interpersonal communication.

Creativity is often associated with doing something new or different, as in the extracts above where people play with the patterns of English or bend linguistic rules. Carter comments that his pattern-reforming examples 'involve new words and novel expressions, implying change and normally involving a single producer who brings about "novel" changes to language ' (Carter, 2004, p. 102). However, such practices are not entirely novel. There is a long tradition of creating punning names for certain kinds of shop or service (although generally not for those engaged in more 'serious' professions, such as doctors or lawyers). And while particular examples may be distinctive, the types of features drawn on are not unique (e.g. it is common to play with email and other digital conventions such as dots and '@'s). Furthermore, while Carter refers to the skill of a 'single producer', in conversational examples there is also usually an element of collaboration and joint construction of utterances. (See also discussion of collaborative storytelling in Chapter 1.)

Poetics in context

I have given examples above of some of the forms that poetic language may take in English, but, as in all utterances, such poetic forms are embedded in particular contexts of use. In order to understand what is going on as people play with language, it's important to know something of the context in which this occurs. The concept of **performance**may be useful here – a term proposed by linguistic anthropologist Richard Bauman as an extension to Jakobson's poetic function. For Bauman, performance is 'the enactment of the poetic function, the essence of spoken artistry' (Bauman, 1986, p. 3). 'Performance' suggests something that happens at a particular time and place, so context becomes important. It also suggests an activity that stands out in some way. This applies to special events, such as theatrical performances, and more impromptu performances – for example, of a song, story or comedy routine. It may also apply, however, to episodes

'Performance' in this context should not be confused with 'performativity' – see Chapter 1.

that stand out much more fleetingly, providing a 'micro break' within everyday communication, as in the example below.

Allow about
10–15 minutes

Activity 5.3

Look at the example below of conversational wordplay. As you read this, think about how the wordplay works and what participants need to know to find it funny. How well do you think the idea of performance accounts for this?

Context: A family is having a picnic in the park and throwing scraps to pigeons. They discuss a somewhat bedraggled pigeon who has driven away another bird.

1 A: He might look scruffy but he's seen off that one over there
2 B: Obviously a thug amongst pigeons
3 C: Al Capigeon
4 D: The godfeather
   [*Laughter overlaps C & D*]

(Maybin and Swann, 2007, p. 506)

Comment

The phrases in lines 3 and 4 may be analysed as wordplay, as in Activity 5.2 above. In line 3 there is a blend of *pigeon* and *Al Capone*, and in line 4 there is a near pun based on *The Godfather*. They can also be seen as performances in that they stand out (very briefly), and there is also an audience response in the form of laughter. The audience clearly plays an important part in performance: for Bauman it is part of the definition, where the performer assumes 'responsibility to an audience for a display of communicative skill' (Bauman, 1986, p. 3).

However, we need to adapt the idea of performance slightly in conversational contexts. In the extract above, lines 3 and 4 don't spring out of nowhere: *The godfeather* is a response to *Al Capigeon*, itself a response to *thug amongst pigeons* which, in turn, builds on *seen off that one over there*. In terms of how the play works within the interaction, this doesn't simply depend on the skill of an individual performer (or a 'single producer' in Carter's terms). While speakers C and D utter the puns, there is a sense in which the performance is collaboratively accomplished by all speakers. Sometimes episodes of language play extend over a longer period with several speakers chipping in, as in the example in the box below. This becomes more like a joint performance or, drawing on Jennifer Coates's musical analogy, a '[j]am session' (Coates, 1996, p. 118) where speakers all pitch in together.

Extended wordplay: store door

A family is eating at a table outside a restaurant. Across the street is a tall building with a door high in the wall, leading to the loft to allow access for storage. The door is divided into four sections. Someone remarks: 'It's a four-door store door.' Instantly, others begin to extend the phrase: 'If there was a battle here it would be called the four-door store door war;' 'If someone kept going on and on about the battle they'd be the four door store door war bore' ... etc. The game runs sporadically through the meal accompanied by laughter as well as mock-despairing cries ('Not again!') before it finally peters out.

(personal example)

I mentioned above that the idea of performance emphasises the importance of context: the time and place of the performance, the participants who take part in it. In the 'pigeons' example, the family's understanding and appreciation of the wordplay – how they come to find it striking, or funny – depends on joint cultural reference points: in this case, common knowledge of US gangsters and gangster movies, without which it would not be successful. The play works in this sense because everyone understands the incongruity – the humorous juxtaposition of the worlds of gangsters, and of parks and pigeons.

The success of the performance also depends on what works in a particular time and place. It is possible here to make joking references to violent people or events that are distant in time and place – an early twentieth-century US gangster; and distant by virtue of being 'unreal' or fictional – a gangster movie. But it may be much less acceptable to make joking references to violent crime in the here and now.

Such playful activity is partly about the creation of pleasure, seen in the extracts above in participants' laughter. However, it is also located within a particular set of social relations and it serves certain interpersonal functions. In the 'pigeon' example, speakers are family members who habitually chat together. If the joke falls flat, there is no serious threat to anyone's face (see Chapter 1), and in fact various types of joking are common in the family. Play partly *reflects* social relations – people are at ease and so they can play. But it also *produces* these – the act of joking and playing helps to make social relations informal and friendly.

Carter has commented (e.g. 2004) that in his data, too, creative episodes are associated with informal friendly talk. But the performance of wordplay, or some other form of creative language, may also function as a form of critique. The 'shallows' example discussed in Activity 5.2, for instance, is a humorous put-down. As a skilled communicator and the compère of the quiz, the speaker is in a relatively powerful position compared to the contestants who are the butt of the joke: it would be unusual for a similar comment to be made in the opposite direction. Guy Cook (2000), in an extended analysis of playful language, comments that this may be collaborative (as in the 'pigeons' example) or competitive (as in verbal duelling, when people try to better one another's insults, or as in witty repartee). It may also be both (the 'store door' example is collaborative, but speakers may also humorously be 'scoring points' in seeking out ever more bizarre rhymes). Similarly, play may be a form of inclusion (bringing a family together) or exclusion (a child taunting another in the playground). Again, the two may work together – by excluding one pupil in the playground, a speaker may well be including others.

Janet Holmes, whose study of workplace discourse you encountered in Chapter 4, notes that humour – in this instance play with various discourse patterns in English – is frequently used in workplace discourse. In this context it may be tied in with institutional power relations, as in the box below. Used by someone in authority, it may serve to maintain power relations between speakers, but in other contexts it may alternatively subvert or destabilise these.

Reinforcing and subverting power relations in the workplace

Extract 1

Context: Manager, Beth, addresses administrative assistant, Marion, who is chatting to secretary, Amy.

Beth: OK Marion I'm afraid serious affairs of state will have to wait we have some trivial issues needing our attention.

          [*General laughter*]

(adapted from Holmes and Marra, 2002, p. 66)

Beth uses irony here to mark a shift from chatting to work, but this also highlights a difference in power between herself, Marion and Amy.

Extract 2

Context: Members of a team discuss a proposal and come to a decision. Eric then challenges this decision.

Eric: don't do it

Jacob: no?

Eric: please put it in the minutes that Eric does not think this is [*laughs*]: a good idea

          [*General laughter*]

(adapted from Holmes and Marra, 2002, p. 73)

Here Eric shifts to a formal register, inappropriate for the group, highlighting his disagreement with the group decision. Holmes and Marra argue that, in doing so, '[h]e challenges the group and thus potentially destabilizes it' (2002, p. 73).

In considering 'poetics in context' in this section I have suggested that context is important in several respects:

- It highlights the need to consider all participants in a creative performance – particularly in everyday interactions, creativity is rarely the responsibility solely of an individual speaker or performer.

- Creative performances also need to be understood in context – they will make sense (or possibly not, of course) in relation to a particular time, place and set of speakers.

- Performances are also embedded in particular sets of social relations and contribute to the construction of relationships between people.

5.3   Creative transformations

> The creative act does not create something out of nothing, like the God of the Old Testament; it combines, reshuffles and relates already existing but hitherto separate ideas, facts, frames of perception, associative contexts. This act of cross-fertilization … seems to be the essence of creativity …
>
> (Koestler, 1976, p. 645)

In Section 5.2 I discussed Carter's argument that processes of 'pattern-reforming' bring about novel changes to language, and I suggested that we needed to qualify this argument – to recognise that language play is not entirely novel. This chimes with views of creativity that would see this as a process of transformation. In linguistic terms the argument would be that, in speaking and writing, we creatively build on and incorporate elements from prior texts and practices. In this case creativity would be a matter of refashioning language, rather than creating entirely novel utterances. In this section I want to explore this point further: I shall look at examples of what I've termed linguistic recycling, and at broader transformations of 'words and worlds'.

Linguistic recycling

> Why is there repetition in conversation? Why do we waste our breath saying the same thing over and over?
>
> (Tannen, 2007 [1989], p. 58)

Repetition of one sort or another is common in language, and it is particularly evident in spoken interaction where speakers frequently repeat their own and others' words. It's hard to see anything creative in repeating someone else, but in fact utterances are never *simply* repeated. Even an utterance that seems to be repeated word for word comes to mean something different because the act of repetition itself is meaningful. More usually, however, repeated utterances are elaborated or recast in some way. Alastair Pennycook sees repetition in this sense as 'an act of difference' (Pennycook, 2007b, p. 580), and I have used the term 'recycling' above to break away from the idea of 'pure' repetition.

Immediate repetition – where a speaker repeats, and recasts, elements from an immediately prior turn – is common in the conversations analysed by Carter, Tannen, Coates and other researchers. The extract below, from Tannen's study, comes from an extended Thanksgiving dinner conversation at which Tannen was one of the guests. It is a short exchange between Deborah (Tannen) and Peter, another guest.

Context: Deborah and Peter have been discussing how, on first getting divorced, one wants to date many people (Peter and Deborah are both divorced, Peter recently and Deborah long since). Deborah then continues:

1	Deborah:	**Then you get bored**
2	Peter:	**We:ll, I think I got bored**
		[*Deborah laughs*]

3		Well I- I mean basically what I feel is
4		what I really LIKE, … is people.
5		And **getting to know them really well.**
6		And **you just CAN'T get to know**
7		… TEN people **REALLY WELL.**
8		**You can't do it.**

9	Deborah:	Yeah right.
10		You have to- **there's no-**
11		Yeah **there'[s no time**
12	Peter:	**[There's not time.**
13	Deborah:	Yeah … it's true.

(adapted from Tannen, 2007 [1989], p. 77)

Transcription conventions

the colon in 'We:ll' means that the word was extended

[*square brackets*] enclose descriptions of speech and other sounds

CAPITALS indicate emphasis

[shows the start of overlapping speech

instances of repetition, or near-repetition, are **emboldened**

In this extract I have used spacing to distinguish what Tannen sees as three verses: an opening, or theme setting (lines 1–2); a closing, or coda (lines 9–13); and a middle section that contains the main substance of the interchange, like the filling in a sandwich. Tannen notes that episodes within a larger conversation often take this form, bounded by repetition at the beginning and the end.

Tannen suggests that Peter's transformation of her statement from line 1 ('Then you get bored') into line 2 ('We:ll, I think I got bored') is an amusing comeback (to which she responds with laughter). The humour comes partly from the rhythm and pace of the utterance:

> [Peter] draws out 'well' and then utters 'I think I got bored' in a quick, sardonic manner. The humor derives from the fact that it is a repetition, the quickness of his utterance conveying, iconically, that the boredom I predicted he would eventually experience has already, quickly, overtaken him.

(Tannen, 2007 [1989], p. 77)

In the middle section, Peter expands on and explains his statement in line 2 about getting bored – namely, that you can't get to know several people well. This is structured by self-repetition. Lines 3 and 4 repeat a syntactic structure:

What I feel is

What I really like is

And all lines pick up a word or phrase from a previous line. This complex pattern of repetition is set out schematically in Figure 5.1.

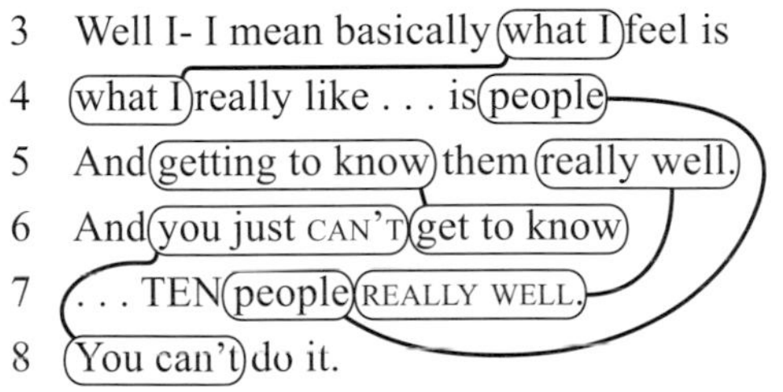

3   Well I- I mean basically what I feel is
4   what I really like . . . is people
5   And getting to know them really well.
6   And you just CAN'T get to know
7   . . . TEN people REALLY WELL.
8   You can't do it.

Figure 5.1   Repetition patterns in the middle section of a conversational episode (Tannen, 2007 [1989], p. 78)

Further repetition occurs in lines 9–13, when Peter and Deborah jointly construct the coda (see Chapter 1).

For Tannen, such patterns of repetition help to structure a conversation: they contribute to its coherence, for instance. But repetition also has an interpersonal function – it is a sign of interactional **involvement**, in which people participate actively in a conversation, engaging both with the conversation itself and with one another. Carter, similarly, argues that repetition enables conversationalists to 'converge their way of seeing things and to create a greater mutuality between them' (Carter, 2004, p. 102).

Apart from Peter's joking comment in line 2, the repetition here doesn't stand out or draw attention to itself in the same way as the pattern-reforming examples in Section 5.2, and it is unlikely it would be noticeable to participants in the conversation. Repetition may, however, also be used more artfully, as in the following example from a study carried out by Angela Goddard of online interactions between university students. In this extract, members of an online chat group greet a latecomer:

Laura>>   hey. sorry i am late, this is group nine isn't it?
RyanS>>   hi there
Laura>>   hello
RyanS>>   welcome

Rebecca>>	hello laura
RyanS>>	hi
Laura>>	hello
RyanS>>	hello laura
Laura>>	hello
Rebecca>>	hi
RyanS>>	h
Laura>>	hello
RyanS>>	.....
Rebecca>>	h
Laura>>	hello
RyanS>>	zzzzzz

(Goddard, 2011, pp. 146–7)

The repetition here is playfully exaggerated – people don't normally greet one another repeatedly. It has something in common with the pattern-reforming examples in Section 5.2, except that the greetings are an infringement not of linguistic rules but conventions of discourse, or language use. The episode is capped, again playfully, by Ryan's virtual snoring. Goddard refers to such playfully extended opening (and closing) routines (see Chapter 1) as a 'broken record' and notes that these are not uncommon in her online data.

The extract also points up the contextualised nature of this type of creative language. Goddard comments that, to appreciate such online discursive play, you really need to see it unfolding on the screen – it translates rather poorly into print. The material properties of texts – whether these are spoken (face-to-face, telephone, online) or written (on paper, handwritten or print; on a computer screen, or a wall; static or moving) – will affect how creative episodes work. Different materials – the stuff in which language is presented – offer certain **affordances**; that is, they enable certain practices and constrain others. Here they enable and constrain particular types of creativity.

Transforming words and worlds

In discussing the wordplay associated with pigeons, in Section 5.2, I suggested that the linguistic blends in *Al Capigeon* and *The godfeather* also playfully blended two worlds – of gangsters, and parks and pigeons – and that the play derived from the incongruity of this juxtaposition. Goddard's work includes similar examples in online discourse.

Activity 5.4

Allow about
10 minutes

Goddard comments that, in playing with language in online chat, the students in her sample often recycled, and sometimes transformed, other speakers' or writers' words. The box below includes several examples of this practice from a group of British students, along with extracts from Goddard's commentary. She notes that, as is common in online chat, the students often construct spatial metaphors in which virtual spaces in the chatrooms are represented as particular types of rooms or events.

- How well do you feel you understand what Devin and Ryan, Joanne and Glyn are saying?

- How helpful do you find Goddard's interpretation of these utterances?

Drawing on others' voices in online play

[T]here are constructions of pubs and bars ... : in [a mixed group of UK and Swedish students], one participant asks another whether she had been 'bounced' [i.e. thrown out] after finding herself suddenly outside of the chatroom; while in [a group of UK students], one male participant playfully challenges another to a virtual fight:

Sample 1:

RyanS>>   mr [name] are you threatenning me

Devin>>   Yes mr [name] that is exactly what i'm doing

RyanS>>   come on you and me outside

[...]

Sample 2:

Joanne>>   hello hello hello

This construction [in Sample 2] is difficult to explain, even to some speakers of English ... It is the voice of the stereotypical English village policeman, a stock figure from countless fictional portrayals in light comedy routines. Although the phrase is curiously antique, particularly coming from young speakers now, it is quite well suited to the cyberspace context. For it articulates a whiff of suspicion of

---

others and what they might be getting up to under cover of darkness (in other words, the invisibility of the online environment).

An equally 'antique' voice is used by a participant to express the disappointment of being stood up in a chatroom:

Sample 3:

Glyn>>   I came, I saw, and no one turned up

Phrases such as those in Samples 2 and 3 can be seen as classic pieces of refashioned cultural material, linguistic fragments which carry with them enough of a trace of their history of use to make them readily usable, but which also have sufficient vagueness to make them usefully plastic in their application.

(adapted from Goddard, 2011, pp. 144–5, but with original spelling and punctuation)

Comment

In Sample 1, the construction of a pub in the metaphorical space of the chatroom allows two participants to enact a playful fight that is rooted in stereotypical British pub culture, with its challenge of *you and me outside*. (This may also call up similar scenarios, such as going outside a house, or classroom, to fight.)

In Sample 2, again, the phrase *hello hello hello* has strong cultural associations. Goddard notes that it is the 'voice of the stereotypical English village policeman', which would be difficult for many non-British English speakers to understand. What you make of this will depend on your familiarity with the phrase itself, and with the fact that it is widely recognised as a stereotype – so, here, a playful send-up.

Sample 3 is a playful adaptation of the famous 'I came, I saw, I conquered', attributed to Julius Caesar after a brief but successful war in Asia Minor.

These phrases are not new recyclings. As Goddard comments on Samples 2 and 3, they are 'classic pieces of refashioned cultural material', often drawn on humorously. (As an illustration, try out an internet search on 'I came I saw'.) The students are likely to have come across previous recyclings, and in Samples 2 and 3 it is not clear how familiar they will be with the origins of either phrase. Goddard's interpretation of *hello, hello, hello*, therefore, may not reflect the meanings that Joanne or her fellow students would take from this phrase.

Goddard sees these utterances as examples of **intertextuality**, a term coined by Julia Kristeva (1986). The idea behind the term is that individual utterances, or texts, form part of a 'chain of speech communication'. They are inherently 'intertextual', made up of words and meanings from other texts. A clear example of this is when we cite others' words directly, as in *hello hello hello* and *I came, I saw* … But the argument is that, whenever we speak or write, we draw on words and meanings that we have encountered in prior utterances. In the examples of language use cited earlier, for instance, phrases such as *cutting edge*, *over the moon* and *pigs … moving across the sky* derive their associations from the same or similar phrases in previous contexts of use.

Kristeva was drawing on a model of language associated with literary theorist Mikhail Bakhtin, whom Goddard also refers to, and Bakhtin's idea of language as being 'polyphonic', or containing multiple **voices**, has proved particularly useful in the study of language play as well as literature (see box overleaf). When people reproduce voices (words, phrases, ways of speaking), they may also adapt them, and this adaptation, or transformation, may be a source of play. Transformation occurs on a linguistic level (as in puns and other forms of wordplay), but it may also involve the playful appropriation of alternative or fictional worlds with all their social or cultural associations (shifting gangster thuggishness to pigeons in parks, or pubs to virtual chatrooms). Sometimes play is transformative in another sense – I mentioned above that it often reinforces relationships between people, but that it may also serve to subvert or destabilise relationships, however fleetingly.

Goddard cites a well-known statement from Bakhtin:

> The word in language is half someone else's … Language … is populated – overpopulated – with the intentions of others.
>
> (Bakhtin, 1981 [1935], pp. 293–4)

'Intentions' here can be roughly glossed as 'meanings'. The point is that language brings meanings from other contexts – and other language users. These are taken up, but also refashioned, and imbued with particular meaning in the current context of use. Language play is a further creative, transformative intervention in this process of meaning making.

See discussions of collaborative storytelling in Chapter 1, literary allusion in Chapter 2 and formulaic language in Chapter 3.

A Bakhtinian model of language use

Bakhtin's ideas (e.g. 1981 [1935], 1984 [1929], 1986 [1953]) have been highly influential in the study of creativity in language and also, more broadly, in several areas of contemporary language study. Of particular relevance here is that Bakhtin sees language not as a unified whole, but as highly differentiated.

- Language itself is **heteroglossic** – it includes languages associated with particular social groups and contexts of use (e.g. the language used by different professional groups, by older people or younger people). There are often tensions and struggles between such languages or language varieties.

- At the level of particular utterances, too, language is **polyphonic** or **multi-voiced**: any utterance reproduces the 'voices' of other speakers and contexts of use. Words, phrases, discourses carry with them the 'taste' of these prior speakers and contexts. This is most obvious where speakers are actually quoted, but it permeates language use more generally – the words and phrases we routinely use will derive their associations from previous contexts of use.

- This process is necessarily evaluative: words and phrases bring with them certain sets of values and speakers may align themselves with these, as when someone is cited with approval, or dissociate themselves from them, as when an expression is cited ironically or a speaker or writer is parodied.

- Language use is dialogic, both in the sense that it addresses a particular person/people and a particular context, and in the sense that any utterance is a response to previous utterances, contexts or people.

Activity 5.5

Now turn to Reading A: *Penfriend poetics* by Janet Maybin. As you read, note down the main points made. Maybin discusses creativity in letter writing between US prisoners on death row and their penfriends in Britain. This is a very different context, and a different type of communicative practice, from those discussed by Tannen and Goddard, but the points Maybin makes are broadly consistent with this earlier discussion and should help you review your earlier work.

Comment

Like Goddard, Maybin draws on ideas from Bakhtin in her discussion of creativity. She sees this as a dialogic process, in which creative episodes are progressively developed by writers in response to one another, sometimes over a series of letters. Words, phrases, even whole poetic texts are recycled, extended, commented on and transformed.

Creative activity here both depends on and exploits the affordances of letter writing as a communicative practice. Maybin mentions, for instance, the importance of openings and closings – the preoccupation with delivery time and how this could provide a source for playful exchange; the invocation of an imaginary world to provide an 'upbeat' ending. People have time to think about their writing – maybe to consider their wording carefully, to add quotations and to include other texts, such as a prisoner's booklet of poems.

The letter-writers in Maybin's study are separated by time and space: 'all links and references, and all shared experience, have to be contained within the letters'. The spatial separation is similar to Goddard's electronic chat. There seems to be a much greater difference between the letter writing and the kind of face-to-face friendship talk discussed by Tannen, where people are chatting together over a meal. Maybin's emphasis, however, is similar to Tannen's in that she sees creative dialogue as contributing to mutual alignment (compare Tannen's idea of 'involvement') – in this case bringing together people who are physically separate and lead very different lives, strengthening their experience of friendship.

5.4 Cross-over creativity

[W]hen would Mickey Mouse write the Ramayana?

… When he was a 'Valmiki'.

(Amritavalli and Upendran, 2011, p. 103)

In previous sections I have focused on the use of various 'poetic' forms in English and on how English words and phrases may be creatively recycled and transformed. But most English speakers around the world make use of English alongside other languages, and often switch between languages. Even monolingual speakers may alternate between different varieties of English. Having access to more than one language or language variety offers further opportunities for creative uses of language, and the alternation between languages may itself be creative.

Chapter 1 of this volume shows bilingual speakers switching between languages in conversation. The phenomenon of codeswitching, and bilingual language use more generally, is addressed in a companion book in this series: Seargeant and Swann (eds) (2012).

The example above is a bilingual joke that involves wordplay between English and Hindi/Sanskrit. Valmiki is the fourth-century BC Hindu sage who is credited with writing the Ramayana. The humour here derives from a play with the similarity in sound between *Valmiki* and *Wall Mickey* – a poster of Mickey Mouse on the wall. The initial sound of *Valmiki* is known phonetically as a labio-dental approximant [ʋ]. This is similar to the initial sound of *wall* for many speakers of Indian English, so that the words are jokingly represented as homophones in this context.

The joke involves not only bilingual but also bicultural play, juxtaposing traditional Hindu and Western media cultures. The humour works only for those who share this bicultural understanding. This and similar jokes also serve as a means of displaying a hybrid, bicultural identity: both telling the joke and showing appreciation (in laughter) display familiarity with two cultural realms, allowing participants to identify as (English) educated while also pointing towards their Indian/Hindu identity.

Multilingual shop signs, advertisements and other textual displays form part of the urban linguistic landscape in many parts of the world, and these may also play on the resources of English and other languages. Figures 5.2 and 5.3, taken from research by Rama Kant Agnihotri and Kay McCormick (2010) again combine English and Hindi, here in Indian advertisements for Amul butter, displayed on street hoardings and also reproduced in newspapers and magazines, on TV and on the internet. Hindi is represented in Roman rather than Devanagari script, and Agnihotri and McCormick suggest that this, combined with the bilingual wordplay, targets an educated, middle-class audience, with the advertisements including 'references to popular films and celebrities or to indicators of a middle-class lifestyle' (Agnihotri and McCormick, 2010, p. 72). Recognising and appreciating the wordplay, as in the bilingual joke above, indexes a bilingual and bicultural middle-class Indian identity. (See Chapter 1 for a general discussion of language and social identity.)

Figure 5.2 Amul Butter: First class snack

Here, *Jumbo*, meaning a jumbo jet, or the adjective 'very large', is combined with the word *pav*, referring to a measure of weight (about half a pound) and a loaf of bread (associated with the famous Bombay *pav-bhaji*). In the image a small girl is trying to park a smiling, personified jet using slices of bread as parking placards. At the bottom right of the advertisement, Amul is qualified as a *first class snack*. Agnihotri and McCormick (2010, p. 73) suggest that the advertisement text plays on multiple meanings: 'In the most straightforward reading, "jumbo pav" would mean "a big sandwich"; it could also mean the biggest possible quarter, where pav is read as a weighing measure; it could also mean sandwiches that are served in the jumbo planes, perhaps only in first class.' They also argue that 'if it is the girl who has started eating the bread [in her hands], it would seem that she, too, regards it as a first-class snack' (Agnihotri and McCormick, 2010, p. 73).

Figure 5.3 Amul Butter: Bun, tea aur butterly

Here, the English/Hindi text, *Bun, tea aur butterly* 'simultaneously plays on a variety of texts from different domains – in particular, Bollywood. It reminds one of the famous and popular film *Bunti aur Babli*; the copy of the ad is written exactly in the same style as that in which the title of the film was published. The association is unmistakable, and even the marks that enclose *aur* ('and') are identical. The film was produced by Yash Chopra and starred Abhishek Bachchan, Amitabh Bachchan, and Rani Mukherjee – caricatures of all three actors appear in the hoarding. Abhishek is holding the bun with clearly visible Amul butter; Amitabh the tea; and Rani is, of course, the butterly part, which reminds one of the famous "utterly butterly" of Amul, as well as of "butterfly"' (Agnihotri and McCormick, 2010, p. 75).

Patricia Lamarre (2010) discusses French/English wordplay in a very different linguistic landscape: commercial signs in Montreal, Canada, such as the shop names *Chou Chou* (shoe shop), and *Très hot couture* (a fashion shop). *Chou* (literally 'cabbage') is used as a term of affection, either as a single word or in the reduplicated *chouchou*. *Hot* is a near pun with the French *haute* in *haute couture* and may also convey some of the contemporary associations of the term in English, such as new, exciting, sexually exciting. Lamarre terms such signs 'bilingual winks'. Like the Amul advertisements, they are playful, and draw attention to themselves, but she argues that they also need to be interpreted in the context of language policy in Quebec province, which is designed to protect the French language and ensure its visibility in public spaces. French is meant to be 'markedly predominant' over other languages, but blending English with French subtly challenges this stipulation.

The creative use of English alongside other languages is a recurrent theme in contemporary research on hip-hop, a well-known (and well-studied) global language practice. Alastair Pennycook (2007a), for instance, argues that, while hip-hop originated in the USA, it has been appropriated and reinvented in different local contexts. The use of English itself, while it may serve to connect rappers from different parts of the world, also allows them to index a variety of local meanings and local identities.

Lyrics from Too Phat – a Malaysian hip-hop group

If I die tonight, what would I do on my last day
I know I'd wake early in the morn' for crack of dawn's last pray
Then probably go for breakfast like I used to do
Fried kuey teow FAM and roti canai at Ruja's with my boo.

(cited in Pennycook, 2007a, p. 3)

Much of the imagery above is associated with local meanings. Pennycook comments on the reference to Muslim prayers at dawn, as well as to food – here Chinese and Indian food eaten at stalls for breakfast: 'fried kuey teow … is a popular dish of fried flat noodles, while roti canai … is Indian bread (roti) with canai or channa: boiled chickpeas in spicy sauce. With the even more specific reference to Ruja's, we are taken into the local world of Malaysia' (Pennycook, 2007a, p. 4). In hip-hop more generally, 'boo' is used as a term of familiarity, sometimes referring to girl- or boyfriend.

In a study of the Hong Kong hip-hop group Fama, Angel Lin (2011) illustrates their use of bilingual lyrics – a blend of Cantonese and English – which enables them to 'craft out' a hybridised Cantonese-English identity. Fama's two MCs (rappers) also draw on Cantonese and English in the 'art names' that they have crafted for themselves. A striking example is MC Six-wing, the art name of Luhk Wihng-Kuehn. Lin comments that, in Hong Kong, many young students have pet names or nicknames which are formed by playing on the bilingual features of their names. *Six-wing* represents an example of this cultural practice. The family name *Luhk* sounds the same as the word for 'six' in Cantonese, hence *Luhk Wihng* becomes *Six-wing*. The name is spelt out in the lyrics of the song '456 Wing':

俾支筆我寫歌詞 \<Give me a pen to write lyrics\>

我寫左幾萬字 \<I've written several thousand words\>
俾支咪我 \<Give me a mike to\> **Rap** 我好寫意! \<I'm very happy!\>
我叫做 \<I'm called\> **S-I-X-W-I-N-G, S-I-X-W-I-N-G, Sing!**

> (Lin, 2011, p. 59; English translations in angled brackets \< \> after Chinese originals; original English lyrics highlighted in bold text)

The letters here are rapped in characteristically Cantonese intonation:

$$S^6\text{-}I^6\text{-}X^1\text{-}W^1\text{-}I^2\text{-}N^6\text{-}G^1$$

Lin comments:

> Cantonese has six commonly used contrastive tones (marked 1–6) and each syllable must be marked with a tone … By rapping the spelling of his 'English' name (Six-wing) in a Cantonese tonal way, Six-wing has crafted out his bilingual identity in an innovative manner: in its segmental features, it is an English name, but in its suprasegmental features (tones and intonation), it sounds like a Cantonese name.

> (Lin, 2011, p. 59)

Activity 5.6

Now turn to Reading B: *TXTPL@Y*, an account by Ana Deumert of creativity in South African digital writing (text messaging (SMS), Facebook and an online discussion board). This has some similarities with the online discussion analysed by Angela Goddard (Section 5.3), but South Africa is a highly multilingual country. People therefore have a choice of languages and may also creatively blend English and other languages in their writing. What do you see as the main points that Deumert makes in the reading, and how do these relate to your study in this section – and indeed earlier in the chapter?

Comment

Deumert describes the considerable growth in access to mobile technology in South Africa. She points out that South African texters use a global English SMS standard, but also extend this, with a much heavier density of abbreviations and other texting forms. Deumert sees this as a localisation of global practices – a similar argument to that made by Pennycook (2007a) and Lin (2011) about language use in hip-hop in Malaysia and Hong Kong.

In a context in which most people have access to two or more languages, Deumert also points to the potential of 'multilingualism as a creative resource', giving several examples of playful combinations of English and isiXhosa, isiZulu and South African slang – again this echoes points made throughout this section. Deumert argues that English has also become a catalyst for creative innovations in local languages.

The playful flirting in digital spaces reminded me of speakers' and writers' blending of different worlds, discussed in Section 5.3. In the 'lalaby' example, Deumert suggests that alternating between languages also allows people to invoke different personae; and in the 'Romeo and Juliet' example, the writers blend a 'mock Elizabethan voice' with contemporary texting conventions.

In all cases, playful language is integral to the interaction; for example, drawn on to wish someone a happy birthday, comment on someone's inability to sleep, and discuss arrangements for dinner. For Deumert, as for other researchers discussed in this chapter, such creative linguistic practices exploit features associated with a particular communicative medium – here texting conventions, for instance. They are also embedded within particular sets of social relations, and allow writers to enact and sometimes play with different identities.

5.5   Conclusion

In the sections above I have discussed various ways in which English, on its own or in combination with other languages, may be used playfully, even artfully or poetically, by speakers and writers. Alongside the daily 'getting things done' of interaction with others, people also focus on what Roman Jakobson (1960) termed 'the message' for its own sake: paying attention to imagery and detail, playing with the structures and patterns of English, creatively adapting and refashioning earlier utterances, and sometimes blending the resources of English and other languages. Such practices, often seen in a highly developed form in literary language, are also more routinely prevalent in everyday spoken and written interaction. In this case, they may be seen as creative performances that stand out, however briefly, from the surrounding interaction.

Examples discussed in the chapter suggest that such creative performances are functional within everyday communication: for instance, imagery and detail contribute to the 'point' of a narrative, playful use of English attracts attention in an advertisement or adds emphasis to an expression in online chat. They are also socially, culturally and interpersonally embedded, both in the sense that they need to be understood within particular contexts of use, and that they contribute to the management of relations between people and the performance of particular identities; for example, balancing traditional and Western identities in the sharing of a bilingual pun.

In interactions between people, creativity is often associated with interpersonal involvement, alignment between speakers and the maintenance of informal, friendly relations. On the other hand, similar forms of language may serve to maintain, or subvert, differential power relations. Because it stands out, creative performance may serve to intensify or heighten the expression of interpersonal relations. The situation may also be more nuanced, however. For instance, humorous play with language or patterns of discourse may be a tease – pointing up a critique; it may align some people in the critique of others; it may take the edge off the critique; or it may be ambiguous – potentially serving any or all of these functions.

READING A: Penfriend poetics

Janet Maybin

Specially commissioned for this book.

Introduction

In this article, I bring together Bakhtin's (1981 [1935]) dialogic theory of communication with the idea that communication is full of creative forms of language – rhyme, imagery, wordplay and a range of figures of speech – which people use in constructing and pursuing relationships (e.g. Carter, 2004; Tannen, 2007). I examine a particular corpus of penfriend correspondences, focusing on the role of dialogicality and language creativity in letters between prisoners on death row in the United States and their penfriends in Britain. These correspondences provide an unusual, exclusive written record of relationships between pairs of people with very different backgrounds and life experiences who have never met, and who yet report building close friendships (Maybin, 2006). All links and references, and all shared experience, have to be contained within the letters which, therefore, provide a particularly rich site for examining dialogic dimensions of creativity.

My data comes from research into the experiences of 162 individuals, including fifty-nine prisoners, involved in death row penfriend correspondences, and the subsequent textual analysis of the beginnings of six correspondences (the first six to eight letters written by each individual involved, eighty letters in all; see Table 1 overleaf for key to participants). The letters were all written before the penfriends became involved in the research and gave me permission to analyse their correspondence. While it may seem unusual in this age of digital technology to focus on one of the oldest forms of written communication, letter writing still proves a remarkably versatile channel of communication, and a testament to human creativity, in contexts where other channels are limited or non-existent.

Table 1 Correspondences

Death row	Britain
Richard, 36*	John, 60, retired
Robert, 25	Kim, 29, housewife
Joe, 34, American Indian	Ruth, 50s, part-time teacher
Sam, 37, African American	Karen, 40s, freelance professional
Chris, 57	Patricia, 60s, freelance professional
Danny, 23	Meg, 60s, retired

* Names are pseudonyms. Ages are taken from the questionnaire responses. Respondents (Caucasian unless indicated) reported particularly valuing inter-ethnic friendships.

Cruise ships, friendship and freedom

As a genre, letters are distinctly structured by their beginnings and endings. Openings have to reactivate the contact and the relationship and penfriends often started their letters, after the salutation, by noting the date when they had received their correspondent's last letter, frequently including a calculation of the time it had taken to reach them. The delivery time is a matter of particular significance in a context where letters are sometimes read by prison authorities, can get delayed in the mail rooms and occasionally disappear. Especially in the early stages of a correspondence, writers were anxious to demonstrate that they had answered letters promptly, or to explain and apologise for any delay.

The business of dates and delivery times could also provide a source for playful exchange, as in the extracts below from correspondence between Richard and John. Richard and John frequently responded to each other's use of imagery and language play, sometimes producing dialogic riffs which extended across a number of letters. Here, the openings of their letters are orientated towards the particular contingencies of this correspondence context, but also illustrate, at this early stage of the friendship, the shared humorous dexterity with language which was to become a distinguishing feature of their written relationship. Both men have a number of other penfriends, whom they sometimes mention in their letters.

> Dear John, I received your 5/19 letter today, which confirms my suspicion that our overseas mail is sent by cruise ship. Margaret's

letters sometimes get to me in three days, but over a week both ways is usual.

(Richard, US, letter 3)

Dear Richard, ... if the USA can put people on the surface of the moon, it ought to be capable of sending mail round the world expeditiously, I suppose, though logic does not often enter into the often esoteric behaviour of bureaucratic government departments.

(John, Britain, letter 3)

Dear John, Thank you for your June 4th letter I received yesterday. Three days for mail to get to you, six days to me, the tail wind must blow from the US to the UK.

(Richard, letter 4)

Dear Richard, 'Par for the course', the transit time of your latest letter: PM Jackson 12. 6 AM England 16.6.

(John, letter 4)

The running joke, where the cruise ship becomes a metaphor for slowness, is collaboratively elaborated over four letters through its introduction (Richard, letter 3), a contrast with rocket science (John, letter 3), susceptibility to tail winds (Richard, letter 4) and the mock official note invoking the 'transit time' of a ship's cargo delivery (John, letter 4). In addition to illustrating the typically dialogic nature of penfriends' creative activity at the level of the text, as they pass words and images back and forth, this example also shows the progressive alignment which often emerged over a number of letters, as penfriends echoed and responded to each other. Here, Richard initiates the joke about the cruise ship in his third letter and extends it in his fourth, while John responds in letter 3 initially by a poke at the United States authorities and then, in letter 4, shifts more fully inside Richard's ship metaphor.

Letter closings have the difficult function of managing the rupturing of the connection, and of trying to ensure the continuation of the relationship over the space of time until the next letter arrives. Some penfriends said that the signing off was the first part of the letter they read, as the place where their penfriend's feelings towards them would be most explicitly expressed. As well as expressions of affection, the endings of letters often included references to their correspondent's intimate social circle, as penfriends began to create a shared network of social connections.

Sometimes letter-writers found creative ways of extending and elaborating this affirmation of their relationship, and its continuation, at the close of a letter. For instance, one British woman explained that she and her penfriend always concluded their letters with a written description of an imaginary hike or outing together, to a place they thought the other would enjoy (The Open University, 2006). This imaginary world, where they could walk side by side, provided an 'upbeat' ending, implying the continuation of the friendship beyond the bounds of the letter and creating a shared experience which could be revisited and reimagined while waiting for future letters to arrive.

Penfriends often introduced quotations in their letters, from poetry, newspaper articles or religious writings. A quotation then became the focus for an exchange of ideas and expressions of judgement across a number of letters, providing scope for the discussion of different interpretations and setting up a joint reference point for the letter-writers' interactive exploration of personal beliefs and value positions. Richard and John provide a particularly rich example of the ways in which quotations could be recontextualised, elaborated, commented on and transformed (omitted text is indicated by a series of dots ....):

> A co-worker told his mother who was worried about his health that he still goes fishing every Saturday. He told her the old prison saying; 'you can lock up our bodies, but you can't lock up our minds'.
>
> (Richard, letter 4)

> I cannot find the quote from Oscar Wilde about his spirit being free when his body was imprisoned, but at the close of his De Profundis he writes

All trials are trials for one's life just as all sentences are sentences of death.... Society, as we have constituted it, will have no place for me, has none to offer. But Nature, whose sweet rains fall on just and unjust alike, will have clefts in the rocks where I may hide, and secret valleys in whose silence I may weep undisturbed.....

(John, letter 4)

John goes on to quote a Bosnian cellist playing Albinoni's Adagio at the site of a mortar bomb massacre:

'My father was a Muslim like my grandfather. But my nationality is music. Music is universal' he says [...]. I like that '...my nationality is music'. It is almost on a par with my favourite quote, from Thomas Paine's The Rights of Man. 'My country is the world and my religion is to do good ...'.

(John, letter 4)

I love the quotes you send, and especially like Wilde's De Profundis quote. A popular version of it here goes: 'Nobody gets out of life alive'. I will also paraphrase the Bosnian cellist and Thomas Paine: My nationality is human, and my religion is friendship. Margaret sent me a quote from John Donne I had been looking for:

No man is an island each onto himself
Each is a part of the whole
Any man's death diminishes me
Ask not for whom the bell tolls, it tolls for me.

If possible, could you please check the punctuation and form of that poem for me. Margaret is a dear friend, but punctuation is not her forte.

(Richard, letter 5)

Here, a number of related images quoted from popular axioms, an essay, a newspaper and poetry are passed back and forth. The image of the mind being able to transcend imprisonment in the popular axiom from Richard (letter 4) is paralleled and elaborated by John (letter 4) in his quotations from Wilde, and the Bosnian cellist and Thomas Paine's comments about nationality and religion. These ideas about a larger, all-embracing humanity are neatly encapsulated and brought back to the correspondence context by Richard (letter 5) 'My nationality is human, and my religion is friendship', who then goes on to express his alignment with John, in terms of language expertise, using the contrast with Margaret to highlight the men's affinity. The use of quotation and metaphor across these three letters generates a rich range of intertextual resources for interactional work and facilitates the discussion of difficult topics like imprisonment, justice and death.

In the letters, whole poems, as well as poetic quotations, provided a shared communicative resource which could be drawn on and reinvoked. Some prisoners included poems written by themselves, either as enclosures or incorporated into the body of their letters, and these were invariably commented on by their correspondent. For instance, Joe, who was half Cherokee, sent his penfriend Ruth a booklet of poems he had written, with his first letter. A recurring motif in these poems was the dream of one day returning to his people: for example, 'I shall burst forth upon the world from behind mountains and trees/ To resume my life of liberty'. While Ruth thanked Joe for the poems in her second letter, she also invoked their imagery in her fourth letter: 'I imagine you to be a soul of the open spaces.' In her fifth letter, in the course of commenting on how his case was progressing, she referred to an image in one of his poems – 'I am like a bird in a cage' – in her comment: 'any intimation that the caged bird will fly free again makes me very happy'. Ruth's expression of hope regarding the outcome of Joe's case is intensified through a reference to the image of himself which Joe sent her right at the beginning of their correspondence. Ruth's response serves both to accept and value the feelings and identity that Joe presented in his poems, and also to mark the continuing, consistent nature of their relationship over time.

In contrast to Joe and Ruth, Sam and Karen's first twelve letters only included one poetic quotation from Karen (letter 4), to which Sam failed to respond. Sam, however, frequently used metaphor: for example, 'all my life I've ran against the wind so this struggle is nothing new to me' (letter 3); 'in my mind I can hear your voice' (letter 5). Karen also produced her own metaphors, especially as the correspondence got going: for example, 'you wouldn't let yourself be "bought"' (letter 5). She also, on two occasions, quoted Sam's metaphors back to him (the only occasions in which she quoted any language from his letters). For instance, in his fifth letter, Sam commented: 'it hurt me because they don't seem to care, or is it they forget how to care after so many years of pain' and Karen responded 'I suspect it's because it is one of their few pleasures after, as you say, "so many years of pain"' (letter 6).

This kind of progressive echoing and mutual alignment can also be found in the rhetorical device of three-part lists which appeared in many correspondences: for example, 'I write to you because sometimes I'm scared, and lonely, and I need a friend' (Danny, letter 4); 'I did not love, like or respect him' (John, letter 2). In some cases, the interactive use of these was very striking. For example, three-part lists were only used once each by Joe and Ruth in their first six letters, but this single reciprocal use coincided with the moment of 'opening up', which penfriends often reported experiencing once trust had been established in the correspondence. Opening up often involved the prisoner revealing details of their conviction, despite the fact that they were expressly instructed by their lawyers never to discuss this on paper. In her seventh letter Ruth wrote 'I am always your friend, now, tomorrow and for ever' and Joe's response included an answering three-part structure 'I was arrested and charged with murder, kidnapping and robbery.' While these two statements might not seem immediately connected at a literal level, the patterns of relationship found within the penfriend correspondences suggest that the structural echo signified a specific response: Ruth's strong expression of friendship prompted a disclosure from Joe which, if Ruth still accepted him as a friend, could take their relationship to a deeper level.

Conclusion

The penfriends' dialogic passing backwards and forwards of jokes, quotations, imagery and three-part lists, in the context of discussions ranging from the everyday to the deeply philosophical, illustrate how language play and creativity are inherently interactional and are enabled, shaped and limited by the writers' circumstances and by the affordances of a particular channel of communication: letter writing. Particular kinds of creative forms predominated in particular correspondence relationships, suggesting a kind of interactional convergence. Significantly, Robert and Kim's correspondence, where there was virtually no use of creative language at all, was not sustained beyond the first year. Since all these relationships were managed entirely by letter, in the early stages at least, I would argue that where the penfriends' use of language creativity met with a similarly creative response from their correspondent, the ensuing dialogic chains knitted together an emotionally and imaginatively intense shared discursive world which supported and strengthened both the paper correspondence and the penfriends' experience of friendship.

References for this reading

Bakhtin, M. (1981 [1935]) 'Discourse in the novel' in Holquist, M. (ed.) *The Dialogic Imagination: Four Essays by M. M. Bakhtin* (trans. C. Emerson and M. Holquist), Austin, TX, University of Texas Press.

Carter, R. (2004) *Language and Creativity: The Art of Common Talk,* London and New York, Routledge.

Maybin, J. (2006) 'Death row penfriends: configuring time, space and self', *Auto/Biography*, vol. 21, no. 1, pp. 58–69.

Tannen, D. (2007 [1989]) *Talking Voices: Repetition, Dialogue and Imagery in Conversational Discourse*, Cambridge, Cambridge University Press.

The Open University (2006) Recorded interview in E301 *The art of English*, Study Guide 1 'The art of English: everyday creativity', Unit 9, CD-Rom Band 23 'Death row penfriends', Milton Keynes, The Open University.

READING B: TXTPL@Y. Creativity in South African digital writing

Ana Deumert

Specially commissioned for this book.

New spaces for literacy: the South African context

In a recent publication, de Bruijn et al. (2009) describe mobile phones as the 'new talking drums of Africa', a quintessentially modern communication technology which is appropriated and adapted to local everyday realities. The growth of mobile access in Africa has been remarkable during the last decade: while in 2000 only one in fifty Africans had access to mobile technology, the figure is now close to one in two. South Africa – followed by Kenya and Nigeria – has the highest user rates in sub-Saharan Africa: over thirty million South Africans (between 70 and 80 per cent of the population) are regular users of mobile phones. Among the youth in particular, mobile phones have opened up new spaces for the creative and playful leisure literacies associated with friendship and affection/love/desire. These include txting/SMSing and mobile chatting, as well as social network applications such as Facebook. The linguistic practices associated with these media are transient and in flux: new forms and variants occur regularly, and norms are continuously changing.

In South Africa, English exists in a multilingual environment. The majority of South Africans are multilingual, with English being just one of their two or more languages. A much smaller group is monolingual in English only. English, although spoken as a home language by less than 10 per cent of South Africans, is dominant in the public sphere and education and is strongly associated with technology, and is thus the dominant language of digital writing. Nevertheless, multilingual users regularly employ their other language(s) in this domain. This article provides a brief overview of South African digital (leisure) writing from a perspective of language creativity.

Creative transformations of the global English SMS standard

Digital writing, or txtspeak, is a non-standard form of writing. It is highly dynamic and creative, characterised by orthographic strategies such as letter omissions and substitutions. Both monolingual and bilingual South African txters are well versed in what has been called a 'global English SMS standard' (Deumert and Masinyana, 2008) or an 'international [English] text-messaging medialect' (McIntosh, 2010). However, unlike their peers in the Global North, South African txters appear to have extended the norms of usage, and employ this new orthography at higher frequencies. Visitors from especially the US have commented on what they see as an unusual, abbreviation-heavy communication practice, a distinctly Southern African form of txting. A US exchange student to South Africa commented as follows:

> My first text message from a boy from Zimbabwe read: *hw ws the rest of ur nyt? only gt hme @ 6- im hurtng. Wnt 2 grab breakfst wit me 2mrw mrning? Wil cal u l8r wit details.* I have never seen this style of texting from any American and after asking my friends, apparently this is how they text message here.
>
> (*Linguistics Research Journal*, University of Cape Town, 2010)

Quantitative analysis supports this view. Figure 1 compares (naturalistic) English-language SMS corpora from South Africa and the UK. South African txters use noticeably higher frequencies of txt variants – which users described as indexing informality and strengthening friendship bonds – across a range of orthographic variables (see Mesthrie and Deumert, forthcoming, for further discussion). South African txting practices constitute a form of localisation in the sense of Pennycook (2007) and Blommaert (2010). Rather than a mere replication or mimicking of usages found elsewhere, South African txting shows how globalised practices are re-enacted and modified in local environments.

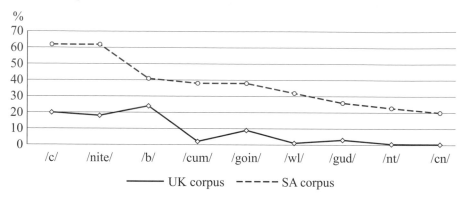

Figure 1 Comparative quantitative analysis of South African and UK SMS data: percentage of text variants for nine English lexical items (*see, night, be, come, going, will, good, not, can*). The SA corpus was collected at the University of Cape Town in 2008 and includes 2269 text messages sent by 110 undergraduate students. The UK corpus, called CorTxt, was collected between 2004 and 2007 and includes 11,067 text messages sent by 251 individuals (see Tagg, 2009, for further details).

Mixing and switching: multilingualism as a creative resource

Being multilingual means that South African txters have more linguistic resources than English-only txters when expressing themselves in the digital domain. This is illustrated in Example (1) below, which shows extracts from a typical Facebook routine: wishing a friend *happy birthday* by posting a message on their 'wall' – a publicly visible space on the user's profile page – is as much an important social ritual as it is an opportunity to display one's linguistic creativity. In this case the participants alternate between various English orthographies, as well as between English, isiXhosa (one of South Africa's indigenous languages) and local South African slang. English material (also in the examples below) is unmarked, isiXhosa is in italics and slang is emboldened.

(1)   Hapi bday *ntömbazana* ('girl', correct spelling *ntombazana*) *mini emandi kuwe* ('a nice day to you')

Hapi vday

hapi brn dae swti

enjoy every minute and every hour, Happi Birthday!

hapee-hav a supa day

♥ HaPpi Be$dae swts♥….paRt¥ lyK a rock¤ stAr.

Happy bday cuz. Enjoy u it 2 da fullest bt dnt go overboard, *hay sana niyakhula* **maan** ('hey baby you are really growing up', correct spelling *hayi*)

Hapi befdae lil'cuz!

Mchana *yayaz* **mos** ('girlfriend you know of course', correct spelling *uayayazi*) ..hapi bdae **ntwana** yam ('my buddy')

eppy birfdae. Nw *asfuni wena sfuni parti* ('we don't want you we want the party', correct spelling *asifuni wena sifun' iparty*)

(Facebook, 2010, wall postings)

Contact with English txting has been a catalyst for creative innovations in local African languages. (1), for example, includes several instances of non-standard orthographic modifications of isiXhosa, reflecting spoken, colloquial pronunciations. Indigenous digital writing also makes use of a limited but growing number of conventionalised abbreviations (such as, for example, *klk* for *kaloku*, an isiXhosa discourse marker, *CC* for *sisi*, an affectionate form of address for female friends) and the light-hearted translation of salient English abbreviations. Thus, ROFL ('rolling on the floor with laughter') now occurs as GPY in multilingual conversations (*giligidi phansi yintsini*, 'falling down with laughter'; the abbreviation is used in both isiXhosa and isiZulu, two closely related South African languages). Examples (2), (3) and (4) come from an online discussion board, where viewers were talking about the local soap opera *Generations*. The conversation and its humour are decidedly local: Example (2) includes two very typical South African exclamations (*eish, tjo*) as well as reference to a popular and jocular song (*Mama Themba's Wedding*); the *Mahotela Queens* in Example (3) are a band who play traditional *Mbaqanga* music (a type of South African jazz) and dress in an outrageous style, mixing modern and traditional fashion items in deliberately incongruous ways. Example (4) is a direct response to (3), celebrating the creative invention of GPY.

(2)   Eish he has this horrible shirt tjo it makes him look like he will sing Mama Thembi is getting married here tonight. I love his character though. GPY!!!! (posted 6 July 2010)

(3) I GPY, when i saw tht, she looked like Mahotela queens …
     LOL (posted 7 July 2010)

(4) Wagagagagagagagagagagagagagagagagaga GPY to the power
     infinity! (posted 7 July 2010)

> (examples taken from TVSA – The South African TV Authority, 2010)

A fine romance: flirting online

New media are centrally involved in the maintenance of our intimate
relationships. Flirting, in particular, has often been associated with txting
and other digital spaces (such as chatrooms and, more recently,
Facebook). McIntosh (2010, p. 343) notes in her discussion of txting
among the Giriama (Kenya) that '[b]ound up with the playful, flexible,
fleet, and future-directed personae of these messages is another figure:
that of the flirt'. This creates specific forms of intimate literacy, new
versions of the old genre of the 'love letter' (Wys, 2008) and classic
epistolary writing.

Playfulness is an integral element of the practice of flirting. In flirting,
we make sexual and romantic innuendos, keep the other guessing about
our actual wishes and intentions. It is a communicative game which
requires cooperation to keep up the momentum of pretence and
imagination – a quintessentially creative and unpredictable type of
interaction, where meaning is always ambiguous. Such playful
interactions are common during courtship as well as between close
friends who are not necessarily real or even potential lovers. The
conversation in Example (5) below starts with a Facebook status update
– a feature which allows users to let their friends know what they are
currently thinking, feeling or doing – from A around midnight. B, C
and D comment in the early hours of the morning.

(5) A   *Akulaleki* ('It's difficult to sleep'), cn u please sing md a
          lalaby nd i wil buy u chocolate 2m0ro. Gud nyt

     B   *Lala lala baby musa ukulila umama uyeza nobisi.* ('Sleep sleep
          baby, do not cry, mama is coming with milk')

     A   Oh thank u B, *unqabile kwezi ncuku* ('you are scarce these
          days', correct spelling *ntsuku*)

     B   *Ndikona* A. ('I am around')

     C   eish *mina* ('myself') i cnt sing bt i cn do smthng tht cn make
          u sleep icely..

     D   @C what is dat?

     C   cnt tel bt i cn do it..

     A   @C, wats dat my love?

A   Why u cnt tel hun? ;(
C   u rily wana knw A?
A   Yes please. I beg u
C   Wil massage u slwly n nicely n er…u knw wat else..y u nt slpn?
A   Am thinkin abt u, nd u hun, why u nt slpn?
C   M at wrk love, wrkn nytshft…
A   K. I c, *usebenze kahle*! ('good luck with the work')
C   Thank u my lovey

(Facebook, 2009)

English idioms of romance – disseminated through literature, popular music and movies – constitute an important script for the playful performance of flirtation and desire. In this case alternation between languages is linked to quite different personae: B, enacting an isiXhosa lullaby, draws on traditional images of motherhood and childhood; C, on the other hand, engages in playful sexual innuendo and teasing using a txt version of English.

Example (6) is an SMS exchange between Zoleka and Thami, two South African university students in their twenties. In this exchange, they artfully articulate a 'mock Elizabethan voice', simultaneously demonstrating (a) their familiarity with the English canon of literary writing (Shakespeare's *Romeo and Juliet*, *Macbeth*), and (b) their ability to recontextualise this canon in medium-appropriate ways (using typical txting conventions; see Deumert and Masinyana, 2008). The dialogue transforms high culture into a flirtatious and imaginary game of one-upmanship between two lovers, who are simultaneously engaged in negotiating the real-life practicalities of meeting up and having dinner together.

(6)   Wherefore out thou… Ahem… Where are u? (Zoleka)
        Is this an sms from my oh-so-dear Julietta I see before me? I am here at last, my luv! What shalt thou cookest for thy sweet Romeo whenfore he visitest u? (Thami)
        So, how's the univsty? There is a bottle of merlot and tofu waiting 4 u. How is ur schedulele? I have 2 c u my everlasting luv… hehaheha. (Zoleka)
        Ur luv guzzling ale at expensive and pretensious but ugly place :-(. No castle here :-)! My gold coins disapearring by the minute!

> With some friends now; they wana come.. They want *die wyn* ['the wine'] Can't get rid of them — out out damned spot! Hahehaha. Or do you wana cum ova rather? Let me knw. (Thami)
>
> Oh Romeo wat u doin there! U r livin large! Wud luv 2 but my minister of transi ('transport') is absent. U guys can take a cab. when do i c u? (Zoleka)

While interactions which fall within the genre of flirtation are commonly conducted in English, 'serious love' is preferably articulated in African languages, without attempts at abbreviation or code-mixing (similar to the contribution by B in (5)). English not only evokes associations of flirtation, but also dramatises a persona that is easy-going, free and uncommitted. IsiXhosa, on the other hand, emphasises the seriousness of 'real love', respect, commitment and obligations to the other. When asked about the difference in meaning between *I love you* and its isiXhosa equivalent (*ndiyakuthanda*) in online interactions, a multilingual (male) teenager responded:

> *Xa esithi* I love you its like *uyamthanda* as a friend or something but *undiyakuthanda* like *ngesiXhosa* it's like *ufuna* **sijole** *kunzima ke ukutsho uba* okay *kufuneka* **sijolile** (Cape Town, 2009)
>
> (When a person says *I love you, it's like* you love them *as a friend or something, but* when you talk love in isiXhosa *it's like* you want a serious relationship, that's more complex, you want a love relationship)

The languages thus derive much of their meaningfulness from their juxtaposition and associated language ideologies: English as the marker of modernity and change, African languages as the carriers of traditional norms and values (see also McIntosh, 2010).

Conclusion: globally inspired, locally meaningful

Txtspeak is emblematic of the modern, ludic self: youthful, unconstrained and endlessly playful. In multilingual settings such as South Africa, multilingual users have more than one language on which they can draw in creating a wide range of online identities: playful or serious, as well as many shades in between.

When studying digital language in contexts where access to phones, the internet and literacy has less time-depth than in the Global North, one needs to be aware that practices are often in flux. When we first studied

Time-depth refers to the amount of time a phenomenon (here literacy, the internet) has existed in a particular place. The concept is discussed more fully in a companion book in this series: Seargeant and Swann (eds) (2012).

isiXhosa txting in 2007 (published as Deumert and Masinyana, 2008), there was no indication that isiXhosa was ever abbreviated and the two languages were treated in a strictly asymmetrical manner. A year later we encountered the first abbreviations and today forms such as *CC* and *klk* (see above) are increasingly common, as are the non-standard orthographic practices illustrated in Example (1). Careful attention to context, time and space is therefore central when studying digital writing as a new type of leisure literacy which is deeply embedded in (global) technological innovations and creatively engages local and global practices in ever-shifting constellations in the negotiation and articulation of friendship and intimacy.

References for this reading

Blommaert, J. (2010) *The Sociolinguistics of Globalization*, Cambridge, Cambridge University Press.

De Bruijn, M., Nyamnjoh, F. and Brinkman, I. (eds) (2009) *Mobile Phones: The New Talking Drums of Everyday Africa*, Leiden, African Studies Centre.

Deumert, A. and Masinyana, O. (2008) 'Mobile language choices – the use of English and isiXhosa in text messages (SMS), evidence from a bilingual South African sample', *English World Wide*, vol. 29, pp. 117–47.

McIntosh, J. (2010) 'Mobile phones and Mipoho's prophecy: the powers and dangers of flying language', *American Ethnologist*, vol. 37, pp. 337–53.

Mesthrie, R. and Deumert, A. (forthcoming) 'Contact in the African area' in Hickey, R., Nevalainen, T. and Traugott, E. (eds) *Rethinking the History of English*, Oxford, Oxford University Press.

Pennycook, A. (2007) '"The rotation gets thick. The constraints get thin": creativity, recontextualization, and difference', *Applied Linguistics*, vol. 28, no. 4, pp. 579–96.

Seargeant, P. and Swann, J. (eds) (2012) *English in the World: History, Diversity, Change*, Abingdon, Routledge/Milton Keynes, The Open University.

Tagg, C. (2009) 'A Corpus Linguistics Study of SMS Text Messaging', Unpublished PhD Thesis, University of Birmingham.

TVSA – The South African TV Authority (2010) [online], http://www.tvsa.co.za/default.asp?blogname=generationsteasersandArticleID=14617 (Accessed 4 November 2010).

Wys, E. L. (2008) 'From the bridal letter to online flirting: changes in text type from the nineteenth century to the internet era', *Journal of Historical Pragmatics*, vol. 9, pp. 225–54.

6 Persuasion in English

Guy Cook

With grateful acknowledgement to Sarah North for input on earlier drafts of this chapter.

6.1 Introduction

A girl pesters her father to buy another ice cream. A teacher exhorts his pupils to pay more attention. Pickets ask other workers to join the strike. Advertisers set out to boost sales. An activist drums up support for a new political movement. A lawyer argues for the innocence of the accused. A scientist marshals evidence for a new theory. A politician asks people to vote for her. An evangelist seeks to convert his audience. A blogger posts her ideas on the internet.

Figure 6.1 The Reverend Jesse Jackson speaks at an AIDS rally in New York, circa 1992.

These examples all involve persuasion. It would be easy to add others, because persuasion is everywhere in human communication. It happens at every stage of life, and in every kind of encounter, from the most intimate to the most public.

This ubiquity is hardly surprising. Humans are social animals and need to work together in groups of all sizes: family, tribe, nation, international bodies. But we are also independent thinkers with differing and often conflicting ideas. We are assertive, often aggressively so, wanting others to share our views and behave the way we would like them to. Sometimes this constant attempt to influence others can have benefits for all, bringing out the best ideas and solutions, and allowing influence to be achieved in more civilised ways than through the use of brute force. At other times and in the wrong hands it can be used to whip up irrationality and violence.

Just as with any other language, persuasion is a major part of what we do with English. Understanding persuasion is therefore an essential part of your exploration of the 'worlds of English'; it permeates all the uses of English, whether old or new, formal or informal, playful or utilitarian, juvenile or adult. We find it every time we speak to others, switch on a TV or computer, or read a newspaper or book. This pervasiveness is reflected in the large number of English verbs which denote one aspect of persuasion or another; for example: 'advise', 'argue', 'beg', 'beseech', 'blackmail', 'bribe', 'cajole', 'charm', 'coax', 'coerce', 'convince', 'entice', 'entreat', 'flatter', 'implore', 'inveigle', 'plead', 'recommend', 'seduce', 'sway', 'sweet-talk', 'urge', 'wheedle', 'win over'.

Persuasion begins very early in life, well before the point when infant behaviour starts to diverge into different cultures and languages. A baby's first sounds are instinctive, expressing inner states involuntarily: hunger, discomfort, tiredness or fear. But this involuntary expression soon merges into deliberate strategies to change the behaviour and attitudes of others (see Chapter 3). The baby begins to seek attention deliberately. She or he cries *in order* to be fed, entertained or reassured. She or he uses signals artificially, to manipulate, to control, to persuade. And with that, communication in all its cultural diversity begins to be layered on initial instincts. At this early stage it is not language but sound and body movement which are used to persuade. When the infant does start to speak, however, these other channels of communication are not replaced by language. They work alongside it, and for this reason are known in linguistics as 'paralanguage' from the Greek *para*, meaning 'alongside' (see also Chapter 1).

Paralanguage figures prominently in persuasion throughout life, even when language has become the most potent implement in the adult's communicative toolkit. Adults can still use tears, smiles and raised voices to get their way, and sometimes such behaviour is more important and more effective than what they actually say. Saying 'Nice to see you' in a morose way is likely to be less convincing than using body language which communicates an overall feeling of connection and warmth. This chapter concentrates mostly on the language of persuasion rather than the paralanguage. But we should not forget that in influencing others, much more is involved than just words. This is true of public as well as personal persuasion, especially perhaps in political and commercial spheres. Think of rallies and parades which incorporate colour, music, rhythmic chanting, banners and hierarchical processions. To take an extreme example, such features played a key role in the Nazi rallies which helped Hitler promote his racist programme of military expansionism. Or, closer to our own time and concerns, think of the extensive use of emotive music and images in advertising. In such examples, language may seem to play only a partial role. Nevertheless, it is through language that persuasion takes on its most complex forms.

Persuasion, then, is of great academic interest in the study of any language as it is one of language's major uses. It is also of great personal concern to all of us. We all have a vested interest in promoting our own wishes and views – hopefully in the belief that they are of benefit to others as well as ourselves – and in understanding how others are trying to influence us, and thus in resisting malign manipulation.

This chapter explores different forms, purposes and effects of persuasion through consideration of examples from a variety of contexts and media. As such, it will add to the repertoire of ideas you can draw on in analysing spoken and written discourse. We deal first with examples of persuasion in the public sphere, and from there move on to its use in more personal encounters. In a final section we look briefly at how persuasive language can be evaluated.

Activity 6.1

The photo in Figure 6.2 was taken in September 2010, during a rally by the Free Burma Coalition outside the embassy of Myanmar (Burma) in Manila. Who are the demonstrators trying to persuade? What means are they using to do this?

Allow about 5 minutes

Figure 6.2   Free Burma Coalition rally, Manila, September 2010

Comment

You might think that the demonstrators are trying to persuade the
Myanmar government, but in this case, why are they using English rather
than Burmese? It seems more likely that they want to influence world
opinion to bring pressure on the Myanmar government, and for this
purpose, English has more chance of carrying their message effectively
around the world. Their verbal messages are accompanied by
paralanguage, including raised fists and raised voices. The placards
include visual images that symbolise the struggle against political
repression, and use colour both to highlight particular words and to
provide a uniform background to the different slogans. Finally, the mere
fact that the demonstrators have all banded together at the same time
and place is also part of their persuasive strategy; a single demonstrator
is unlikely to make so much of an impact.

6.2   Classical rhetoric

One indication of the importance of persuasion is that its study has a
very long history, predating modern linguistics and discourse analysis by
many centuries. In Europe, enquiry into **rhetoric** – the art of
persuasion – dates back at least to the fourth century BC, and was
energetically pursued first in Ancient Greece and then in Ancient Rome.
There are also traditions from outside Europe, such as Indian rhetoric,

dating from the fifth century BC, and Buddhist debating, formalised by the sixth century AD, but in this chapter we will focus predominantly on Graeco-Roman ideas.

The early studies of rhetoric had the very practical purpose of teaching people how to construct and execute a convincing and effective case, and they arose in two institutional contexts which are still with us today: adversarial law and political campaigning. The most systematic and influential early formulation of the principles of rhetoric was Aristotle's *Ars Rhetorica* (*The Art of Rhetoric*) composed during the fourth century BC, probably in Athens.

Some scholars, such as Vickers (1998), have argued that it is no coincidence that an interest in rhetoric emerged in Athens at the same time as democracy (albeit a 'democracy' limited to male citizens and excluding women and slaves). In this political system, where decisions were taken through votes in the Athenian marketplace, it was necessary for the proponents of a policy to win over their fellow citizens. A view or a decision could not simply be imposed through force or by unchallenged authority, as it was in some other Greek city states. Where government is through consent and agreement, persuasion takes on a new importance. Thus, rhetoric and democracy are perhaps necessarily linked. We might wonder whether a society without a forum for open and equal debate between opposed views, or where political contenders do not present substantial alternatives, can be classed as a democracy.

Ancient rhetorical theory and practice was much preoccupied with categorising rhetorical types, purposes and devices. While some of its finer distinctions became quite arcane, its broader categories are still useful, and form the basis of the study of rhetoric, today – suggesting that perhaps, despite all the intervening changes in societies over the last two and a half thousand years, the techniques of persuasion have remained essentially the same.

Contrasting persuasive strategies

We can gain insight into contrasting persuasive techniques, as they were characterised in rhetorical theory, by considering two famous speeches from Shakespeare's *Julius Caesar*. Although this play was written over 400 years ago about events 1500 years earlier, its central event dramatises two approaches to persuasion still highly relevant today.

The situation is as follows. Caesar's personal power has grown and he is seen as a threat to Roman republicanism and democracy. (Similar

concerns are levelled in our day at leaders from Moscow to Harare.)
A combination of public motives and private jealousies leads a group of
senators to conspire in assassinating Caesar, but they fail to plan fully
for the aftermath of that violent action. They are unprepared for the
power vacuum which follows Caesar's death, and the key role in it of
persuasive language (or, as we might say, 'spin'). After the assassination,
the conspirators face a 'multitude, beside themselves with fear'
(Shakespeare, 1955 [1599/1623], Act III, Scene I, line 180), and need to
win public opinion over to their cause.

Two speeches to the crowd decide the course of events. The first is by
Brutus, the most respected and influential of the conspirators, a man
who would have had high ratings for trustworthiness in Roman opinion
polls, had they existed, and who apparently acted out of genuine
concern for the public interest rather than out of jealousy or personal
interest.

Brutus adopts a particular strategy to win over the crowd. His speech is
calm, balanced and factual. He lists Caesar's vices, but also his virtues.
He gives reasons for and against the murder, explaining why, when he
weighed them up, he decided regretfully to join the conspiracy:

> As Caesar loved me, I weep for him; as he was fortunate, I rejoice
> at it; as he was valiant, I honour him: but, as he was ambitious,
> I slew him. There is tears, for his love; joy, for his fortune;
> honour, for his valour; and death, for his ambition.

> (Act III, Scene II, lines 25–9)

The crowd listen respectfully to this measured prose, and seem
reassured, although there is a gasp when Caesar's protégé Mark Antony
appears during Brutus's speech, bearing Caesar's bloody corpse.

The second speech is by Antony, left alone with the crowd. Brutus has
allowed this out of a sense of fair play, on condition only that Antony
should not 'blame us', but it proves a fatal mistake. Antony is
determined to turn the crowd around, against Brutus. He adopts a quite
different approach, and his speech is presented in resonant rhythmic
verse. He begins with the famous, apparently democratic opening of
'Friends, Romans, countrymen, lend me your ears', professes

understanding of the killers' motives and praises Brutus as 'an honourable man' (Act III, Scene II, lines 75, 84). But he is also apparently distraught, so overcome with grief for Caesar that he breaks off at one point to weep:

> Bear with me.
> My heart is in the coffin there with Caesar,
> And I must pause till it come back to me.

> (Act III, Scene II, lines 107–9)

Then, gradually, skilfully, eloquently, with vivid and emotive imagery, he turns both his meaning and the crowd around, while at the same time denying his intention to do so, talking, in a phrase still used by twenty-first century politicians, about influencing 'hearts and minds':

> O masters! if I were dispos'd to stir
> Your hearts and minds to mutiny and rage,
> I should do Brutus wrong, and Cassius wrong,
> Who, you all know, are honourable men.
> I will not do them wrong; I rather choose
> To wrong the dead, to wrong myself and you,
> Than I will wrong such honourable men.

> (Act III, Scene II, lines 123–9)

Thus 'honourable' comes to mean the opposite of what it did, and the word here lends itself to being interpreted as sarcastic.

Antony has more than words in his persuasive armoury, however; his tactics are visual as well as verbal. He makes good use of paralanguage and exploits his props: his own grief-stricken appearance, Caesar's bleeding body and, lastly, a mysterious document which he waves at the crowd (rather as the British Prime Minister Chamberlain did after meeting Hitler in Munich in 1938), without actually showing anybody what it contains.

Figure 6.3 Marlon Brando as Antony in *Julius Caesar*

Figure 6.4 British Prime Minister Neville Chamberlain waving document in Munich, 1938

> But here's a parchment with the seal of Caesar;
> I found it in his closet; 'tis his will.
> Let but the commons hear this testament,
> Which, pardon me, I do not mean to read,
> And they would go and kiss dead Caesar's wounds,
> And dip their napkins in his sacred blood,
> Yea, beg a hair of him for memory

(Act III, Scene II, lines 130–6)

It is supposedly Caesar's will, which Antony implies leaves lavish legacies to the people of Rome. By adding this appeal to greed, Antony has the crowd now completely in his hands. Brutus and his accomplices are forced to flee. Antony and his allies take power. The persuasive power of emotion has triumphed over reason.

Allow about 20 minutes

Activity 6.2

These two speeches by Brutus and Antony encapsulate two opposite approaches to persuasion and two ways of relating to an audience. How would you summarise the key differences between them? Can you think of any modern examples of these approaches?

Comment

One strategy is to set out, as clearly and objectively as possible, the evidence and the reasons for holding a point of view, but let the audience decide. It implies an optimistic, respectful view of public opinion, although it can be open to charges of smugness and political naivety. The other strategy is an appeal to emotion and self-interest, clouding the listeners' judgement and reason, and skilfully manipulating them into agreement. This second strategy implies a lack of respect and low opinion of the audience, seeing them as ignorant, uncritical and easily swayed, but it can be presented by its proponents as realistic and necessary.

In the modern media, newspapers provide good examples of both approaches to rhetoric. Broadsheet newspapers, such as *The Guardian* in the UK, *The Washington Post* in the USA or *The Times of India*, typically appeal to reason, while tabloids such as *The Sun* in the UK, *The National Enquirer* in the USA or *MiD DAY* in India, typically appeal to emotion. The media provide many other examples of these approaches that you might also have identified.

Rhetorical styles and strategies

These contrasting approaches reflect categorisations of rhetoric which were widely accepted in both Caesar's and Shakespeare's time. Aristotle's *The Art of Rhetoric* (e.g. 1991) distinguishes three strategies of persuasion:

- reasoned proof (*logos*)
- emotional appeal (*pathos*)
- appeal to the good reputation of the speaker (*ethos*).

Logos, *pathos* and *ethos* are still the basis of prevalent types of persuasion today. Thus, modern science aspires to carry a point by *logos* alone. Many charity advertisements use *pathos* when exhorting people to give money – appealing to emotion with pictures of disaster victims, for example (although this is not to say that there are not also rational reasons to give them money). Advertisements using endorsement, whether by a celebrity or an authority figure, use *ethos* – working on the principle that people will transfer their trust or admiration for the speaker to the product itself.

Other useful categories formulated in ancient rhetoric concern the style of persuasion. Is its use of language grand, or plain, or somewhere in between? Does it seek to overwhelm its hearers, or to be sparse and economical, or to create a perfect balance between the two? And what are its purposes: to judge past events (as in law), to determine the course of future events (as in politics), or for ceremony (as in a wedding speech or funeral oration)?

These categories are well illustrated by Brutus and Antony. Both seek to influence the opinion and behaviour of the crowd; both rely on their own good reputations. Brutus, however, attempts reasoned proof, presented economically, whereas Antony appeals to emotion, seeking to overwhelm his hearers, while all the time professing the opposite:

> I come not, friends, to steal away your hearts.
> I am no orator, as Brutus is,
> But (as you know me all) a plain blunt man
>
> (Act III, Scene II, lines 218–20)

While Brutus speaks in a grand style, Antony affects a plain style, although his speech is in fact very carefully crafted. Brutus deliberates on what has happened and urges the crowd to support him. Antony appears to be speaking only ceremonially, but turns his funeral oration into an incitement.

Within classical rhetoric, a good deal of attention was paid to rhetorical figures and devices which could be used by the successful speaker. One of these – the so-called **rhetorical question** – simulates dialogue by taking an interrogative form, but does not expect a response, either because the answer is too obvious or because the speaker proceeds to answer the question him- or herself. 'You ask, what is our aim? I can answer that in one word: victory', said Winston Churchill in one of his wartime speeches, delivered in the House of Commons in May 1940 (*Collins Dictionary of Quotations*, 2003). Repetition is also an obvious, well-known and apparently effective rhetorical figure. Martin Luther King's famous 1963 address to Civil Rights marchers at the Lincoln Memorial, contains no fewer than eight ringing reiterations of its most famous words 'I have a dream', and is full of other similar repetitions. Near the end, for example, we find:

> This is the faith with which I return to the South. With this faith we will be able to transform the jangling discords of our nation into a beautiful symphony of brotherhood. With this faith we will

be able to work together, to pray together, to struggle together, to go to jail together, to stand up for freedom together, knowing that we will be free one day.

> (King, 1984 [1963], p. 97 – note that this quotation is from the written version of his speech, not the actual oration)

Here King uses a device known as a **rhetorical triplet**, using the phrases 'This is the faith', 'With this faith' and 'With this faith' as the openings of three consecutive sentences, building up to a climax 'knowing that we will be free one day'. In addition, these sentences, like many other parts of the speech, not only contain verbatim repetition, but also place grammatical constructions in parallel. That is to say, they repeat the same construction with different words – in this case infinitive clauses:

to transform the jangling discords of our nation ...
to work together,
to pray together,
to struggle together,
to go to jail together,
to stand up for freedom together ...

Figure 6.5 Dr Martin Luther King Jnr addressing a Civil Rights rally at the Lincoln Memorial, Washington DC (1963). His lapel badge depicts a white and a black hand linked together, and reads 'March on Washington for Jobs and Freedom August 28 1963'.

Activity 6.3

The Indian politician Jawaharlal Nehru was one of the main founders of an independent India in the period after the Second World War. The most famous and influential figure in the struggle for Indian independence, however, was Mahatma Gandhi. In Reading A: *'The light has gone out': Indian traditions in English rhetoric* by Sen et al., you will find a transcript of the speech Nehru made to the Indian nation on the death of Gandhi. First, read the three introductory paragraphs of the reading. Then read the speech (which is reproduced as an appendix to the reading), and consider the degree to which it uses the same kind of rhetorical techniques discussed so far, or draws on some more specifically Indian rhetorical tradition. Finally, read the analysis of the speech by Sen et al. (which begins at the heading 'The influence of Indian rhetorical traditions').

Comment

Sen et al. point to the essentially oral and impromptu character of Nehru's speech, with its effective use of cohesive devices (such as the use of 'and') and 'purposeful repetition'. They also show how Nehru, like other Indian political speakers, drew on Indian rhetorical practices established by Kautiliya in the fourth century BC. So the reading offers a glimpse of another analytical perspective on the rhetorical use of English: one which has similarities to, but also important differences from, the speeches we looked at earlier in this chapter.

6.3   Attitudes towards rhetoric

An underlying assumption in Greek and Roman rhetorical theory was that the art of rhetoric can and should be taught. It was not regarded as something which comes naturally, nor was it seen as right simply 'to let the facts speak for themselves'. The Roman orator Cicero believed that a well-constructed argument showed respect for the audience, and also aided decision making, enabling hearers to judge it effectively. Rhetoric, in short, was seen as a virtuous activity for the public good. In many places this educational tradition continues – notably in the USA – where public speaking is taught and examined in high schools, and promoted by numerous organisations and publications as well.

There is, of course, an alternative point of view which suspects the accomplished speaker of being involved in some kind of deceit. In this view, enshrined in popular wisdom about the virtues of plain speaking, any artful endeavour to sway an audience should be treated with suspicion. Like rhetoric itself, this counter view of professional persuasion also dates back to classical times. According to Plato, Socrates equated all rhetoric with deceit, arguing that honest speakers should do no more than simply state their evidence and reasons, and then let the audience decide on that basis.

If justified, this distrust of professional persuasion has important implications. Is it the case, for example, in criminal trials, that the conviction or acquittal of the accused depends more on the eloquence of their counsel than on the truth of the accusation? Is it the case in elections that voters are swayed more by candidates' charm than by their policies? On a more intimate level, is there an association in personal relations between eloquence and insincerity, or being tongue-tied and being honest? There is a strong tradition that holds this to be true – as in the saying 'the deepest feelings lie too deep for words'. The idea is prominent in the novels of Jane Austen, where the best suitors always have a problem expressing themselves. 'I cannot make speeches' says Mr Knightley, the hero of *Emma*, to his beloved:

> If I loved you less, I might be able to talk about it more. But you know what I am. – You hear nothing but truth from me.
>
> (Austen, 2003 [1816], p. 338)

In our time, one reason for a negative view of professional efforts to persuade is the discredited political propaganda associated with totalitarian regimes in the mid-twentieth century, particularly Nazi Germany and the Stalinist USSR. Given the pernicious nature of these regimes, the term 'propaganda' has since assumed a largely pejorative sense, associated with oppression, deception and misinformation. Yet while there is now widespread condemnation of propaganda, there is less agreement on the extent to which its characteristics are also present in subtler forms in contemporary persuasive practices in democratic societies. The negative associations of 'propaganda' mean that those professionally engaged in persuasion no longer wish to have their activities equated with it. Contemporary attempts to influence opinion – such as advertising, public relations (PR) and election campaigning – are seen as quite different. This was not always so, however, and in the 1920s, early practitioners of PR were quite happy to equate their activities with propaganda (Moloney, 2006, p. 46). Thus, Bernays, one of the founders of public relations, wrote that:

> The conscious and intelligent manipulation of the organised habits and opinions of the masses is an important element in democratic society. Those who manipulate this unseen mechanism of society constitute an invisible government which is the ruling power of our country.
>
> (Bernays, 1928, cited in Moloney, 2006, p. 46)

We have, then, two distinct views of contemporary persuasion and its relation to totalitarian propaganda. One would see the two as quite separate, and indeed claim that operations such as advertising and PR are an important component of market-oriented economies and liberal democracies, as they keep the public informed, promote choice between alternatives and allow healthy competition. Proponents of this view would point to the multiplicity of views current in democracies, and use of similar techniques both by ruling interests and by campaigners against them, including non-governmental organisations (NGOs) such as Amnesty International or Greenpeace. They would also insist on distinguishing between arguments which aim to persuade, artfully but not deceptively, and those which set out to distort facts, as malign propaganda does.

The opposite view would see contemporary persuasion as essentially similar in kind to classic propaganda, perhaps even worse, as it uses subtler and more effective techniques. Such critics point to the disproportionate funds and resources available to politicians and corporations, making grass-roots democratic opposition to them comparatively powerless. For example, in his analysis of debate in 'the public sphere', the philosopher Jürgen Habermas suggests that public relations and propaganda are equally manipulative and oppressive, and quite antithetical to genuine democratic decision making (Habermas, 1989). Herman and Chomsky (1988) use the phrase 'manufacturing consent' to express their view that the notion of a public mandate for government policies in Western democracies masks the manipulation of public opinion in favour of the establishment. In their view, corporate-owned news media have vested interests in the status quo, and consequently distort how news is selected and reported, resulting in guaranteed endorsement of establishment policy by the media.

6.4   Advertising

As we have seen in the example of Martin Luther King, political rhetoric is prone to repetition at the micro level of words, phrases and grammatical constructions within the same speech. There is also the phenomenon of **wholesale repetition**, where an entire message is repeated many times. Propaganda relies heavily on such wholesale repetition, as a kind of substitute for reasoned argument. This is part of a general elevation of emotion over evidence, making propaganda, in Aristotle's terms, very much argument by *pathos* rather than *logos*. In the contemporary commercial sphere, advertising campaigns demonstrate this same faith in the persuasive power of wholesale repetition, and consumers repeatedly encounter the same advertisement.

In addition to this wholesale repetition, advertisements also employ a range of rhetorical devices to attract attention and make the message memorable. For example, the launch of a new low-fat salad dressing began with the words *New Year, New Look – Dressing to Impress* (see Cook, 2008, p. 7). Here we have two parallel noun phrases with the same premodifier ('New') but different head nouns ('Year' and 'Look'), an internal rhyme ('*dres*sing to im*press*') and a pun ('*dres*sing' seems initially to be about clothes rather than 'salad').

Activity 6.4

Pick out two or three advertisements that catch your attention. What devices do they use to do so? Why do you think they are effective?

Allow as much time as you like

Comment

There is really no exhaustive list of the techniques used by advertisements, precisely because they are always seeking to attract attention with a device which has not been used before. Nevertheless, however 'original' they may appear, they do usually resort to some kind of established trope. For example, one memorable advertisement from the 1980s was unusual in that it had no words at all, not even the name of the product. All you could see was a shimmering piece of purple silk, with a cut slashed through the middle. This is a good example of a visual pun, where the image itself calls up the name of the product, *Silk Cut* cigarettes.

This type of wordplay is generally appealing, figuring prominently in poetry and song as well as rhetoric, but it is difficult to pin down quite why it should contribute to persuasive power. McQuarrie and Mick (1996) point to the way that incongruity can attract our attention, and to the 'pleasure of the text' that we find in decoding the more complex types of figuration. Perhaps such language also plays on our emotions, lowers our guard and establishes a sense of intimacy, or jokey familiarity, which deters the reader from approaching claims critically (Cook, 2000, 2001).

Advertisements, like propaganda, rely heavily on emotion, often representing idealised versions and visions of people's aspirations, expressing and influencing the values of the society in which they occur: in the UK, bucolic images of farms and countryside, welcoming grannies with traditional home cooking, happy families round the breakfast table, loving couples in fast cars on empty roads. Classic propaganda also represented idealised versions of people – blond Aryans marching to the front, muscular factory workers, or happy peasants bringing in bumper harvests. Like propaganda, advertisements are heavily reliant on modes of communication other than language. They seek the memorable and striking symbol; the contemporary golden arches on a red background used by an international burger restaurant chain are strikingly similar to the old yellow hammer and sickle on the red flag of the Soviet Union!

Figure 6.6   Burger restaurant sign   **Figure 6.7**   Soviet flag (detail)

As we are beginning to see, there are many similarities which cut across genres of public persuasion, and are also – curiously – shared by literary genres too. Many of the devices and uses of language taught in classical rhetoric, and still occurring in political oratory today, have also been deployed in political propaganda campaigns and are the stock-in-trade too of contemporary advertising. Thus, advertisers are inordinately fond, not only of repetition, whether wholesale or internal, but also of figures of speech such as hyperbole, punning, paradox, irony, metaphor and metonymy.

6.5 Public relations

Advertising can be seen as a branch of a more general phenomenon of persuasive self-presentation, public relations (PR), in which organisations of all kinds seek to portray themselves in a favourable way, both to outsiders (e.g. customers) and to insiders (e.g. their own employees). Recent decades have witnessed an exponential growth in PR. It has its own theory, a burgeoning workforce, a growing literature, thriving academic courses. It consumes a growing proportion of the budgets of organisations from businesses (where it originated) to churches, political parties, trade unions, clubs and societies, universities and schools, charities and NGOs, as well as individuals such as royalty and celebrities (Moloney, 2000, pp. 17–18). Indeed, it is hard to find people or organisations engaged in public life who are not also engaged in PR.

This very ubiquity makes PR extremely hard to define and therefore vague. Given this, most definitions are very general. Moloney regards PR as:

> mostly a category of persuasive … communications done by interests in the political economy to advance themselves materially and ideologically through markets and public policy-making.

(Moloney, 2000, p. 60)

Moloney also lists discourse features which are typical of PR. Sources, purposes and originator are often undeclared, and therefore unclear. Points are asserted rather than argued or supported by evidence. Information is factually accurate, but partial – in both senses of the word (i.e. both biased and incomplete). Contrary views and evidence are omitted. One publication on corporate responsibility by a leading tobacco company, for example, contained the following vague, selective and unsupported claims (also incidentally displaying the kind of parallelism we have encountered in political rhetoric):

> We value people with good ideas who are willing to engage in constructive debate

We have created a culture where realism and open communication are valued

We acknowledge hard work, good cost control and goal achievement

We place strong emphasis on personal accountability

We encourage employees to voice their opinions

(Cook, 2007, p. 29)

The language of PR is often as vague as the content and favours, for example, general quantifiers ('many people', 'some people', 'more people'), hedges ('could be because', 'tend to', 'may contribute') and lack of detail ('a poll in 2005'). Perhaps most strikingly of all, it often adopts a familiar chatty tone, as though the message were a casual one between friends rather than any kind of official announcement. This false friendliness has been dubbed **synthetic personalisation** or **conversationalisation**, defined as a 'tendency to give the impression of treating each of the people "handled" *en masse* as an individual' (Fairclough, 2001, p. 52).

Synthetic personalisation means that, unlike the genres we have looked at so far, PR is by no means confined to the public sphere, but extends into face-to-face encounters between individuals. When the person at the check-out asks how you are, smiles and wishes you a nice day, there is no longer any way of telling whether their voice is their own or that of the supermarket chain for which they work, or indeed whether these two voices can any longer be completely disentangled, even in the mind of the speaker. This phenomenon is present as much on screen as in writing or speech. When I complained about an unexplained charge on a utility bill and received a refund, I also received the following email:

Good Morning Guy

We try to provide the best service possible to our customers. I'm happy that you're pleased with the service we provide.

Thank you for taking your time to tell it to us.

Have a nice day!

Kind regards

Fahad [a pseudonym]
Customer Service

These emails are presumably sent out automatically rather than customised as this one purports to be – and I had certainly never said I was pleased. Such insidious penetration of corporate persuasion into individual communication provides a link to the next section of this chapter, leading us from the public to the private sphere.

Activity 6.5

Before you begin Reading B: *Forcing a smile: customer care and 'superior service'* by Deborah Cameron, think about your own experience as a supermarket customer. What kinds of communicative behaviour from staff give you a favourable impression, making you more likely to shop there, and what kinds give you an unfavourable impression? Then, as you go through Reading B, note the three features of synthetic personalisation that it mentions, and the main dangers of this approach to customer care. How do these points relate to your own views of customer care?

Comment

In her account of synthetic personalisation, Cameron identifies the way in which a company may require staff to carry out normal speech acts, such as greetings (see Chapter 1), as an obligatory feature, to carry out other speech acts that are not normally expected, such as suggesting extra purchases, and to perform all speech acts in a 'sincere' and friendly way. The dangers of this approach, she suggests, are that customers may find it artificial, that it may be inappropriate to the particular context, and that it ignores cultural differences about what constitutes friendly, polite, appropriate behaviour. Finally, it may devalue staff members' own customer service skills by preventing them from using their own discretion.

6.6   Personal persuasion

So far we have dwelt very much on persuasion in the public sphere – in politics and advertising, PR and service encounters – rather than in intimate relations and everyday encounters. What, though, of persuasion at a more personal level – within families, between friends, in relationships? While few people make major speeches or launch propaganda campaigns, everyone has had disagreements at home and tried to persuade those close to them to see things differently. These everyday acts of persuasion do not have the benefit of the immense investment of professional time, expertise and extensive preparation that goes into advertising or political campaigning or service training. They are more likely to be spontaneous and untutored. Yet there may still be some fundamental similarities between the persuasive language and techniques used on the smallest and the largest scales, rather as – as we have seen in Chapter 5 – there are parallels between everyday and artistic creativity.

In order to examine this more personal face of persuasion, let us return to the earliest and most intimate relationship of all, that of small child and parent. Erftmier and Dyson (1986) examined the persuasive strategies of children, comparing their informal strategies in speech with those they are taught to develop more formally in writing. They illustrate a point in their argument with the following exchange. At 9.30 one morning, a mother discovers her six-year-old son Bruce climbing on the kitchen counter to take packets of his favourite food out of the cupboard ('jello', known in British English as 'jelly'). The following dialogue ensued.

Bruce: (replying) Well, see, they're gonna be for this afternoon in the army *[a game he and his friend Elizabeth like to play]*. I'm getting ready for then 'cause when Liz gets home she needs a little snack 'cause she always says, 'I'm hungry.' So, this is gonna be for her evening snack.

Mother: So it all has to be made now?

Bruce: We'll make the jello first 'cause it takes longer and we can cook it shorter *[meaning that jello takes longer to congeal, but a shorter time than popcorn to 'cook']*.

Mother: OK. (Mother tears open jello package to begin the cooking.)

Bruce: Let me taste it.

Mother: Why?

Bruce: I've never tasted peach flavoring before. I just want to taste a little bit and I'm not gonna get a big chunk.

Mother: OK.

(adapted from Erftmier and Dyson, 1986, pp. 91–2)

The first thing to notice here is the dialogic nature of the argument (see Chapter 1). Unlike the largely monologic oratory and advertising we have looked at so far, this is an argument developing in interaction. Point answers point, and the two speakers presumably do not know at any given moment what is going to happen next, or what they are going to say. In other words, this encounter is not preplanned, or rehearsed, or informed by theory, as public rhetoric generally is. In answer to each challenge from his mother, Bruce quick-wittedly deflects her points with answers calculated to undermine and reverse her view. In so doing, he uses an impressive variety of strategies, challenging both the facts and her interpretation. First, he asserts that his motive is altruistic rather than selfish – the food is for his friend Elizabeth rather than primarily for himself. Second, he claims it is not for now, as his mother suspects, but for later. Third, he advances a reason for the early start – the time jello takes to set. Then, having won the argument, he builds on his success by persuading his mother to let him eat some jello even at this early time in the morning, on the grounds that he needs to expand his experience of flavours. We can never know, as in so many encounters, how far the boy's argument corresponds to his original motivations, and how far it develops as he goes along. In the course of an argument, people often find that they have persuaded themselves as much as others!

It is not the case, however, that personal persuasion is dialogic in this way while public rhetoric is entirely monologic. Even the most public persuasion draws on some of the features of face-to-face encounters. Even when there is no actual response from the audience, the shape of a speech or campaign is determined by the responses which are projected or assumed by the speaker or writer. The good orator responds to the crowd; effective advertisers carefully monitor consumer reaction. There are also formal and public instances of persuasion which are structured in dialogue form. These include adversarial justice, when counsels for defence and prosecution pick up and rebut each other's cases, and parliamentary debate, where political adversaries score points. Like the argument in the kitchen, these too may follow unpredictable paths, with contestants having to think on their feet, rather than rely wholly on preformulated plans. Indeed, the distinction between public and personal persuasion is by no means straightforward. There are many face-to-face encounters which play out in public spaces, such as supermarkets and law courts, and in which some participants speak on behalf of organisations, rather than as individuals. Such a situation is examined in the next activity.

Activity 6.6

Consider the following extract, from a job interview cited by Ragan and Hopper (1981). Can you see any similarities between this dialogue and the encounter between mother and son in the kitchen?

I[nterviewer]: Uh, why did you decide to leave something that seemed to be – you seemed to be pretty well equipped for and go on into something else, – huh?

A[pplicant]: Well, even though I enjoyed optometry, I've been interested in health services administration field for quite a bit longer than that. Ah, as my resume says, I've worked in the hospital as a nursing assistant and I'd say that's about when I decided that I was interested in health services administration. So the optometric work was kind of a fill-in type thing until I could get into graduate school and work directly in the administrative field.

(Ragan and Hopper, 1981, p. 90)

Comment

A job interview is a formal situation, governed by convention and law, with clearly demarcated power relations, and with serious consequences for all involved – gaining desired employment on the part of the interviewee, hiring the best person on the part of the interview panel. Yet the relationship between question and answer in this exchange has much in common with the dialogue in the kitchen. (Although from an adult point of view the decisions of an interview panel are more important than those about jello, this is not necessarily the case for the child.)

The interview question implies a criticism, even if it does not state it directly, and the answer rebuts this criticism by giving a coherent alternative view of the challenged behaviour. Similarly, the mother's questions ('So it all has to be made now?' and 'Why?') represent a challenge to the child. As with Bruce and his jello, there is no way of telling from the words alone whether the applicant is telling the truth or merely inventing reasons to justify his or her behaviour. In both cases, the speakers are thinking on their feet, reacting to and trying to anticipate the responses from their interlocutor.

Such dialogues are as pervasive on screen as in face-to-face interaction. Internet forums are full of exchanges where a point made by one participant is countered by another as each writer seeks to persuade their fellow discussants of a point of view in a process, as in this extract from a discussion of climate change:

> LivingEco: Maybe, we know that disasters are given already since our ecosystem is not balance already but the effect of it during typhoons and other related disaster is absolutely unpredictable. …
>
> emrld1122: Yes, of course natural disasters have an effect. But as human beings must we be ignorant to the things we can do to help? …
>
> Wickerman: Some things are predictable, many others are not. One of the reason's we tend to use the term Climate Change more than Global Warming is to reflect the fact that temperatures are fluctuating. The trend though Globally is upward. …
>
> Jasonnjon: you cannot predict climate change.. but you can definitely see the changes .. places where it rains normally now get a lot of rain and then flooding its the same in some regions where there is no or less rain .well it just got worse
>
> (The Environment Site, 2010, reproduced with the original spelling and punctuation)

Although written, such exchanges have many of the characteristics of language usually associated with speech: 'maybe', 'yes, of course', 'well', etc.

We have here very different contexts. Yet there is a sense in which the more public and the more formal genres of persuasion evolve out of the more personal ones, both ontogenetically (i.e. in our individual lives) and phylogenetically (i.e. in society at large). It is possible to conceive of a continuum from the unschooled persuasive art of the child through the conventions of more formalised debate sometimes taught at school to the grand skills of the public orator. With some important caveats, we might posit two opposite types of persuasion, each with a cluster of characteristics; we could then locate particular instances of persuasion along continua between the two extremes.

At one extreme we have persuasion which is carefully planned, formal and serious, and delivered as a monologue, without significant adjustment to interjections from the audience. Persuasive language at this more planned and formal end of the spectrum may also be a collaborative effort, as in the case of advertising or propaganda campaigns, or even – despite appearances – political speeches. At the other extreme, we have persuasion which is unplanned, informal and interactive or dialogic. These concurrent continua can be represented schematically as follows:

Unplanned   -   Planned
Informal   -   Formal
Dialogic   -   Monologic

There is some general correlation too between these continua and that of speech and writing – although one which should be approached with great caution. There are plenty of instances of planned and formal speech on the one hand, and unplanned informal writing on the other, especially in online and mobile communication (see Chapter 2.) We should also remember that many of the weightiest pieces of persuasive language, such as speeches, although delivered orally, have in fact been written in advance.

Dimensions of persuasion

Allow about
30 minutes

Activity 6.7

Thinking back over the last few days, try to recall four or five different occasions on which you tried to persuade people. For each occasion, identify where it lies on the three continua shown above. Did it involve speech or writing?

How did these factors affect the rhetorical style, strategies and devices that you used? Were there any other factors that influenced the way you tried to persuade people?

One key factor which is omitted by this schematic representation is the relationship between those involved. Intimacy and affection can fundamentally determine the ability of the speaker to persuade and the propensity of the listener to be persuaded. The task facing Bruce is much easier and less threatening than that facing Brutus or Martin Luther King; consequently, the forms of persuasion are likely to be different.

Here is another example from Erftmier and Dyson (1986), this time relating to a later stage in development, when two teenage girls (J and T) are in dispute over whether to play softball or soccer:

J: OK. Now what sport are we gonna do it on? How about softball?

T: How about soccer?

J: No. Let's do softball.

T: Why?

J: Because it's an easier sport to do. *(giggling)*

T: Well, do you know the rules to it?

J: Yeah.

T: What are they?

J: *(laugh)* T, I don't wanna go to … Well you know, it's an easier game than soccer. You don't know the rules to soccer, do you?

T: No.

J: Well, softball rules are easier to look up in the book. I already have the books for it.

T: OK. We'll try it …

J: OK. Deal.

T: Deal.

(adapted from Erftmier and Dyson, 1986, pp. 103–4)

In this case T uses a similar strategy to Bruce, in that she counters and undermines every point made by her interlocutor, but with an important addition, indicated by the references to laughter and giggling. There are dimensions here which are likely to be lacking in more public and formal persuasion: an affection between the two participants, and a commitment to the argument simultaneous with an ironic distance from it, by which the speaker both makes a case and laughs at it, and thus perhaps prevents this dispute from becoming too serious. It is a lightheartedness and sense of closeness which public persuaders, particularly advertisers and PR people, try to emulate – but of which their audiences should be wary.

6.7   Evaluating persuasion

At the heart of the prevalence of persuasion in human life is the fact that human beings are collaborative animals whose current evolutionary success (however temporary it may prove to be) derives from an ability to coordinate ideas and activity and to tackle problems in very large social groups. No other animal approaches this ability to share ideas across time and space, or make joint decisions in such large groupings. As collaborating and choosing the best solutions to problems necessarily entails differences of opinion, joint reasoning is often more fruitful than lone activity, hence the prevalence of persuasion, in both small- and large-scale groups – families, friendship groups, workplaces or entire nations. Language is the unique attribute of our species which underpins these abilities, and some linguists have seen language, and a child's propensity to acquire the particular language around him or her, as fundamentally shaped by these two requirements: to share information and experience, and to form relationships with others (Halliday, 1973). (See fuller discussion of the ideational and interpersonal functions of language in Chapter 1 and of child language acquisition in Chapter 3.)

If we take this view of persuasion as an inevitable consequence of a need for collaboration and reaching the 'best' conclusion, then we might also be interested in how to identify the 'best' arguments. In pursuit of this, we might make a simple and stark evaluative contrast between 'good' and 'bad' persuasive arguments. 'Good' persuasion, we might say, appeals to reason and evidence, weighing the consequences, laying out its arguments as clearly and elegantly as possible to facilitate the judgement of the audience. 'Bad' persuasion, on the other hand, is driven by a lust for power rather than a quest for the general good. It lacks logic and evidence, and confuses and distracts its audience with appeals to emotion. In reality, however, as with our earlier continua, actual instances are likely to combine elements of both extremes.

An attempt to understand the processes of argument, and to make judgements about them, is found in the interdisciplinary enterprise of **argumentation theory** – which studies how humans do and should reach conclusions through collaborative reasoning (for a survey, see Grootendorst et al., 1996). A part of the theory of argumentation, especially in early work, involves formulating universal and absolute aspects of a good case, setting out, for example, the stages and components of an argument and how each can be assessed (Toulmin, 1958). Thus, an argument can be broken down into components such as the initial claim, the evidence for it, the warrant for making it, rebuttal of counter-arguments, exceptions to the claim, and the degree of commitment in the argument – that is, is this something the speaker feels to be definitely, probably or just possibly the case? (van Eemeren et al., 2002).

Yet while there may be criteria relating to each of these components which hold across all arguments, there are also (as later argumentation theorists, such as Willard, 1989, have stressed) important criteria which vary between different fields of argument. The criteria applying in 'marketplace' or everyday arguments, such as those between Bruce and his mother or among the teenage friends, for example, are different from those in more formal and institutional arenas, while within such institutional discourses there may also be disciplinary differences between fields such as medicine, law and politics. The criteria for assessing what constitutes a good argument are therefore subject to variation.

Another source of variation is cultural difference – an issue already touched on, in connection with political speeches, in Activity 6.3. The way that cultural differences affect writing is studied under the heading of **contrastive rhetoric**, which focuses in particular on how students and scholars writing in a second language may be disadvantaged by unfamiliarity with the relevant rhetorical conventions. Early work in this field tended to be Anglocentric and impressionistic, characterising English writing as linear and direct, and 'oriental' writing as circular and indirect. Such claims have now been subjected to more rigorous examination, based on analysis of coherence and discourse patterns. Hinds (1987), for example, argues that Japanese, Chinese and Korean writers have a preference for a 'quasi-inductive' style in which the topic or thesis statement is implied rather than stated directly. He relates this to the idea that these are 'reader-responsible' languages, where readers are expected to draw their own conclusions from what they read, as opposed to 'writer-responsible' languages like English, where it is up to writers to make their argument explicit to the reader.

Such approaches run the risk of over-generalising and stereotyping a particular culture without acknowledging the different practices and groups which exist within it. It makes little sense to talk about an

Indian or an American way of writing, when these national labels encompass so many different styles and approaches, including some which cross national boundaries. The best contrastive rhetoric does not simply identify features of texts from a particular place or in a particular language, but relates those features to complex ideologies, values and attitudes that are present in and across cultures. Writers and speakers do not just blindly follow a cultural blueprint, but make their own strategic decisions about how best to present their case. Like Brutus and Antony, they have personal as well as cultural preferences, and may make different choices depending on their individual purposes, their understanding of the situation and their relationship with the audience.

Acknowledgement of contextual and cultural variation in persuasion recognises that attempts to formalise and calculate what makes a 'good' argument are in danger of omitting from analysis a sense of the humanity of persuasion and the role within it of factors other than reason and evidence. Like the theories of classical rhetoric with which we began, it acknowledges that there is much more involved in persuasion than the bare underlying bones of claim and support. As we have seen, a good deal revolves around the personality and relationship of those involved, and remains today as entwined with such elusive factors as eloquence, charm, humour, irony and presence as it was in ancient times.

6.8   Conclusion

In this chapter we have explored the ubiquity of persuasion in human life, in both the most public and the most private of situations, and in different ages, media and cultures. We have seen how, despite this variety of contexts, many of the issues and strategies in persuasive discourse remain largely unchanged.

READING A: 'The light has gone out': Indian traditions in English rhetoric

Julu Sen, Rahul Sharma and Anima Chakraverty

Source: Sen, J., Sharma, R. and Chakraverty, A. (1996) '"The light has gone out": Indian traditions in English rhetoric' in Maybin, J. and Mercer, N. (eds) *Using English: From Conversation to Canon*, London, Routledge/Milton Keynes, The Open University.

Although English has been used in India since 1600, and we are familiar with Indian writing in English, we have only recently begun to study the speeches in English of well-known Indian orators, such as Gandhi and Nehru. Since India is a multilingual country, most of the broadcasts to the nation are in Hindi as well as in English. Although Gandhi spoke mostly in Hindi or Gujarati, his speeches delivered in south India and in South Africa were generally in English.

While studying these speeches, we have discovered that spontaneous impromptu speeches were very different from prepared addresses. The formal written addresses of both Gandhi and Nehru resemble their writing in English, while in their impromptu speeches we find features of oral speech – additive, aggregative, redundant, conservative, close to human life world, empathetic and participatory. Their transcribed speeches also show evidence of the influence of Indian rhetorical traditions. We will illustrate and discuss some of these features here, with reference to one famous impromptu speech by Jawaharlal Nehru, entitled 'The light has gone out' (as transcribed in Gopal, 1987).

The assassination of Mahatma Gandhi on 30 January 1948 was a national catastrophe. The brutal murder of the Father of the Nation, barely a few months after independence, sent shock waves throughout the country and plunged millions of Indians into gloom and mourning. In this hour of crisis, Nehru, the then prime minister of India and a trusted lieutenant of Gandhi, addressed the nation on the radio. Widely regarded as one of Nehru's immortal speeches, this spontaneous address to the nation made an indelible impact on the hearts and minds of millions of Indians.

[We recommend that you read now the complete speech, reproduced as an appendix to this reading.]

Figure 1   Jawaharlal Nehru, Indian prime minister, addressing a public meeting in May 1957

The influence of Indian rhetorical traditions

A salient feature of this speech is that the expression of 'grief' is accomplished without the use of the word 'grief' or any of its synonyms. This is because the feeling is too deep to be directly expressed in conventional words. It can only be evoked or suggested indirectly, and Nehru expresses the inexpressible in the following manner:

> The light has gone out from our lives and there is darkness everywhere.

(lines 2–3)

This manner of dealing with grief indirectly is in accord with one of the principles of Indian aesthetics, *dhvani*, 'the use of poetic or dramatic words to suggest or evoke a feeling that is too deep, intense and universal to be spoken' (Coward, 1980, p. 148). *Dhvani* forms part of a theory of language propounded by the fifth-century Sanskrit grammarian and philosopher of language, Bhartrahari, and has also been drawn on by other Indian scholars in the analysis of figurative speech.

The speech also embodies several principles of effective communication that can be traced back to the *Artha Sastra*, a series of books dealing with politics, thought to have been written by the scholar Kautiliya in the fourth century BC. Kautiliya advises his readers that:

> Arrangement of subject-matter, connection, completeness, sweetness, exaltedness and lucidity constitute the excellences of communication. Among them, arranging in a proper order, the statement first of the principal matter, is *arrangement of subject-matter*. The statement of a subsequent matter without its being incompatible with the matter in hand, right up to the end, is *connection*. Absence of deficiency or excess of matter, words or letters, description in detail of the matter by means of reasons, citations and illustrations, (and) expressiveness of words, is *completeness*. The use of words with a charming meaning easily conveyed is *sweetness*. The use of words that are not vulgar is *exaltedness*. The employment of words that are well-known is *lucidity*.
>
> (Kangle, 1988, pp. 92–3; emphasis added)

Later in the same chapter Kautiliya refers to two further principles: *relevance* and *empathy* with the audience. We shall give examples of these principles in Nehru's speech, beginning with *arrangement of subject matter* and *connection*.

In a spontaneous speech like this, unlike in a written/prepared speech, one has to think on one's feet, and the textual order reflects the order in which impressions occur in the mind. Despite the fact that this is a spontaneous speech, it is a good example of arrangement of subject matter and connection, as described by Kautiliya. These can be seen in the sequence of topics in the speech:

assassination – funeral – homage

Nehru starts with the principal matter of Gandhi's assassination by articulating his deep sense of dismay bordering on helplessness:

> I do not know what to tell you and how to say it
>
> (lines 3–4)

This is how he identifies himself with the Indian masses and shares their sorrow. At the same time, however, as their undisputed leader, he is conscious of his responsibility to warn them of the dangers of communalism [i.e. sectarianism], and to impress upon them the need to strengthen the bonds of unity to face challenges boldly. With all the force at his command, he reminds his people that the likes of Gandhi never die and that the best homage to Gandhi would be a solemn pledge to work for peace, unity and brotherhood. In the midst of all this, Nehru keeps his cool, pauses, and finds time to give details of the funeral arrangement:

> May I now tell you the programme for tomorrow?
>
> (line 58)

Finally he advises his listeners on how they can best pay homage to Gandhi.

Nehru is concerned about the welfare of India so he repeats this concern before turning to the funeral arrangements and afterwards at the very end of his speech. Compare these two sentences:

> As in his life, so in his death he has reminded us of the big things of life, the living truth, and if we remember that, then it will be well with us and well with *India*.
>
> (lines 55–7; emphasis added)

> That is the best prayer that we can offer to *India* and ourselves.
>
> (lines 96–7; emphasis added)

The speech illustrates other principles suggested by Kautiliya. One of these is *completeness*. Although it is an impromptu speech, Nehru has chosen his words very carefully, whether they concern bringing the first news of the assassination to the nation (lines 1–23), his own reactions (lines 24–57), his plans for the funeral arrangements and advice on paying homage (lines 58–95) or finally the 'prayer' (lines 95–7). We can't strike out any part, claiming it is irrelevant, or deficient. It seems *complete* in all respects.

Sweetness can be found in Nehru's choice of words, word order, sentence construction, elegant variation and purposeful repetition. The first two sentences of the speech comprise a virtual string of 25 monosyllables. This aptly reflects the speaker's deep sense of anguish and helps create an atmosphere of mourning. However, this is soon followed by a little drama and the element of suspense. 'Bapu … is no more. Perhaps I am wrong to say that … The light has gone out, I said, and yet I was wrong' (lines 4–13). (*Bapu*, meaning 'Father', is the affectionate name Indians gave Gandhi.)

One of the best examples of Nehru's oratorical skill can be found in:

> The light that has illumined this country for these many, many years will illumine this country for many more years, and a thousand years later that light will still be seen in this country, and the world will see it, and it will give solace to innumerable hearts.
>
> (lines 15–19)

This rather extraordinary construction effectively illustrates the 'extraordinariness' of Gandhi, and places him far above not only common mortals but also most leaders of men and women. The magnitude of Gandhi's contribution to India's freedom struggle and the eternal relevance of his teachings is communicated most effectively through expressions like 'these many, many years', 'many more years' and 'a thousand years later'.

Nehru concludes the speech with the words:

> That is the best prayer that we can offer him and his memory.
> That is the best prayer that we can offer to India and ourselves.
>
> (lines 95–7)

The use of repetition here not only emphasizes the fact that the best prayer would be a life-long commitment to Gandhi's ideals of non-violence and communal harmony but also (by equating 'him' with

'India') acclaims Gandhi as the architect of India's freedom and the Father of this Nation.

The speech also shows great *dignity*: Nehru has not uttered a single word that could be termed socially offensive. That he had suffered a great blow may be gauged from the expression: 'A *madman* has put an end to his life, for I can only call him *mad* who did it' (lines 30–1; emphasis added). And 'We must face this *poison*, we must root out this *poison*, and we must face all the perils that encompass us, and face them, not *madly* or *badly*, but rather in the way that our beloved teacher taught us to face them' (lines 34–7; emphasis added). Yet he advises his people to be strong and determined. He maintains the dignity of his state and office, as prime minister, and talks about the funeral arrangements in a very calm manner.

The speech is *relevant* to the needs of the moment because in the hour of 'grief', through his 'love for his country', Nehru is making an appeal to his people to remain calm. The style is *lucid*, expressed in simple language so that this request reaches the masses. And finally, anticipating and sharing their love for Bapu, he can *empathize* with the audience. His use of the term *Bapu* itself is an illustration of this.

References for this reading

Coward, H. G. (1980) *The Sphota Theory of Language – A Philosophical Analysis*, Delhi, Motilal Banarasidass.

Gopal, S. (ed.) (1987) *Selected Works of Jawaharlal Nehru*, second series, vol. 5, New Delhi, Jawaharlal Nehru Memorial Fund.

Kangle, R. P. (1988) *The Kautiliya Artha Sastra – Parts 1 and 2 – An English Translation with Critical and Explanatory Notes,* trans. from the Malayalam manuscript of the twelfth century AD, Delhi, Motilal Banarasidass.

Appendix to Reading A

On 30 January 1948 at about 5 p.m., Mahatma Gandhi was late by a few minutes for the prayer meeting in the grounds of Birla House, New Delhi, because he had been held up by a meeting with Vallabhbhai Patel. With his forearms on the shoulders of his grandnieces, Abha and Manubehn, he walked briskly to the prayer ground where about 500 persons had gathered. He raised his hands and joined them to greet the congregation who returned the greeting in a similar manner. Just at that moment Nathuram Vinayek Godse pushed his way past Manubehn, whipped out a pistol and fired three shots. Mahatma Gandhi fell instantly with the words *He Ram* (Oh God!) on his lips.

The following speech is Nehru's broadcast to the nation announcing the death of Gandhi (30 January 1948, All India Radio tapes).

The Light Has Gone Out

1   Friends and Comrades,

The light has gone out from our lives and there is
darkness everywhere. And I do not know what to tell
you and how to say it. Our beloved leader, Bapu, as we
5   called him, the Father of the Nation, is no more.
Perhaps I am wrong to say that. Nevertheless, we will
not see him again as we have seen him for these many
years. We will not run to him for advice and seek
solace from him; and that is a terrible blow, not to me
10   only, but to millions and millions in this country. And
it is a little difficult to soften the blow by any advice
that I or anyone else can give you.

The light has gone out, I said, and yet I was wrong. For
the light that shone in this country was no ordinary
15   light. The light that has illumined this country for these
many, many years will illumine this country for many
more years, and a thousand years later that light will
still be seen in this country, and the world will see it,
and it will give solace to innumerable hearts. For that
20   light represented something more than the immediate
present; it represented the living, eternal truths
reminding us of the right path, drawing us from error,
taking this ancient country to freedom.

All this has happened when there was so much more
25   for him to do. We could never, of course, do away with
him, we could never think that he was unnecessary, or
that he had done his task. But now, particularly, when
we are faced with so many difficulties, his not being
with us is a blow most terrible to bear.

30   A madman has put an end to his life, for I can only call
him mad who did it. And yet there has been enough
of poison spread in this country during the past years and
months, and this poison has had effect on people's

35   minds. We must face this poison, we must root out this
poison, and we must face all the perils that encompass
us, and face them, not madly or badly, but rather in the
way that our beloved teacher taught us to face them.
The first thing to remember now is that none of us dare
misbehave because we are angry. We have to behave

40   like strong, determined people, determined to face
all the perils that surround us, determined to carry out
the mandate that our great teacher and our great leader
has given us, remembering always that if, as I believe,
his spirit looks upon us and sees us, nothing would

45   displease his soul so much as to see that we have
indulged in unseemly behaviour or in violence. So we
must not do that. But that does not mean that we
should be weak, but rather that we should, in strength
and in unity, face all the troubles that are in front of us.

50   We must hold together, and all our petty troubles and
difficulties and conflicts must be ended in the face of
this great disaster. A great disaster is a symbol to us to
remember all the big things of life and forget the small
things of which we have thought too much. Now the time

55   has come again. As in his life, so in his death he has reminded
us of the big things of life, the living truth, and if we remember
that, then it will be well with us and well with India.

May I now tell you the programme for tomorrow? It
was proposed by some friends that Mahatmaji's body

60   should be embalmed for a few days to enable millions
of people to pay their last homage to him. But it was
his wish, repeatedly expressed, that no such thing
should happen, that this should not be done, that he
was entirely opposed to any embalming of his body,

65   and so we decided that we must follow his wishes in
this matter, however much others might have wished
otherwise.

And so the cremation will take place tomorrow in
Delhi city by the side of the Jumna river. Tomorrow

70   morning, or rather forenoon, about 11.30, the bier will
be taken out from Birla House and it will follow the
prescribed route and go to the Jumna river. The

75   cremation will take place there at about 4.00 p.m. The
exact place and route will be announced by radio and
the press.

People in Delhi who wish to pay their last homage
should gather along this route. I would not advise too
many of them to come to Birla House, but rather to
gather on both sides of this long route, from Birla
80   House to the Jumna river. And I trust that they will
remain there in silence without any demonstrations.
That is the best way and the most fitting way to pay
homage to the great soul. Also, tomorrow should be a
day of fasting and prayer for all of us.

85   Those who live elsewhere, out of Delhi and in other
parts of India, will no doubt also take such part as they
can in this last homage. For them also let this be a day
of fasting and prayer. And at the appointed time for
cremation, that is 4.00 p.m. tomorrow afternoon,
90   people should go to the river or to the sea and offer
prayers there. And while we pray, the greatest prayer
that we can offer is to take a pledge to dedicate
ourselves to the truth and to the cause for which this
great countryman of ours lived and for which he has
95   died. That is the best prayer that we can offer him and
his memory. That is the best prayer that we can offer to
India and ourselves. *Jai Hind.*

(Cited in Gopal, 1987, pp. 35–6)
(Note: *Jai Hind* roughly translated means 'Long live India'.)

READING B: Forcing a smile: customer care and 'superior service'

Deborah Cameron

Source: Cameron, D. (2000) *Good to Talk? Living and Working in a Communication Culture*, London, Sage, pp. 73–8.

[Commonly] the primary focus of linguistic training and regulation in retail businesses is the way staff interact with customers. Since the perceived standard of a company's service is a function of its employees' behaviour, the 'customer care' approach means that companies are essentially selling the qualities of their staff. Consequently, they must take a close interest in the qualities staff actually display to customers: in their appearance, their demeanour and, not least, their speech.

In October 1998, the *Washington Post* reported on a controversy that had broken out on the internet[1] around a 'superior service' programme initiated by the Safeway supermarket chain in the USA. Under the title 'Service with a forced smile: Safeway's courtesy campaign also elicits some frowns' (October 18: A1), reporter Kirstin Downey Grimsley explained the background. The rules of 'superior service' required employees to 'make eye contact with the customer, smile, greet him or her, offer samples of products, make suggestions about other possible purchases that could go with the items being purchased, accompany customers to locate items they can't find … thank shoppers by name at the checkout using information from their credit, debit or Safeway card'. To monitor compliance, Safeway employed 'mystery shoppers', people who impersonated real customers but were actually in the store to grade staff on a 19-point checklist. These gradings were used in subsequent performance evaluations; good grades could attract bonuses, while poor grades might result in the employee being sent for remedial customer service skills training at what some workers interviewed by the *Post* derisively referred to as 'smile school' or 'clown school'. […] The immediate cause of the furore, which occurred when the programme was already several years old, was that several women Safeway workers in California had complained at a union conference that the company's policy exposed them to sexual harassment. Some male customers interpreted displays of friendliness as signs of 'romantic interest' or as cues to make 'lewd comments'. These complaints sparked off a discussion of the rights and wrongs of the superior service programme.

Much of the behaviour that is regulated by the superior service programme is 'communicative' – in the jargon, verbal, vocal or visual – behaviour. In some cases, regulation takes the form of making speech acts and routines which would be expected to occur in service encounters – such as greetings, thanks and farewells – *categorical*: that is, employees do not choose whether and when to perform these acts, but are required to perform them at every opportunity, and may be 'written up' for any omission. This requirement can have bizarre consequences. The *Post* report begins with a vignette in which a clerk in a Safeway store in Reston, Virginia spots a customer coming down the aisle where he is stacking shelves:

The clerk sprang into action, making eye contact, smiling and greeting her warmly … The woman nodded briefly in return and continued shopping. The clerk moved on to another part of the store, going about his duties, and passed her again. Knowing that he might earn a poor grade on the company's 19-point friendliness report card if he failed to acknowledge her fully each time, the clerk again made eye contact and asked her how she was doing. This time she looked quizzical … But after it happened a third time, the woman's face darkened as he approached. 'That poor lady', the clerk said ruefully. 'You could see her thinking, "what is his problem?"'.

His problem, of course, was that the rules were enforced without regard to such obvious contextual considerations as whether an employee had already greeted a particular shopper. It is only mildly unnatural to be 'warmly greeted' by a store clerk *once*, but it becomes extremely unnatural if the routine is repeated every time the same clerk comes within greeting distance.

Regulation of employees' linguistic behaviour may also take the form of instructing them to do things that would not ordinarily be expected to occur even once in the context of a supermarket. For instance, Safeway staff are exhorted to 'make suggestions about other possible purchases that could go with the items being purchased' – in other words to initiate conversations with people who are in the middle of doing their shopping. Since in context this is a 'marked' action – conversing with staff about what they are buying is not part of most customers' existing schema for visiting a supermarket – it is interactionally quite difficult to 'bring off'. A student of mine, Karen MacGowan, carried out observations in a supermarket in the UK where staff had been furnished with a set of opening gambits for initiating conversation at the checkout (such as 'are you using coupons with your shopping today?'). She noted that although the gambits themselves were perfectly straightforward, some customers appeared to have great difficulty framing a response to them, because they could not fathom the checkout operator's underlying intentions. (Ultimately, of course, the intention both in the Safeway case and in the 'coupons' case is to persuade the customer to buy *more*.)

Finally, employees' behaviour is regulated by instructions to perform all communicative acts in a prescribed manner: smiling, making eye contact, using the customer's name, greeting him or her 'warmly' and selecting personalized formulas like 'how are you doing?' which incorporate direct second person address. These linguistic and paralinguistic preferences are designed to express particular dispositions, notably friendliness and sincere concern for the customer's wellbeing, and thus to construct a particular kind of interpersonal relationship between the customer and the employee.

All these types of regulation, especially the last, exemplify 'synthetic personalization', which [...] (following Fairclough, 1989) is a way of designing discourse to give the impression of treating people as individuals within institutions that, in reality, are set up to handle people *en masse*. [...]

As the term '*synthetic* personalization' implies, however, this impression is achieved by interactional sleight-of-hand. It remains a way of handling people *en masse* rather than a genuinely individualized approach: the supposed expressions of personal concern are actually standard formulae, pre-packaged at head office and produced indifferently for every customer. Even the most markedly individualizing strategy, the use of customers' names, is a piece of artifice, and it draws mixed responses from customers. Whereas one customer told the *Post*'s reporter, 'It makes you feel good when you're spending $50 to have them know your name', another said: 'it doesn't make me feel better. I know they are looking me up in the computer. It's not because they know me'. Some people judge Safeway's superior service programme the very opposite of 'personal', because they believe employees are only following a formula: their friendliness is not genuine. [...]

If one problem with 'synthetic personalization' is that people may perceive it as more synthetic than personalized, another is that some find personalization *per se* inappropriate to the context. One customer who was interviewed by the *Post* remarked, for instance, that he was annoyed and embarrassed by staff commenting on what he had bought. He also disliked having his name used at the checkout: 'it's almost too personal, if you don't know the person'. Safeway's corporate spokesperson admitted that the use of names had attracted many complaints – especially from foreign-born customers whose names were invariably mispronounced.

These comments raise the issue of variation. The Safeway spokesperson's assertion that 'in general, people like people to be friendly to them' sounds like a statement of the obvious, but what it conceals is individual, social and cultural differences affecting what behaviours people define as 'friendly' – one person's 'friendliness' may be another's 'over-familiarity' – and what contexts they see as requiring what degree of 'friendliness'. Politeness in general is an area where national and cultural differences can be quite pronounced, even when people speak the same language. In Britain, for instance, there are hazards associated with importing signifiers of friendliness from the US – a common practice, since many US-based companies do business in Britain, and in addition there is a widespread belief that service in the US is better than in Britain. (One UK railway company's manual urges employees to 'put American-style friendliness into your voice', as if friendly service were as intrinsically American as Coca-Cola.) Many people are irritated by formulas like 'have a nice day', partly just because they are marked as 'American', and so Americanize public space in ways that offend some British sensibilities, but partly also because they arise from ways of relating to others which are themselves experienced as foreign. Although there is variation in both countries, generally speaking the British have traditionally had a greater distrust of anything that smacks of effusiveness, especially between strangers. Karen MacGowan reported that an initiative whereby shoppers in the Scottish town of Coatbridge were met at the store entrance by a 'greeter' saying 'enjoy your shopping experience' had evoked varying degrees of embarrassment, puzzlement and hilarity: exhortations to 'enjoy' are more Californian than Caledonian. Another difference, crudely stated, is that in Britain polite behaviour between unacquainted equals tends to involve the reciprocal marking of social distance. For people who have internalized this norm, the (increasingly common) practice of workers being identified by their first names only may not connote what it is intended to connote, namely friendliness, but instead may seem to demean the worker by denying her or him the social distance one accords to non-intimates of equal status.

In other parts of the world, where English is not widely spoken or is spoken as a second language, the linguistic and cultural difference issues may be far more extreme. There is much to be said about the implications of the fact that 'globalization' tends to mean 'Americanization'. [...] the importation of American-style 'friendly' service into post-communist Hungary is disrupting the complex formal system of address in Hungarian; and [...] Black South Africans entering service sector jobs previously reserved for white workers have been obliged to learn forms of interpersonal behaviour which are viewed in their community as alien and bizarre. It has also been pointed out to me that some societies have their own highly formalized service styles with which the 'globalized' style is in conflict. An example is Japan, where training for customer service workers has long given considerable attention to their speech and body language. The Japanese style now increasingly coexists, however, with the totally different style favoured by American-owned companies like Disney and McDonald's.

But even within one society, everyone will not necessarily share the same understanding of particular linguistic strategies, nor the same expectations of language-use in service encounters. Making and enforcing invariant rules for 'friendly' behaviour and language-use compels staff to ignore their own readings of what particular customers want or need, and to discard their understanding that, for instance, one might wish to address people differently on the basis of age or gender. An employee quoted in the *Washington Post* pointed out that often someone's body language would tell you that they wanted to be left alone. As she also said, however, if you used your own judgement in such a case and there happened to be a 'mystery shopper' around, you would be 'written up' for poor customer service skills. In this example we see how what employers describe as 'skills' may in fact be no such thing; employees may actually be penalized for making use of their learned ability to interact successfully with others.

Note

[1]   The source is an internet discussion group, 'Forced smiles at Safeway'. For drawing my attention to the *Washington Post* report I am grateful to Scott Kiesling, and for additional assistance I thank Keith Nightenheiser.

References for this reading

Fairclough, Norman (1989) *Language and Power*. London: Longman.

Grimsley, Kirstin Downey (1998) 'Service with a forced smile: Safeway's courtesy campaign also elicits some frowns'. *Washington Post*, 18 October: A1.

7   Material English

Daniel Allington

7.1   Introduction

As the previous chapters of this book have emphasised, texts do not exist outside of time, space and social institutions. Instead, they are produced, reproduced, exchanged and consumed in the course of social practices. This chapter aims to show that those practices rely not only on social convention, but also on technologies that in turn rely on economic systems.

As you will see, it is useful to think of the English language and its history in material terms – taking account of the physical nature of text – as well as in materialist terms – taking account of the economic bases of textual production and reproduction. Thinking in this way means analysing 'the human motives and interactions which texts involve at every stage of their production, transmission, and consumption' as well as investigating 'the roles of institutions, and their own complex structures, in affecting the forms of social discourse' (McKenzie, 1999 [1986], p. 15). This material(ist) approach has been described both as the sociology of texts and as the history of the book. It sees written, printed and digital texts as the products of complex 'communications circuits' involving not only writers and readers, but also printers, distributors, booksellers and others (Darnton, 1990). As this chapter will show, such an approach can teach us much about the history and sociology of the English language.

7.2   Materialising language

Most people are able to speak and hear language without the need for anything that would normally be called a technology, but the same cannot be said when it comes to writing and reading. Giving language material form has always required technologies – starting with what we call **writing systems**.

A writing system is a set of symbols used for producing linguistic expressions in textual form. Linguists have sometimes assumed that the writing system of a language does (or should do) no more than represent the way the language sounds: Ferdinand de Saussure, for example, saw any tendency of spelling to influence pronunciation as 'really pathological' (Saussure, 1960 [1916], p. 31). But it may be more helpful to view writing and speech as equivalent.

The alphabetic and logographic *principles* in writing were explained in Chapter 3. A contrast can in fact be made between alphabetic writing systems, such as those which have been used for English, and logographic writing systems, such as those which are most commonly used for Chinese. In logographic writing systems, the logographic principle dominates, so that each symbol, often called a 'character' or more accurately a 'logogram', stands for a word. Written Chinese is the most influential logographic writing system still in use: for example, all three Japanese writing systems used today derive from earlier Chinese systems (although only one of them is logographic). Other kinds of writing systems exist, including syllabic writing systems, in which each symbol corresponds to a whole syllable in the spoken language, and alpha-syllabic writing systems, in which individual symbols may correspond to whole syllables or to single sounds. Syllabic writing systems include the Hiragana and Katakana scripts used in written Japanese, and alpha-syllabic writing systems include Devanagari, used in written Hindi, Marathi and many other languages of the Indian subcontinent.

In alphabetic writing systems, the alphabetic principle dominates. This means that most or all of the symbols used correspond in some way to sounds, enabling words to be spelled out using sequences of symbols roughly corresponding to the sequences of sounds produced when the same words are spoken. In practice, any correspondence may be very rough indeed, as we see when we consider the 'silent' letters demanded by the orthographies (i.e. spelling systems) of many modern languages, including English.

The writing systems or scripts used to write English, most other languages of European origin and many other languages today, are collectively called the 'Roman' or 'Latin' alphabet. This is because all of them closely derive from the system used by the Ancient Romans to write their language, now called Classical Latin. This system was itself derived from an earlier Greek alphabet, which was developed from the still more ancient Phoenician alphabet: a vowel-less writing system devised in the second millennium BC in a land roughly corresponding to modern Lebanon. You can get an idea of the continuities between these scripts from Figure 7.1, which is a simplified depiction of the first six letters of the Phoenician, Greek and Roman alphabets (note that what is here given as the sixth Greek letter is in parentheses because it was dropped from the Greek alphabet early in the first millennium BC). Each letter in the second and third columns derives in shape from the older letter to its left, and many are associated with similar sounds. In Figure 7.2, you can see how the 'Roman' alphabet used for Modern English derives from the alphabet used for Classical Latin (note that in Classical Latin the letter K was rarely used and the letters Y and Z were used for words 'borrowed' from Greek, while in English the letters U and J did not become distinct from V and I until the seventeenth century). A Greek alphabet was also the model for the Cyrillic alphabet now used to write Russian and many other languages, while the Hebrew and Arabic alphabets derive from the Phoenician alphabet via the Aramaic alphabet. Hangul, used for written Korean, is one of the rare alphabetic writing systems to have no historical link to the Phoenician alphabet.

Figure 7.1 From left to right, the first letters of the Phoenician, Ancient Greek and Roman alphabets

The degree of historical continuity between most alphabetic writing systems is one reason for their inability to reflect pronunciation exactly. Certain sounds in modern European languages correspond to no single letter in the Roman alphabet, and pronunciation generally changes faster than writing systems. A good example is the sound that falls at the end of the English word 'English' when it is spoken. You might like to think of this as the 'sh' sound, but in the International Phonetic Alphabet it is represented by ʃ.

Figure 7.2 The Roman alphabet as used for writing Classical Latin (left) and Modern English (right)

ʃ played no role in the pronunciation of Classical Latin and Greek, so there is no letter that might correspond to it in the alphabets developed for those languages. Nonetheless, ʃ plays an important role in the pronunciation of several later European languages, presenting a problem that has been dealt with in different ways. Written Russian employs a letter adapted from the Phoenician alphabet, Ш. Written Czech employs a Roman letter combined with a diacritic mark, Š. Written German employs a sequence of three Roman letters, SCH, or (when at the start of a word and followed by certain consonants) the single Roman letter S. Spoken Polish uses two contrasting sounds similar to ʃ, in correspondence with which, written Polish contrasts a sequence of two Roman letters, SZ, with a single Roman letter with a diacritic mark, Ś (or, before a vowel, the sequence SI).

For written English, the situation is complicated in a different way, as we see from the dominant British and American pronunciation of words like 'cash', 'confection' and 'confession'. In the case of the first of these words, we have a regular correspondence between sound and symbol: it is S and H that we generally reach for when we want to represent the sound itself on the page ('"Sh!" said the librarian'). But in the case of the second and third words, we see the results of spelling not keeping pace with pronunciation: at the time when the spelling of these words settled on its current form, their dominant pronunciation did not involve ʃ.

Further technologies are needed to put writing systems to use. Symbols can be shaped with a pen, brush or chisel, printed on a variety of surfaces or substituted with numbers (see Chapter 2 on ASCII and Unicode). In medieval Europe and the ancient world, the wax tablet was a common erasable medium (see Figure 7.3), and some of the oldest texts in existence – the cuneiform tablets of Sumeria – were written by pressing the tip of a reed into wet clay (see Figure 7.4). Patterns of raised dots form the symbols used in Braille, a writing system read with the fingertips rather than the eyes (Figure 7.5). And a person producing text by pressing buttons on a keyboard is said to be 'writing' – unless he or she is copying a text or taking down dictation, in which case 'typing' is the usual word.

Figure 7.3 A wax tablet inscribed with early Cyrillic script

Figure 7.4 A clay tablet inscribed with cuneiform script

Figure 7.5 Braille, read by touch

7.3 Symbols and spaces in early medieval British literacy

Take a look at Figures 7.6 (a), (b) and (c). These show the Ruthwell Cross: a red sandstone monument, roughly five metres high. It was probably constructed in the eighth century AD, when the surrounding area was encompassed not (as now) by Scotland but by the now-vanished kingdom of Northumbria. It was reconstructed in the nineteenth century, when a modern horizontal crosspiece was added. On the broad front and back of its massive upright are small figurative carvings in low relief, with letters from the Roman alphabet engraved upon the borders. The narrow sides are carved with twining vines and birds, surrounded by strings of symbols that you may find unfamiliar, as they are unused by any modern language. These symbols are known as **runes** and belong to a family of alphabets called the **Futhorc**. Similar alphabets were once widely used in parts of north-western Europe and especially Scandinavia, but today they only serve decorative purposes.

Figure 7.6(a) The Ruthwell Cross

(b) Latin inscription on the Ruthwell Cross

(c) Runic inscription on the Ruthwell Cross

The Futhorc was certainly influenced by the Roman alphabet, although it was adapted to the specific needs of Germanic peoples. Some runes can be treated as roughly equivalent to letters in the Roman alphabet while others correspond to sounds that had no corresponding Roman letter. The sound at the beginning of the modern English word 'thorn', for example, was represented by a rune known as 'thorn': Þ. This rune continued to be employed long after the abandonment of the Futhorc, with Y substituting for it in the scribal abbreviation 'yᵉ', meaning 'the' (a version of which can be seen in the second line of Figure 2.5 in Chapter 2).

The Roman letters on the Ruthwell Cross form long lines that run around the relief panels in horizontal lines of vertical letters (like the ones in this paragraph) and vertical lines of horizontal letters (like the ones on the spine of this book). These spell out short Latin texts, which describe the events depicted in the accompanying relief carvings. The runes, however, are all vertical and are arranged in horizontal lines, most of which are extremely short. They were not deciphered until the mid-nineteenth century, when the philologist John Kemble recognised a connection between them and an English manuscript recently discovered in the north of Italy. As Kemble realised, the runes on the Ruthwell Cross spell out words similar to some of those of a poem contained within that manuscript, and now known as 'The Dream of the Rood'.

'The Dream of the Rood' was written in the tenth century in the West Germanic language variety that we now call West Saxon, whose usual writing system combined letters from the Roman alphabet with certain non-Roman symbols (including thorn). The runic verses on the Ruthwell Cross, however, were carved in the West Germanic language variety that we now call Northumbrian, and are generally assumed to be much older. Like 'The Dream of the Rood', the runic text narrates the crucifixion of Jesus from the point of view of his cross (or 'rood'). Although the runic text is much shorter, the (reconstructed) shape of the Ruthwell Cross gives it a special depth of meaning: it is almost as if the cross itself speaks the poem.

Activity 7.1

Look at Figure 7.7. In it you can see a short excerpt from the runic text on the Ruthwell Cross, a longer excerpt from 'The Dream of the Rood' (Anon., 1970 [10th century], l. 52–8) and a key to the runes used (this is *not* a complete futhorc, and is in Roman alphabetical order). Note that the 'Dream of the Rood' extract uses several characters that may be

Allow about 30 minutes

unfamiliar to users of Modern English: not only Þ (in lower case, þ), but also Ð (in lower case, ð, again roughly equivalent to the Modern English letter combination TH) and Æ (in lower case, æ, a vowel).

Which part of the 'Dream of the Rood' extract corresponds to the Ruthwell Cross extract? The activity of matching the two together has been made much easier than it would have been in the mid-nineteenth century: these are extracts, we all know that correspondences are there to be found, the 'Dream of the Rood' excerpt is printed with modern punctuation and letterforms, and I redrew the runes to make them easier to read (compare the originals, most of which are visible on the right-hand side of Figure 7.6(c)). But it is still a demanding task – what makes it so hard?

a æ c d e ea f h i k l m n o r s t th u w

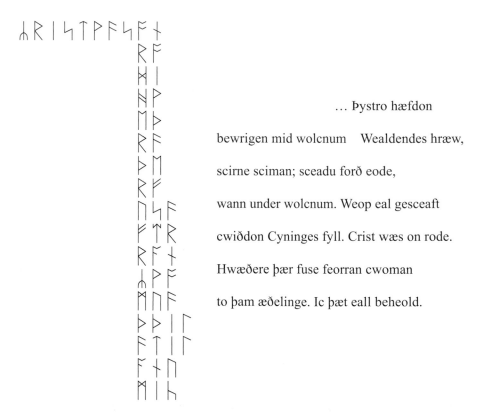

... Þystro hæfdon

bewrigen mid wolcnum   Wealdendes hræw,

scirne sciman; sceadu forð eode,

wann under wolcnum. Weop eal gesceaft

cwiðdon Cyninges fyll. Crist wæs on rode.

Hwæðere þær fuse feorran cwoman

to þam æðelinge. Ic þæt eall beheold.

Figure 7.7 The Ruthwell Cross poem (left) and 'The Dream of the Rood' (right), with a key to the runes used (above)

Comment

Written out in Modern English orthography, using the additional letter Æ, the runic text reads:
'kristwæsonrodihwethrætherfusæfearrankwomuæththilætilanumic'.
If we capitalise the first letter, add word spaces, and drop the last two letters (which begin a new clause), we are left with 'Krist wæs on rodi hwethræ ther fusæ fearran kwomu æththilæ til anum'. These words have been poetically translated into Modern English as 'Christ was on the cross / But eager ones came thither from afar / Noble ones came together' (Ó Carragáin, 2005, p. xxvi). They have a clear parallel in the last four words of the fifth line of the 'Dream of the Rood' extract ('Crist wæs on rode') and the whole of its sixth line ('Hwæðere þær fuse feorran cwoman'). After that, the correspondence between the two extracts is harder to trace: for example, 'til' was the Northumbrian equivalent of the West Saxon word 'to', which appears in the seventh line of the 'Dream of the Rood' extract (and was the ancestor of the Modern English word 'to').

Further differences between the two language varieties may have been a stumbling block ('kwomu' versus 'cwoman', etc.). But perhaps the key difficulty is the way in which the runes are divided up on the Ruthwell Cross.

On the Ruthwell Cross, words are run together without spaces or punctuation marks. This means that the Latin text appears in continuous streams of letters, while the Northumbrian text is broken up into small groups of runes that might contain parts of as many as three different words. This was one of the reasons why the Northumbrian text was so hard for nineteenth-century scholars to decipher. Similar runes had once been used in Scandinavia, which gave Scandinavian philologists a degree of expertise when it came to the Ruthwell Cross. But knowing neither where the words spelled out by the runes started and finished, nor what language those words were in, all they could find were isolated textual fragments that happened to look like Scandinavian words, and completely meaningless sequences like 'ashlafardahl' (arbitrarily supposed to have been the name of a place).

Natural though it seems to us today, word spacing was not commonly used in ancient alphabetic writing systems. It was an Irish innovation that was only beginning to be used in Britain at the time the Ruthwell Cross was made. Paul Saenger (1997) argues that it was the reading practices of the first millennium AD that enabled un-spaced alphabetic writing to persist for so long. Reading was largely confined to the church hierarchy, for which the most important text was the Bible: a book read letter-by-letter, and aloud, as a ritual practice carried out in the course of an existence devoted to ritual. Reading thus, one hardly needs the words separated: one has reached the end of a word when one has said all the sounds of that word. Saenger argues that breaking up words with spaces enables the reader to perceive their meaning without first having to reconstruct their sound. This is because, when isolated on the page, a word has a unique shape and can be recognised as a whole unit – much as in a logographic writing system. According to Saenger, the fast, silent reading of European languages was a second Irish invention that spread alongside word spacing. It made possible new uses of text: uses not confined to the purposes of a narrow religious elite.

7.4 To write, to print and to read

Allow about 10 minutes

Activity 7.2

Think for a moment about Figure 7.8, a reproduction of the title page of a sixteenth-century edition of a fifteenth-century text. What is depicted in the illustration? What is the illustration's connection to the text it accompanies?

Comment

To begin with the obvious, the image shows a monk writing on a page, alone in a room with other books. We can see that he is not copying from these books because they are all closed. Thus, he is composing a new text as he writes. He may even be at the very beginning of his composition: we see him writing on the right-hand half of a sheet whose left-hand half is blank, suggesting that the sheet is intended to be folded into a four-page booklet (or 'folio') with the current words at the front. (Only a supremely confident writer would embark on a book in such a way – but we should not suppose this to be a realistic depiction.) The words above the illustration suggest that the text the monk is depicted writing is the text to which the frontispiece belongs: 'Here begynneth the testame[n]t of Iohn Lydgate monke of Berry: which he made hymselfe/ by his lyfe dayes'. (Note the lower-case e with a line over it – a scribal abbreviation for 'en' – and the use of I where a writer of Modern English would use J; see Figure 7.2.)

Figure 7.8 Title page, Lydgate 1520 [fifteenth century]

John Lydgate wrote his testament in fifteenth-century England: a very different place from that discussed in the preceding section of this chapter. The kingdom of Northumbria was long gone, its lands divided between the newer kingdoms of England and Scotland. England's Anglo-Saxon aristocracy had in the eleventh century been displaced by invaders who brought with them a new socio-economic system (feudalism) and a new language variety (now known as Norman French) whose influence had transformed the language varieties of the Anglo-Saxon peoples into what scholars now call 'Middle English'. Great changes had also come to intellectual culture. Since the twelfth century, scribal copying had increasingly been the work of paid professionals rather than monks, and a book trade had developed. Partly as a result of these changes, a secular literary culture was starting to appear, and Lydgate was one of its brightest stars – like Geoffrey Chaucer, whom he evidently admired (Lydgate's *Seige of Thebes* draws heavily on Chaucer's *The Canterbury Tales*, and begins with an extended pastiche of that work's opening lines; see Figure 2.5).

But that is not the world in which the page in Figure 7.8 was made. The sort of books with which Lydgate would have been familiar were written by hand on sheets of vellum, or other types of cured animal skin. Soon after Lydgate's death, however, a new device had been invented for manufacturing documents (including the page in Figure 7.8). This device was the **printing press**, and its introduction was accompanied by the increasing replacement of vellum with paper (invented in China).

The first use of printing was not to reproduce text, but to reproduce images, using the technology of the **woodcut**. The first stage was to cut the required design into a block of wood with a knife. The block would then be smeared with ink, which would be transferred to a sheet of paper from the raised parts of the block. If you ever made potato prints as a child, you will understand the general principle! Like paper, this technology was invented in China, where from the eighth century onwards it was used not only in the reproduction of pictures, but also in the reproduction of whole pages of text: one can cut logograms or letters into a woodblock much as one would incise it with the lines of a detailed drawing. Before long, whole books and newspapers were being manufactured in this way, and by the fifteenth century, a crude form of woodblock printing had reached as far as Europe, where it was used to produce playing cards and religious images.

In the mid-fifteenth century, however, European printing technology was radically improved by Johannes Gutenberg. A goldsmith from Mainz (in present-day Germany), Gutenberg seems to have realised that he didn't have to cut each page of text into a fresh block of wood and then press paper or vellum on to it by hand. Instead, he could produce metal blocks bearing letters and punctuation marks, which could be fitted together and printed in a device probably inspired by a medieval wine press; as in Figure 7.8, these pieces of **type** could be combined with woodcuts to produce an illustrated text. We do not know much about the actual process and materials Gutenberg used, but it is probably fair to regard him as the inventor of the hand press and the pioneer of printing European languages with moveable type (see Figure 7.9).

Figure 7.9   Type on a compositing stick, ready to be placed in a chase (see box overleaf)

In the beginning, Gutenberg's workshop produced short printed texts such as indulgences (church-issued certificates supposedly entitling the bearer to preferential treatment in the afterlife). But it is mostly remembered for issuing Europe's first printed book: a magnificent Latin bible. Printed on vellum in black-letter type (see Chapter 2), this book closely resembles a high-quality handwritten bible of the same era – yet it was unquestionably far more difficult to produce. Why did Gutenberg bother? Preparing to print a book by letterpress requires expensive equipment and is extremely time-consuming. Because of this, it requires a much larger capital investment than hand-copying. But if enough copies of the resulting book can be sold, it yields much larger profits, since production costs *per copy* are greatly reduced, yielding economies of scale. This made printing into a lucrative although somewhat risky business: many of those engaged in it did very well (including Gutenberg's financial backer, Johann Fust), but many others were ruined (including Gutenberg himself). The net result, however, was an exponential growth in the amount of text available to read – which in turn effected a cultural and linguistic revolution.

The common press

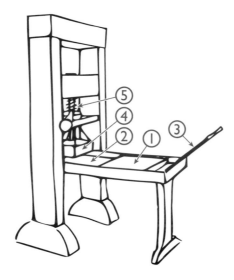

Figure 7.10   Simplified diagram of a wooden hand press

Figure 7.10 shows the basic components of a common press or hand press. Woodcuts and type are arranged in a frame called a chase (1) that lies upon the bed of the press (2). The pieces of type must be arranged to spell words backwards, because anything to be printed will appear in mirror image. Once ink has been applied to the type, a piece of paper is placed upon a hinged frame called a tympan (3), which folds down upon the chase, bringing the paper into contact with the type. The bed then slides under a slab of wood called a platen (4), which is forced down on to the back of the tympan with a lever-operated screw (5). This action drives the paper on to the type, transferring ink from the latter to the former.

Figure 7.11   Type set in a chase

No comparable revolution took place in China, even though printing with moveable type had been practised there since the tenth century AD. In contrast to the situation that unfolded in Europe, moveable type was in China used only by state authorities, and even then in a comparatively restricted way. One possible explanation for this is technological. The printing press was not invented in China, so sheets of paper had to be pressed on to the type by careful rubbing with a hand-held tool – a much slower process than that pioneered by Gutenberg. Another possible explanation, proposed by Benedict Anderson, is economic: capitalism had not yet begun to develop in China, which meant that it would have been harder both to raise the necessary investment and to realise profits through high-volume sales (Anderson, 2006 [1983], p. 44, f.n. 21). But it is also apparent that moveable type is a technology better suited to alphabetic than to logographic writing systems. To print a page of Classical Latin, one needs many pieces of type for each letter, but the total number of letters is relatively small (fewer than for Modern English; see Figure 7.2). By contrast, the classical Chinese writing system requires many thousands of different individual characters. Producing so many different type-casting moulds would have been very expensive, and there are huge problems with storing, using and re-storing so many tiny objects. Indeed, it appears that the hand-cut woodblock remained the most economical way of printing Chinese texts until the late nineteenth century (Edgren, 2007, p. 105).

Printing the English language

Gutenberg's invention spread rapidly across Europe, reaching the British Isles in 1475 or 1476 when a printing shop was set up at Westminster Abbey by William Caxton, an English merchant who had entered the printing business in Bruges (in present-day Belgium). Westminster was an auspicious location for a new venture in the communications industry: it was the political centre of England and was located just a few miles from the commercial centre of the kingdom, the City of London. Although Caxton was not a technical innovator like Gutenberg, he was a very successful businessperson and seems to have been keenly aware of his audience. The first book he printed at Westminster was his 1477 edition of Chaucer's *The Canterbury Tales* (discussed in Chapter 2): a fourteenth-century work that was still very popular in Caxton's time. Although *The Canterbury Tales* had been one of the most widely hand-copied works of the day, its circulation increased enormously once it was available in print. Moreover, the copies in circulation became much more linguistically similar to one another, since they were no longer subject to change by individual scribes. Late medieval scribes tended to 'translate' texts between language varieties when they copied them: a practice that appears to have arisen along with cursive (i.e. 'joined up') styles of handwriting, which encouraged writers to copy texts word-by-word rather than letter-by-letter (Benskin and Laing, 1981). Thus, medieval manuscript copies of *The Canterbury Tales* reveal a huge range of spellings, variant words, and forms of punctuation, but different copies of Caxton's first *Canterbury Tales* seem, by contrast, to be almost identical.

Printing also had an impact on the way that language was used, bringing more and more people into direct contact with the written word. The literary critic, Marshall McLuhan (1962), argued that the technology of printing transformed Western society, producing a new kind of person that he called 'typographic man': he asserted that '[t]he interiorization of the technology of the phonetic alphabet translates man from the magical world of the ear to the neutral visual world' (McLuhan, 1962, p. 18). This position has been described as **technological determinism**: the view that social and personal change is driven by the introduction of new technologies. On a historical level, it can be misleading, in part because technology usually develops in response to existing needs. Gutenberg's invention caught on so quickly in western and central Europe because the demand for books there was already too great to be satisfied through scribal production; where existing demand was lower (as in Russia), it was much longer before the new technology was taken up.

A subtler view of the relationship between printing and social change was provided by the historian, Elizabeth Eisenstein (1979), who contrasted **print culture** with **scribal culture**. Eisenstein argued that as printing came to supersede hand-copying by scribes as the primary means of textual reproduction, texts came to be more widely disseminated and more standardised (as with *The Canterbury Tales*) – and readers came to be more critical of what they read. According to Eisenstein, this was less because of the technology itself than because of its deployment in an industry primarily owned by entrepreneurs: instead of trying to impose texts on people through the exercise of authority, printers and booksellers competed with one another to produce the best editions and to sell them as widely as possible. Economic history shows that this picture is idealised, since laws of copyright limit direct competition between publishers of new texts, resulting in a tendency to produce relatively expensive editions for relatively exclusive audiences (St Clair, 2004). But despite this, the audience for print certainly became far larger, and far less exclusive, than the medieval audience for hand-copied manuscripts had been.

Activity 7.3

Allow about 10 minutes

Think for a moment about the likely impact of such a change. (It might be easier to begin by imagining the change in reverse: what do you think would have been lost if the English language had never been printed?)

Comment

The coming of print gave more and more people access to news, information and ideas. And it also had a transformative effect on speech communities, exposing readers to language produced in geographically distant locations. In the days before television, radio and the telephone, text was the only medium through which this could occur.

Mass literacy and social change

Print culture was not experienced in the same way by all levels of society. Until the nineteenth century, the only books that the working poor could afford were chapbooks: small, shoddily printed booklets with outdated contents. This suited many people. As Richard Altick (1957) shows, the possibility of mass literacy was feared by British politicians, and when modern literature began to come within the economic reach of ordinary people, church leaders did everything possible to discourage them from reading it. Moreover, with the Stamp Act of 1712, the British government deliberately prevented poor people from reading the news by imposing a heavy tax on newspapers – a tax that was not abolished until 1855. But despite all obstacles, English-language print became a part of life for an ever-wider public.

Nineteenth-century Britain saw a tremendous increase in the number of different books and newspapers being published, the number of individual copies of those books and newspapers being printed and the total volume of printed posters, fliers and other ephemera. At the same time, the proportion of the population possessing some degree of literacy also rose enormously: while just 60 per cent of males and 45 per cent of females in England and Wales appear to have been literate in 1800, these figures had risen to 94 per cent and 93 per cent by 1891 (Eliot, 2007). Many different factors drove these changes, perhaps the most important being the rapid technological developments that have characterised the printing business from the end of the eighteenth century to the present day. In the early nineteenth century, steam power began to replace human muscle as the motive power for the printing press; in the late nineteenth century, hand-compositing of type began to be replaced by mechanical compositing; in the late twentieth century, chemical and photographic processes overtook metal type as the most efficient tool for reproducing large volumes of text; by the end of the twentieth century, printing with metal type had all but disappeared in the developed world.

To many, the increasing availability of text appeared to be bringing about a new world order, as we see from one of John Keats's political works. This was written in response to Edmund Spenser's *The Faerie Queene*, in which a character called Sir Artegall, introduced as the 'Champion of true Iustice' (Spenser, 1609 [1596], v i 3, l. 2; note the use of the letter I where we would now use J; see Figure 7.2) engages in what now seems very unjust behaviour. Early in his adventures, Artegall encounters a giant who wishes to make all people equal, suppressing '[t]yrants that make men subiect to their law' (v ii 38, l. 6) and drawing 'all the wealth of rich men, to the poore' (v ii 38, l. 9). The knight engages the giant in a brief debate, which ends when Artegall's squire, Talus, takes the would-be revolutionary by surprise and shoves him over the edge of a cliff. In witty pastiche of Spenser, Keats added an epilogue to the tale:

> In after time, a sage of mickle lore,
> Yclep'd Typographus, the Giant took
> And did refit his limbs as heretofore;
> And made him read in many a learned book,
> And into many a lively legend look;
> Thereby in goodly themes so training him,
> That all his brutishness he quite forsook;
> When meeting Artegall and Talus grim,
> The one he struck stone-blind, the other's eyes wox dim.

(Keats, 1839 [1821])

In this stanza, believed to have been Keats's last, the poet imagines the printing industry as the wise Typographus, enabling the disenfranchised masses at long last to educate themselves. Not only restored, but refined through extensive reading of what we would now call fact and fiction, the working-class giant triumphs over its 'grim' feudal oppressors in this radical fairy story.

7.5 'English' and the market for English-language texts

The first printers had strong incentives to print in Latin: it was an international language, and its readers constituted an international market. As a result, printing in the vernacular languages of continental Europe did not become established until the sixteenth century. English, however, had something of a head start in this regard, because England's printers were unable to break into the Latin market. Vernacular printing therefore made economic sense for them: as many as 63 per cent of surviving books printed in England before 1501 are in English, as against 28 per cent in Latin and 9 per cent in French (Hellinga, 2007, p. 214).

The question of which variety of English to print arose quickly, and Caxton at least was consciously aware of making a choice. We know this because he discusses the matter in the foreword to his translation of Virgil's *Eneydos* (Caxton, 1490). In this text, Caxton tells the story of some merchants who stopped for provisions while sailing down the Thames towards the sea. The merchants' request for a common foodstuff ('eggys'; in Modern English, 'eggs') was not even recognised as English by the woman to whom it was presented until it was reiterated using the equivalent word in a local language variety ('eyren'). Caxton uses the story to illustrate the problem that, in choosing which word to use, 'it is harde to playse euery man / bycause of dyuersite & chauge of langage' (Caxton, 1490; 'it is hard to please everyone, because of linguistic diversity and change'; note that V and U were two versions of the same letter, one for use at the start of words and one for use in the middle: see Figure 7.2).

From this point of view, it seems inevitable that printers should have tried to settle on some kind of standard language, for the sake of the greatest possible comprehensibility and the widest possible market. Setting type by hand was a time-consuming task requiring skilled and educated workers: producing a special edition of each book for each part of the country would have eroded the printer's economies of scale, and in Europe, printing was from the very beginning a commercial enterprise. Caxton did not ask his readers to consider his profit margins, but he did ask them to accept that he had to adopt *some* sort of standard.

The question of which standard to adopt was far from neutral, however. Caxton had set up shop in Westminster, and Fleet Street in the nearby City of London rapidly became established as the centre of the English book trade. It is therefore hardly surprising that early English printers should in their linguistic choices have favoured language varieties used in this part of the world. But the printing industry established itself in Westminster and the City of London because it was there that the kingdom's wealth and power were concentrated (a state of affairs that still holds today). The English language in its printed form thus took for its model the language of money and of political authority. In fact, in a less frequently quoted passage of his foreword to *Eneydos*, Caxton goes on to explain that though the words he uses may be difficult for many people to understand, that should not be a problem because he writes for an exclusive audience. As he put it, 'this booke is not for euery rude dna vnconnynge man to see / but to clerkys and very gentylmen that vnderstande gentylnes and scyence' (Caxton, 1490; 'this book is not for every uneducated and ignorant man to see, but for clerks and true gentlemen who understand courtesy and learning'; 'dna' was an error by the compositor, who must have set the word 'and' forwards by mistake). A clerk was a churchman or a scholar, and a gentleman was a man of high social standing; English as it was to be printed was thus a language variety defined not only by geography, but also by education and social class. In (re)producing this English, Caxton and the early printers of London – most of whom appear to have been immigrants from continental Europe – were not imposing the language varieties that they happened to have grown up speaking, but meeting the expectations of their most important customers. As a merchant, Caxton himself was neither a clerk nor a gentleman – and like the woman who understood 'eyren' but not 'eggys', he hailed not from London, but from Kent.

Print-English

The idea that more standard forms of English are 'better' than less standard forms is discussed in more detail in another book in this series: Hewings and Tagg (eds) (2012), *The Politics of English*, Chapter 8.

Benedict Anderson coined the term 'print-languages' to refer to the language varieties used for printing (Anderson, 2006 [1983]). The use of a standard print-language enables printers to cater not only to readers who speak the language varieties on which that print-language is based, but also to readers who speak language varieties that are, in Anderson's terms, 'assimilable' to the standard; that is, similar enough for the print-language not to seem *completely* foreign. Such readers might not be in a position to demand their own print-language. But without one, they find themselves in a position of inferiority, since print comes to define the standard for speech as well as for writing. Pierre Bourdieu (1992 [1975]) argues that utterances of non-standard form have less value on the 'linguistic market', resulting in material disadvantage for speakers who struggle to produce the standard form of a language in situations where it is required (hence the idea that they lack 'linguistic capital'; see Chapter 4 of this book). And in his analysis of the psychological aspects of colonialism, Frantz Fanon (2008 [1952], p. 11) draws an analogy between speaking 'like a book' and speaking 'like a white man'.

Although proposed as a general theory, Anderson's ideas are applicable to the social history of language in the British Isles. What we might call print-English was based on the West Germanic language varieties spoken in the powerful and wealthy 'Golden Triangle' of Oxford, Cambridge and London/Westminster. The Celtic language varieties spoken in Wales, Ireland and the Scottish Highlands were not 'assimilable' to this printed form: for monolingual speakers of these language varieties, learning to read print-English will have involved not just learning to read, but learning an entirely new language. On the other hand, most of the language varieties that we now think of as dialects of Middle English evidently *were* assimilable to the print-form of Middle English. This is arguably why we consider them – and their modern descendants – to be dialects of a single language. Speakers of these varieties may have had to learn, for example, that the word spelled 'eggys' meant the same thing as the word they might have preferred to spell 'eyren' – but they will not have had to learn an entirely new grammar.

The West Germanic language varieties spoken in lowland Scotland were a very different matter, however. These resembled the speech of northern England, and were often referred to in Scotland as 'Inglis' (i.e. English). But England and Scotland were separate (and mutually hostile) kingdoms. As the royal court of Scotland became more closely identified with the lowlands than with the highlands, it increasingly communicated in Inglis – or as it was coming to be known, 'Scots'. In the sixteenth century, books began to be printed that followed Scottish lowland linguistic norms, rather than the norms of the printers working in London, and it is certainly conceivable that these developments could eventually have given rise to a standard form of print-Scots.

That this did not come to pass is usually put down to the coronation of King James VI of Scotland as King James I of England in 1603. Although James moved his court to London, he was unable to unify his two kingdoms. However, he was able to ensure that both the Church of England and its counterpart, the Scottish Kirk, would adopt the same text as their holy book: the 1611 Authorised Version of the Bible, popularly known as the King James Bible. Under state direction, this text was translated into English (not Scots), and authorised for reproduction by licensed printers in London, Edinburgh and elsewhere. In consequence, the 'written' language most familiar to Scots speakers was increasingly likely to be print-English. After the early eighteenth century unification of England and Scotland, Edinburgh became a centre for the book-producing industry, but it did so by catering less to the relatively small markets of Scots- and Gaelic-readers than to the much larger market of English-readers that by then existed both in England and in Scotland – as well as in the colonies that the two nations were jointly acquiring overseas and shaping into what would become their British Empire.

This did not prevent the first dictionary of Scots from appearing in 1808. Today, popular dictionaries of so-called 'dialect words' are often light-hearted, even trivialising, but studies of currently unprestigious language varieties can be very serious, both on a scholarly and on a political level. To publish a dictionary, a grammar or a history of a language variety is a very potent way of giving it material form, and thus of asserting its difference from existing print-languages – even when there currently exists little or no market for texts written in that language variety. A great many such publications appeared from the late eighteenth century onwards, often in conjunction with nationalist political movements (Anderson, 2006 [1983], pp. 71–5). On the basis of vernacular speech, existing writings and the authors' ingenuity, these books attempted (often successfully) to establish standard writing systems, orthographies, syntaxes and vocabularies for new print-languages.

When it comes to publications on the English language, however, none can compete for influence with Noah Webster's *American Dictionary of the English Language* (1828). Webster was well aware of the polemical potential of lexicography, using definitions and example sentences to promote his political and religious views. But his legacy was the establishment of British and American English as *visibly* different language varieties.

Activity 7.4

Now turn to Reading A: *Noah Webster and the diffusion of linguistic innovations for political purposes* by Brian Weinstein. Why were Webster's reforms so minor – yet so significant?

Comment

While Benjamin Franklin had proposed a new writing system, and justified it on grounds of its more accurate representation of spoken English, Webster's proposed reforms were limited to English orthography, and appear to have been motivated by nationalist concerns: on the one hand, the wish to unify English-users within America, and on the other hand, the wish to establish differences between them and English-users in Britain. However, the orthographic changes Webster succeeded in introducing were much fewer and less radical than those he had initially advocated.

As Weinstein notes, the very people whose help Webster needed in promoting his spelling reforms, from politicians to printers, were reluctant to endorse any radical changes. But the orthography that Webster eventually settled on was just different enough to distinguish American from British texts on the visual level.

In view of the idea that a writing system should do no more than represent the sound system of a language in visual form, it is worth emphasising that such systematic differences as now exist between British and American spelling bear no relation whatsoever to the equally systematic differences between British and American pronunciation. Webster's reforms did not respond to a pre-existing difference in American talk; instead, they produced a difference in American text.

7.6   Access to texts

The final section of this chapter looks at the ways in which readers may be materially obstructed from reading particular texts. We have already considered the most ubiquitous of these; that is, price. By today's standards, the Stamp Act seems monstrous, but high prices still act to exclude people from many forms of textual culture. In the developed world, mass-market books may now be a relatively cheap commodity, but the same books are prohibitively expensive for many people in the developing world: people who have in many cases lost access to public library provision in recent decades (for a range of reasons, including externally mandated restrictions on government spending). And many specialist publications are beyond the means of individuals everywhere. The subscription fees commanded by leading scientific journals (including medical journals) are now so high that even the best-funded research libraries struggle to pay them: in 2010, the University of California threatened to boycott the Nature Group over proposals to raise the average cost of its journals to more than $17,000 per year (Krupnick, 2010). Moreover, although many university libraries allow members of the public access to their collections of printed books and journals, access to electronic books and journals is in most cases legally restricted to students and staff. This means that, as electronic publication becomes the norm, access to the latest scientific knowledge will fall – at least while commercial publishers continue to control the market. State and commercial control of the internet is not unlimited, as was proven by the US government's inability to prevent confidential diplomatic materials from appearing on the WikiLeaks website in 2010. But as the example of academic publishing shows, digital technology is not *in itself* sufficient to democratise the circulation of texts: just as with print, it all depends on how the technology is used. And in recent years, public policy has been shaped far less by the imperative to secure public access to knowledge than by the commercial interests of wealthy corporations like Disney and Google – which is why the book historian, Robert Darnton, argues that 'we live in a world designed by Mickey Mouse, red in tooth and claw' (Darnton, 2009, p. 10).

Access to text is thus facilitated and limited by political and commercial forces, as well as by technology. But it is also facilitated and limited by language – or rather, by the interaction of language with politics, commerce and technology. We see this clearly with the example of the Republic of South Africa. During the apartheid era, when South Africa was ruled by white supremacists, the dominant language was Afrikaans. This might seem unsurprising, as it was the language of the Afrikaner community, which encompassed the majority of white South Africans. However, the political existence of the Afrikaner community as such was in large part the product of nineteenth- and early twentieth-century language politics. Until South African nationalists began campaigning on its behalf, Afrikaans was not widely regarded as a language, but simply as the non-standard speech of white 'Boer' colonists whose print-language was Dutch. The creation of a standardised print-form was necessary to establish Afrikaans as a language in its own right – which in turn helped to establish its speakers as a distinct ethnic community able to assert itself against the British Empire (which had subjected

Afrikaans-speaking civilians to inhuman atrocities during the Second Boer War). Rudi Ventner thus argues that '[t]he Afrikaner's rise to power did not start with the foundation of a political party but with the foundation of the language movements' (Ventner, 2007, p. 100). This rise not only involved state recognition for the Afrikaans language, but also state support for the new Afrikaans-language publishing industry. Had it not been for such support, Afrikaans would have had great difficulty in competing with longer-established print-languages such as English and Dutch, much as indigenous African languages continue to do to this day.

In a detailed history of apartheid-era censorship, Peter D. McDonald (2009) shows that books in Afrikaans were less often banned than books in other languages. But it should be noted that, despite this advantage, Afrikaner authors were in some ways more vulnerable than English-language authors. This was because Afrikaans books had virtually no audience outside South Africa: an unintended consequence of the Afrikaans language movement and its rejection of print-Dutch norms. South African books in English were, by contrast, much more likely to reach a worldwide audience, even when they could not legally be sold in South Africa itself. For this reason, André Brink responded to the banning of his novel *Kennis van die aand* (1973) by translating it into English: a move that 'had a profound effect on Brink's international career and his position, today, as the most widely translated Afrikaans author' (Ventner, 2007, p. 106). Nonetheless, it was books in indigenous African languages such as Xhosa that were in the worst position, since they were denied both the favoured status of Afrikaans and the international audience of English – and since their racially oppressed potential readers were for the most part trapped in poverty (as they and their descendants largely remain today).

The picture is not uniformly gloomy, however. No state has ever managed to achieve total control over textual circulation, and opponents of the apartheid regime went to great lengths in their efforts to read and reproduce forbidden texts. Proscribed books could be smuggled into the country like any other contraband and (with a little ingenuity) could even be printed in South Africa itself; for example, the anti-apartheid publisher Taurus used to send banned Afrikaans texts to a printer who could not read that language (Ventner, 2007). Moreover, texts that could not be sold on the open market were privately reproduced and exchanged on a non-commercial basis, creating what

Rachel Matteau calls an 'underground communication system' in which 'books ... circulated from hand to hand, either in their original form or as photocopies or extracts' (Matteau, 2007, pp. 81, 84).

Activity 7.5

Apartheid censorship was at its most extreme in South African prisons, with political prisoners being prevented from accessing many texts that were freely available outside the prison walls. Turn now to Reading B: *'Blood from stones': censorship and the reading practices of South African political prisoners, 1960–1990* by Archie Dick. What role did language difference play in the censorship regime – and how did political prisoners adapt their literacy practices to cope?

Comment

Dick describes a general lack of texts in indigenous African languages as well as a deliberate withholding of texts in languages that specific prisoners were thought able to read. However, lack of proficiency in particular languages could also prevent effective censorship. Moreover, as in the world outside prison, books written in Afrikaans were less tightly censored, permitting Afrikaans-reading inmates access to texts that would have been denied them in other languages.

Many of the literacy practices Dick describes testify to the value that reading and texts assumed in the repressive (and information-starved) environment of prison, including the intensive reading of personally important texts, the rescuing of newspapers from foul places, and the speed-reading, copying, translation and secret dissemination of news articles.

7.7 Conclusion

To understand language and communication, we must study the ways in which text technology has been put to use – whether by writers, readers, printers, censors or anyone else. The current chapter has taken a historical approach to such study, ranging from the invention of the alphabet to the present day. This has emphasised the need to look at language use not only in terms of individual or small-group practices, but also in terms of technological, economic and political systems subject to continual change. In the next chapter, you will see that such change continues even today.

READING A: Noah Webster and the diffusion of linguistic innovations for political purposes

Brian Weinstein

Source: Weinstein, B. (1982) 'Noah Webster and the diffusion of linguistic innovations for political purposes', *International Journal of Social Language*, vol. 38, pp. 85–108.

The changes in American English spelling, which have made written English in the United States of America slightly different from written English in Great Britain, are [...] an example of nationalism at work, an effort to create symbols which would unite Americans and draw a cultural frontier between the country and the former colonial power. Language strategists, particularly Noah Webster, and their friends provided a symbol of identity and a means to build cultural conformity. They changed a language rather slightly, as it turned out, and influenced American history without central government intervention.

The roots of this development are in Western Europe and England. Intellectual currents – the Age of Reason – in the late 17th and 18th centuries nurtured the idea that humans could consciously change and improve their societies, once they understood the origins of societies and institutions. John Locke, David Hume, and Montesquieu influenced their own societies and the 13 American colonies across the Atlantic; they analyzed the origins of politics and proposed secular ideals toward which humans could and should strive, including linguistic ones. In his *Essay Concerning Human Understanding,* Locke wrote that people should study the language they already speak, and written language should conform to spoken usage. [...]

This advice fell on receptive ears in England and in America. Why? Leonard has explained that the upper-middle classes in 18th-century England were replacing feudal lords in the seats of power. They were unsure of cultural standards and felt insecure in their own language [Leonard, 1929 [1962], pp. 12–13]. At the same moment and later in the 19th century the middle classes in America, swelled by new arrivals from the lower strata and from other countries, searched for standards. [...] At the same time, Americans put new faith in mass education through the common or public school [Marckwardt, 1976], which opened a huge market for books such as readers, spellers, and eventually dictionaries. [...]

As a result of these and other concerns, many Americans felt a compelling need to correct patterns of speech and writing. Appeals for government action in the form of an academy or a law concerning correctness were rejected. Officialdom refused to make policy or engage in culture planning in those early days, preferring to leave the initiative to private persons [Heath, 1976]. Without government encouragement, writers and printers began to propose an American written standard, and they diffused it along a network of friends and colleagues who played an essential role in the final outcome. The innovations finally accepted were not dramatic despite the radicalism of the very first suggestions. The changes, such as they were, and the extensive discussions justifying them and even attacking them made the English language one important symbol for America, however. As a symbol, American English at first reinforced the frontier between the former colonizing power and the former colony, and it provided one means of promoting internal unity, loyalty, and cultural homogeneity. The changes in orthography finally accepted include the following:

1. dropping 'u' from words like 'colour';

2. using 'ize' endings instead of 'ise' as in 'organize';

3. using 'ice' endings instead of 'ise' as in 'practice';

4. 'ct' instead of 'x' in 'connection';

5. 'er' instead of 're' in 'theater' and 'center';

6. dropping double 'll' in words like 'traveled', 'labeled'.

[…]

From Franklin to Webster

The person who initiated the process of spelling innovation was probably Benjamin Franklin (1706–1790). […] Franklin was a man of at least two worlds; born in America, he had studied printing in England as a youth and always had a special place in his heart for that country, as did other founders of the Republic. He set up his printing establishment in Philadelphia, where he quickly amassed a fortune so large that he could sell his enterprise at the age of 42 and then devote the next 42 years to travel, writing, inventions, and politics.

A year after his retirement Franklin turned his attention to problems of education and language in America [… and] began to experiment with a phonetic writing system. At least by 1768 he had prepared some new alphabet characters and went to the expense of having printing plates made for them. He used his scheme in a little correspondence and published the new system by 1779. According to his proposal, some characters were a radical departure from the Roman alphabet: s for 'sh' as in 'ship'; ɥ for 'u' as in 'umbrage'; and ŋ for 'ng' as in 'walking'. Further, he insisted that one symbol equal one sound only; 'e' would always represent the 'e' in 'men' and 'z' would always represent the sound of 's' in 'wages', for example [Franklin, 1838, p. 296]. Franklin proposed his changes in the name of science and rationality for the benefit of all English speakers. […]

Webster […] knew about Franklin's innovations and wrote to him in an effort to extend his network and to gain approval […] In 1786 Franklin invited the young writer to visit him in Philadelphia: 'Our ideas are so nearly similar, that I make no doubt of our easily agreeing on the plan; and you may depend on the best support I may be able to give it …' [Franklin to Noah Webster, 18 June 1786, in Sparks, 1838, vol. 10, pp. 261–2]. […]

The next year Webster returned to Philadelphia during the Constitutional Convention. Evenings he met and talked with delegates. The following months were spent editing the *American Magazine* in New York City. Promotion of the new constitution was the plain purpose of this publication, and influential federalists appreciated the assistance. Back home in Connecticut in 1789 he published his *Dissertation on the English Language*, dedicating it to Benjamin Franklin. In this text Webster explained the political and economic goals of spelling reform: he says he noted growing regional differences in pronunciation and spelling during his travels through the states to promote copyright legislation. Political division might follow cultural differences. […]

In the essay appended to the *Dissertation on the English Language* Webster made public his radical proposals, such as dropping 'ph' in 'philosophy' for 'f'; 'k' should replace the 'ch' in 'chorus'; removal of 'u' from 'honour'; drop the 'k' in 'publick' and drop silent 'e' at the end of words like 'examine'. 'Th' should be combined in one letter. This essay does not seem to have had much influence, however. He may have been testing the wind for his ideas.

For the next 54 years Webster grappled with reform and proposed standards, first in the name of science and politics and then to promote his Christian ideas. The spelling books and later dictionaries had a greater impact in this effort than his essays and other books. The

American Spelling Book was a great success, and it convinced him he could publish a second edition, which he did in 1790. In order to increase sales, he mobilized his network, particularly those who were federalists, Connecticut Yankees, and alumni of Yale. They sent him testimonials of support which he published in that second edition. As proof that 'the reception of our first Edition of The American Spelling Book has been so favourable [sic] . . ,' he printed the names of important people who approved it. The Lt. Governor of Connecticut, the president of Yale College, the mayor of Hartford, General Samuel H. Parsons, the Reverend Timothy Dwight of Yale, and the former head of Princeton were on the list. [...]

[... I]n 1806 [Webster] published a preliminary dictionary in which he proposed changes in a more systematic way than in the spellers. He stated in the preface that he would not be quite so radical as Franklin or as conservative as others [...]

In the body of the dictionary Webster hedged on some reforms. Although he definitely and consistently dropped the 'u' from words like 'labor' and the 'k' from 'public', and replaced 're' with 'er' in 'center' and 'theater', he wrote the following: 'leather, *more correctly* lether' (Webster's emphasis), 'Tour or Toor', 'Soup or soop', with separate entries for 'Soop' and 'Bild' [i.e. 'build'].

For the 1828 dictionary Webster pulled in his reformist horns a little more. In this book, which has served as the basis for dictionaries down to the present day, he made one last stand for more reforms. He gave up 'soop' but spelled the word 'Söup' and used 'Töur', explaining that the ¨ stood for 'anomalous sounds of the vowels' [Webster, 1830, p. 1]. More important, he set down here rules for spelling which have survived to the present day; they concerned 'u' and other alterations Americans follow today. He admitted that for many words he was obliged to accept custom and usage. Thus, the great lexicographer had wrestled with tradition and had won a few points; he had succeeded in making many people conscious about the issue of a standard language and the desirability of legitimizing some orthographic changes to suit the American experience and custom. [...]

What are the reasons for Webster's hesitation or refusal to apply and promote more radical ideas which would have drawn a clearer line between American and British culture and would have provided a more phonetic spelling? In his preface to the 1828 dictionary he admitted that it was desirable to maintain American and British English close together, 'yet some differences must exist. Language is the expression of ideas; and if the people of one country cannot preserve an identity of ideas, they cannot retain an identity of language' [Webster, 1828 [1970]]. This was a much weaker position than the one he took in the last decades of the 18th century. One reason for Webster's growing conservatism was his fear of radical changes and violence like those taking place in France after the Revolution of 1789. Like many of his federalist friends, he was not a democrat and believed that threats to authority would unleash the worst impulses among the common people. In 1808 he converted to fundamental Protestantism and began to believe that human tinkering with God's world could be sinful.[1] Economic considerations played a role in his conservatism, too. The American and British economies complemented each other, he believed, and France was a threat to both. America would be a great market for the British, he wrote in a letter, and the British West Indies and England would always be a great market for America's agricultural products [letter to Rufus King, New York, 1 June 1797, in Warfel, 1953, pp. 150–9]. (He was doubtless thinking about books, too.)

A third answer is that [...] the people he respected most [...] disapproved of his radical changes. He had tried to influence his friends and acquaintances and found himself being influenced in turn. The people with whom he shared the most in terms of class, region, religion, and political beliefs urged restraint. Even old Franklin had complained about some changes naturally occurring: 'notice' and 'advocate' were being used as verbs, he wrote to Webster in 1789; printers were no longer capitalizing nouns the way tradition demanded, and they were giving up italics [Franklin to N. Webster, 26 December 1789, in Franklin, 1794, pp. 42–8]. Others offered specific objections to changes Webster had tried to introduce. For example, Ezra Stiles, who became president of Yale in 1778, the year Webster was graduated, objected to the idea of dropping silent 'e' at the end of words [Rollins, 1980; Fishman, 1977]. [...] John Jay, governor of New York and the first Chief Justice, explicitly warned the dictionary maker:

> The literary production of Britain and America being interesting to each other, many are of opinion, and I concur in it, that the English language and its orthography should be the same in both countries. Apprehensions have been entertained that your

dictionary would tend to impair that sameness; and those apprehensions may, to a certain degree, have had an unfavourable influence.

[Jay to Webster, 31 May 1813, in Johnson, 1970, pp. 372–3]

What Jay meant by 'unfavourable influence' was that some people were not purchasing Webster's book, and he knew better than most people that Webster needed money. Jay, in fact, had sent him funds to keep him going [Warfel, 1936 [1966], p. 364].

Note

[1]   This is Rollins' [1980] view.

References for this reading

Fishman, Joshua A. (ed.) (1977). Preface. In *Advances in the Creation and Revision of Writing Systems*. The Hague: Mouton: xvi.

Franklin, Benjamin (1794). *Works of the Late Dr. Benjamin Franklin*, vol. 2. New York: Campbell: 42–48.

Franklin, Benjamin (1838). Scheme for a new alphabet and reformed mode of spelling; with remarks and examples. In *The Works of Benjamin Franklin*, Jared Sparks (ed.). Boston: Hilliard Gray, vol. 6: 296.

Heath, Shirley Brice (1976). A national language academy? Debate in the new nation. *International Journal of the Sociology of Language* 11: 33–35.

Johnson, Henry P. (ed.) (1970). *The Correspondence and Public Papers of John Jay*, vol. 4, 1794–1826. New York: Burt Franklin: 372–373.

Leonard, Sterling Andrews (1929 [1962]). *The Doctrine of Correctness in English Usage 1700–1800*. New York: Russell and Russell: 26.

Marckwardt, Albert (1976). The professional organization and the school language problem. *International Journal of the Sociology of Language* 11: 107–123.

Rollins, Richard M. (1980). *The Long Journey of Noah Webster*. Philadelphia: University of Pennsylvania Press: 19.

Sparks, Jared (ed.) (1838). *The Works of Benjamin Franklin*. Boston: Hilliard Gray, vol. 10: 261–262.

Warfel, Harry R. (1936 [1966]). *Noah Webster: Schoolmaster to America*. New York: Octagon: 364.

Warfel, Harry R. (ed.) (1953). *Letters of Noah Webster*. New York: Library Publishers: 150–159.

Webster, Noah (1828 [1970]). *An American Dictionary of the English Language* .... New York: Converse: Preface.

Webster, Noah (1830). *A Dictionary of the English Language Abridged from the American Dictionary for the Use of Primary Schools and the County House.* New York: White, Gallaher, and White: 1.

READING B: 'Blood from stones': censorship and the reading practices of South African political prisoners, 1960–1990

Archie L. Dick

Source: Dick, A. L. (2008) '"Blood from stones": censorship and the reading practices of South African political prisoners, 1960–1990', *Library History*, vol. 24, no. 1, pp. 1–22.

Political imprisonment and prison narratives

Although one source claims that between 1960 and 1990 about 80,000 people in South Africa were detained without trial, there were probably many more political prisoners [Human Rights Commission, 1990]. In 1978 alone there were 440 convicted political prisoners, mostly from the African National Congress (ANC) and Pan Africanist Congress (PAC), of which 400 were on Robben Island and the rest in Pretoria Local and Kroonstad prisons [Schadeberg, 1994, p. 48]. [...]

These prisoners represented a cross-section of South African society that opposed the apartheid state and its policies. They included men and women, old and young, working- and middle-class and black and white members of several political organizations and movements. [...]

A growing body of prison literature – jail diaries, authorized biographies, autobiographies, prison memoirs, interviews, and prison letters – provides personal accounts of the most horrific kinds of torture and humiliation in apartheid South African and other African jails. Several prisoners died in detention, many more suffered psychological and physical harm at the hands of interrogators and security police, and a few attempted suicide in prison.

In these prison narratives, there are also references to struggles for access to reading materials; their uses, abuses, and roles in resisting prison authorities; quarrels with prison censors; reading to shape personal and political lives and to maintain contact with the outside world; and using books to experience as 'normal' a life as possible in traumatic circumstances. [...]

Detention, solitary confinement and the Bible

[...] During spells of detention and solitary confinement the Bible was [...] the only reading material [Kgosana, 1988, p. 38]. Detainees with other religious convictions were sometimes supplied with their own holy books. Abdulla Haron, for example, kissed and placed the Koran on his prayer mat on the day he died in detention [Desai and Marney, 1978, p. 125]. Fatima Meer, a Muslim, was mistakenly given the 'Ramayana' (a Hindu epic poem), which she found 'fascinating reading' [Meer, 2001, p. 33]. And Zubeida Jaffer set herself the task during her second detention to read the Arabic-English Koran from 'cover to cover', with the expectation that: 'When I was finished with this task, I would be released' – and she was [Jaffer, 2003, pp. 133–5]. [...]

Religious leaders were targeted spitefully so that Methodist priest Stanley Mogoba was given a Xhosa-language Bible while in isolation [Mogoba, 2003, p. 48], which ironically he made use of to learn that language. Reverend Frank Chikane was refused a Bible because a warder said 'it makes you a terrorist', and was eventually given an Afrikaans-language version [Chikane, 1988, p. 56]. Tshenuwani Simon Farisani, who was Dean of the Evangelical Lutheran Church, was told that he was 'always reading the wrong verses of the Bible', and [was] regularly denied one [Farisani, 1987, pp. 22, 29, 60].

On the other hand, Michael Dingake was refused a Bible because the warder at Jeppe Police Station did not want to get him 'expelled from the Communist Party' [Dingake, 1987, p. 114]. At John Vorster Square, Emma Mashinini was also refused a Bible on the grounds that she was a communist, but she later received one from her husband and another as a gift from Bishop Desmond Tutu [Mashinini, 1989, pp. 54, 82, 84]. In another cynical twist on this theme, Raymond Suttner was tortured using 'his bible' (works of Marx, Engels and Lenin) to weigh down his outstretched arms while in a crouching position, and forced to read from it while lying flat on a table with just his head raised [Suttner, 2001, p. 26]. [...]

The Bible as a material artefact was also a useful resource for political prisoners. At Port Elizabeth Prison, [Robert] Strachan helped to make a set of dominoes from the thicker back page of the Bible. More irreverent was to smoke the 'actual text of the Bible', even if it earned offenders six days without food. [...]

Library services for political prisoners

Access to reading material in prisons, which were racially segregated, improved only through struggle by political prisoners themselves, and the right of access was withdrawn without explanation from time to time. An Appellate Division judgment relating to conditions of ninety-day detention in Rossouw versus Sachs in 1964, for example, reversed a decision of the lower court. The original decision had held that to deprive a detainee of a reasonable supply of reading and writing material constituted a form of punishment, and it allowed Sachs access to books. The subsequent judgment, though, concluded that 'it was not the intention of Parliament that detainees should as of right be permitted to relieve the tedium of their detention with reading matter or writing materials' [quoted in Foster, 1987, p. 98]. [...]

Some political prisoners were not always given access to books, and language was a discriminating factor. By 1991 at Pollsmoor Prison library's General Section there were still only 140 Xhosa-language books for about 150 Xhosa-speaking women. Of these books, sixty-three were 'Junior Fiction', and when Palesa Thibedi enquired about this she was told that Pollsmoor Prison had been designed for whites and 'coloureds' [i.e. people of mixed race] [Thibedi, 1992, p. 138]. In an attempt to overcome the language and literacy barriers, political prisoners like Caesarina Makhoere became involved in improving the literacy levels of fellow prisoners [Makhoere, 1988, p. 113]. The Department of Prisons also conducted its own literacy classes, and 4,040 prisoners completed a literacy course between 1968 and 1976 [Commissioner of Prisons, 1976, p. 12]. [...]

Censorship and contraband

To achieve its rehabilitation ideals, the Department of Prisons generally allowed all books that were not banned by the state's Censorship Board. But a further regulation enabled a prison commanding officer to prohibit reading matter of an overwhelmingly stimulating and sexual nature, along with stimulating photographs and anything that might promote unrest among prisoners [Suid-Afrika, Departement van Gevangenisse, 1976]. In the case of political prisoners, censor officers had also to apply all the 'B-orders', which stated clearly that 'politics and news from outside was strictly forbidden' [Gregory, 1995, p. 105]. [...]

Some officials took a different approach, and Robben Island censor officer James Gregory, for example, became convinced that censorship laws were harsh and wrong. He argued with other censor officers, and the system of censorship of letters and newspapers on Robben Island was gradually relaxed [Gregory, 1995, pp. 126–7, 239]. Warder Sotheby, moreover, allowed a young prisoner to read the *Cape Times* and tell his comrades the news. He also left the Sunday newspapers where political prisoners could find them [Babenia, 1995, p. 144]. Nelson Mandela's first prison punishment, however, was for being caught 'black-and-white-handed' for possessing a newspaper left for him by a warder [Mandela, 1994, p. 493].

[…] Books with any reference to Marx, marxism, Lenin, leninism, Russia, China, Cuba, socialism, communism, revolution, war, civil war, violence, Africa, anti-Apartheid literature, and historic-political literature written by blacks were almost always automatically withheld. Carl Niehaus [1993, p. 125], for example, was refused *The Way of the black messiah*, and for some time [Jean] Middleton [1998, p. 114] was not allowed to get *Black prophets in South Africa*.

Prison censors had little formal education and were told in crash courses by higher-ranking officers what books or titles to disallow. Some books like Tolstoy's *Resurrection* were refused because prison officials knew too little to tell whether it was suitable or not [Sachs, 1990, p. 249]. Censor officer Aubrey du Toit, for example, only had a matriculation qualification and knew nothing about political science, but had to censor the political science assignments of Unisa [University of South Africa] honours degree student and prisoner Andrew Mlangeni. He says: 'I didn't know what I was looking for … it was a joke for an Afrikaner with Standard 10 to censor these difficult assignments' [quoted in Schadeberg, 1994, p. 47].

Ironically though, under-qualified censors let in many books unknowingly while many actually needed were stopped [Alexander, 1991, p. 302]. [Neville] Alexander admits that he read books in prison that he would never have had the time or chance to read outside. He read classics of European literature, Gibbon, Shakespeare, Dickens, African history, international law, economics, languages, and lots of German literature, and adds: 'I had more banned books inside prison than I ever had outside' [Alexander, 1994, p. 69]. […]

[…] From the 1960s, however, through collusion with common law prisoners, the wall of apartheid censorship was breached through smuggling. Tobacco was used to pay the smugglers for newspapers, and [Dennis] Goldberg started smoking again just to get a prison tobacco ration.

Often more desperately, though, newspapers were fished from toilets [Turok, 2003, p. 160], retrieved from rubbish dumps, lifted from the satchels of unsuspecting or collaborating visiting preachers, and simply stolen [Mandela, 1994, p. 537; Daniels, 1998, p. 165]. […] And then they were read in secret and shared with others [Mphahlele, 2002, p. 123].

In the case of Robben Island, smuggled newspapers were brought to a central point where they were rapidly scanned, then memorized by readers and transmitted to a smaller group that would in turn disseminate the information to another group, and so forth. The news would sometimes be translated and transcribed and then re-transcribed to safeguard individuals. The readers usually developed their own techniques of remembering articles on political, social, cultural, scientific, and sporting categories [Naidoo, 1982, pp. 155–6].

They learned speed reading techniques from Sedick Isaacs and read as quickly as possible, and then got rid of the contraband. Pages were usually soaked because tearing was noisy, and then flushed down toilets in strips. But sometimes reading as consumption assumed a literal meaning when pages were actually swallowed and eaten to avoid detection [Lewin, 1974, p. 108]. […]

[A]t Pretoria Central […] a couple of thousand [books were] bought over the years [by higher-status prisoners] and when they left the books remained behind as prison property. These books were of a high quality. The prison censor had a list of banned books but kept no record of what was ordered, and nothing was removed from their shelves. Censors were not very intelligent, and many 'subversive' books of economic and political theory with fairly innocuous titles were added to the collection [Jenkin, 2003, pp. 195–6]. Afrikaans language books were not screened as closely as those in English, and an Afrikaans book on sabotage circulated freely among prisoners [Robben Island Museum Education Department, n.d., p. 34].

References for this reading

Alexander, N. (1991) in T. Lodge and B. Nasson (eds), *All, here, and now: black politics in South Africa in the 1980s* (Cape Town: Ford Foundation – David Philip) 302.

Alexander, N. (1994) in B. Hutton (ed.) *Robben Island: symbol of resistance* (Johannesburg, Sached; Bellville, Mayibuye Books) 69.

Babenia, N. (1995) *Memoirs of a saboteur: reflections on my political activity in India and South Africa*, as told to Iain Edwards (Bellville: Mayibuye Books) 144.

Chikane, F. (1988) *No life of my own: an autobiography* (London: Catholic Institute for International Relations) 56.

Commissioner of Prisons (1976) Report of the Commissioner of Prisons of the Republic of South Africa for the Period 1 July 1975 to 30 June 1976 (Pretoria: Government Printer) 12.

Daniels, E. (1998) *There and back: Robben Island 1964–1979*, Mayibuye History and Literature Series, No. 83 (Bellville: Mayibuye Books) 165.

Desai, B. and Marney, C. (1978) *The killing of the Imam* (London: Quartet Books) 125.

Dingake, M. (1987) *My fight against apartheid* (London: Kliptown Books) 114.

Farisani, T. S. (1987) *Diary from a South African prison*, edited by J. A. Evenson (Philadelphia: Fortress Press) 22, 49, 60.

Foster, D. (1987) *Detention and torture in South Africa: psychological, legal & historical Studies* (Cape Town: David Philip) 98.

Gregory, J. with Bob Graham (1995) *Goodbye Bafana; Nelson Mandela, my prisoner, my friend* (London: Headline) 105, 126–7, 239.

Human Rights Commission (1990) Violence in detention, in B. McKendrick and W. Hoffmann (eds), *People and violence in South Africa* (Cape Town: Oxford University Press) 410–413.

Jaffer, Z. (2003) *Our generation* (Cape Town: Kwela Books) 133–135.

Jenkin, T. (2003) *Inside out: escape from Pretoria Prison* (Bellevue: Jacana) 239, 195–6.

Kgosana, P. A. (1988) *Lest we forget: an autobiography by Philip Ata Kgosana*, (Johannesburg: Skotaville) 38.

Lewin, H. (1974) *Bandiet: seven years in a South African prison* (London: Heinemann) 108.

Makhoere, C. K. (1988) *No child's play: in prison under apartheid* (London: The Women's Press) 113.

Mandela, N. (1994) *Long walk to freedom: the autobiography of Nelson Mandela* (London: Abacus) 493, 537.

Mashinini, E. (1989) *Strikes have followed me all my life: a South African autobiography* (London: Women's Press) 54, 82, 84.

Meer, F. (2001) *Prison diary: one hundred and thirteen days, 1976* (Cape Town: Kwela Books) 33.

Middleton, J. (1998) *Convictions: a woman political prisoner remembers* (Randburg: Ravan Press) 114.

Mogoba, M. S. (2003) *Stone, steel, sjambok: faith on Robben Island*, edited by T. Coggin (Johannesburg: Ziningweni Communications) 48.

Mphahlele, L. (2002) *Child of this soil: my life as a freedom fighter* (Cape Town: Kwela Books) 123.

Naidoo, I. (1982) *Island in chains – Prisoner 885/63: ten years on Robben Island as told by Indres Naidoo to Albie Sachs* (London: Penguin Books) 155–156.

Niehaus, C. (1993) *Om te Veg vir Hoop* (Cape Town: Human & Rousseau) 125.

Robben Island Museum Education Department (n.d.) *Banned books: images of the word*.

Sachs, A. (1990) *The jail diary of Albie Sachs* (Cape Town: David Philip) 249.

Schadeberg, J. (1994) *Voices from Robben Island* (Randburg: Ravan Press) 47, 48.

Suid-Afrika, Departement van Gevangenisse (1976) Hoofstuk 26, Wysigingstrokie no. 4/76, Biblioteekdienste en Leesstof, 28 junie 1976 (Ongepubliseerd), Staande Gevangenisdiensorder no. B.22.8 (b)(ii).

Suttner, R. (2001) *Inside apartheid's prison: notes and letters of struggle* (Pietermaritzburg: University of Natal Press) 26.

Thibedi, P. (1992) Ayiyo Trongo Yethu Le!, in B. Schreiner, *A snake with ice water: prison writing by South African women* (Johannesburg: COSAW) 138.

Turok, B. (2003) *Nothing but the truth: behind the ANC's struggle politics* (Johannesburg and Cape Town: Jonathan Ball) 160.

8   Digital English

Caroline Tagg

8.1   Introduction

> – Come with me, then, Patrick. Let's go backwards. … Back to a
> country that neither of us would recognize, probably. Britain, 1973.
>
> – Was it really that different, do you think?
>
> – Completely different. Just think of it! A world without
> mobiles or videos or Playstations or even faxes. A world that had
> never heard of Princess Diana or Tony Blair … There were only
> three television channels in those days, Patrick. Three!
>
> (Coe, 2001, pp. 3–4)

How quickly the world has changed in recent decades! In the novel *The
Rotters Club*, Jonathan Coe takes his readers back to 1970s Britain.
Although many differences reflect British concerns at the turn of the
millennium – Princess Diana, Tony Blair – the world of the 1970s was
not only a place 'without mobiles or videos or Playstations' , but one
without search engines and the World Wide Web – and one in which
email and the internet were available only to a tiny minority. The end
of the twentieth century saw a development in technology which has
transformed the way many people communicate. By 2000, for example,
globally over 360 million people were estimated to be online (i.e. able to
access the internet). Such figures continue to rise at a staggering rate,
with the estimated number of internet users rising to nearly two billion
in 2010 (Internet World Stats, 2010a). If the preceding half-millennium
can be described as the age of print, then the twenty-first century has
quickly become the digital age: the age of computer and information
technology.

Figure 8.1 From the age of print to the digital age

The internet and the World Wide Web

The **internet** is a network of interconnected computer networks. It was developed by public and private US research organisations in the 1970s on the basis of the ARPANET, an earlier network organised and funded by the US Department of Defence and employing technologies developed at RAND Corporation and the UK National Physical Laboratory.

The **World Wide Web (WWW)** is a network of interlinking 'web pages' available via the internet and viewable using a computer program called a browser (e.g. Mozilla Firefox). These pages are grouped into 'websites'. Individual pages or sites are usually found either through search engines (e.g. Google), or by navigating from one page to the next via 'hyperlinks': images or pieces of text that instruct the browser to view a different page when selected by the user. The Web was invented in 1989 by Tim Berners-Lee, a British scientist working for CERN, the publicly funded European Organisation for Nuclear Research; in 1991, CERN hosted the world's first web page.

'Digital' describes the technique of storing, transmitting and processing data which sits behind these advances: as discussed in Chapter 2, it involves transforming information of every kind, from text to sound to image, into sequences of numbers. Most electronic gadgets are now driven by digital technology: watches, cameras and washing machines, as well as computers and mobile phones. Developments in these technologies appear to be having a profound and potentially lasting impact on English, affecting both the forms of the language itself and the communicative practices in which its speakers engage. The term 'digital English' encompasses both the changing language and the emerging practices. **Online communities** – for example, the users who contribute to and consult entries in online resources such as Wikipedia and Urban Dictionary – are developing new literacy practices around **digital texts**; that is, texts that are stored in a digital medium rather than printed, written or engraved on a physical surface (as discussed in the previous chapter). In this chapter, I look at some of these digital practices and explore the implications for what it means to be literate in the twenty-first century. I also look at how digital technology facilitates 'interactive written discourse' (Ferrara et al., 1991) or **digital talk**: a form of language use which has characteristics of what earlier chapters in this book have called 'talk' and 'text'. To what extent can online written exchanges be compared to spoken conversation? Should we worry when these fast and informal exchanges appear to be changing spelling and grammar conventions? In this chapter, I argue that digital technologies in fact provide unregulated spaces where people feel free to play with language, often in creative and meaningful ways.

Digital 'talk', digital 'text'

This chapter defines talk and text somewhat differently from other chapters in this book. 'Talk' in digital contexts does not necessarily refer to oral communication. Although it is possible to communicate orally online (through a program such as Skype, for example), most linguistic research on digital communication focuses on cases where textual media, such as email and online messaging, are used in a 'speech-like' way. The term 'digital text' is, by contrast, used to describe more stable resources such as ebooks and individual blog postings. This is a useful distinction, but (as we shall see) no clear divide can be assumed.

Why digital English and not digital French or digital isiXhosa? The issues and controversies surrounding digital communication are relevant across languages, and English cannot easily be discussed in isolation from other languages with which it coexists online. However, given its particular position in the world today and in the development of communications technology, English holds a unique position in the digital sphere. At the end of this chapter, I look at the impact that digital technology has had on the balance and relationship between English and other languages – that is, the extent to which the global status of English is reflected in, and sustained by, online usage – and the opportunity for language contact that the internet provides.

What I want to highlight throughout this chapter is the fact that, despite the impact of digital technology on how people communicate, ultimately it is the people who use it who choose what they will do with it. Rather than being constrained by technology (as is assumed in technological determinism: see Chapter 7), individuals can potentially exploit different technologies in different ways. One way of understanding this is to see the features or potential constraints of a medium as its affordances (see Chapter 5). This term describes the possible ways in which a technology can be used. For example, SMS (Short Message Service) may have appeared to be a constraining and unlikely medium of communication when it was added to mobile phones in the 1990s as a way for engineers to communicate. However, the people who took up the technology and used it for various social purposes (the start of text messaging as we know it!) saw and exploited possibilities that the phone manufacturers had underestimated. They had perceived its affordances. This is an important point to which I will return throughout the chapter.

Allow about
10 minutes

Activity 8.1

Before reading on, take a moment to reflect on the importance of digital technology to your communicative practices. List the forms of digital communication you use (including phone calls and text messaging, as well as the internet). How often do you use them and what do you use them for?

Comment

I'll briefly describe one use of digital communication technology that is important in my life. As of the beginning of 2011, instant messaging is perhaps my principal means of digital communication (after email). I use Windows Live Messenger daily to chat – in the sense of sending typed messages – to friends and family abroad, as well as to my mother who uses Messenger at work. My conversations with my mother tend to be on practical topics; and when I chat to a British friend in Chile, we both write in Spanish (to practise).

Should the technology or practices seem odd or unfamiliar to you, there are various explanations. First, digital technology continues to change so fast that what you or I were doing in 2011 may not be what either of us is doing by the time you read this book. Think about the digital technology you were using this time last year, and how it differs from your current list; keep the list and see how quickly it dates. (You may also bear this in mind as you read through this chapter.) Second, online options are increasingly diverse: Messenger, for example, now offers many of the same facilities as Skype; there are numerous national and international social network sites (SNS); and often it is simply a question of what the people you want to communicate with are themselves using.

8.2   Digital Englishes

Figure 8.2   People – as well as machines – shape digital communication.

Let's look more closely at what is meant by 'digital English' and highlight the diversity encompassed by the term.

Computer-mediated communication has been defined by Susan Herring as 'predominantly text-based human–human interaction mediated by networked computers or mobile telephony' (Herring, 2007). By breaking down this densely packed definition, we can identify the following characteristics of digital interaction:

- It is produced, disseminated and accessed through computers or mobile phones (which are in reality small computers). Digital communication is a product not only of computer technology, but also of the communication and information technology by which it is disseminated – usually the internet, but also local computer networks or 'intranets'. These may affect, respectively, the size of message that can be sent and the speed of delivery.

- It takes place between people (human–human), rather than between people and machines or machines and other machines. It is important to remember that people – as well as machines – shape digital communication.

- It is largely 'text based' in the sense of being written rather than spoken: despite its name, even online 'chat' involves short, typed messages rather than speech. At the same time, a characteristic feature of digital English is its multimodality: while previous chapters in this book have argued that all language use involves non-linguistic forms of communication, digital communications technology provides genuinely new multimodal affordances, such as the possibility of embedding digital images, video and sound files in a web page.

Allow about 20 minutes

Activity 8.2

Look through the following extracts of digital Englishes and decide where they come from. What features, if any, do they have in common? What are the main differences? This activity should start you thinking about the different forms of digital English and the linguistic features which characterise them. Note that because this chapter is primarily concerned with linguistic (as opposed to paralinguistic, bibliographic or multimodal) features, data are not given in the form of authentic screenshots (as in Chapter 2).

Extract 1

\<Wizard\>	Come, brave Knight! Let me cast a spell of protection on you ….. Oooops – wrong spell! You don;t mind being green for a while- do you???
\<Prince\>	Lioness: please don't eat him…
\<storm\>	*shivers from the looks of lioness*
\<Knight\>	Wizard: Not at all.
\<Bel_letre\>	*hahahah*
\<Lioness\>	Very well, your excellency. *looks frustrated*
\<Prince\>	*falls down laughing*.
\<Knight\>	Wizard: as long as I can protect thou ass, I'd be utter grateful! :-)
\<Bel_letre\>	*Plays a merry melody*
\<storm\>	*walks over to lioness and pats her paw*
\<Wizard\>	*Dispells the spells cast on Knight!*
\<Wizard\>	Knight: Your back to normal!!!
\<Prince\>	*brings a pallete of meat for Lioness*
\<Lioness\>	*licks Storm*
\<storm\>	*Looking up* Thank You for not eating me!

(Reid, 1991, p. 23)

Extract 2

Brur its 2bed one matras my darling is going 2 put me in shid in church. My money i have save have been decrease due 2 da Aunt Mayoly's funeral,& miner problst. So da case is coming very soon 3months preg. I'll c then. Sharp. (Mzwakhe)

(Deumert and Masinyana, 2008, p. 126)

Extract 3

Finland (/ˈfɪnlənd/; Finnish: *Suomi*; Swedish: *Finland* (help info)), officially the **Republic of Finland**,[5] is a Nordic country situated in the Fennoscandian region of Northern Europe. It is bordered by Sweden in the west, Norway in the north and Russia in the east, while Estonia lies to its south across the Gulf of Finland.

(adapted from http://en.wikipedia.org/wiki/Finland, accessed 31 July 2011)

Extract 4

I've never told anyone this story, and never thought I would – not because I was afraid of being disbelieved, exactly, but because I was ashamed … and because it was mine. I've always felt that telling it would cheapen both me and the story itself, make it smaller and more mundane, no more than a camp counselor's ghost story told before lights-out. I think I was also afraid that if I told it, heard it with my own ears, I might start to disbelieve it myself. But since my mother died I haven't been able to sleep very well. I doze off and then snap back again, wide awake and shivering. Leaving the bedside lamp on helps, but not as much as you might think. There are so many more shadows at night, have you ever noticed that? Even with a light on there are so many shadows. The long ones could be the shadows of anything, you think. Anything at all.

(King, 2000a)

Comment

Extract 1 is from an early digital communications technology called Internet Relay Chat (IRC). In IRC, any number of users, who often do not otherwise know each other, enter a public online forum and send short messages to the group or direct them to one particular user, such as the user 'Knight' as in *Knight: Your back to normal!!!* IRC is **synchronous**; that is, the turns follow quickly on the heels of the others and conversation takes place in near-real time. (Email, in contrast, is potentially **asynchronous**, because delays of days or even weeks may occur between messages.) IRC comprises short turns, as in spoken conversation. It features speech-like abbreviated phrases such as *Very well* and *not at all*, and a similar sense of interactivity to that seen in speech: *do you????* At the same time, another defining feature of IRC is its distinctive **graphology**; that is, orthography, punctuation and layout. In this case, the most distinctive graphological feature is the way in which imaginary actions are signalled with asterisks (*) as in *shivers from the looks of lioness*. This particular IRC exchange is part of an online fantasy role-playing game (hence the actions and the particular nicknames).

Extract 2 is an SMS text message, sent from a mobile phone by Mzwakhe, a South African bilingual in English and isiXhosa. An SMS message is limited to 160 characters, although more than one message can be sent at one time, if the texter is willing to pay for that. Mzwakhe's SMS is one relatively short 'turn' in a longer texted conversation. A distinct graphology can be seen in the spelling variants or **respellings**; for example, *due 2 da* (due to the) and *3months preg* (three months pregnant). (The term 'respellings' avoids judgements about correctness, and instead focuses on the role that unconventional spellings can play in conveying identity.) As with Extract 1, you may notice that the language is difficult for an outsider to understand. In this case, this is not so much because of respellings, like *da* for 'the', or *2* and *c* for 'to' and 'see', but because of the number of 'local' forms which occur in it. These include respellings and other features characteristic of the region of South Africa from which the message is sent: *Brur* is 'brother', *sharp* is 'cheers' or 'see you', and *2bed one matras* refers to a local joke about a missing mattress which hinges on the mispronunciation of 'too bad' as 'two bed' (Deumert and Masinyana, 2008, p. 127). These give a strong sense of local identity to the text message: a theme I return to later.

Extract 3 is from an online wiki: a website which allows users to create, add or delete content. This particular wiki is the online collaborative encyclopaedia, Wikipedia, set up in 2001 and, at the time of writing, by far the most widely used and well-known wiki. What identifies this extract as digital is the hyperlinks (which are here underlined and in the original would have been differently coloured). By clicking on a 'hyperlinked' word, the user is directed to the relevant page and can navigate his or her own way through the text. In its original form, the extract also included an embedded sound file.

Extract 4 perhaps has fewer features which identify it as a digital text. It is from a book by Stephen King, *Riding the Bullet* (2000b). The book was published online and became the world's first mass-market ebook, or electronic book. Users paid a small sum to download the text, which they could either print or read on a computer screen. Although the ebook format offers certain affordances (a computer screen can be read in dim light; a digital text is searchable), the text of *Riding the Bullet* is linguistically indistinguishable from the sort of text that might have appeared in a printed book – and very different from what we see in media such as SMS and IRC. It could easily have been printed on the pages of a physical book: as, indeed, it very soon was (see King, 2002).

What initial observations can be made about digital English? The first aspect to which I would like to draw your attention is the *diversity* of digital practices. The texts given in the extracts above suggest that digital English cannot be thought of as one homogenous form of language. Instead, digital technology provides a number of distinct media, which are associated with distinctive varieties of English: IRC, text messaging, wikis, and so on. To capture this variety accurately, the title of this chapter would have to be *Digital Englishes*. This title would also reflect the variation seen across users from different regions (as seen in the local forms in the South African message) and social backgrounds (the texter in question was from rural South Africa; urban South Africans in the study used fewer local forms).

A second aspect is that of multimodality. As well as linguistic forms, the distinctive features that characterise digital Englishes include images that accompany texts, as well as the hyperlinks and embedded sound files, and specific graphological practices, such as particular forms of respelling. Although many of these features are necessarily lost when transferred to the pages of a printed book like this one, these forms of multimodality form an essential part of digital Englishes.

Activity 8.3

Allow about 10 minutes

The nature of these different types of digital English is determined in part by the technology. For example, the fact that IRC is text based, and does not involve audio or video functions, may encourage people to signal actions textually. However, the users themselves shape digital practices. For example, there is no technological reason why asterisks had to be used to signal actions. And Mzwakhe exploits possibilities for spelling when he texts in order to 'sound' South African. Note down further aspects of the technology you think might impact on digital interaction. Then consider other factors to be taken into account when we consider how users may also shape digital Englishes.

Comment

According to Herring (2007), differences between digital media include:

- Their synchronicity (i.e. to what extent the communication takes place in real time). To use IRC, users must be logged on at the same time, while the author and reader of an ebook or a wiki do not need to be. Synchronous communication is likely to use less complex language, and has also been seen to involve more respelling and more codeswitching.

- Their **persistence**, or how long messages are stored. Words typed into an IRC conversation last longer than spoken words, but are unlikely to be saved in the way that changes to a wiki are. However, as changes to wikis can be overridden or deleted, they are not as permanent as words in an ebook. We might posit that the greater persistence of digital English over speech heightens users' awareness of the language they use, and that this might encourage language play.

- **Message size**, or how many characters the system allows: only 160 per SMS text message but millions (if not limitless) for an ebook. Character allowance has a bearing on the amount of abbreviation: shorter messages are more likely to be abbreviated.

As suggested above, digital varieties of English are shaped not only by the medium through which they are conveyed, but also by the users, the online communities they form and the practices they engage in. As Herring (2007) points out, distinctions may arise from the following variables:

- **Participant characteristics**: people's background, skills, experiences, beliefs – all of which depend on the particular individuals involved.

- **Distribution of participation**: in the IRC group, all participants are able to participate fairly equally in the discussion; by contrast, only very few users of Wikipedia are likely to actually contribute to the wiki. The relationship between participants in the ebook is that of author and readers, and so is even less equally divided.

- **Purpose**: not only of the domain itself, but also the individuals involved – for example, the purpose of Wikipedia may be to act as an encyclopaedic resource, but the goals of individual contributors might be to put forward a particular view or to compete with other contributors.

What the list given above suggests is that any one technology may differ according to who is using it. Thus, it becomes difficult even to say that IRC (for example) is a homogenous variety, because the purpose for which it is used, the topics followed and the activities carried out will depend on the particular community that is using it. An online community comprises a group of people who orient around a digital space, and who are linked by shared interests and purposes – these may be online fantasy role playing, as in the IRC example above (hence the actions and the nicknames); or special interests, such as politics or parenting; or the motivations may be social. Digital communities often cut across existing social and geographical distinctions – so that the online fantasy game above may be played by men and women, old and young, from any part of the world – and it is likely that practices and forms of language peculiar to particular online communities will emerge. The language used in the IRC community above may therefore differ from other IRC communities.

8.3   Digital texts

In this section, I explore the challenges posed by digital technology for traditional material culture and consider the extent to which everyday digital practices can and should be exploited in teaching literacy. First, however, to illustrate some attributes of what may be an emerging digital culture, I start with a contrastive look at two online reference sites: Urban Dictionary and Wikipedia. Both these sites are wikis.

Urban Dictionary, established in 1999 by Californian computer student Aaron Peckham, is a web-based dictionary of English slang with millions of entries, which by 2009, were coming in at a rate of 2000 a day. It attracted 15 million visitors in April 2009, according to one commentator (Heffernan, 2009). What is significant about Urban Dictionary is that the entries themselves are submitted by users.

Activity 8.4

Allow about 20 minutes

Look at the following definitions of 'lol', which at the start of 2011 included a total of 287 entries. What overall definition would you draw from these varying definitions and how would you evaluate each one?

277. **lol** 36 [thumbs] up, **228** down

lots of laughs, used when talking online to friends

lol!! that was funny

by **Khjil** Mar 13, 2005 **share this**

(adapted from www.urbandictionary.com/define.php?term=lol&defid=1118929, accessed January 2011)

148. **lol** **1** thumb down

A slang that used to stand for 'laugh out loud' but now frequently represents slight humor and acknowledgement of what is said. If someone was seriously laughing, instead of lol they would type LMAO or LMFAO! Lol is just another way to bump the conversation.

Someone: omfg, my dad took my car away from me!

Someone2: lol... yea now we can't go to wal-mart.

by **anonymous_user** Jun 16, 2005 **share this**

(adapted from www.urbandictionary.com/define.php?term=lol%20slang&page=2, accessed January 2011)

21. **LOL** 28 [thumbs] up, **14** down

A term often seen in text messages, typically used when the sendee is too polite to tell the sender what they really feel about them or generally written in the absence of personality. Very contagious phrase. Lol.

message sender 1: Hey. Lol. How are you?

message sender 2: Good. Lol

message sender 1: Lol

message sender 2: Lol

lmfao haha hehe teehee muahaha

by **Phyllis Birkenfloyd** Feb 4, 2009 **share this**

(adapted from http://www.urbandictionary.com/define.php?term=lol&page=4, accessed January 2011)

Comment

To understand the significance of Urban Dictionary, it is necessary to remember the authority bestowed on lexicographers since the 1700s. Dictionaries both document language change and provide the last word in language disputes. Urban Dictionary challenges the traditional authority of the lexicographer in a number of ways. Its purpose is to document slang usage as defined by its users, and it accepts multiple and contrasting definitions of the same word. It also accepts neologisms invented for the purpose of entering them into the dictionary. These often serve to document or highlight existing concepts or practices, such as 'cheappuccino' (1 September 2010), a flavoured coffee drink offered at convenience stores at half the price of a coffee shop cappuccino. Like more conventional dictionaries, Urban Dictionary tries to reflect usage, but unlike its professionally published counterparts, it does not include information on parts of speech, etymologies or spelling. It has numerous affordances that printed dictionaries don't have; for example, that definitions can be continually updated (by those who use the words) and that pages are hyperlinked. You may have noticed the 'thumbs' 'up' and 'down' at the top right-hand corner of each entry, by which users evaluate entries. Urban Dictionary is not as freely compiled as it first appears: before an entry can be posted, it is vetted – but by self-appointed users rather than by lexicographers.

Like Urban Dictionary, the online and multilingual Wikipedia challenges its paper predecessor, the encyclopaedia, in its apparent prioritising of collaboration over credentials. As of 2010, Wikipedia had 16 million articles (with over three million in English). However, it differs from Urban Dictionary in that contributors alter as well as add content, and in that the aim is to present users with something more like a conventional printed reference work, written from what aspires to be a neutral or collective point of view. In a further difference from Urban Dictionary, it also recognises the authority of traditional academic sources of knowledge.

Activity 8.5

Allow about 10 minutes

Extracts 5, 6 and 7 are adapted from the Wikipedia entry for 'wiki' (the kind of web page of which Wikipedia is an example). These represent successive states in the ongoing revision of the entry (Wikipedia, 2002, 2006 and 2011). Read through the versions, without worrying too much if you don't understand all the content. Which year do you think each one comes from? Can you see a progression, or other clues suggesting improvement?

Extract 5

A **wiki** (/ˈwɪki/ WIK-ee) is a website that allows the creation and editing of any number of interlinked web pages via a web browser using a simplified markup language or a WYSIWYG text editor. [1][2][3] Wikis are typically powered by wiki software and are often used collaboratively by multiple users. Examples include community websites, corporate intranets, knowledge management systems, and note services. The software can also be used for personal notetaking.

Extract 6

A wiki (<u>IPA</u>: ['wI.kiː] <WICK-ee> or ['wiː.kiː] <WEE-kee>[1]) is a type of <u>Web site</u> that allows the visitors themselves to easily add, remove, and otherwise <u>edit</u> and change some available content, sometimes without the need for registration. This ease of interaction and operation makes a wiki an effective tool for <u>collaborative authoring</u>. The term wiki also can refer to the <u>collaborative software</u> itself (<u>wiki engine</u>) that facilitates the operation of such a Web site, or to certain specific wiki sites, including the computer science site (an original wiki), <u>WikiWikiWeb</u>, and on-line encyclopedias such as <u>Wikipedia</u>.

Extract 7

The term **WikiWiki** ('wiki wiki' means '<u>quick</u>' in the <u>Hawaiian language</u>; 'wee kee wee kee') can be used to identify either a type of <u>hypertext</u> document or the <u>software</u> used to write it. Often called 'wiki' for short, the <u>collaborative software</u> application enables web documents to be authored collectively using a simple <u>markup</u> scheme and without the content being reviewed prior to its acceptance. The resulting collaborative hypertext document, also called either 'wiki' or '<u>WikiWikiWeb</u>,' is typically produced by a community of users. Many wikis are immediately identifiable by their use of <u>CamelCase</u>, produced by capitalizing words in a phrase and removing the spaces between them; this turns the phrase into an automatic link.

Comment

Extract 5: 2011; Extract 6: 2006; Extract 7: 2002. We can see a slight reduction in length over the period (although this may have more to with the reorganisation of subsequent paragraphs – not included above – than any overall conciseness). The main clue placing Extract 7 as the 2002 entry is the use of the earlier term 'Wikiwiki', from which 'wiki' derives. To me, the 2006 entry (Extract 6) shows a clear improvement in terms of clarity and in highlighting the difference between a wiki and other websites, which may reflect a growing wider interest in wikis, beyond computer communities. Extract 5 also gives examples, acknowledging the popularity of Wikipedia (as well as WikiWikiWeb, the first wiki, established in 1995). Keeping to our criteria of clarity, the 2011 entry seems to me to be more dense and technical than the 2006 entry.

As in all well-edited Wikipedia entries, the overall change in the entry 'wiki' from 2002 to 2011 occurred not through redrafting by a single author, but as the result of thousands of edits made by numerous contributors. These contributors arguably form an online community. However, they may not share a common goal: some may be trying to present a balanced account of an issue, for example, while others may be interested only in promoting their personal views.

Each entry on Wikipedia is accompanied by a 'Talk' page (which preserves the discussions and arguments behind the entry's construction) and a 'History' page (a comprehensive list of all changes made to an entry, making clear which editors made which changes at what times). However, it is fair to say that most *users* of Wikipedia will not seek out this information. This matters, insomuch as the collaborative nature of Wikipedia attracts contributions from experts and non-experts alike. It is thus arguably harder to evaluate Wikipedia for its veracity and bias than most books, whose authors (and often editors) are named. (A similar point can be made about many websites. Next time you visit a site, try to find an author's real name or the date when a page was last edited.) Moreover, as discourse analyst Greg Myers insists, Wikipedia entries can only hope to be reliable if they are frequently edited yet relatively uncontroversial: if an entry's content has not been well checked, or has been the cause of 'edit wars' between contributors with incompatible views, then it should be treated with great caution (Myers, 2010, p. 142). To assess the value of a particular Wikipedia entry, then, you often need to look behind the scenes by reading its associated Talk and History pages.

On Urban Dictionary, however, it is clearly apparent that there are competing and individual voices. As its founder, Aaron Peckham puts it, 'Every single word on here is written by someone with a point of view, with a personal experience of the word in the entry' (quoted in Heffernan, 2009). The contrast between Wikipedia and Urban Dictionary is similar to that between Wikipedia and blogs, which Myers has theorised in terms of conflicting models of knowledge. According to Wikipedia's 'public' model, knowledge is a group endeavour: 'anyone can contribute, but … only with the agreement of others can one's own contribution stand' (Myers, 2010, p. 146). But in the 'private' model of the blogosphere, knowledge is an individual possession: 'everyone is entitled to say what they want' and 'everyone has the right to be heard' (Myers, 2010, pp. 157, 146). As Peckham's statement would suggest, these assumptions also underpin Urban Dictionary.

Wikis illustrate changing notions of what it means to be an author, in a number of ways: providing a forum for anyone to contribute to a text, encouraging the collaborative creation of texts and arguably eroding the authority of the named and expert author (Warschauer and Grimes, 2007).

Activity 8.6

Authorship is not the only way in which the traditional values associated with print culture are challenged by digital practices. The following characteristics are sometimes considered typical of print culture:

- particular means of textual reproduction and dissemination, such as printing and the postal service
- valuing of writing over speech – words in print may be more binding or more authoritative than that which is spoken
- the notion that reading and writing means grappling with ideas in a distinct way.

Do these characteristics also apply to a digital world? Jot down some notes on how computer technology (personal computers, laptops, mobile devices) and new communications media (particularly the internet) may have changed the world with regard to these three points.

Now turn to Reading A: *Under the microscope: facets of modern written culture* by Naomi Baron. In this reading, Baron suggests five 'facets' of online practice that together transform what it means to be literate. As you read, make notes under her five headings. Do her views resonate with your own literacy practices, as shaped by digital technology? To what extent is her view technologically determinist?

Comment

I find myself recognising much of what Baron describes, often in relation to my own literacy practices. For example, I often let Microsoft or Google check my spelling with a red wavy line from Word or a curt 'Did you mean to type heterogeneous?' from the search engine. I don't disagree with Baron's views, but the negative aspects of digital advances are only part of the picture. If we accept the rise of 'snippet literacy', for example, the practices it involves show that people are very much able to discern what they need to read and can even learn to do the same when faced with a million Google results. Others may use online technology to find books to buy and read: books that may be purchased online as printed editions and delivered to the reader by post. Technology does not *determine* behaviour in the way Baron seems to suggest, but offers possibilities – affordances – which can be exploited in myriad ways according to the goals and capabilities of the individuals involved.

One of the possibilities offered by digital technologies is that they open up global spaces for vernacular writing. The second reading in Chapter 2 looked at the Edwardian practice of sending postcards: one of the many ways in which people have engaged in vernacular writing. Digital technologies encourage us to revisit what vernacular writing means. Communicating via networked technologies adds to the many ways in which people can participate in everyday acts of writing, in some cases enabling new interactions and ways of communicating between people in different locations; and, in others, transforming existing writing practices.

Activity 8.7

Now turn to Reading B: *Researching language practices on a photo-sharing website* by David Barton. In this reading, Barton describes the writing practices that surround the creation of photo albums and profiles on Flickr, an online photo-sharing site. Read the first half of the reading, up to the heading 'Vernacular practices revisited', in which Barton describes the site and looks at the significance of users' language choices, and then jot down your answers to the following questions. (If necessary, look back to Chapter 2 of this book.) Then compare your answers with the account given in the second half of the reading. To what extent do you agree with Barton?

- What do you think is significant about the language in which users choose to write?

- In what ways are the practices that Barton describes a reflection (or extension) of offline activities?

- To what extent are these practices new?

- How do you think online technologies, such as photo-sharing sites, have changed the nature of vernacular writing? (Think about how vernacular writing is valued; where it takes place, and who people are in contact with; how people view social networking).

Comment

Barton makes the interesting point that practices on Flickr are shifting, as people get to know the technology and become comfortable with moving away from familiar practices, such as sharing wedding albums with friends, towards new practices made possible by the technology: tagging their photos, commenting on others' photos and making links between these and their own photos. By involving users in collaborative activities and knowledge sharing, these new practices seem to be having a fundamental effect on how people engage in vernacular writing and the roles they take on. One interesting difference between offline and online vernacular writing is the arena in which it takes place. The internet allows local discussions and experiences, which would once have been carried out in the home or in a local institution, to be carried out in a public, global forum. The choices that users make in terms of which languages they use reveal their awareness that they are interacting with a complex configuration of both local and global readerships. Users move between English, uncritically accepted as the lingua franca of the site, and other languages in order to balance the need or desire to include a wider audience while addressing more immediate friends. One could argue that, through sites such as Flickr, as well as learning how to become better photographers, users are also learning crucial new communication and presentation skills in an increasingly globalised and online world. While you may disagree with Barton's conclusions regarding some of the practices he documents, his engagement with how Flickr users build on offline practices to develop new ways of interacting with a changing world warns us against positing online activities in absolute and unfavourable contrast to traditional writing practices.

8.4   Digital talk

Figure 8.3   'Talking' on the net

In the previous section, we looked at online practices in the sense of texts located on the World Wide Web. In contrast, digital talk is formed through synchronous interaction between users of the internet. What I want to explore in this section is how similar digital talk is to spoken talk (discussed in Chapter 1) and how playful and creative digital talk can be (see Chapter 5), as users draw creatively on the linguistic and technological resources available to them.

Activity 8.8

Allow about 15 minutes

Read through the following online conversation, which took place on the instant messaging tool Windows Live Messenger. I will be drawing on this to illustrate a number of points about online interaction, but first I would like you to consider in what ways it resembles spoken conversation, and what the differences are.

Dream and Tee are both from Thailand. At the time, Tee was doing a PhD in neuroscience in Thailand, and for this exchange he had access to a computer which allowed the input of Thai script (such as อือ translated below as 'yes'). Dream, on the other hand, was writing from her phone in London and could not input Thai script (although she could receive and read it). For this reason, many of her turns comprise 'romanised Thai': that is, the rendering of Thai in Roman script (e.g. *Gin rai pai ja?* in line 1).

1	Dream:	Gin rai pai ja?	*[What did you eat?]*
2	Tee:	Blueberry cheese pie	
3	Dream:	Dinner nia na?	*[As your dinner?]*
4	Tee:	อือ	*[Yes]*
5	Dream:	Save some for me pao?	*[Did you save some for me or not?]*
6	Tee:	ม่าย	*[No]*
7	Tee:	เด๋วนกอ้วน	*[Nok'll get fat* (Nok is Dream's nickname)*]*
8	Dream:	Auan kor me kon love :D	*[I will be loved although I am fat]*
9	Tee:	เหรอ	*[Really?]*
10	Dream:	Uhmmm	
11	Dream:	Young ngai mother, p'ni, p'na kor love	*[(My) mother, Nini* (Dream's sister), *Nana* (Dream's other sister) *love me anyway]*
12	Tee:	จ๊ะ	*[Yes]*
13	Dream:	Laew p'tee la? :P	*[How about Tee?]*
14	Tee:	ทามมาย	*[What?]*
15	Dream:	Mai mee arai	*[Nothing]*
16	Dream:	:(	

...

17	Dream:	Mai disturb u laew naka	*[I won't disturb you any longer]*
18	Dream:	Bye byeee	
19	Tee:	อ้าว ไปซะแระ	*[Are you logging off?]*
20	Dream:	Kor u r busy	*[Because you are busy]*
21	Dream:	And don't wanna chat with me nee	
22	Tee:	นกหัวล้านนน	*[a bald Nok (In Thailand there is the belief that the bald tend to be sensitive)]*

(author's own data)

Comment

Like much spoken conversation, the focus of the above exchange is mainly phatic as participants work at maintaining their friendship. As we saw with the IRC exchange, digital communication can resemble spoken conversation in terms of its turn taking. This exchange also comprises short, synchronous turns resembling those in spoken dialogue, characterised by adjacency pairs:

1	Dream:	Gin rai pai ja?	*[What did you eat?]*
2	Tee:	Blueberry cheese pie	
3	Dream:	Dinner nia na?	*[As your dinner?]*
4	Tee:	อือ	*[Yes]*

As in speech, turns do not always constitute full sentences – *Mai mee arai* ('Nothing') – while responses such as Tee's *Really?* (เหรอ) and Dream's *Uhmmm* heighten the sense of speech-like interactivity. Note that in most cases turns are ended by the participant hitting send, but this is not always the case. In line 7, Tee replies *No* and sends it, but then extends his turn with *Nok'll get fat*. Dream similarly makes a contribution which spans turns 17 and 18. Rather than disrupting the turn-taking sequence, the practice allows users to achieve communicative effects: pausing for effect, indicating a change in topic or marking an utterance as an afterthought.

Not all digital exchanges exhibit similar turn taking. Take the email conversation, shown in Figure 8.4 (opposite), among a family making plans for Christmas, where different fonts (see Chapter 2) indicate different contributors.

Turns in this exchange are harder to relate to spoken interaction, in that replies are inserted into the initial email message like comments scribbled on to a printed text. This allows users to respond to several different points and in so doing create distinct 'threads' of conversation. In this respect, digital turns resemble *formal* spoken encounters, where a speaker may respond to various questions ('I'll take your second question first … and moving on to your other point …'). Thus, we see in the two exchanges how the affordances of different digital technologies encourage varied practices which differ from spoken conversation.

> Well everyone, Xmas is fast approaching and decisions must be made. Here follows a list of statements, please give your thoughts and reactions and add any more statements you can think of to help in our quest.
>
> We won't have Xmas pudding (? ok) but have a nice chocolate pud of some kind (Nellie, will you be eating choc?)
> *Also fine by me. I'll make something! Nellers, let me know what you'd like / can eat.* Choc choc choc choc!
> *Right, i'm onto it.* **Yum yum**
>
> I agree. Perfect.
>
> I am going to make a Xmas cake. Somebody else could make some mince pies? *Homemade Xmas cake is lovely idea. Can do – or me and Ernie can do them the weekend before we go.*
> Yup
>
> I would be happy to help make mince pies with floss.

Figure 8.4 'Xmas decisions' (personal correspondence)

The digital medium affords graphological resources which users exploit in order to compensate for the fact that their distinct voices cannot be heard. For example, participants in the email exchange above use typography to indicate which contributions are their own. The MSN exchange between Dream and Tee contains some abbreviations now strongly associated with digital English: *u* and *r* are letter homophones, while *wanna* is an attempt to capture an informal spoken pronunciation. One other practice in the exchange is the repetition of letters in both Thai and English, as in *Uhmmm* (line 10), *byeee* (18) and *nee* (line 21), which serve to show emphasis or represent how a word might be said. This appears to be a widely used resource in digital encounters. In this message posted on Twitter during the 2010 World Cup, one tweeter writes:

RT @PaulaAbdul: AHHHHHHHHHHHHHHHH!!! SO EXCITED FOR THAT GOOOOOOOOOOOOOAAAAAAAAAAAAALLLLLLLLLLL!!! #World Cup #USA

(Twitter, 2010)

Tee and Dream also use a range of 'emoticons', including :D and :P (a grinning face and a tongue sticking out), as well as a sad face :(. These symbols constitute attempts to capture paralinguistic aspects of communication conveyed in speech by facial expressions or intonation; as with the respellings, these graphical resources are used to give the written text a sense of speech-like intimacy.

Although spelling manipulations are perhaps the most distinctive feature of digital talk and the one which people most readily associate with texted or online language, it cannot be assumed that all digital talk is characterised by such a degree of spelling variation. In her reading for Chapter 5, Ana Deumert points out that although South African texters are heavy users of 'txtspeak', this is in contrast to UK texters who have been found to use many fewer respellings. Second, it also becomes evident that in some contexts respellings are not used to shorten messages, but to heighten the sense that participants are speaking: *Uhmmm* and *Bye byeee* seem to suggest that particular sounds are drawn out (see Chapter 1). Despite the written medium, it is how people choose to exploit it that determines how speech-like digital talk can be.

A strong sense of the participants' social identities – that is, how they choose to present themselves in any given interaction – comes across from the conversation. Dream appears to drive the conversation, eliciting only one-word answers from Tee, and towards the end she plays at being hurt:

17	Dream:	Mai disturb u laew naka	*[I won't disturb you any longer]*
	...		
19	Tee:	อ้าว ไปซะแระ	*[Are you logging off?]*
20	Dream:	Kor u r busy	*[Because you are busy]*
21	Dream:	And don't wanna chat with me nee	

These 'identities' are not necessarily either stable or permanent ways in which the people involved present themselves; instead, they constitute the roles which they have chosen to adopt at particular points within this exchange.

As well as individual identities, respellings and other choices can indicate national or local identity. You saw at the beginning of the chapter how forms such as *Brur*, *shid* and *da* were used by South African texters to capture local expressions and pronunciation. Another localised practice in the Arabic-speaking world is the use of number homophones to represent sounds which do not have a correspondence in English. In the following example from Al-Khatib and Sabbah's (2008) study in Jordan, '2' represents the English word 'to' in 'I wont 4get 2 bring' and the syllable 'to' in 'tomorrow': '2mr'. However, it is also used in a way that may not be familiar to non-Arabic speakers, to capture Arabic sounds that cannot easily be transcribed from Arabic script into romanised script. Examples of this can be seen below in 'AL2O5T ALFADILAH' where the numerals 2 and 5 have been used in the romanised script to represent sounds in the word الأخت الفاضلة ('sister').

A: [...] الأخت الفاضلة...الرجاء إحضار آتاب صقر معك غدا

B: ☺ this z the 1st time someone calls me **"AL2O5T ALFADILAH"**... ☺ lol. Anyway, don't worry, I wont 4get 2 bring the book *2mr*. Take care.

(Al-Khatib and Sabbah, 2008, p. 53)

In many pre-digital texts, the sound would be omitted in romanised Arabic. In online communication and text messaging, however, people across the Arabic-speaking world have started to represent such sounds using numbers and they have become an everyday feature of digital talk. The following examples are from Kuwait and Egypt respectively:

Ra7aroo7 ma3a e'7ty 7aneen el7 f.la

('I'll go to the party with my sister Haneen.')

(Haggan, 2007, p. 440)

Hello Dalia, 7amdellah 3ala el-salama ya Gameel. we alf mabrouk 3alal el-shahada el-kebeera. Keep in touch ... I really hope to see you all Soooooooooooooon

('Hello Dalia, Thank God for the safe return, my sweet. Congratulations for the big certificate [...]. Keep in touch ... I really hope to see you all Soooooooooooooon')

(Warschauer et al., 2007, p. 312)

As Warschauer et al. (2007) explain, although this form of respelling is now a widespread practice among Arabic speakers, it arose in an ad hoc manner as users responded to the constraints of writing romanised Arabic. Respellings such as 'da' or '3ala' are not prescribed: users do not learn them by studying dictionaries or at school. Instead, like many other language practices, they are picked up through interaction. As Shortis (2007, p. 2) puts it, 'Txt' spellings are 'interpreted and replicated by immersion rather than by formal instruction'. This view of language use helps to explain how different respellings emerge within communities.

Another way in which identities are forged within digital communities is through codeswitching (see Chapter 1). As in much spoken conversation, it is difficult to identify any patterns in the mix of languages used in the exchange between the two Thai speakers. For example, *Auan kor me kon love* alternates between Thai and English, while *Mai disturb u laew naka* is largely a Thai sentence with the inserted phrase *disturb u*. One of the reasons for the romanised Thai is interpersonal: Tee is older than Dream and for this reason Dream has stated in interview that she feels she should follow Tee's lead in language choice. However, it is interesting then that she also chooses to mix romanised Thai with English. Sometimes, this is because the English word is a loanword, at least in such digital encounters, as in *Bye byeee* used by Dream and *Blueberry cheese pie* used by Tee.

Given difficulties in ascribing clear motivations for each language switch, how can we explain this hybrid practice? It appears that the practice affirms the participants' identities as young, cosmopolitan English-knowing Thai speakers. Theirs is a code which draws on specific language knowledge and excludes those who are not English–Thai bilingual or who are unfamiliar with particular online practices (such as the emoticons or typical digital English abbreviations). If you do not speak Thai, how well can you follow the above exchange, even with the English glosses? And conversely, how much do you think could be understood by someone who only spoke Thai? Each example of digital talk must be understood not only as a result of the technology involved, but in the context of a particular digital (and linguistic) community.

8.5 Digital globe

So far I have been treating English as just another language using the digital medium; to an extent, of course, that's exactly what it is. At the same time, however, the relationship between English and the internet is somewhat different from that of other languages, due to the prominent role that English, or varieties of English, play in the world today.

One question is whether the internet is further promoting the use of English globally or whether it is facilitating the use and spread of other languages. A related question is how much linguistic *diversity* there is online; that is, how many languages are represented on the internet. It would appear by most accounts that the dominance of English is declining. For example, Table 8.1 shows that English speakers accounted for over a quarter of all internet users in 2010, down from nearly a third in 2005 (Gardner, 2007). However, despite this decline, English still appears to be the most used language on the internet.

Table 8.1 Languages online (number of internet users by language as of 30 June 2010)

Top ten languages on the internet	Internet users by language	Growth in internet use (2000–2010)	% of total internet users	World population for this language (2010 estimate)
English	536,564,837	281.2%	27.3%	1,277,528,133
Chinese	444,948,013	1277.4%	22.6%	1,365,524,982
Spanish	153,309,074	743.2%	7.8%	420,469,703
Japanese	99,143,700	110.6%	5.0%	126,804,433
Portuguese	82,548,200	989.6%	4.2%	250,372,925
German	75,158,584	173.1%	3.8%	95,637,049
Arabic	65,365,400	2501.2%	3.3%	347,002,991
French	59,779,525	398.2%	3.0%	347,932,305
Russian	59,700,000	1825.8%	3.0%	139,390,205
Korean	39,440,000	107.1%	2.0%	71,393,343
Top 10 languages	1,615,957,333	421.2%	82.2%	4,442,056,069
Rest of the languages	350,557,483	588.5%	17.8%	2,403,553,891
World total	1,966,514,816	444.8%	100.0%	6,845,609,960

(adapted from Internet World Stats, 2010b)

**Allow about
10 minutes**

Activity 8.9

(A)   Using the table, answer these questions:

1   Which three languages saw the largest increase in internet users between 2000 and 2010?

2   Which group of languages represented only 17.8% of internet users in 2010?

3   There are three languages for which more than half of the speakers were internet users in 2010. Which languages are they?

(B)   Now consider the following questions:

•   What do the statistics show with respect to the *relative* use of the top ten languages online since 2000?

•   Look at the third column: 'Growth in internet use'. Do the figures in this column suggest that linguistic diversity is increasing, decreasing, or neither?

•   Do these figures tell the whole story? Think about the distinction made in this chapter between digital text and digital talk, and the points made particularly in relation to the latter. Think also about multilingualism.

Comment

Answers to (A):

1   Arabic, Russian and Chinese.

2   Speakers of other languages not mentioned in the 'top ten'.

3   Japanese, German and Korean.

The questions in (B) are addressed in the discussion that follows.

The statistics show that, although English-speaking internet users in 2010 outranked even Chinese (the language with the most speakers), the number of people using English is not increasing as quickly as for some other languages. The biggest increases in internet presence since 2000 have been for Arabic, Russian and Chinese. Why? Possible reasons include population size and recent growth in the wealth and infrastructure necessary for online access. Korea, Japan and the German-speaking nations are all technologically advanced countries with relatively small populations, which became relatively dominant on the internet before reaching market saturation (Japanese, German and Korean being the only languages represented for which over half of all speakers have internet access); they have since been overtaken by languages with more speakers. The prime example of this is Chinese, with over a billion speakers; Arabic and Russian also have sizeable populations of speakers, but for a variety of reasons these have been slower to gain internet access. The implication for English is that although it was still dominant in 2010, other languages were 'catching up'.

To what extent, however, does this imply greater linguistic diversity? The increasing use of Chinese, for example, and its possible overtaking of English in the future, does not increase the number of languages represented online. It simply replaces one dominant language with another. The 'rest of the languages' account for only 17.8 per cent of the total number of internet users. On the one hand, the internet can be a useful forum for minority or endangered languages 'that bridge geographically dispersed speakers or that have insufficient resources to make use of more expensive media' (Warschauer et al., 2007, p. 304). However, the number of online users of 'the rest of the languages' is in fact down from 20.4 per cent in 2005 (Gardner, 2007, p. 209), suggesting that we saw a general trend away from the use of 'other' languages online in the period.

It is worth probing a little deeper into how statistics concerning internet use are arrived at, and what they do and don't imply. First, however, I will look briefly at why English was so quick to dominate the internet.

Why English?

One reason for the initial dominance of English was the use of the ASCII coding system for the digital representation of text (see Chapter 2). This was best suited to languages using the Roman alphabet (see Chapter 7). Although the multilingual Unicode system has gradually superseded ASCII since the 1990s, it still does not cover every script, and such factors may account for some of the inequality in internet language use and for the continued exclusion of certain languages (Paolillo, 2007).

The dominance of English online is also tied up with its role as the global language of politics and business. For example, in their study of internet use in Egypt, Warschauer et al. (2007) suggest that English is used because much business in the oil-rich Gulf countries is conducted with English-using foreign and multinational companies. Another reason Warschauer et al. give is the apparent perception in Egypt that English is the appropriate choice for computer-mediated literacy practices. This is often because users' past experience of computer literacy – in school and university – has been in English. At the time of Warschauer et al.'s study, only 0.7 per cent of Egyptians had online access, and these tended to be the English-educated elite. Similar elite usage may explain why some of the largest proportions of English-speaking websites are in countries where internet penetration is low: Turkey (62 per cent), Latvia (75 per cent), Bulgaria (86 per cent) (Paolillo, 2007, p. 421): countries where such internet resources as there are, are in English and accessed by English-speaking elites. What we see is a have and have not relationship between those who can use English to access English-language websites, and those who cannot. However, what we *don't* have is a dichotomy between those who speak English and those who speak other languages, as Table 8.1 seems to imply. The 1,277,528,133 English speakers mentioned in the table are not only mother tongue speakers, of whom there may be less than 400 million. They also include speakers of other languages who, for political, business or personal reasons, access the internet in English. For a discussion of the number of English speakers and issues involved in identifying them, see Crystal (2012).

Evaluating the statistics

This leads us on to the question of how 'internet use' is measured. Many surveys such as those discussed above are based on the languages used in websites; that is, what we have been calling digital texts. Digital talk, for practical reasons, is generally not included in the counts. Why might this omission be problematic?

It can be an issue, first, because certain synchronous modes of communication tend to penetrate sooner into populations with limited internet access (Paolillo, 2007, p. 421), and so statistics will present an unbalanced (or outdated) picture of actual online usage. Second, it can create a misleading picture of how languages are used online. Languages other than English tend to be used more in informal digital talk (while, as mentioned above, English tends to be the language of choice for business and formal purposes). Warschauer et al. (2007) find that romanised Egyptian Arabic rather than English was used in informal email and online chat, particularly for the expression of personal content: greetings, humour and sarcasm, and religious expressions.

The exclusion of digital talk can also be misleading because it is there that we see more switching between languages. As illustrated in the previous section, codeswitching occurs more often in synchronous chatrooms than it tends to on websites. This is an important challenge to internet usage statistics. Such surveys tend to assume that internet use can be categorised into one distinct language or another. However, no such division can be made in cases where participants are drawing on various resources, from various 'languages'. To take another example from the same Thai-speaking community, to what extent can we say that the following exchange on the social networking site, Facebook, is either in English or in romanised Thai?

Mint: ****** seng mak loey gae sia dai roob a! kong ha mai jer laew cus lost nai maddox anyway thanks mak mak na jaa see you soon na noon :)

Sun at 21:58 Comment Like

Aum: ****** thank u jaa… love u lots naaaa :)) xxx

Sun at 00:31 Comment Like

(author's own data)

Does this imply a dichotomy between digital text (dominated by English) and digital talk (characterised by a more fluid use of languages)? Again, that is too simplistic a picture, given the diversity of digital texts on the Web.

8.6 Conclusion

In this chapter, I have given an idea of the diversity of practices which have grown up in response to the digital medium. I have explored some of the varied, often creative and highly interpersonal ways in which people have exploited affordances of the digital medium. Two points emerge from discussion of these digital practices. First, the impact of a digital medium on language and on society depends on how particular users choose to exploit it. Its impact is not an inevitable result of particular features of the technology, but is forged through people's purposes, interactions and relationships. This brings us to the second point, which is that digital English cannot be seen as representing a clean break from practices that could previously have taken place only through written and printed texts or through speech. Much of what we have explored in this chapter – multimodality, codeswitching, creativity and the formation of communities characterised by distinct literacy practices – has been discussed in other chapters, with regard to non-digital forms of communication. It appears that the digital media have not just caused the appearance of entirely new forms of language use, but afforded us new ways of mediating existing communicative practices.

READING A: Under the microscope: facets of modern written culture

Naomi Baron

Source: Baron, N. S. (2008) *Always On. Language in an Online and Mobile World*, Oxford, Oxford University Press, pp. 183–212.

Text in the fast lane

[…]

The virtues of saving time have historically been an important motivation for devising techniques to speed production of written text. One early strategy, practiced by medieval scribes, was to use abbreviations [Rodriguez and Cannon, 1994]. With fewer distinct characters to be copied, fewer animal skins were needed to produce a manuscript.

The coming of the telegraph fostered its own truncated writing style ('BROKE. SEND MONEY.'), reflecting the fact that telegrams were priced by the word. The fewer words you wrote, the less you paid. In fact, businesses in the early twentieth century raised abbreviated text to a near art form, developing elaborate cryptograms for transmitting boilerplate phrases and sentences. For instance, the British Society of Motor Manufacturers and Traders created its own codebook. If the single word *ixuah* was transmitted, the recipient decoded it to mean 'Quote price and earliest day of shipment,' resulting in substantial savings at the telegraph office [Saunders, 1921, pp. x–xi]. […]

The real speed revolution came about with introduction of first typewriters and then computers. Once you learned to type, you could turn out more text in a given time interval than by hand. Accurate? Not always. But fast.

[…] But fast thinking has not historically been associated with the written word.

[…] [I]t was the sixteenth-century humanist Desiderius Erasmus who proposed that individuals could strengthen their minds through guided use of the written word. In his manual *On Copia of Words and Ideas,* Erasmus counseled young men to read the works of great (inevitably dead) writers and then copy out important passages into a commonplace book, following an older medieval tradition. These passages were to be organized into conceptual categories, committed to memory, and then incorporated through paraphrase into the young man's own thinking and writing. The Renaissance commonplace movement, of which Erasmus was the best-known proponent, thrived up into the nineteenth century, with a gentleman's commonplace book serving both as a vehicle for and a chronicle of his intellectual development. The initial scribal act was a necessary component in this stepwise development in the life of the mind. […]

Flooding the scriptorium

[…] Once the computer turned us all into typists, the ever-growing online and mobile options engendered yet more text. I have come to call this phenomenon 'flooding the scriptorium.' Given all the writing we increasingly are doing, can we any longer afford, Governor, to pay careful attention to the words and sentences we produce? The proliferation of writing, often done in a hurry, may be driving out the opportunity and motivation for creating carefully honed text. The 'whatever' attitude toward the written word may be the inexorable consequence.

In principle, there is no reason we can't do some writing the old-fashioned way: multiple drafts, time between them to think, a couple of rounds of proofreading. In practice, though, word-processing programs beckon us to push 'print,' while email entices us to hit 'send.' The convenience of electronically-mediated language is that it tempts us to make a Faustian bargain of sacrificing thoughtfulness for immediacy. […]

Eriksen tells the story of an Internet company official who made no apologies for errors in materials the company issued. Instead, he informed a group of Scandinavian journalists that since Internet journalists had to work very fast, rarely taking time to check sources, it was now the job of the reader, not the writer, to assume this responsibility [Eriksen, 2001, p. 67]. […]

Then there's the case of the late Stephen E. Ambrose, director of the Eisenhower Center for American Studies, founder of the D-Day Museum, and author of twenty-four books, many of them bestsellers. Respected for his thorough research and incisive analyses, he was widely praised as a media consultant and historical expert. In January 2002, Ambrose was accused of plagiarism, a charge he acknowledged as valid. Why would a capable scholar stoop to plagiarizing? The reason, said Ambrose, was time – he was in too much of a hurry to check whether the notes he used were made in his own words or directly lifted from published works written by others. Two hundred years of written culture requiring authors to have something original to say went down the tubes in the name of pressure to flood the scriptorium. [...]

The print paradox

For the year 2005, there were $2.6 billion in sales of hardcover juvenile books, up 60 percent since 2002 [*Wall Street Journal*, March 15, 2007, D1]. Harry Potter obviously accounted for a sizable chunk of those revenues, but $2.6 billion (and just for hardcover) is hardly small change. [...]

On Saturday afternoons, it's impossible to find a seat in the cafe of my local bookstore. Customers fill the space, spilling over into the aisles and making themselves at home in spare nooks and crannies, often ensconced with piles of potential book purchases. Judging from the crowd, Americans would seem to be reading up a storm.

[... W]rong.

Start with the question of quantity. A study by the National Endowment for the Arts reported that, in 2002, only about 47 percent of the respondents had read *any* fiction, poetry, or plays in their leisure time during the preceding twelve months – down from 54 percent in 1992. (Rates for reading any book – fiction or nonfiction – also declined, from 61 percent in 1992 to 57 percent in 2002.) Not surprisingly, rates of reading literature increased with education and income, and females read more than males. However, when the data are broken down by age cohort, a troubling pattern emerges. The highest reading rate (52 percent) was for those aged 45–54. Outside of those 75 and older, the lowest rate (43 percent) was among adults aged 18–24.[1]

Are younger readers simply preoccupied with other activities such as television, movies, and the Internet, and later destined to mature into active readers? A recent study of the reading skills of college-educated adults seems to squelch the maturation hypothesis. Comparing literacy levels over time for Americans who had gone through college, scores declined significantly between 1992 and 2003. In fact, in 2003, only a quarter of college graduates were deemed to have 'proficient' literacy skills. (The percent for those with some graduate school training was only slightly higher: 31 percent.)[2] [...]

Snippet literacy

A few years back, one of the items I assigned my undergraduates to read was Robert Putnam's book *Bowling Alone*. The class was discussing the effects of the Internet on social interaction, and Putnam's carefully documented analysis of social capital in America offered a good frame of reference.

The students balked. Was I aware that the book was 541 pages long? Didn't I know that Putnam had written a précis of his argument a couple of years earlier, which they easily found on the web? One memorable freshman sagely professed that people should not be reading entire volumes these days anyway. She had learned in high school that book authors (presumably fiction excepted) pad their core ideas to make money or enhance their resumes. Anything worth writing could be expressed (I was informed) in an article of twenty or thirty pages, tops.

Back in the day, assigning a book a week in university humanities and social science courses was typical (and still is in some select schools). Now, though, many of us in academia feel lucky if students are willing to sign on for our pared-down curricular Book of the Month Club. In the words of Katherine Hayles, professor of literature at UCLA, 'I can't get my students to read whole books anymore.' [Hayles, 2006] [...]

To be fair, my own era had Cliff Notes, not to mention Readers Digest Condensed Books. We also relied on introductions and secondary sources when we were too busy, lazy, or confused to work through primary texts. Yet today's college crowd has available a tool we did not: the search engine.

Search engines are a blessing. Unquestionably, they save all of us vast amounts of time, not to mention their democratizing effect for users without access to substantial book collections. But there's a hitch. Much as automobiles discourage walking, with undeniable consequences for our health and girth, textual snippets-on-demand threaten our need for the larger works from which they are extracted. Why read *Bowling Alone* – or even the shorter article – when you can airlift a page that contains some key words? [...]

Admittedly, in the pre-online era when research necessitated opening dozens of books in hope of finding useful information, one rarely read each volume cover to cover. It's also fair to say that given how scattershot our searches sometimes were (and the inadequacy of many back-of-the-book indexes), we often missed what we were looking for. But that said, we also happened upon issues that proved more interesting than our original queries. Today's snippet literacy efficiently keeps us on the straight and narrow path, with little opportunity for fortuitous side trips. […]

The future of written culture

[…] Whatever eventually becomes of modern written culture, it seems unlikely that its material manifestations will be disappearing any time soon. People will still read and write, paper mills will continue to do a brisk business, and manufacturers can count on making bookcases for years to come. Despite the growth of open source and Creative Commons licenses, there is no immanent threat to authorial copyright on published works that have substantial sales potential. […]

One plausible scenario is what we might call 'print culture sans print.' Writing might continue to be culturally valuable, but handwritten missives or printed codices would decline in importance. Under this scenario, we would become increasingly comfortable relaxing with ebooks or studying complex texts online. We might learn to produce well-edited works without resorting to printing out physical copies to mark up by hand, and could expect developments in computer hardware and software to facilitate annotating online text so as to rival the affordances of paper.

This scenario would encourage some additional changes in our notion of written culture. Printed books that continued to be produced might become essentially collectors' items; concerns about spelling and punctuation could slacken (following the present trend) without denying the importance of writing as a cultural artifact. We can imagine a society in which many of the values of print culture would be maintained without relying primarily upon familiar print technology and editorial assumptions.

An alternative scenario would be 'print sans print culture.' Print might remain a physically prominent component of our cultural universe, but the multifaceted aspects of Western written culture would diminish in importance. Printed works might persist but for different ends. Think of university diplomas that are still written in Latin. The text looks impressive (and highly suitable for framing), although practically none of the recipients can decipher it.

What might the future look like? It's tempting to fall back on history, to the sixteenth and seventeenth centuries, when printing presses were starting to proliferate, but before print had helped create the Western European cultural assumptions that we have identified as print culture.

Tempting, yes, but perhaps not very useful. The early modern European citizenry, who possessed minimal literacy skills and had restricted access to reading or writing materials, has little in common with a population that is overwhelmingly literate, is awash in books, and has cheap paper and pens – and computers. The future of written culture will be a product not only of education and technology but of the individual and social choices we make about harnessing these resources.

Notes

[1]   The full NEA report is available at http://www.nea.gov/news/news04/ReadingAtRisk.html.

[2]   The National Assessment of Adult Literacy is available at http://nces.ed.gov/naal/pdf/2007464.pdf.

References for this reading

Eriksen, Thomas H. 2001. *Tyranny of the Moment: Fast and Slow Time in the Information Age.* London: Pluto Press.

Hayles, Katherine. 2006. Address at the Phi Beta Kappa 41st Triennial Council Meeting, Atlanta, GA, October 25–29, 2006.

Rodriguez, Felix, and Garland Cannon. 1994. 'Remarks on the Origin and Evolution of Abbreviations and Acronyms.' In *English Historical Linguistics, Papers from the 7th International Conference on English Historical Linguistics,* ed. F. Fernandez, M. Fuster, and J. Calvo, 261–272. Amsterdam: John Benjamins.

Saunders, W. M. 1921. *The Motor Trade Telegram Code.* London: The Society of Motor Manufacturers and Traders, Limited.

READING B: Researching language practices on a photo-sharing website

David Barton

Source: Barton, D. (2010) 'Vernacular writing on the web' in Barton, D. and Papen, U. (eds) *The Anthology of Writing: Understanding Textually Mediated Worlds*, London, Continuum, pp. 112–25.

Writing on Flickr

Writing is obviously central to blogs and Wikipedia but this [reading] examines a place where it may be less obvious that there would be writing, that is, in photo sharing sites. The focus here is on Flickr, one of the most well-known photo sharing sites internationally, www.flickr.com; Flickr is a site where people can upload and display their photos, effectively creating an online photo album. This [reading] draws upon data which has been collected as part of a larger ongoing study of the literacy practices associated with Flickr to address the question […] about what is happening to vernacular writing as people use new technologies. […]

Flickr is a website which provides a frame or interface and people add their own content, primarily photographs. As a first step, when someone uploads a photo, they can add a title and a description of the photo. They can also add tags: these are individual descriptive labels which can be used when searching for photos.

Figure [1] shows a Flickr page where a photo has a title, description and tags. Users can form sets of their own photos, which they give a name to, and sets can be grouped into collections, which are also named. The photo in Figure [1] belongs to a set called *nw yrk 2007*. Users can also share their photos with other Flickr members by adding their photos to groups representing common interests across users. These groups also have spaces for discussion and sometimes members run blogs. People also make contact with other members by listing friends and family members they want to keep in touch with, known as their contacts. People can also comment on each others' photos. Figure [1] shows a comment and response below the photo, and when scrolling down there are further comments. Users can join discussions of photos and they can send messages to other photographers. These are all optional activities and people using Flickr may do none of them, some of them or all of them. The list of possible activities continues, and examples will be given below of how people use Flickr for complex social networking and how people situate their Flickr activities within a web of other ever changing Web activities.

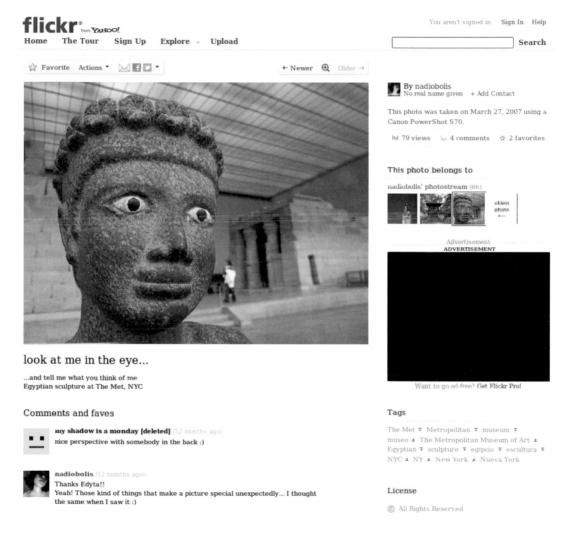

Figure [1] A Flickr photo page [advertisement removed]

There is a separate page for people to write a profile of themselves. The page might be empty or it might contain several screens of writing. For example, [a user calling herself] Carolink wrote a description in Spanish with a translation into English below it:

> The only person that takes awful photos with the most expensive camera. I am not in this thing for the photo, with all my respects.

I make photos to write. This is a permanent learning for me and I have nothing to teach. Knowing all that, if you still like my pictures, be my guest.

There are some general categories which people fill in, optionally, when joining Flickr, such as gender and location. The profile also contains a list of people's contacts and of the public groups they belong to. On their profile page people can provide links with internet activities, such as their blogs, other photo sites and websites. People can also add widgets, small programs, to show such things as the number of hits they have received, what countries viewers have come from and their most popular photos. The framing provided by Flickr is currently available in eight different languages, but people can write in any language they want to. In these different ways Flickr encourages social participation; it provides a range of affordances which people take up.

Researching Flickr

[…]

The study focussed on multilingual activity on Flickr for several reasons. First, it is the only way to include the range of international activity represented there and people's deployment of different languages is essential to the global communication seen on such sites. In addition, language choice can be quite revealing about issues of identity and sense of audience. This can be analysed on people's websites and followed up in individual questions for them. Crucially for this [reading], language choice illuminates what is happening to vernacular practices.

The first step in the analysis was to get a gauge of multilingual activity on Flickr. A set of 100 randomly selected Flickr users who were members of a major English-based group, FlickrCentral, were examined. Of these, 75 users of the 100 users had their profile in only English, a further 12 had a bilingual profile including English. Seven had it in a language other than English and 6 had no written profile. This demonstrates that even on an English-based site there are significant numbers of users of other languages.

For the next stage of the research, the online interviews, a different group of people were studied: people were selected who were active on Flickr and who used at least two languages, Chinese and English or Spanish and English. These are the two most common languages on Flickr after English, and are languages which the researchers know. […]

Language choice [...]

[... L]anguage choices are revealing about people's sense of identity and the audience they are addressing. [The Flickr users in our study] combined the resources of the different languages they knew in various ways. The titles and descriptions would be in either language, with titles more likely to be in English than the descriptions. In terms of tagging, people drew on various languages, sometimes translating directly and at other times having particular reasons for having a tag in a specific language. Carolink, for example, said she was participating in new practices and she had a strong sense of the global: *I try to fit all the tags both in English (universalism) and in Spanish (my immediate Flickr public) and, since I know a little French, I put the French word when I remember it.* Elsewhere she talked of her Spanish audience and her international audience: *Spanish flickrs is too limited for these internet times. I do not leave Spanish, but I try to use English when I can* and later she responded to our questions: *Well, I try to put all my photos available to any kind of public, and it is not a mistery that English is more universal than Spanish* ... For her and for several of the people interviewed English provides access to a global culture, especially a music culture, which was drawn upon for titles and comments about photos, providing a common reference uniting people from many different countries. This shows the importance of music to people's global identities and how people used it to identify themselves as global cosmopolitans.

Often, the profile contained more than one language, and commonly it was in two languages – a rough translation with the English usually being below the first language. However, the languages were deployed in many different ways with translation being only one use of people's linguistic resources. One Chinese person, Tiong, for instance, wrote in English 'My English is not v good' and in Chinese 'neither is my Chinese' – a joke which only people with a knowledge of both languages would understand. Often the English translation was shorter than the original, but people also used the two languages to provide different information. Where people left comments or wrote testimonials they wrote them in a range of languages. [...]

Vernacular practices revisited

Returning to examining this data in terms of vernacular writing practices [...], the first thing to point out is that the activities which people are engaging [in] include new practices. Based on the responses which people gave us in the interviews, it is clear that some things people are doing, like creating a wedding album or sharing a photo with a friend or relative who lives at a distance, consist of carrying out existing practices in new ways. And, for several people, their engagement with Flickr began with a desire to continue existing practices. However, once people saw the affordances of the medium, they extended what they did into new practices. Their new practices included a range of specific activities such as commenting on and evaluating photos taken by other people, classifying their own photos and making links between different photos. Most people said they had not done these things before, particularly with people they did not know offline.

Tagging is a good example where most people could not think of an earlier activity around photography where they had classified their photos in this manner. The only example we found was where one person had used tags effectively on his blog. By inventing tags, and putting their photos into sets and collections they were organizing and classifying their photos in new and more complex ways. This made their photo collections searchable more easily by themselves and by others and it opened up the possibilities for new uses of their photos.

These specific activities contributed to broader social practices which resulted in people relating to the world in new ways. As a way of examining these broader social practices which the writing was located in, it is worth returning to the areas of life where reading and writing were seen to be of central importance to people [see Chapter 2 of this book]. People engaged in these areas of vernacular activity in new ways. For example, there were the new forms of social participation which developed with a wider and more geographically dispersed group of people. Flickr served new purposes for them. They became involved in social networking, in deliberately setting out to get more views for their photos and trying to get a higher chance of being searched for and getting more comments and other activity around their pictures. They were also documenting their lives in new ways and their personal leisure activities were changing as Flickr took up more and more of their time.

[…] Vernacular literacy practices [have been] described as voluntary and self-generated and this is true of people's participation in Flickr and in the internet more generally. What people do on Flickr has its roots in everyday experience – albeit within a framework provided by a private company driven by commercial concerns. The software developers provide the possibilities and constraints within which people act. Companies such as Yahoo, the owners of Flickr, can be seen, in

Brandt's (1998, 2009) terms, as sponsoring particular practices. The people we studied saw it as providing many possibilities for them. They appreciated the freedom they had and did not refer to any perceived restrictions.

Vernacular practices like the activity on Flickr may also be a source of creativity, invention and originality, and the vernacular writing did give rise to new practices which embody different values from dominant literacies, as in the sharing of knowledge and the support which people said they gave each other around photography, which they mentioned in the interviews. […]

Vernacular practices have been thought of as more rooted in and restricted to personal spheres rather than to public spheres. Whilst people can keep areas of their Flickr site private if they want to, and many do, our research focussed on the public arena. Here, as in other areas of the internet, what counts as being private and personal in vernacular activity has changed. People are making available to the world activities which before were kept local. These vernacular practices are not private and they are not hidden from other people or from authority. On the internet, photos can have a different circulation. What is happening is that people are making the local global. There were several examples of people wanting to tell the world about their local activity. They were putting up photos to inform the world, *showing people how we live*, as one person put it, for example, when people added explanations of local sites or customs. People project global identities by making their photos available for other people to see, by participating in global discussions of them and by switching between their local language and English, the perceived global language. […] We see practices which are at the same time both vernacular and cosmopolitan. Technologies make these connections possible and people take up the affordances offered and develop new practices.

References for this reading

Brandt, D. (1998), 'Sponsors of Literacy'. *College Composition and Communication*, 49, 165–185.

Brandt, D. (2009), *Literacy and Learning: Reflections on Writing, Reading and Society*. San Francisco, CA: Jossey-Bass.

References

Agnihotri, R. K. and McCormick, K. (2010) 'Language in the material world: multilinguality in signage', *International Multilingual Research Journal*, vol. 4, pp. 55–81.

Aitchison, J. (1994) *Words in the Mind: An Introduction to the Mental Lexicon* (2nd edn), Oxford, Blackwell.

Al-Khatib, M. A. and Sabbah, E. H. (2008) 'Language choice in mobile text messaging among Jordanian university students', *SKY Journal of Linguistics*, vol. 21, pp. 37–66.

Altick, R. (1957) *The English Common Reader: A Social History of the Mass Reading Public, 1800–1900*, Chicago, IL and London, University of Chicago Press.

Amritavalli, R. and Upendran, S. with Jayalakshmi, G. D. (2011) 'Word play across languages and cultures' in Swann, J., Pope, R. and Carter, R. (eds) *Creativity, Language, Literature: The State of the Art*, Basingstoke and New York, Palgrave Macmillan.

Anderson, B. (2006 [1983]) *Imagined Communities: Reflections on the Origin and Spread of Nationalism* (revised edn), London, Verso.

Anon. (1970 [10th century]) The Dream of the Rood (ed. M. Swanton), Manchester, Manchester University Press.

Aristotle (1991) *The Art of Rhetoric* (trans. H. C. Lawson-Tancred), London, Penguin.

Austen, J. (2003 [1816]) *Emma* (ed. J. Kinsley), Oxford, Oxford University Press.

Austin, J. L. (1962) *How to Do Things with Words*, Oxford, Oxford University Press.

Bakhtin, M. (1981 [1935]) 'Discourse in the novel' in Holquist, M. (ed.) *The Dialogic Imagination: Four Essays by M. M. Bakhtin* (trans. C. Emerson and M. Holquist), Austin, TX, University of Texas Press.

Bakhtin, M. (1984 [1929]) *Problems of Dostoevsky's Poetics* (trans. and ed. C. Emerson), Manchester, Manchester University Press.

Bakhtin, M. (1986 [1953]) 'The problem of speech genres' in Emerson, C. and Holquist, M. (eds) *Speech Genres and Other Late Essays* (trans. V. W. McGee), Austin, TX, University of Texas Press.

Bakhtin, M. (1986 [1979]) 'The problem of speech genres' in McGee, V. W., Emerson, E. C. and Holquist, M. (trans.) *Speech Genres and Other Late Essays*, Austin, TX, University of Texas Press.

Bakhtin, M. M. (1981 [1975]) *The Dialogic Imagination* (trans. M. Holquist; ed. C. Emerson and M. Holquist), Austin, TX, University of Texas Press.

Bakhtin, M. M. (1986 [1952]) 'The problem of speech genres' in Emerson, C. and Holquist, M. (eds) *Speech Genres and Other Late Essays* (trans. V. W. McGee), Austin, TX, University of Texas Press.

Bancroft, D. (2007) 'English as a first language' in Mercer, N., Swann, J. and Mayor B. (eds) *Learning English*, Abingdon, Routledge.

Bamberg, M. (2004) 'Form and functions of "slut bashing" in male identity constructions in 15-year-olds', *Human Development*, vol. 47, no. 6, pp. 331–53.

Barthes, R. (1967 [1964]) *Elements of Semiology* (trans. A. Lavers and C. Smith), London, Jonathan Cape.

Barthes, R. (1972 [1957]) *Mythologies* (trans. A. Lavers), London, Paladin.

Barton, D. and Hamilton, M. (1998) *Local Literacies: Reading and Writing in One Community*, London, Routledge.

Bauman, R. (1986) *Story, Performance and Event: Contextual Studies of Oral Narrative*, Cambridge, Cambridge University Press.

BBC (2010) *A History of the World in 100 Objects*, BBC Radio 4 programme, first broadcast Wednesday, 20 January 2010, 09.45.

Benskin, M. and Laing, M. (1981) 'Translations and Mischsprachen in Middle English manuscripts' in Benskin, M. and Laing, M. (eds) *So meny people longages and tonges: philological essays in Scots and medieval English presented to Angus McIntosh*, Edinburgh, M. Benskin & M. L. Samuels.

Biber, D., Johansson, S., Leech, G., Conrad, S. and Finegan, E. (1999) *Longman Grammar of Spoken and Written English*, Harlow, Longman.

Bissex, G. (1984) 'The child as teacher' in Goelman, H., Oberg, A. and Smith, F. (eds) *Awakening to Literacy*, London, Heinemann Educational.

Blum-Kulka, S. and Snow, C. E. (2002) *Talking to Adults: The Contribution of Multiparty Discourse to Language Acquisition*, Mahwah, NJ, Lawrence Erlbaum.

Bourdieu, P. (1986 [1983]) 'The forms of capital' in Richardson, J. G. (ed.) *Handbook of Theory and Research for the Sociology of Education*, New York, Greenwood Press.

Bourdieu, P. (1992 [1975]) *Language and Symbolic Power* (trans. G. Raymond and M. Adamson; ed. J. B. Thompson), Cambridge, Polity Press.

Bourdieu, P. (1992 [1982]) 'Price formation and the anticipation of profits' in Bourdieu, P. *Language and Symbolic Power* (trans. G. Raymond and M. Adamson; ed. J. B. Thompson), Cambridge, Polity.

Bourdieu, P. and Passeron, J.-C. (1990 [1970]) *Reproduction in Education, Society, and Culture* (trans. R. Nice), London, Sage.

Braine, M. D. S. (1971) 'On two types of models of the internalisation of grammar' in Slobin, D. I. (ed.) *The Ontogensis of Grammar: A Theoretical Symposium*, New York, Academic Press.

Brink, A. P. (1973) *Kennis van die aand*, Cape Town, Buren.

Brown, R. (1973) *A First Language: The Early Stages*, London, George Allen and Unwin.

Cambourne, B. and Turbill, J. (1987) *Coping with Chaos*, Rozelle, NSW, Primary English Teaching Association.

Cameron, D. (1998) 'Performing gender identity: young men's talk and the construction of heterosexual masculinity' in Coates, J. (ed.) *Language and Gender: A Reader*, Oxford, Blackwell.

Cameron, D. (2007) *The Myth of Mars and Venus*, Oxford, Oxford University Press.

Carter, R. (1999) 'Common language: corpus, creativity and cognition', *Language and Literature*, vol. 8, no. 3, pp. 195–216.

Carter, R. (2004) *Language and Creativity: The Art of Common Talk*, London and New York, Routledge.

Carter, R. and McCarthy, M. (2006) *Cambridge Grammar of English: A Comprehensive Guide*, Cambridge, Cambridge University Press.

Caxton, W. (1490) Untitled foreword to *Virgil, The boke yf Eneydos*, London, William Caxton.

Chaucer, G. (1477) Untitled; known as *The Canterbury Tales*, Westminster, William Caxton.

Cheepen, C. and Monaghan, J. (1990) *Spoken English: A Practical Guide*, London, Pinter.

Chomsky, N. (1980) 'Rules and representations', *Behavioral and Brain Sciences*, vol. 3, no. 1, pp. 1–15.

Chomsky, N. (1986) *Knowledge of Language: Its Nature, Origin and Use*, New York, Praeger.

Coates, J. (1996) *Women Talk: Conversation between Women Friends*, Oxford, Blackwell.

Coates, J. (2003) *Men Talk: Stories in the Making of Masculinities*, Oxford, Blackwell.

Coe, J. (2001) *The Rotters Club*, London and New York, Viking.

Coleridge, S. T. (1827) *Specimens of the Table Talk of S. T. Coleridge* (ed. H. N. Coleridge 1821–1834), Project Gutenberg [online], http://www.gutenberg.org/catalog/world/readfile?pageno=1&fk_files=1471099 (Accessed 23 May 2011).

Collins Dictionary of Quotations (2003) London, Collins. Credo Reference [online], http://www.credoreference.com (Accessed 28 February 2011).

Connor, U. (1999) '"How like you our fish?" Accommodation in international business correspondence' in Hewings, M. and Nickerson, C. (eds) *Business English: Research into Practice*, Harlow, Longman.

Cook, G. (2000) *Language Play, Language Learning*, Oxford, Oxford University Press.

Cook, G. (2001) *The Discourse of Advertising* (2nd edn), London, Routledge.

Cook, G. (2007) '"This we have done". The different vagueness of poetry and PR' in Cutting, J. (ed.) *Vague Language Explored*, London, Palgrave.

Cook, G. (2008) 'General introduction' in Cook, G. (ed.) *The Language of Advertising (Volume 1)*, London, Routledge.

Copperfield, D. (2006) *Wasting Police Time: The Crazy World of the War on Crime*, Wolvey, Monday Books.

Craft, A. (2005) *Creativity in Schools: Tensions and Dilemmas*, London and New York, Routledge.

Crystal, D. (1986) *Listen to Your Child: A Parent's Guide to Children's Language*, Harmondsworth, Penguin.

Crystal, D. (1995) *The Cambridge Encyclopedia of the English Language*, Cambridge, Cambridge University Press.

Crystal, D. (2012) 'A global language' in Seargeant. P. and Swann, J. (eds) *English in the World: History, Diversity, Change*, Abingdon, Routledge/Milton Keynes, The Open University.

Darnton, R. (1990) 'What is the history of books?' in *The Kiss of Lamourette: Reflections in Cultural History*, London and Boston, MA, Faber and Faber.

Darnton, R. (2009) 'Google and the future of books', *New York Review of Books*, 12 February, pp. 9–11.

Deuchar, M. and Quay, S. (1998) 'One vs. two systems in early bilingual syntax: two versions of the question', *Bilingualism: Language and Cognition*, vol. 1, no. 3, pp. 231–43.

Deumert, A. and Masinyana, S. O. (2008) 'The use of English and isiXhosa in text messages (SMS): evidence from a bilingual South African sample', *English World-Wide*, vol. 29, no. 2, pp. 117–47.

de Villiers, P. A. and de Villiers, J. G. (1979) *Early Language*, London, Open Books.

Dondis, D. A. (1973) *A Primer of Visual Literacy*, Cambridge, MA, MIT Press.

Downing, J. (1973) *Comparative Reading*, New York, Macmillan.

Downing, J. and Leong, C. K. (1982) *Psychology of Reading*, New York, Macmillan.

Drew, P. and Heritage, J. (eds) (1992) *Talk at Work*, Cambridge, Cambridge University Press.

Eckert, P. and McConnell-Ginet, S. (2003) *Language and Gender*, Cambridge, Cambridge University Press.

Edgren, J. S. (2007) 'China' in Eliot, S. and Rose, J. (eds) *A Companion to the History of the Book*, Oxford, Blackwell.

Eisenstein, E. (1979) *The Printing Press as an Agent of Change: Communications and Cultural Transformations in Early-Modern Europe*, vol. 1, Cambridge, Cambridge University Press.

Eliot, S. (2007) 'From few and expensive to many and cheap: the British book market 1800–1890' in Eliot, S. and Rose, J. (eds) *A Companion to the History of the Book*, Oxford, Blackwell.

Eliot, T. S. (2004 [1922]) 'The waste land' in Eliot, T. S. *Complete Poems and Plays of T. S. Eliot*, London, Faber and Faber.

Erftmier, T. and Haas Dyson, A. (1986) '"Oh, ppbbt!": differences between the oral and written persuasive strategies of school-aged children', *Discourse Processes*, vol. 9, no. 1, pp. 91–114.

Ervin-Tripp, S. M. (1969) 'Sociolinguistics' in Berkowitz, L. (ed.) *Advances in Experimental Social Psychology*, New York, Academic Press.

Fairclough, N. (1995) *Critical Discourse Analysis: The Critical Study of Language*, London, Longman.

Fairclough, N. (2001) *Language and Power* (2nd edn), London, Longman.

Fanon, F. (2008 [1952]) *Black Skin, White Masks* (trans. R. Philcox), London, Pluto Press.

Ferrara, K., Brunner, H. and Whittemore, G. (1991) 'Interactive written discourse as an emergent register', *Written Communication*, vol. 8, no. 1, pp. 8–34.

Firth, A. (1996) 'The discursive accomplishment of normality: on "lingua franca" English and conversation analysis', *Journal of Pragmatics*, vol. 26, no. 2, pp. 237–59.

Fraser Gupta, A. F. (1994) *The Step Tongue: Children's English in Singapore*, Clevedon, Multilingual Matters.

García, O. (2007) 'Intervening discourses, representations and conceptualizations of language, Foreword' in Makoni, S. and Pennycook, A. (eds) *Disinventing and Reconstituting Languages*, Clevedon, Multilingual Matters.

Gardner, C. (2007) 'English and new media' in Goodman, S., Graddol, D. and Lillis, T. (eds) *Redesigning English*, London, Routledge/Milton Keynes, The Open University.

Garfield, S. (2010) *Just My Type: A Book About Fonts*, London, Profile.

Genesee, F. (2000) 'Early bilingual language development: one language or two' in Li Wei (ed.) *The Bilingual Reader*, London, Routledge.

Georgakopoulou, A. (2006) 'The other side of the story: towards a narrative analysis of narratives-in-interaction', *Discourse Studies*, vol. 8, no. 2, pp. 235–57.

Giles, H., Coupland, J. and Coupland, N. (1991) *Contexts of Accommodation: Developments in Applied Sociolinguistics*, Cambridge, Cambridge University Press.

Gillen, J. (2003) *The Language of Children*, London, Routledge.

Gimenez, J. C. (2000) 'Business e-mail communication: some emerging tendencies in register', *English for Specific Purposes*, vol. 19, pp. 237–51.

Gleason, J. B. (1973) 'Code switching in children's language' in Moore, T. E. (ed.) *Cognitive Development and the Acquisition of Language*, London, Academic Press.

Goddard, A. (2011) '.   look im over here: creativity, materiality and representation in new communication technologies' in Swann, J., Pope, R. and Carter, R. (eds) *Creativity, Language, Literature: The State of the Art*, Basingstoke and New York, Palgrave Macmillan.

Goffman, E. (1959) *The Presentation of Self in Everyday Life*, New York, Doubleday Anchor.

Goffman, E. (1967) *Interaction Ritual*, Harmondsworth, Penguin.

Goodwin, M. H. (1990) *He-Said-She-Said: Talk as Social Organisation among Black Children*, Bloomington, IN, Indiana University Press.

Goodwin, M. H. (1998) 'Cooperation and competition across girls' play activities' in Coates, J. (ed.) *Language and Gender: A Reader*, Oxford, Blackwell.

Goodwin, M. H. (2006) *The Hidden Life of Girls: Games of Stance, Status and Exclusion*, Malden, MA, Blackwell.

Goswami, U. (2010) 'Phonology, reading and reading difficulties' in Hall, K., Goswami, U., Harrison, C., Ellis, S. and Soler, J. (eds) *Interdisciplinary Perspectives on Learning to Read: Culture, Cognition and Pedagogy*, London and New York, Routledge.

Graddol, D. (2006) *English Next: Why Global English May Mean the End of 'English as a Foreign Language'*, London, The British Council.

Grafton, K. (2010) *Paying Attention to Public Readers of Canadian Literature: Popular Genre Systems, Publics, and Canons*, Unpublished PhD thesis, Vancouver, University of British Columbia; available online at https://circle.ubc.ca/bitstream/handle/2429/27707/ubc_2010_fall_grafton_kathryn.pdf (Accessed 30 September 2010).

Gray, J. (1992) *Men Are from Mars, Women Are from Venus*, New York, HarperCollins.

Gregg, J. (1844) *Commerce of the Prairies, or, the Journal of a Santa Fe Trader During Eight Expeditions Across the Great Western Prairies, and a Residence of Nearly Nine Years in Northern Mexico*, Vol. 1, New York, Henry G. Langley.

Grootendorst, R., Snoeck Henkemans, F. and van Eemeren, F. H. (1996) *Fundamentals of Argumentation Theory: A Handbook of Historical Backgrounds and Contemporary Development*, London, Routledge.

Habermas, J. (1989) *The Structural Transformation of the Public Sphere* (trans. T. Burger with the assistance of F. Lawrence), Cambridge, MA, MIT Press (original German edition 1962).

Haggan, M. (2007) 'Text messaging in Kuwait. Is the medium the message?', *Multilingua*, vol. 26, no. 4, pp. 427–49.

Hakuta, K. (1986) *Mirror of Language: The Debate of Bilingualism*, New York, Basic Books.

Halliday, M. A. K. (1973) *Explorations in the Functions of Language*, London, Edward Arnold.

Halliday, M. A. K. (1975) *Learning How to Mean*, London, Arnold.

Halliday, M. A. K. and Hasan, R. (1976) *Cohesion in English*, London, Longman.

Harris, R. (1981) *The Language Myth*, London, Duckworth.

Harste, J., Burke, C. and Woodward, V. (1981) *Children, Their Language and World: Initial Encounters with Print*, National Institute of Education, Bloomington, IN, Indiana University Press.

Hatch, E. M. (ed.) (1978) *Second Language Acquisition*, Rowley, MA, Newbury House.

Heath, S. B. (1982) 'Protean shapes in literacy events: ever-shifting oral and literate traditions' in Tannen, D. (ed.) *Spoken and Written Language*, Norwood, NJ, Ablex.

Heath, S. B. (1983) *Ways with Words: Language, Life and Work in Communities and Classrooms*, Cambridge, Cambridge University Press.

Heffernan, V. (2009) 'Street smart', *New York Times*, 5 July, Section MM, p. 16.

Hellinga, L. (2007) 'The Gutenberg revolutions' in Eliot, S. and Rose, J. (eds) *A Companion to the History of the Book*, Oxford, Blackwell.

Herman, E. and Chomsky, N. (1988) *Manufacturing Consent*, New York, Pantheon.

Herring, S. C. (2007) 'Faceted classification scheme for computer-mediated discourse', *Language@Internet*, vol. 1.

Hester, S. and Hester, S. (2010) 'Conversational actions and category relations: an analysis of children's argument', *Discourse Studies*, vol. 12, no. 1, pp. 33–48.

Hewings, A. and Tagg, C. (eds) (2012) *The Politics of English: Conflict, Competition, Co-existence*, Abingdon, Routledge/Milton Keynes, The Open University.

Hewings, M. (1991) 'The interpretation of illustrations in ELT materials', *The ELT Journal*, vol. 45, no. 3, pp. 237–44.

Hinds, J. (1987) 'Reader versus writer responsibility: a new typology' in Silva, T. J. and Matsuda, P. K. (eds) *Landmark Essays on ESL Writing*, Philadelphia, Lawrence Erlbaum Associates.

Hofstede, G. (2005) *Cultures and Organizations: Software of the Mind* (2nd edn), New York, McGraw Hill.

Holmes, J. and Marra, M. (2002) 'Over the edge? Subversive humor between colleagues and friends', *Humor*, vol. 15, no. 1, pp. 65–87.

Hoyle, S. M. and Adger, C. T. (eds) (1996) *Kid's Talk: Strategic Language Use in Later Childhood*, New York and Oxford, Oxford University Press.

Huang, J. and Hatch, E. M. (1978) 'A Chinese child's acquisition of English' in Hatch, E. M. (ed.) *Second Language Acquisition*, Rowley, MA, Newbury House.

Hymes, D. H. (1972) 'On communicative competence' in Pride, J. B. and Holmes, J. (eds) *Sociolinguistics: Selected Readings*, Harmondsworth, Penguin.

Internet World Stats (2010a) *Internet Usage Statistics* [online], http://www.internetworldstats.com/stats.htm (Accessed 30 May 2011).

Internet World Stats (2010b) *Internet World Users by Language: Top 10 Languages* [online], http://www.internetworldstats.com/stats7.htm (Accessed 30 May 2011).

Jakobson, R. (1960) 'Closing statement: linguistics and poetics' in Seboek, T. A. (ed.) *Style in Language*, Cambridge, MA, MIT Press.

Jenkins, J. (2000) *The Phonology of English as an International Language*, Oxford, Oxford University Press.

Jensen, A. (2009) 'Discourse strategies in professional e-mail negotiation: a case study', *English for Specific Purposes*, vol. 28, no. 1, pp. 4–18.

Keats, J. (1839 [1821]) 'In after time, a sage of mickle lore', *Plymouth and Devonport Weekly Journal, and General Advertiser for Devon, Cornwall, Somerset and Dorset*, p. 3.

King James Bible (1611) *The Holy Bible, Conteyning the Old Testament, and the New*, London, Robert Barker.

King, M. L. (1984 [1963]) '"I have a dream": excerpt from the speech given August 28, 1963' in King, C. S. (ed.) *The Words of Martin Luther King*, London, Fount.

King, S. (2000a) *Riding the Bullet*, Scribner/Philtrum Press [online], http://www.readersread.com/excerpts/ridingthebullet.htm (Accessed 31 July 2011).

King, S. (2000b) *Riding the Bullet*, New York, Simon and Schuster.

King, S. (2002) 'Riding the bullet' in King, S., *Everything's Eventual: 14 Dark Tales*, London, Hodder and Stoughton.

Koester, A. (2004) *The Language of Work*, London, Routledge.

Koester, A. (2006) *Investigating Workplace Discourse*, London, Routledge.

Koestler, A. (1976) 'Association and bisociation' in Bruner, J. S., Jolly, A. and Sylva, K. (eds) *Play: Its Role in Development and Evolution*, London, Penguin.

Kramsch, C. and Whiteside, A. (2008) 'Language ecology in multilingual settings: towards a theory of symbolic competence', *Applied Linguistics*, vol. 29, no. 4, pp. 645–71.

Kress, G. (2003) 'Perspectives on making meaning: the differential principles and means of adults and children' in Hall, N., Larson, J. and Marsh, J. (eds) *Handbook of Early Childhood Literacy*, London, Sage.

Kress, G. and van Leeuwen, T. (1996) *Reading Images: The Grammar of Visual Design*, London, Routledge.

Kristeva, J. (1986) 'Word, dialogue, and the novel' in Moi, T. (ed.) *The Kristeva Reader*, New York, Columbia University Press.

Krupnick, M. (2010) 'UC to publishers: price off', *Contra Costa Times* (California), 10 June, p. 1.

Labov, W. (1972) *Language in the Inner City*, Philadelphia, PA, University of Pennsylvania Press.

Labov, W. and Waletzky, J. (1967) 'Narrative analysis: oral versions of personal experience' in Helms, J. (ed.) *Essays on the Verbal and Visual Arts*, Seattle, WA, University of Washington Press.

Lachter, J. and Bever, T. G. (1988) 'The relation between linguistic structure and associative theories of language learning – a constructive critique of some connectionist learning models', *Cognition*, vol. 28, pp. 195–247. (Reprinted in Pinker, S. and Mehler, J., 1988, eds, *Connections and Symbols*, Cambridge, MA, MIT Press.)

Lakoff, R. (1975) *Language and Women's Place*, New York, Harper & Row.

Lamarre, P. (2010) 'Bilingual winks', Paper presented at *Sociolinguistics Symposium 18*, 1–4 September, University of Southampton.

Liberman, K. (1981) 'Understanding Aborigines in Australian courts of law', *Human Organization*, vol. 40, no. 3, pp. 247–54.

Lin, A. (2011) 'The bilingual verbal art of *Fama*: linguistic hybridity and creativity of a Hong Kong hip hop group' in Swann, J., Pope, R. and Carter, R. (eds) *Creativity, Language, Literature: The State of the Art*, Basingstoke and New York, Palgrave Macmillan.

Louhiala-Salminen, L. (1999) 'From business correspondence to message exchange: what is left?' in Hewings, M. and Nickerson, C. (eds) *Business English: Research into Practice*, Harlow, Longman.

Lydgate, J. (1520 [15th century]) 'Here Begynneth the Testamet of Iohn Lydgate Monke of Berry: Which he Made Himselfe/by His Lyfe Dayes', London, Richard Pynson.

Magoffin, S. S. (1962 [1846]) *Down the Santa Fe Trail and Into Mexico: The Diary of Susan Shelby Magoffin, 1846–1847* (ed. S. E. Drumm), New Haven, CT and London, Yale University Press.

Malinowski, B. (1923) 'The problem of meaning in primitive languages', supplement to Ogden, C. K. and Richards, I. M. *The Meaning of Meaning*, London, Routledge & Kegan Paul.

Mampe, B., Friederici, A. D., Christophe, A. and Wermke, K. (2009) 'Newborns' cry melody is shaped by their native language', *Current Biology*, vol. 19, no. 23, pp. 1994–7.

Matteau, R. (2007) 'The readership for banned literature and its underground networks in apartheid South Africa', *Innovation*, vol. 35 (December), pp. 81–90.

Maybin, J. (2006) *Children's Voices: Talk, Knowledge and Identity*, Basingstoke, Palgrave.

Maybin, J. and Swann, J. (2007) 'Everyday creativity in language: textuality, contextuality, and critique' in Swann, J. and Maybin, J. (eds) *Language Creativity in Everyday Contexts*, Special Issue of *Applied Linguistics*, vol. 28, no. 4, pp. 497–517.

McDonald, P. D. (2009) *The Literature Police: Apartheid Censorship and its Cultural Consequences*, Oxford, Oxford University Press.

McGann, J. (1991) *The Textual Condition*, Princeton, NJ, Princeton University Press.

McKenzie, D. F. (1999 [1986]) *Bibliography and the Sociology of Texts*, Cambridge, Cambridge University Press.

McLuhan, M. (1962) *The Gutenberg Galaxy: The Making of Typographic Man*, Toronto, University of Toronto Press.

McQuarrie E. F. and Mick, D. G. (1996) 'Figures of rhetoric in advertising language', *Journal of Consumer Research*, vol. 22, pp. 424–38.

Miller, C. (1984) 'Genre as social action', *Quarterly Journal of Speech*, vol. 70, no. 2, pp. 151–67.

Miller, C. and Shepherd, D. (2004) 'Blogging as social action: a genre analysis of the weblog' in Gurak, L., Antonijevic, S., Johnson, L., Ratcliff, C. and Reyman, J. (eds) *Into the Blogosphere: Rhetoric, Community, and Culture of Weblogs* [online], http://blog.lib.umn.edu/blogosphere/ blogging_as_social_action_a_genre_analysis_of_the_weblog.html (Accessed 24 May 2011).

Mitchell-Kernan, C. and Kernan, K. T. (1977) 'Pragmatics of directive choice amongst children' in Ervin-Tripp, S. and Mitchell-Kernan, C. (eds) *Child Discourse*, New York, Academic Press.

Moloney, K. (2000) *Rethinking Public Relations: The Spin and the Substance*, London, Routledge.

Moloney, K. (2006) *Rethinking Public Relations: PR Propaganda and Democracy*, London, Routledge.

Mullis, I. V. S., Martin, M. O., Kennedy, A. M. and Foy, P. (2007) *IEA's Progress in International Reading Literacy Study in Primary School in 40 Countries*, Chestnut Hill, MA, TIMSS & PIRLS International Study Center, Boston College.

Myers, G. (2004) *Matters of Opinion: Talking about Public Issues*, Cambridge, Cambridge University Press.

Myers, G. (2010) *Discourse of Blogs and Wikis*, London, Continuum.

Myers, G. (2010) *Discourse of Blogs and Wikis*, London and New York, Continuum.

National Writing Project (1989) *Becoming a Writer*, Walton-on-Thames, Thomas Nelson.

National Writing Project (1990) *A Rich Resource: Writing and Language Diversity*, Walton-on-Thames, Thomas Nelson.

Nelson, K. (1981) 'Individual differences in language development: implications for development and language', *Developmental Psychology*, vol. 17, no. 2, pp. 170–87.

Ó Carragáin, E. (2005) *Ritual and the Rood: Liturgical Images and the Old English Poems of the Dream of the Rood Tradition*, London, British Library.

Ochs, E. (1979) 'Introduction: what child language can contribute to pragmatics' in Ochs, E. and Schieffelin, B. B. (eds) *Developmental Pragmatics*, New York, Academic Press.

Ochs, E. and Schieffelin, B. B. (eds) (1979) *Developmental Pragmatics*, New York, Academic Press.

OECD (2010) PISA 2009 Results: What Students Know and Can Do, *Student Performance in Reading, Mathematics and Science (Volume I)* [online], http://dx.doi.org/10.1787/9789264091450-en (Accessed 15 May 2011).

o-jenny (2010) 'Been gone for a few days', posted to *–insert clever title here–* on 6 January 2010 [online], http://o-jenny.livejournal.com/489739.html (Accessed 12 April 2010).

Pandharipande, R. (1992) 'Defining politeness in Indian English', *World Englishes*, vol. 11, no. 2/3, pp. 241–50.

Paolillo, J. C. (2007) 'How much multilingualism? Language diversity on the internet' in Danet, B. and Herring, S. C. (eds) *The Multilingual Internet: Language, Culture and Communication Online*, New York, Oxford University Press.

Peccei, J. S. (1994) *Child Language*, London, Routledge.

Pennycook, A. (2007a) *Global Englishes and Transcultural Flows*, London and New York, Routledge.

Pennycook, A. (2007b) '"The rotation gets thick. The constraints get thin": creativity, recontextualization, and difference', *Applied Linguistics*, vol. 28, no. 4, pp. 579–96.

Pinker, S. (1994) *The Language Instinct: A New Science of Language and Mind*, London, Penguin.

Poncini, G. (2002) 'Investigating discourse at business meetings with multicultural participation', *International Review of Applied Linguistics in Language Teaching,* vol. 40, no. 4, pp. 345–73.

Potter, J. (2001) 'Wittgenstein and Austin' in Wetherell, M., Taylor, S. and Yates, S. J. (eds) *Discourse Theory and Practice*, London, Sage.

Pye, C. (1986) 'Quiché Mayan speech to children', *Journal of Child Language*, vol. 13, no. 1, pp. 85–100.

Radford, A. (1990) *Syntactic Theory and the Acquisition of English Syntax: The Nature of Early Child Grammars of English*, Oxford, Blackwell.

Ragan, S. L. and Hopper, R. (1981) 'Alignment talk in the job interview', *Journal of Applied Communication Research*, vol. 9, no. 2, pp. 85–103.

Raney, K. (1999) 'Visual literacy and the art curriculum', *International Journal of Art and Design Education*, vol. 18, no. 1, pp. 41–7.

Ravem, R. (1974) 'The development of *wh-* questions in first and second language learners' in Richards, J. (ed.) *Error Analysis: Perspectives on Second Language Acquisition*, London, Longman.

Reed, L. (1971) 'Goodnight ladies' on *Transformer*, RCA Records, Track 11.

Reid, E. M. (1991) 'Electropolis: communication and community on internet relay chat', University of Melbourne, Department of History.

Ritchie, L. D. (2010) '"Everybody goes down": metaphors, stories, and simulations in conversations', *Metaphor and Symbol*, vol. 25, no. 3, pp. 123–43.

Roberts, C. and Campbell, S. (2006) *Talk on Trial: Job Interviews, Language and Ethnicity*, Department for Work and Pensions Research Report No. 344, Leeds, Corporate Document Services.

Romaine, S. (1995) *Bilingualism* (2nd edn), Oxford, Blackwell.

Sacks, H. (1998 [1995]) *Lectures on Conversation*, Vol. 1 (ed. G. Jefferson), Malden, MA, Blackwell.

Sacks, H., Schegloff, E. and Jefferson, G. (1974) 'A simplest systematics for the organization of turn-taking in conversation', *Language*, vol. 50, no. 4, pp. 696–735.

Saenger, P. (1997) *Space Between Words: The Origins of Silent Reading*, Stanford, CA, Stanford University Press.

Saussure, F. de (1960 [1916]) *Course in General Linguistics* (trans. W. Baskin; ed. C. Bally and A. Sechehaye in collaboration with A. Reidlinger), London, Peter Owen.

Saxena, M. (1993) 'Literacies among the Panjabis in Southall' in Hamilton, M., Barton, D. and Ivanič, R. (eds) *Worlds of Literacy*, Clevedon, Multilingual Matters.

Schegloff, E. (1999) 'Discourse, pragmatics, conversation, analysis', *Discourse Studies*, vol. 1, no. 4, pp. 405–35.

Schegloff, E. A. and Sacks, H. (1973) 'Opening up closings', *Semiotica*, vol. 8, no. 4, pp. 289–327.

Sealey, A. (2000) *Childly Language: Children, Language and the Social world*, Harlow, Pearson Education.

Seargeant, P. and Swann, J. (eds) (2012) *English in the World: History, Diversity, Change*, Abingdon, Routledge/Milton Keynes, The Open University.

Seidlhofer, B. (2004) 'Research perspectives on teaching English as a lingua franca', *Annual Review of Applied Linguistics*, vol. 24, pp. 209–39.

Seymour, P. H. K., Aro, M. and Erskine, J. M. (2003) 'Foundation literacy acquisition in European orthographies', *British Journal of Psychology*, vol. 94, no. 2, pp. 143–74.

Shakespeare, W. (1604) *The Tragicall Historie of Hamlet, Prince of Denmarke*, London, Nicholas Ling.

Shakespeare, W. (1955 [1599/1623]) *Julius Caesar* (ed. T. S. Dorsch), London, Methuen.

Shortis, T. (2007) 'Revoicing txt: spelling, vernacular orthography and "unregimented writing"' in Posteguillo, S., Esteve, M. J. and Gea, M. L. (eds) *The Texture of Internet: Netlinguistics*, Cambridge, Cambridge Scholar Press.

Shuy, R. (1978) 'What children's functional language can tell us about reading or how Joanna got herself invited to dinner' in Beach, R. (ed.) *Perspectives on Literacy: Proceedings of the 1977 Perspectives on Literacy Conference*, Minneapolis, MN, University of Minnesota.

Snow, C. E. and Blum-Kulka, S. (2002) 'From home to school: school-age children talking with adults' in Blum-Kulka, S. and Snow, C. E. (2002) *Talking to Adults: The Contribution of Multiparty Discourse to Language Acquisition*, Mahwah, NJ, Lawrence Erlbaum.

Spencer-Oatey, H. (2000) *Culturally Speaking: Managing Rapport through Talk across Cultures*, London and New York, Continuum.

Spenser, E. (1609 [1596]) *The Faerie Queene, Disposed into XII Bookes, Fashioning Twelue Morall Vertues*, London, Mathew Lownes.

St Clair, W. (2004) *The Reading Nation in the Romantic Period*, Cambridge, Cambridge University Press.

Street, B. (1984) *Literacy in Theory and Practice*, Cambridge, Cambridge University Press.

Swales, J. M. (1990) *Genre Analysis: English in Academic and Research Settings*, Cambridge, Cambridge University Press.

Swann, J., Deumert, A., Lillis, T. and Mesthrie, R. (2004) *A Dictionary of Sociolinguistics*, Edinburgh, Edinburgh University Press.

Tannen, D. (1984) *Conversational Style: Analyzing Talk Among Friends*, Norwood, NJ, Ablex.

Tannen, D. (2007 [1989]) *Talking Voices: Repetition, Dialogue, and Imagery in Conversational Discourse* (2nd edn), Cambridge, Cambridge University Press.

Teale, W. and Sulzby, E. (1988) 'Emergent literacy as a perspective for examining how young children become writers and readers' in Mercer, N. (ed.) *Language and Literacy from an Educational Perspective, Volume 1 Language Studies*, Milton Keynes, The Open University.

The Environment Site (2010) [online], http://www.theenvironmentsite.org/forum/climate-change-forum/24321-climate-change-really-unpredictable.html (Accessed 1 June 2010).

The Open University (1997) U210 *The English language: past, present and future*, Study Guide 5, Extract 4, 'Children's use of language varieties', Milton Keynes, The Open University.

Toulmin, S. (1958) *The Uses of Argument*, Cambridge, Cambridge University Press.

van Eemeren, F. H., Grootendorst, R. and Snoeck Henkemans, A. F. (2002) *Argumentation: Analysis, Evaluation, Presentation*, Mahwah, NJ, Lawrence Erlbaum Associates.

Ventner, R. (2007) 'Inventing an alternative through oppositional publishing: Afrikaans alternative book publishing in apartheid South Africa – the publishing house Taurus (1975–1991) as a case study', *Innovation*, vol. 35 (December), pp. 91–124.

Vickers, B. (1998) *In Defence of Rhetoric*, Oxford, Clarendon.

Warschauer, M., El-Said, G. and Zohry, A. (2007) 'Language choice online: globalisation and identity in Egypt' in Danet, B. and Herring, S. C. (eds) *The Multilingual Internet: Language, Culture and Communication Online*, New York, Oxford University Press.

Warschauer, M. and Grimes, D. (2007) 'Audience, authorship, and artifact: the emergent semiotics of Web 2.0', *Annual Review of Applied Linguistics*, vol. 27, pp. 1–23.

Webster, N. (1828 [1970]) Preface, *An American Dictionary of the English Language*, New York, Converse.

Wells, C. G. (1985) 'Language and learning: an interactional perspective' in Wells, G. and Nicholls, J. (eds) *Language and Learning: An Interactional Perspective*, London, Falmer.

Wenger, E. (1998) *Communities of Practice: Learning, Meaning and Identity*, Cambridge, Cambridge University Press.

Wikipedia (2002) http://en.wikipedia.org/w/index.php?title=Wiki&oldid=425967(Accessed 31 July 2011).

Wikipedia (2006) http://en.wikipedia.org/w/index.php?title=Wiki&oldid=86036912 (Accessed 31 July 2011).

Wikipedia (2011) http://en.wikipedia.org/wiki/Wiki (Accessed 31 July 2011).

Willard, C. A. (1989) *A Theory of Argumentation*, Tuscaloosa, AL and London, University of Alabama Press.

Wimsatt, W. K. and Beardsley, M. C. (1946) 'The intentional fallacy', *The Sewanee Review*, vol. 54, no. 3, pp. 468–88.

Wray, A. (2002) *Formulaic Language and the Lexicon*, Cambridge, Cambridge University Press.

Yates, J. and Orlikowski, W. (1992) 'Genres of organizational communication: a structurational approach to studying communication and media', *Academy of Management Review*, vol. 17, no. 2, pp. 299–326.

Acknowledgements

Grateful acknowledgement is made to the following sources:

Text

Page 34: Sacks, H. and Jefferson, G. (1995) 'Lecture 1: Rules of conversational sequence', *Lectures on Conversation*, Vol. 1, Blackwell Publishing Ltd. Copyright © 1992, 1995 The Estate of Harvey Sacks. Reproduced with permission of Blackwell Publishing Ltd; page 40: Eades, D. (1991) 'Communicative Strategies in Aboriginal English', in Romian, S. (ed.), *Language in Australia*, Cambridge University Press. Copyright © 1991 Cambridge University Press, reproduced by permission; page 77: McNeill, L. (2005) 'Genre Under Construction: The Diary on the Internet', *Language@Internet*, Vol. 2, Copyright © 2005 Laurie McNeill; page 83: Gillen, J. and Hall, N. (2010) 'Edwardian postcards: Illuminating ordinary writing' in Barton, D. and Papen, U. (eds.) *The Anthropology of Writing: Understanding Textually Mediated Worlds*, Continuum International Publishing Group. Copyright © 2010 David Barton and Uta Papen. By kind permission of the Continuum International Publishing Group; page 120: Hanley, R. J. (2010) 'English is a difficult writing system for children to learn: evidence from children learning to read in Wales' in Hall, K. (ed.) *Interdisciplinary Perspectives on Learning to Read: Culture, Cognition and Pedagogy*, pp. 117–129, Routledge. Copyright © 2010 Kathy Hall, Usha Goswami, Colin Harrison, Sue Ellis and Janet Soler; page 127: Kenner, C. (2004) 'Living in simultaneous worlds', *Becoming Biliterate*, Trentham Books Limited. Copyright © 2004 Trentham Books Limited; page 164: Markus, A. T. and Cameron, D. (2002) 'Why language matters' in *The Words Between the Spaces: Buildings and Language*, Routledge. Copyright © 2002 Thomas A. Markus and Deborah Cameron. Reproduced by permission of Taylor and Francis Books UK; page 171: Holmes, J. and Stubbe, M. (2003) 'Humour and workplace culture', *Power and Politeness in the Workplace*, Pearson Education Limited. Copyright © 2003 Pearson Education Limited; page 261: Reproduced by permission of SAGE Publications, London, Los Angeles, New Delhi and Singapore, from Cameron, C., *Good to Talk? Living and working in a communication culture*. Copyright © Deborah Cameron, 2000; page 293: Weinstein, B. (1982) 'Noah Webster and the diffusion of linguistic innovations for political purposes', *International Journal of Social Langauge*, Vol. 38, pp. 85–108. Reprinted by permission of the publisher; page 299: Dick, L. A. (2008) 'Blood from Stones', *Censorship and the Reading Practices of South African Political*

Figures

page 240 (right): © imgmaker/Alamy; page page 254: © AFP/Getty Images; page 271 (top left): © Anatoly Maltsev/epa/Corbis; page 271 (middle right): © peace portal photo/Alamy; page 271 (bottom left): © Ireneusz Skorupa/iStockphoto; page 272 (left): © South West Images Scotland/Alamy; page 272 (middle): © David Lyons/Alamy; page 272 (right): © South West Images Scotland/Alamy; page 277: © The British Library Board. C.21.c.3; page 279: thanks to Nigel Roche of the St. Bride Library; page 308: © Andy Hendry; page 311: © Andy Hendry; page 324: © John Birdsall.

Tables

Page 331: data taken from Internet World Stats Usage and Population Statistics, www.internetworldstats.com.

Every effort has been made to contact copyright holders. If any have inadvertently been overlooked the publishers will be pleased to make the necessary arrangements at the first opportunity.

Acknowledgement is made to Daniel Allington as author of the figures on page 10 and page 280.

Index